Early Modern Cultural Studies

Ivo Kamps, Series Editor

PUBLISHED BY PALGRAVE MACMILLAN

REMAPPING THE MEDITERRANEAN WORLD IN EARLY MODERN ENGLISH WRITINGS

Edited by

Goran V. Stanivukovic

PR
129
.M48
R45
2007

First published in 2007 by
PALGRAVE MACMILLAN™
175 Fifth Avenue, New York, N.Y. 10010 and
Houndmills, Basingstoke, Hampshire, England RG21 6XS
Companies and representatives throughout the world.

PALGRAVE MACMILLAN is the global academic imprint of the Palgrave Macmillan division of St. Martin's Press, LLC and of Palgrave Macmillan Ltd. Macmillan® is a registered trademark in the United States, United Kingdom and other countries. Palgrave is a registered trademark in the European Union and other countries.

ISBN-13: 978–1–4039–7557–7
ISBN-10: 1–4039–7557–4

Library of Congress Cataloging-in-Publication Data

Remapping the Mediterranean world in early modern English writings / edited by Goran V. Stanivukovic.
    p. cm.—— (Early modern cultural studies)
    Includes bibliographical references and index.
    ISBN 1–4039–7557–4 (alk paper)
    1. English literature—Mediterranean influences. 2. English literature—Early modern, 1500–1700—History and criticism. 3. Mediterranean Region—In literature. 4. Multiculturalism in literature. 5. Imperialism in literature. 6. Mercantile system in literature. 7. English literature—Turkic influences. 8. Turkey—In literature. 9. Islam in literature. 10. Turkey—History—Ottoman Empire, 1288–1918. I. Stanivukovic, Goran V. II. Series.
    PR129.M48R45 2007
    820.9′321822—dc22   2006042960

A catalogue record for this book is available from the British Library.

Design by Newgen Imaging Systems (P) Ltd., Chennai, India.

First edition: January 2007

10 9 8 7 6 5 4 3 2 1

Printed in the United States of America.

69028461

Contents

LIST OF ILLUSTRATIONS

Series Editor's Foreword

The Early Modern Cultural Studies series is dedicated to the exploration of literature, history, and culture in the context of cultural exchange and globalization. We begin with the assumption that in the twenty-first century, literary criticism, literary theory, historiography, and cultural studies have become so interwoven that we can now think of them as an eclectic and only loosely unified (but still recognizable) approach to formerly distinct fields of inquiry such as literature, society, history, and culture. This series furthermore presumes that the early modern period was witness to an incipient process of transculturation through exploration, mercantilism, colonization, and migration that set into motion a process of globalization that is still with us today. The purpose of this series is to bring together this eclectic approach, which freely and unapologetically crosses disciplinary, theoretical, and political boundaries, with early modern texts and artifacts that bear the traces of transculturation and globalization.

This process can be studied on a large as well as on a small scale, and the books in this series are dedicated to both. It is just as concerned with the analyses of colonial encounters and native representations of those encounters as it is with representations of the other in Shakespeare, gender politics, the cultural impact of the presence of strangers/foreigners in London, or the consequences of farmers' migration to that city. This series is as interested in documenting cultural exchanges between British, Portuguese, Spanish, or Dutch colonizers and native peoples as it is in telling the stories of returning English soldiers who served in foreign armies on the continent of Europe in the late sixteenth century.

Ivo Kamps
Series editor

ACKNOWLEDGMENTS

This book owes its existence to several institutions for their support and to a number of individuals for their enthusiasm, advice, or invitation to present my work. I am grateful to the Newberry Library, Social Sciences and Humanities Research Council of Canada, and Saint Mary's University for awarding me grants that enabled my research at The Newberry Library, The Folger Shakespeare Library, The Huntington Library, The British Library, and The Bodleian Library. I am indebted to Alan Stewart for sharing with me his knowledge of things Anglo-Mediterranean; Ivo Kamps for his enthusiastic support from start to finish; the press's scrupulous reader for deft reading of the manuscript and for making important suggestions how to improve it; and to Daniel Goffman, an Ottomanist, for accepting to join this project at the right moment and for changing it in a number of ways. I am pleased to thank Elissa Asp, Jerry Brotton, Bradin Cormack, Julia Cohen, Maran Elancheran, Teresa Heffernan, Renée Hulan, Elizabeth Hulse, Natasha Hurley, Ian McAdam, Carla Mazzio, Randall Martin, Greg Nepean, Lori Humphrey Newcomb, Mary and Richard Keshen, Farideh Koohi-Kamali and William Sherman for their help with this book in differing ways along the way. Basil Chiasson was an exemplary research assistant; I only wish I could rely on his attentiveness and endurance again. My colleagues at Saint Mary's University and The University of Sheffield remain in my debt for providing me with a stimulating and joyful working environment. I am grateful to Duke University Library for the permission to reproduce the two images in Edmund Valentine Campos's essay.

ABOUT THE CONTRIBUTORS

Bernadette Andrea teaches in the English Department at the University of Texas at San Antonio. She has published numerous articles, book chapters, and reviews on early modern women, imperial studies, and orientalism. Her book, *Women and Islam in Early Modern English Literature*, will be published by Cambridge University Press.

Leeds Barroll is a Scholar-in-residence at the Folger Shakespeare Library and former Editor of *Shakespeare Studies*. He is the author of a number of books and articles, including *Plague, Politics, and Shakespeare's Theatre* (1991), and *Anna of Denmark, Queen of England: A Cultural Biography* (2001).

Emily C. Bartels is an Associate Professor of English at Rutgers University (New Brunswick) and Associate Director of the Bread Loaf School of English (Middlebury College). Her publications include *Spectacles of Strangeness: Imperialism, Alienation, and Marlowe* (1993), and edited collection, *Critical Essays on Christopher Marlowe* (1997), and numerous essays on Marlowe, Shakespeare, and early modern representations of Africa and the Moor, the topic of her current book-in-progress.

Adam R. Beach is Assistant Professor of English at Ball State University. He has published articles on English colonialism in *The Eighteenth-Century: Theory and Interpretation* and *Texas Studies in Literature and Language* and is currently researching nationalist and colonial literature of the Renaissance period.

Matthew Birchwood is Lecturer in English at Kingston University, London. His interests lie in the role of Islam and the East in literary-political discourses of the seventeenth century and the related topic of Anglo-Dutch rivalry in relation to the Eastern trade. His book, *Staging Islam in England: Drama and Culture, 1640–1685*, is coming out with Boydell and Brewer in 2007.

Jonathan Burton is Assistant Professor of English Literature at West Virginia University. He is the author of *Traffic and Turning: Islam and English Drama, 1579–1624* (2005) and other essays in early modern studies. He is currently working on a documentary companion to the study of race in the Renaissance.

Edmund Valentine Campos is Assistant Professor of English at Swarthmore College where he teaches Renaissance transatlantic literature and culture. He is currently writing a book about Anglo-Spanish literary exchange during the Age of Discovery.

Daniel Goffman is Professor and Chair in the Department of History at DePaul University. He is the author, most recently, of *The Ottoman Empire and Early Modern Europe* (2002), as well as other books and articles. He also has served as editor of the *Turkish Studies Association Bulleting* (1989–92), as president of the Turkish Studies Association (1995–96), and as editor of the *Middle East Studies Association Bulletin*.

Constance C. Relihan is Hargis Professor of English Literature at Auburn University. She is the author of *Fashioning Authority: The Development of Elizabethan Novelistic Discourse* (1994) and *Cosmographical Glasses: Geographical Discourse, Gender, and Elizabethan Fiction* (2004). She is also the editor of *Framing Elizabethan Fictions: Contemporary Approaches to Early Modern Narrative Prose* (1996) and (with Goran V. Stanivukovic) *Prose Fiction and Early Modern Sexualities in England, 1570–1640* (2003).

Elizabeth Sauer is Professor of English at Brock University, where she holds a Chancellor's Chair for Research Excellence. She has authored *"Paper-Contestations" and Textual Communities in England, 1640–1675* (2005) and *Barbarous Dissonance and Images of Voice in Milton's Epics* (1996). She also edited the following books: *Imperialisms: Historical and Literary Investigations 1500–1900* (with Balachandra Rajan, 2004); *Reading Early Modern Women* (with Helen Ostovich, 2004); *Books and Readers in Early Modern England: Material Studies* (with Jennifer Anderson, 2002); *Literature and Religion in Early Modern England* (with Jennifer Anderson, special issue of *Renaissance and Reformation* 25:4 [2001; date of issue 2003]); *Milton and the Imperial Vision* (with Balachandra Rajan, 1999), winner of the Milton Society of America Irene Samuel Memorial Award; and *Agonistics: Arenas of Creative Context* (with Janet Lungstrum, 1997). She is currently completing *Toleration and Milton's "Peculiar" Nation*, a book funded by the Social Sciences and Humanities Research Council of Canada.

Goran V. Stanivukovic is Lecturer in Shakespeare and Early Modern Literature at The University of Sheffield. He is the editor of *The Most Pleasant History of Ornatus and Artesia* by Emanuel Ford (2003), *Prose Fiction and Early Modern Sexualities in England, 1570–1640* (with Constance C. Relihan, 2003) and *Ovid and the Renaissance Body* (2001). He is currently completing a book on prose romances, Mediterranean travels, and narratives of sexuality.

Alan Stewart is Professor of English and Comparative Literature at Columbia University in New York, and Associate Director of the AHRB Center for Editing Lives and Letters in London. His publications include *Close Readers: Humanism and Sodomy in Early Modern England* (1997), *Hostages to Fortune: The Troubled Life of Francis Bacon 1561–1626* (with Lisa Jardine, 1998), *Philip Sidney: A Double Life* (2000), and *The Cradle King: A Life of James VI and I* (2003). He is currently working on a monograph on the Portingale community in Elizabethan London, tentatively called *Killing Dr Lopez*.

Daniel Vitkus is Associate Professor, Florida State University. He specializes in cross-cultural texts, travel literature, Renaissance drama, and the cultural history of early modern England. He is the editor of *Three Turk Plays from Early Modern England* (2000) and *Piracy, Slavery and Redemption: Barbary Captivity Narratives from Early Modern England* (2001), and he is the author of *Turning Turk: English Theater and the Multicultural Mediterranean, 1570–1630* (2003). He is currently coediting the Bedford Texts and Contexts edition of Shakespeare's *Antony and Cleopatra* and working on a study titled *Islam and the English Renaissance*.

Richard Wilson holds Professorship and Chair at Cardiff University. He is the author of *Will Power: Essays on Shakespearean Authority* (1993) and *Secret Shakespeare: Studies in Theatre, Religion and Resistance* (2004). He has edited *Christopher Marlowe and New Historicism* (1999) and *Renaissance Drama* (1996) in the Longman Critical Reader series, and *Lancastrian Shakespeare: Essays on Theatre and Religion* (2005).

Introduction: Beyond the Olive Trees: Remapping the Mediterranean World in Early Modern English Writings

Goran V. Stanivukovic

> *The Mediterranean is not merely history . . . not merely belonging.*
>
> —Predrag Matvejević, *The Mediterranean: A Cultural Landscape*[1]

The broad yet poignant reflection on the Mediterranean as a cultural signifier in this epigraph points to the route taken by the essays in this book. The word "remapping" in the title refers to discursive representations of the Mediterranean in early modern English literary and nonliterary writings. The essays in *Remapping the Mediterranean World in Early Modern English Writings*[2] address the Mediterranean from a variety of perspectives, reflecting recent scholarly interests in, and definitions of, Anglo-Mediterranean contacts. Some of those definitions in these essays take the Mediterranean to mean a geographical reality and an area of Anglo-Ottoman trade and diplomacy. For others, it implies early modern imperialism. In this volume, the Mediterranean is subsumed under a more specific category of the eastern Mediterranean as a region onto which Renaissance England projected discursively, if not in reality, its colonizing fantasies. The essays in *Remapping the Mediterranean World* examine how early modern English imagination conceptualized the intermingling categories of sameness and difference, of otherness and familiarity, which were produced through complex and often ambiguous contacts between Renaissance England and the Mediterranean, especially the eastern Mediterranean.

The rift that divided East and West in the ideological realm, however, was not always matched by rivalry in the realm of culture. As Daniel Goffman argues, "at . . . the societal level, there never has been an enduring rapprochement between the Christian and Islamic worldviews" since "a host of common interests always counterbalanced this doctrinal abyss."[3] The degree to which the interwoven cultures, religions, and complex politics of the Mediterranean feature in the volume's essays varies. Yet at times, the approaches in these essays overlap, reflecting the historical situation in which commerce, cultural interaction, religious divisions, and uneasy diplomacy occurred simultaneously. It is this interaction of the aspects of engagement that prevents us from creating clear-cut categories within the Mediterranean framework. How does one speak about Mediterranean commerce without engaging with Anglo-Turkish relations? How does one investigate colonialism without taking into account internal differences between the Turkish and North African parts of the Ottoman Empire? How does one separate mercantilism from the proto-colonialism that underpinned these contacts? Can one speak about travel and geography without addressing the Anglo-Turkish politics that underpin the representations and discourses of cultural differences within the Mediterranean? Thus the epigraph from Matvejević also indirectly sheds light on the possibilities of critical approaches to the study of the early modern Mediterranean. The editor of a recent history poses a similar query about the boundaries of the scholarly approach to the Mediterranean in the following way: "the question is whether to identify the Mediterranean in terms of its waters, its islands, its coasts or indeed the civilizations and states that have emerged along its coasts."[4] This question articulates some of the concern with the definition of the Mediterranean as an object of cultural analysis, an issue that is crucial for the methodologies and approaches taken in *Remapping the Mediterranean World.*[5]

Relevant for this volume, then, is the definition of the Mediterranean in early modern English literature. Is it the geography, urban topography, cultures, and peoples of its shores and islands that we are looking for? Or does the Mediterranean suggest a looser, more conceptual, and broader political allegory of empire, unrelated to a specific location in the Mediterranean but emerging out of the idea of early (proto-) colonial discourses associated with the region? Literary scholars and historians alike grapple with the problem of defining the Mediterranean. Recently, one scholar has formulated this issue of definition in the following way: "the history of the Mediterranean Sea is not just the history of fleets and trades . . .; the movement of ideas

and religions need to be documented as well. It is not just with politics, but with the way that objects and ideas moved across this space."[6]
The essays in this volume address the Mediterranean both as a cultural
and geographical space, and they approach it as a symbolic set of ideas
produced by the Mediterranean.

What parameters do we use to determine the work's indebtedness
to the Mediterranean? Multicultural interaction, as in *Othello*, can be
taken as one of those parameters. Recent work argues that the
Mediterranean content matters when, for instance, plays take an interest in the specific kinds of cross-cultural interaction that occurred
between England and the Ottoman Empire.[7] Speaking about
Mediterranean multiculturalism in drama, Daniel Vitkus observes:
"Many of the plays set in the Mediterranean merely deploy the foreign
setting as an exotic framework in which to depict English concerns
and English behavior, but the texts that I will analyze . . . are plays
that have a tighter referential relation to contemporary events and
conditions in the Mediterranean world."[8] And he continues: "Drama
was an important medium through which the different appearances,
behaviors, and beliefs of other cultures were imported, distorted,
mimicked, and displayed."[9] In addition to making a case for multiculturalism as a topic that gave rise to a new type of drama dealing with
the Anglo-Ottoman Mediterranean, Vitkus also suggests why drama,
more than other genres, engaged with the Mediterranean to such a
degree. I would add that, as a cultural conduit for new ideas and attitudes toward the new diplomacy and the Anglo-Ottoman markets
that started to open up in the 1580s, theater's capacity to "display"
and bring the distant Mediterranean to London audiences with
immediacy made the transmission of the new ideologies regarding the
eastern Mediterranean more effective. Because London was an important center for commercial traffic in Mediterranean goods, for foreign
merchant-bankers and also for the theater, itself an economic institution, theater became a fruitful space for Mediterranean stories. Thus it
both reflected and also shaped the new English subject looking for
opportunities for personal and economic profit in travel and trade.
Further arguing for the connection between the Mediterranean and
theater, Vitkus says: "Theater represented the world of foreign
trade on stage, and foreign trade (and later, colonization) became an
endeavor through which new roles, new forms of self-fashioning,
could be staged . . . The playhouses were exoticized by representing
and selling exotic difference in many different forms."[10] Just as
the region was crucial to the emergence of capitalism, so were the
theaters central to disseminating ideas about, and challenges to,

early capitalism in the burgeoning capitalist market of early modern London.

Other literary genres, especially lyric poetry and to a lesser extent the epic, did not beat to the pulse of the market and the commercial aspect of cultural production in the way that drama was. These genres were governed more by literary conventions (for example, Petrarchism or pastoralism) than they were influenced by the topical issues of trade and politics in the Mediterranean, as was the case with drama. Poetry was dependent upon literary conventions and it targeted a select group of mostly aristocratic readers. In poems such as "The Fishermans tale" by Francis Sabie, "Upon the picture of Achmat the Turkish tyrant" by Phineas Fletcher, and "To my Noble and Judicious friend Sir Henry Blount" by Henry King, the Mediterranean features minimally, and mostly as a background, not a primary topic.[11] Some writers of prose romances, however, not only set their narratives in the eastern Mediterranean but employed it to promote discourses of English nationalism vis-à-vis an imagined colonialism in the region and in North Africa.[12] Accounts of travel, merchant-adventurers' records and diaries, border annotations and illustrations in geographical maps, descriptions of places in atlases, manuscript portolan charts, and treatises on trade and shipping in the Mediterranean, all these represent rich resources for our knowledge of the area. This material that we can classify under the broad category of travel literature has not been dealt with in a separate contribution in this volume, but to varying degrees, all the essays resort to a number of travel documents in generating historical contexts for their arguments. Early modern English travel literature, from the period before the transatlantic voyages to North America, inspired early modern literary narratives and plays.[13] As most of the essays in this volume demonstrate, discourses on the Mediterranean in travel writing and imaginative literature often overlap. And sometimes it is not clear which way the influence went: from literature to travel writing or the other way round.

Two particularly fascinating phenomena in the field of the Mediterranean studies at present are that the Ottoman Empire has been superimposed on the concept of the Mediterranean and that a shift has occurred from looking at the Mediterranean from the perspective of the West, with a focus on Spain, Italy, and Greece as topics of scholarly investigation, to a focus on the eastern Mediterranean.[14] The absence in this volume of essays on Italy and Greece, which one would expect to find in a book such as this, should not be read as a lacuna in the examination of the Mediterranean. Rather, the effort has been to create room for the emerging study of the Ottoman

Mediterranean's impact on early modern English literature.[15] In recent scholarship, to study the Mediterranean has increasingly meant to focus on the Anglo-Ottoman Mediterranean; thus the *remapping* in the title suggests the predominantly Ottoman-orientation of this book. A point made recently in connection with the Ottoman involvement in the defeat of the Spanish Armada in July 1588 represents a good example of how the new scholarly tilt toward Anglo-Turkish Mediterranean diplomacy can alter the perspective from which we view a major event in English history. The defeat of the Armada, hitherto thought to have resulted only from the combination of Sir Francis Drake's naval skills and the weather, was also enabled by the Ottomans' maneuvers of ships in the Mediterranean, splitting and thus weakening the Spanish fleet.[16] *Remapping the Mediterranean World*, then, demonstrates the growing interest in the eastern Mediterranean in early modern studies. It thus moves forward from the vision of the Mediterranean as a socioeconomic and Eurocentric place, a view represented in the important work of Ferdinand Braudel.[17] Given that most of the essays explore the Ottoman Mediterranean, the dividing line is no longer along the West-East border but along the new, "forgotten" geopolitical frontier between the north and the south, where "north" stands for the European Mediterranean and "south" for its African, mostly Ottoman coast.[18]

The Ottoman Empire occupies a pivotal role in the cultural imagination and political reality of early modern England because, as the only real empire in the sixteenth-century Mediterranean, it was the obvious entity for England to engage with, if it was to battle the older maritime powers, particularly Spain, Italy, and France, for dominance on the seas and in the markets. England had to constantly reimagine, refashion, and adjust its role in precapitalist Europe, in which warring for dominance on the sea meant conquering new markets and ensuring one's power in the Mediterranean. One of the most exhaustive collections of early modern travel literature on the Mediterranean, Richard Hakluyt's 1589 *The Principal Navigations: Voyages, Traffiques and Discoveries of the English Nation*, provides persuasive evidence of the early English focus on and obsession with Turkey. Most of the sea roads in this collection of seafaring accounts lead to the Ottoman Empire, especially Constantinople. Perceived by early modern England as at once a political menace and an economic opportunity, the Ottoman Empire, on one hand, enabled England to develop pragmatic, discursive strategies for negotiating its own power and place in the eastern Mediterranean, as the essays in *Remapping the Mediterranean* demonstrate. On the other, its interaction with the

Ottomans opened up ways for it to construct its own nationalism and create nationalistic subjects in its citizens. The "transactional power" that came out of those contacts, however, "problematize[s] the cultural binaries" in writing about the Anglo-Turkish relationship in the early modern period.[19] Yet while providing England with a cause to fantasize nostalgically about its heroic (Christian) omnipotence that was no longer promoted within the culture of chivalry at home but in the eastern Mediterranean—in the Ottoman Empire—that territory also enabled England to project onto it its own anxieties over differences in race, ethnicity, religion, social status, and sexuality.

The burgeoning economic and cultural life of London provided for lively contacts between Turkey and England in the sixteenth and seventeenth centuries. Although not all the essays in this volume are concerned with the Ottoman Empire, the overwhelming emphasis in most of them is on the differing influences it had on literature, especially drama. Drawing on new archival sources and the historicism that attempts to situate the Mediterranean in the larger context of the boundaries between Christian Europe and the primarily non-Christian Mediterranean Africa and the Near East, the essays in this volume open up a new critical field in the study of early modern England. In that field the eastern Mediterranean features as a formative influence on and a storehouse of themes in literature.[20] In a period in which frontiers were determined more by religion than by territory, the Mediterranean was considered to be at once familiar and strange. It was familiar because of the long history of the Crusades in the Holy Land and because of a more recent sense that Christians living in the old lands of Christianity, such as Armenia, were cut off by the Ottoman Empire from the Christian lands of Europe. Discursive travel to Christian North Africa and Natolia as well as the mercantile enterprises in those lands should thus be seen as examples of the symbolic connection of England with Mediterranean Christianity. It was the non-Christian parts of the Ottoman Empire, areas that were religiously different, that early modern England conceptualized as remotely unfamiliar.

The essays in *Remapping the Mediterranean World* examine how literature reflected and reacted to two competing attitudes toward the Mediterranean: as a region of cultural and commercial interaction and productive engagement and as an arena of political tensions at a time of "cultural collisions" and divisions between its cultures and religions.[21] Thus the Mediterranean that emerges from this book represents not only a place but a concept and a cultural construct, a source of ideas about the complexly ambiguous West-East diplomacy, and an imagined space for literature. This Mediterranean, then, becomes an allegory for the exercise of the imperial imagination and a zone in which imperialism is critiqued; it turns into a hiding place for converts and gives rise to a cultural narrative of the intersection between an early modern linguistic debate and a vast area of danger and trade; it becomes a meeting place for strangers, and for infidels and Christians; and it emerges as an arena that liberates desires bottled up in English subjects by the strict codes of Protestant morality. In the early modern English imagination, then, the Mediterranean is both a world apart from and a part of England.[22] Because the Mediterranean world is one "where borders are notoriously obscure and where cultural identities are impossible to fix,"[23] it becomes a good resource for the shaping of the new English subject.[24] Hence the Mediterranean animates in early modern English literature some of the most controversial and most ambiguous discourses of race, gender, religion, and proto-ethnography.

From Ephesus to Valencia, from Tunis to Venice—that is, from Turkey to Spain and from North Africa to the Adriatic Sea—the Mediterranean infuses the political and literary map of early modern England in ways that have been only partially explored. The Mediterranean, especially the eastern region, features centrally in the expanding English power in Europe. In the sixteenth and seventeenth centuries, to trade globally, wage global wars, mingle with the world-wide population, and become a world traveller meant shipping one's fleets, navigators, cartographers, and merchant-adventurers to the Mediterranean, especially to the Ottoman Empire. England embarked on Mediterranean activities more prominently after the 1580s, when William Harborne, Elizabeth's intelligencer and ambassador in Turkey brokered for the Queen a network of trading opportunities with the Ottomans and helped to open the market for goods in both directions. From the 1580s, one notices a pronounced interest in the Mediterranean in early modern English literature that started to imagine the English presence in the Mediterranean.

England's intensive focus, manifested in travel and trade, on the Ottoman Empire starting in the 1580s and culminating in the 1590s did not come without antecedents. The end of the war over Lepanto in 1571 (in which the naval armies of the Holy League of Christian states defeated the Ottomans) marks a period of slow weakening in the powerful Ottoman state, shattered by the losses it had suffered during the Battle of Lepanto.[25] At the same time, that battle marks the entry of England onto the political and commercial stage of the eastern Mediterranean, where it had few contacts before the 1580s. Since after the Battle of Lepanto, Europe shifted "the center of her creative activity north and east,"[26] England's activities and interests in the eastern Mediterranean in the 1580s and 1590s were both politically and commercially justified. In turn, one could look at them as the English expansion of Christian power in the eastern Mediterranean. Lisa Jardine's essay "Alien Intelligence," for example, has charted the route for our thinking about the network of power between the West and the eastern Mediterranean, which involves simultaneous transactions of diplomatic intelligence and mercantile profit.[27] While the merchant-bankers of early modern England used the eastern Mediterranean to establish new trading colonies in port cities such as Algiers, Tunis, Tripoli, Smyrna(Izmir), and Constantinople, they also sifted through the historical ruins of the eastern Mediterranean in search of antiquities. A growing interest in the Levant as a region of opportunities for trade, travel, and privateering encouraged the study of the ancient languages of the East, including Arabic.[28] Mediterranean travels stimulated historiographic writing about the lands of classical antiquity.[29] The opening up of Mediterranean trade resulted in the importation of silk, carpets, olive oil, wine, spices, amber, and other luxury commodities desired by the ruling and mercantile classes.

England's interest in the Mediterranean comes out of the old, symbolic connection with its own cultural roots in the classical and early Christian Mediterranean and out of the plethora of new opportunities for political and commercial prestige in a world of mercantile competition, especially with France and Italy. The political and commercial opportunities that the sea offered provided an arena for the swelling ambitions of an insular northern country to place itself in the vortex of activity among a number of Europe's emerging maritime powers. The new European nations fought for advantage on the seas and in markets with the more established centers of the "ancien regime" in the Mediterranean, such as Italy, Turkey, Aleppo, Alexandria, Tunis, and Algiers.[30] When England's interests in the eastern Mediterranean became more pronounced, it entered the battle "between . . . [the] ancient regime and the 'northern intruders,' France, Holland, and, later on, Russia. They upset the balance in the Mediterranean not because they were Christian but because they were new. Their newness derived from the fact that their world, unlike the Venetian and Ottoman worlds, was larger than the Mediterranean."[31] Literature that grew out of a new history of Anglo-Mediterranean contacts registered many ways in which this clash between the old and new powers gave rise to writing about the Mediterranean.[32]

Although the thesis that English political and commercial interests in the Mediterranean represented a precursor to the country's colonial projects in the New World of the Atlantic continues to attract attention, one can challenge it on the grounds that the Anglo-Mediterranean connection should be considered on its own terms, given the specificity of the Ottoman Empire that ruled a large part of the eastern Mediterranean, including North Africa. For example, encouraged by new research on the politics of the early modern Mediterranean, literary historians may wish to start reconsider their attitudes toward the "Bermuda pamphlets" syndrome that has for a while compelled critics to juxtapose the politics of the Mediterranean *Tempest* with the colonialism of the New World of the Atlantic.[33] Some critics have seen in *The Tempest* Shakespeare's attempt to bring together two most radical manifestations of the English hegemony outside its borders: colonialism in the New World and England's entry into the diplomatic arena of the Mediterranean. These critics have argued that the play should be seen as fusing (albeit ambiguously) the Mediterranean and Atlantic frames of reference.[34] As Jerry Brotton has argued, "if *The Tempest* carried traces of England's earliest encounters with the Americas, then it also is concomitantly and crucially inflected with English involvement in the trade and diplomacy of the Mediterranean world."[35]

Searching for sources elsewhere, early modern English literature picked up on the cultural push toward the Mediterranean that swept Europe and started to emulate ideas about the Mediterranean in its narratives of the nation. But it did not stop at that, and like other countries of northern Europe, especially Holland, England also became an integral part of the Mediterranean because it became crucial for the advancement of its trade and empire. *Remapping the Mediterranean World* complicates these arguments about early modern English colonialism either by linking it analogically to other historical imperial projects, especially in Ireland, or by showing how discourses of empire started to formulate themselves in some of the writing about the Mediterranean in the late sixteenth and early seventeenth centuries.

Yet the book challenges some of the postcolonial arguments about imperialism by discussing them, as Jonathan Burton does in his essay here, in terms of the specific engagement with the Mediterranean, seen as different in intent from the colonization of territories in the Americas. Burton's thesis represents a call to those working in early modern Mediterranean studies to move beyond the confining models of colonial rhetoric, especially as used to discuss historical colonization in the Americas and elsewhere. At the same time, Burton voices skepticism toward criticism of the Mediterranean that privileges exchanges over other kinds of encounter. He argues that such an approach to the Mediterranean creates its own critical fictions by privileging points of exchange over the anxiety, misapprehensions, and prejudice about the alien that the Mediterranean evoked in the consciousness of early modern England. Burton's contribution serves as a frame for the writing about empire in this book, whose essays approach the imperial discourses from a number of perspectives, involving both exchanges and differences. Daniel Goffman's afterword, which engages more specifically with individual essays, approaches the issue of Anglo-Ottoman relations from yet another angle, that of the Ottomanist historian interested in how Ottoman sources regarded the interaction with the English. Thus, rather than offering a univocal approach to empire, this volume brings together a polyphony of critical voices about Mediterranean imperialism.

Through its pragmatic engagement with the political and religious complexities of the Mediterranean, early modern England, in fact, soon became one of the countries that exerted influence in that region. A number of highly popular plays, such as Marlowe's *Tamburlaine the Great*, George Peele's *The Battle of Alcazar*, the lost *Mully Mollocco*, and William Shakespeare's *The Comdey of Errors* and The *Merchant of Venice*, as well as *The Turkish Mahomet and Hiren the Fair Greek*, *Selimus, Emperor of the Turks*, and *Tamar Cham*, filled the coffers of London's theater owners, demonstrating that the playgoers were "hungry for drama with a Mediterranean connection."[36]

Like the theaters, the burgeoning print market in early modern London benefited from the growing interest in the Mediterranean. In the period between 1576 and 1620, there was more prose fiction than drama printed in London. Since a significant number of these texts constituted romances set in the Mediterranean, one could say that their authors competed with the dramatists who set their plays in the Mediterranean. The region became a topic that sold well, and the writers who resorted to it were imaginatively bringing England and Mediterranean closer together. A cursory look at the early modern prose romances and at the manuscript or printed literature of travel in the Mediterranean (Purchas, Moryson, Nicolay, Botero, Lithgow, Ramusio, Biddulph, Hakluyt) shows that the line that separates narratives and discourses of the Mediterranean in travel writing from those in romances appears to be rather thin. In both romances and travel literature the serendipitous and the strange are at the center of stories about encounters between England and the Mediterranean.

The study of the imperial Mediterranean is intricately connected with the recent historicization of race, ethnicity, nation, gender, sexuality, colonialism, and mercantilism—approaches that have expanded the scholarship on power, the circulation of ideologies, and the representation of places and subjects in early modern England.[37] The new historicist and theoretical approaches to the Mediterranean also point to the shift from source studies to the study of the Mediterranean as a political reality and a network of signifiers that shaped England's diplomatic, mercantile, and literary responses to the most dynamic world (the Ottoman Empire) of "otherness" at its doorstep. I call these early imperial ambitions "fantasies" because they represent imagined, discursive strategies designed to acquire a symbolic control over and offset anxieties about the Ottoman omnipotence in the Mediterranean. In reality, however, as Andrew Hadfield has argued, "[t]here were no attempts to establish colonies on the far shores of the Mediterranean, showing that the relationship between Englishmen and Muslims was simply not the same as that between the Englishmen and the native Americans."[38] Recent scholarship about the relationship between imperialism in the Mediterranean and the colonization of the New World of the Americas has produced subtle arguments that address imperialism as a precursor to "the transatlantic perspective" that enabled the specificities of the knowledge transaction between early modern Europe and the Mediterranean.[39] Yet the specific traits of imperialism in the Mediterranean, especially English fantasies of imperialism, still remain to be explored. In some writings, imperialism and colonialism are not imagined as pragmatic undertakings, but more as discursive enterprises or even nostalgic fantasies for the lands of early Christianity and antiquity lost to the Ottomans. This is very often the case in prose romances of the period, typically set in the Aegean archipelago, Turkey, or North Africa, even on the shores of the Black Sea. The Christian knights' travels and adventures, sometimes crowned with marriage to one of the Levantine princesses, have more to do with the fictionalized discursive "conquests" of the territories of old Christianity and the lands in which the Crusaders displayed their heroic skills and virtues than with the imagined strategies, or projections, of colonizing those lands, or with trade.

While the topic of early modern imperialism has occupied scholarly attention for some time, the ambiguities, even elusiveness, of early modern responses to the discourses of colonialism have not been sufficiently investigated. The period produced works that record the Englishmen's push toward the new continents of exotic goods and natural resources, but at the same time it has given us texts that voice a vigorous critique of such greedy and ambitious enterprises. Here is, for example, an early criticism of the English colonial practice articulated by Richard Eden, as given in Richard Willes's commentary:

> What is the matter, you Christian men, that you so greatly esteeme so lytle portion of golde more then your owne quietnesse, whiche neyerthelesse you entende to deface from these fayre ouches, and to melt the same into a rude masse. If your hunger of golde be so insatiable, that onlye for the desire you haue thereto, you disquiet so manye nations, and you yourselues also susteyne so many calamities and incommodities, lyuyng lyke banished men out of your owne countrey, I wyll shewe you a region flowing with golde, where you may satisfie your rauenyng appetites: But you must attempt the thing with a greater power, for standeth in your hand by force of armes to ouercome kings of great puissaunce, and rigorous defendours of theyr dominions . . . Albeit that the greedie hunger of golde hath not yet vexed us naked men, yet do we destroy one another by reason of ambition and desire to rule. Hereof spryngeth mortal hatred among us, and hereof commeth our destruction. (sig. K7^r)[40]

Eden's criticism of Christian men's hunger for gold, their self-inflicted calamities and their disruptions of other nations also represents his critique of the thirst for rule that obsessed Christians and spread hatred among them. His account is an early example of the counter-colonial discourse. It demonstrates how the values of empire, as the early modern period conceived it, are a product of, but also clash with, aspiring human affections and the humanist ideals of harmony and order.[41] This kind of rhetoric, however, has been neglected by much postcolonial theory and criticism that focus on the violent and unjust advantage the colonizers took of the colonized. Yet, the coexistence of colonialist and anticolonialist rhetoric in early modern England signals tension between the imperial ideology and the ideology of heroic individualism that started to emerge early in the colonial projects. Peter Hulme has argued that in *The Tempest* we see how as England and other nations of the West took on an imperialist role, "the classical world of the Mediterranean grew in importance as a repository of the images and analogues by which those nations could represent to themselves the colonial activities."[42] The classical Mediterranean is not free from contemporary ideologies when used in early modern literature; often, in fact, it becomes the principal conduit for early modern ideas. In Marlowe's play *Dido, Queen of Carthage*, for example, the narratives of the division between Rome and Carthage are coupled with the tensions between North Africa and Spain, and that in a play that dramatizes the sentimentalism of the Dido-Aeneas romance and Aeneas's misogyny and ambition.[43]

Although references are scattered throughout this book, *Remapping the Mediterranean World* does not contain a separate essay on William Shakespeare, one of the two early modern English writers most fascinated by the Mediterranean. (The other is Christopher Marlowe.)[44] There are two reasons for this exclusion. First, *Shakespeare and the Mediterranean*, a recent volume of essays, provides a selection of writings on this topic. The focus on Shakespeare and the Mediterranean inevitably raises the question of sources (broadly conceived) and discursive influences on a specific set of texts. *Remapping the Mediterranean World*, however, addresses a larger set of issues. It contains essays on John Milton and empire, on Samuel Pepys's diary, on commerce in a number of plays, on sexuality in popular prose romances, on the colonial discourses of Ireland, on Malta, on religious conversion, and on Anglo-Spanish cultural interaction. Second, the present volume provides room for Christopher Marlowe and the Mediterranean, especially for one of the most Mediterranean of early modern English works, *The Jew of Malta*.

In a field of overlapping historical activities in which traveling, trading, and fantasizing empire sometimes seamlessly mix in literature, creating clear-cut categories for essays that are often concerned with more than one aspect of the Anglo-Mediterranean contacts poses its own difficulties. Mindful of the underlying chronologies of the writings discussed, which range from the sixteenth to the early eighteenth century, and bearing in mind the wide array of topics, I have organized the essays chronologically.

The book opens with Jonathan Burton's essay that frames the volume and foregrounds those essays in the volume that are implicitly or explicitly concerned with issues of alterity. Burton defines the boundaries of the use of postcolonial theory as applied to the study of Anglo-Mediterranean interaction, and he proposes new directions in applying that theory to Mediterranean studies. Making a strong argument as to why the Mediterranean, especially the Ottoman Mediterranean, became so popular in drama, Daniel Vitkus implicitly foregrounds the tilt toward drama in a number of essays in this volume. His essay explores the relation between English diasporic trading communities in the Mediterranean and the conversion plots in English drama. Captivity discourses provide a rich resource for the subtleties and depth of the contacts between early modern England and the Muslims of the Mediterranean. In the words of Nabil Matar, narratives of captivity and conversion have demonstrated "that the *corpus captivities* provides the most extensive description of England's early modern encounter with Islam and Muslims in North Africa."[45] This point is developed in Vitkus's essay. Captives and converts put to test, in differing ways, the religious and cultural dominance of Christianity and, in narratives of such transgressions, reveal as much about Christianity as about its fears over the potential hegemony of Islam in the Mediterranean. The fear of "turning Turk," of abandoning one's Christianity "to go over to the other side,"[46] not only represents cultural instability, but also reveals the desired goals of the captives and their attitudes toward England and its authorities. Those goals are more tied to the captives' personal aspirations and motives than to "international polemic against Islam."[47] Goran V. Stanivukovic's essay explores homoerotic charges in early modern prose romances set in the eastern Mediterranean. The early modern anti-Turkish sentiments in these romances are co-opted by the erotic narratives in romances imagined to be suited to geographically remote, and hence morally unrestrained regions that become spaces in which the traveling youths of prose romances, away from the moral restraints of Protestant England, find pleasures that transgress normative sexuality. Though using romances as a test case, the essay makes a larger argument about how we might employ the Mediterranean as a resource for discussing multicultural differences, colonial ambitions, and geographical knowledge in the study of the multiple ways in which the early modern Mediterranean signifies.

Several essays deal with the varieties of cultural interaction between England and the Mediterranean. They concern actual travelers exploring the Mediterranean, as well as the appropriation of the idea of the Mediterranean. Thus Edmund Valentine Campos studies Anglo-Iberian linguistic interactions mediated through the Mediterranean. He examines the proliferation of imperial discourses from a different angle, conceptualized as "imperial lexicography" and imperial pedagogy emerging from the Anglo-Spanish war in the Mediterranean. While Campos is interested in Mediterranean imperial philology, two essays on drama inspired by the Battle of Alcazar examine early modern cultural constructions of non-Christian ethnicity. Emily Bartels, for example, analyzes George Peele's *The Battle of Alcazar* (1588–89), the first play to present a Moor in the English theater, and the construction of the Moor as an agent whose presence on the stage of the public theater in London symbolically connected England to the world outside. Leeds Barroll, however, takes a somewhat different trajectory of ethnographic construction in analyzing the mythologized, the imagined, and the alien represented in the figure of the Ottoman, in a number of plays featuring Ottomans.

Several essays explore the ways in which the mercantile Mediterranean of sixteenth- and seventeenth-century profit making combined the commercial with the imperial charges in early modern English literary representations of the Mediterranean. Richard Wilson discusses in a larger context the politics of Mediterranean trade and the role of factors (merchants) and financiers in *The Jew of Malta*. Alan Stewart approaches Robert Wilson's play *A Right excellent and famous Comedy, called The Three Ladies of London* (c. 1581) by examining the economic position of London as a growing center of global trade. Constance Relihan's essay juxtaposes Barnaby Riche's ideas about North African Mediterranean peoples with his ideas about the Irish in *A Short Survey of Ireland* (1609) and *The Irish Hubbub; or, the English Hue and Crie* (1619). Next, the essays by Elizabeth Sauer, Adam Beach, and Matthew Birchwood deal with the constructions of the notion of empire in early modern literature. Sauer examines Turkish and Mediterranean aspects of John Milton's *Paradise Lost* and *Paradise Regained*, while Matthew Birchwood analyzes conversion as a topic that animates the plot in William Davenant's play *The Siege of Rhodes* (1663). Both these essays explore Levant politics and post–1642 conflations of eastern violence and English political crisis. Bringing us close to the end of the seventeenth century, Adam Beach analyzes Samuel Pepys's *Diaries* and *Tangier Papers* against the notion of empire. The last essay, by Bernadette Andrea, spans the period between the sixteenth and early eighteenth century. It explores early modern constructions of Malta in terms of separateness, even otherness, from the surrounding world of the Mediterranean.

Remapping the Mediterranean World reimagines the Mediterranean, not only as part of a recent scholarly interest in East-West exchanges, but also within the early modern history of that region. The volume's post-Braudelian orientation manifests itself in its emphasis on culture and specifically on literature on areas germane to the construction of the Mediterranean's golden age in the consciousness and records of the sixteenth and seventeenth centuries. As a contribution to cultural history and the history of literature, this volume attempts not only to explore literary and nonliterary writings of the Mediterranean but, in so doing, also to expand a field that, at the moment, provides us with some of the most exciting research in early modern studies.

NOTES

1. Predrag Matvejević, *Mediterranean: A Cultural Landscape*, trans. Michael Henry Heim (Berkeley, Los Angeles, and London: University of California Press, 1999), pp. 10, 12.
2. For the sake of brevity, I will further refer to the title of this volume as *Remapping the Mediterranean.*
3. Daniel Goffman, *The Ottoman Empire and Early Modern Europe* (Cambridge: Cambridge University Press, 2002), p. 7.
4. David Abulafia, "Introduction," in *The Mediterranean in History*, ed. David Abulafia (Los Angeles: The Paul Getty Museum, 2003), p. 11.
5. This is a different question (it concerns scholarly approaches and methods) from the questions of the etymology and meanings of the "Mediterranean Sea," succinctly summarized by Daniel Vitkus, *Turning Turk: English Theater and the Multicultural Mediterranean, 1570–1630* (New York: Palgrave, 2003), p. 33.
6. Abulafia, "Introduction," p. 13.
7. Vitkus, *Turning Turk*, pp.1–14.
8. Ibid., p. 29.
9. Ibid.
10. Ibid., p. 28.
11. I am indebted to Jonathan Burton for drawing these poems to my attention.
12. For the list of romances set in the Mediterranean, see my essay "Recent Studies of English Literature of the Mediterranean," *ELR* 32:1 (2002): 168–86, on pp. 185–6.
13. See Andrew Hadfield, *Literature, Travel, and Colonial Writing in the English Renaissance 1545–1625* (Oxford: Clarendon Press, 1998).
14. The volume *Shakespeare and the Mediterranean* brings out a number of essays on Italy and the Mediterranean that mostly look at Italy as a discursive influence, intertext, or direct influence in Shakespeare's works. Other sources that deal with the Anglo-Italian connections in the Renaissance, include: Mario Praz, *Shakespeare e l'Italia* (Firenze: F. le Monnier, 1963), Ernesto Gillo, *Shakespeare and Italy* (Glasgow: Privately printed by Robert Maclehouse and Co., the University of Glasgow, 1949), David C. McPherson, *Shakespeare, Jonson, and the Myth of Venice* (Newark: University of Delaware, 1990), Michèle Marrapodi, A.J. Hoenselaars, Marcello Cappuzzo, and L. Falzon Santucci, *Shakespeare's Italy: Functions of Italian Locations in Renaissance Drama* (Manchester and New York: Manchester University Press, 1993), Murray J. Levith, *Shakespeare's Italian Settings and Plays* (London: Macmillan Press, 1989), and Michèle Marrapodi and A.J. Hoenselaars, *The Italian World of English Renaissance Drama: Cultural Exchange and Intertextuality* (Newark: University of Delaware Press, London: Associated University Presses, 1998), and Jonathan Bate, "The Elizabethans in Italy," in *Travel and*

Drama in Shakespeare's Time, ed. Jean-Pierre Maquerlot and Michèle Willems (Cambridge: Cambridge University Press, 1996), pp. 55–74. In her essay "Shakespeare's Greek World: The Temptations of the Sea" (in *Playing the Globe: Genre and Geography in Renaissance Drama,* ed. John Gillies and Virginia Mason Vaughan [Madison, Teaneck: Fairleigh Dickinson University Press, London: Associated University Presses, 1998], pp. 107–28), Sara Hanna provides a good survey of early modern, especially Shakespeare's, appropriations of Greece.

15. The limited Portuguese presence in the Mediterranean, especially its role in importing slaves to the European markets and the commercial trade through Marseilles, is explored in *Le Portugal et la Méditerranée,* ed. Luísa de Oliviera (Paris: Centre Culturel Calouste Gulbenkian, 2002).

16. I am referring to Jerry Brotton's argument, presented at the literary festival in Hay-on-Wye in June 2004 and reported by John Ezard in an article in the British newspaper *The Guardian,* that a hitherto unnoticed letter from Sir Francis Walsingham, Elizabeth I's "security chief and spymaster," to William Harborne shows that it was the Ottomans' maneuvers off the Mediterranean coast of Africa meant to occupy and split King Philip II's fleet and not Sir Francis Drake's "swashbuckling" that helped to defeat the Spanish Armada. Ezard quotes Brotton as saying: "So alongside all the stories we're told at school of why the Spanish Armada failed to conquer Britain and destroy Protestantism, we should add another reason: the Anglo-Ottoman alliance brokered by Elizabeth, Walsingham [and others]." See John Ezard, "Why we must thank the Turks, not Drake, for defeating the Armada," *The Guardian,* June 1, 2004. See, http://www.guardian.co.uk/uk_news/story/0,3604,1228687,00.html (accessed June 20, 2006). While Brotton has made the connection between the letter and the historical event, the material about the letter can be found in S[usan] A. Skilliter, *William Harborne and the Trade with Turkey, 1578–1582: A Documentary Study of the First Anglo-Ottoman Relations* (London: Oxford University Press for The British Academy, 1977). I am grateful to Jerry Brotton for sharing the context for his argument.

17. See Fernand Braudel, ed., *La Méditerranée: les homes et l'héritage* (Paris: Arts et métiers graphiques, 1978); ed., *La Méditerranée: l'espace et l'histoire* (Paris: Arts et métiers graphiques, 1977); *The Mediterranean and the Mediterranean World in the Age of Philip II,* 2 vols., trans. Siân Reynolds (London: Collins, 1972).

18. Andrew C. Hess, *The Forgotten Frontier: A History of the Sixteenth-Century Ibero-African Frontier* (Chicago: University of Chicago Press, 1978).

19. Lisa Jardine and Jerry Brotton, *Global Interests: Renaissance Art between East & West* (Ithaca: Cornell University Press, 2000), p. 61.

20. Points made about the English trade and financial activities in the Mediterranean in this volume go beyond those made in the essays in *Money and the Age of Shakespeare: Essays in New Economic Criticism*, which are not concerned with the Mediterranean mercantile transactions. See Linda Woodbridge, ed., *Money and the Age of Shakespeare: Essays in New Economic Criticism* (New York: Palgrave Macmillan, 2003).

21. I borrow the term "cultural collision" from Andrew C. Hess, who uses it to write about the "division[s] between Mediterranean civilizations" in the context of his study about the north-south barrier on the sixteenth-century Hispano-Muslim frontier. See Andrew C. Hess, *The Forgotten Frontier: A History of the Sixteenth-Century Ibero-African Frontier* (Chicago and London: The University of Chicago Press, 1978), p. 3.

22. Looked at from the Mediterranean perspective, early modern England illustrates Fernand Braudel's observation that "Northern Europe, beyond the olive trees, is one of the permanent realities of Mediterranean history." See Fernand Braudel, *The Mediterranean and the Mediterranean World in the Age of Philip II*, trans. Siân Reynolds (Glasgow: William Collins Sons & Co, 1972), p. 24.

23. Robert Boerth, "The Mediterranean and the Mediterranean World on the Stage of Marlowe and Shakespeare," *Journal of Theatre and Drama* 2 (1996): 36.

24. In her essay "The Psychomorphology of the Clitoris," *GLQ: A Journal of Lesbian and Gay Studies* 2:1–2 (1995): 83–113, Valerie Traub shows how a number of travel accounts in Turkey animated early English anxieties over female-female eroticism.

25. Daniel Goffman, *The Ottoman Empire and Early Modern Europe* (Cambridge: Cambridge University Press, 2002), p. 113. On the consequences of the Battle of Lepanto, see also Andrew C. Hess, "The Battle of Lepanto and Its Place in Mediterranean History," *Past and Present* 57 (1972): 53; and Colin Imber's review of Hugh Bicheno's *Crescent and Cross: The Battle of Lepanto* (London: Weidenfeld and Nicolson, 2003), *Times Literary Supplement* (October 2, 2003): 25.

26. Hess, "The Battle of Lepanto," p. 53.

27. Lisa Jardine, "Alien Intelligence: Mercantile Exchange and Knowledge Transactions in Marlowe's *The Jew of Malta*," *Reading Shakespeare Historically* (London and New York: Routledge, 1996), pp. 98–113.

28. See G.D. Ramsay, *English Overseas Trade During the Centuries of Emergence: Studies in Some Modern Origins of the English-Speaking World* (London: Macmillan, 1957), p. 61.

29. One such book is Lodowick Lloyd's *The Consent of Time, Deciphering the Error of the Grecians in their Olympiads* (London: George Bishop and Ralph Newberie, 1590). In the preface to this book, Lloyd says

that his travels inspired him to retell and comment on the history of antiquity in Greece and the Levant.

30. Molly Greene, *A Shared World: Christians and Moslems in the Early Modern Mediterranean* (Princeton: Princeton University Press, 2000), p. 5.

31. Ibid.

32. England registers the shifts between the new emerging powers and the "ancient regime." This new power shift involved even Russia, which was the last to join, in the seventeenth century, eastern Mediterranean mercantile activities. Marlowe's *Tamburlaine the Great* and the Muscovy Company's Asian trade, see Richard Wilson, "Visible Bullets: Tamburlaine the Great and Ivan Terrible," *ELH* 62:1 (1995): 47–68.

33. *The Tempest* has recently been restored to its Mediterranean context in *The Tempest and Its Travels*, ed. Peter Hulme and William H. Sherman (Philadelphia: University of Pennsylvania Press, 2000). In "Voyage to Tunis: New History and the Old World of *The Tempest*," *ELH*, 64:2 (1997): 333–57, Richard Wilson makes arguments about the Mediterranean context of *The Tempest* in "The Island of *The Tempest*," *On Shakespeare: Jesus, Shakespeare, and Karl Marx, and Other Essays* (Oxford: Basil Blackwell, 1989], pp. 322–40), Brockbank argues for the indebtedness of *The Tempest* to the Mediterranean setting and politics. D.D. Carnicelli, in his essay "The Widow and the Phoenix: Dido, Carthage, and Tunis in *The Tempest*," *Harvard Library Bulletin* 27:4 (1979): 389–433), also locates this within the sixteenth century's thinking about Dido, Carthage, and Tunis.

34. Peter Hulme, "Hurricane in the Carribees: The Constitution of the Discourse of English Colonialism," in *1642: Literature and Power in the Seventeenth Century, Proceedings of the Essex Conference on the Society of Literature*, ed. Francis Barker, Jay Bernstein, John Coombes, Peter Hulme, Jennifer Stone, Jan Stratton (n. p., 1980), pp. 55–83.

35. Jerry Brotton, " 'This Tunis, sir, was Carthage': Contesting Colonialism in *The Tempest*," in *Post-Colonial Shakespeare*, ed. Ania Loomba and Martin Orkin (London and New York: Routledge, 1998), p. 24.

36. Roslyn L. Knutson, "Elizabethan Documents, Captivity Narratives, and the Market for Foreign History Plays," *ELR* 26:1 (1996): 95.

37. A recent collection of travel and discovery includes texts that reveal early travelers' interest in ethnography as part of the proto-colonial writing about the Mediterranean. See *Travel Knowledge: European "Discoveries" in the Early Modern Period*, ed., Ivo Kamps and Jyotsna G. Singh (New York: Palgrave, 2001).

38. Andrew Hadfield, ed., *Amazons, Savages & Machiavels: Travel & Colonial Writing in English, 1550–1630* (Oxford: Oxford University Press, 2001), p. 119. In his book *Turks, Moors and Englishmen in the Age of Discovery* (New York: Columbia University Press, 1999), Nabil

Matar suggests that England's representations of the Mediterranean ought to be seen as precursors of the colonial projects of the New World of the Atlantic. On the gendering of empire, see Bernadette Andrea, "Pamphilia's Cabinet: Gendered Authorship and Empire in Lady Mary Wroth's *Urania*," *ELH* 68 (2001): 335–58.

39. See Barbara Fuchs, *Mimesis and Empire: The New World, Islam, and European Identities* (Cambridge and New York: Cambridge University Press, 2001), p. 3.

40. *The History of Trauayle in the West and East Indies, and other countreys lying eyther way, towards fruitfull and ryche Moluccaes. Gathered in parte, and done into Englyshe by Richarde Eden, newly set in order, augmented, and finished by Richarde Willes* (London: by Richard Iugge, 1577).

41. For an earlier interpretation of empire represented in Shakespeare's mercantile cities, see Philip Brockbank's "Urban Mysteries of the Renaissance: Shakespeare and Carpaccio," in his book *The Creativity of Perception* (Oxford: Basil Blackwell, 1991), pp. 145–61.

42. Peter Hulme, *Colonial Encounters: Europe and the Native Caribbean, 1492–1797* (London and New York: Methuen, 1986), p. 35.

43. This line of argument relies on Margo Hendrick's reading of Marlowe's play in "Managing the Barbarian: *The Tragedy of Dido, Queen of Carthage*," *Renaissance Drama* NS 23 (1992): 165–88.

44. On Marlowe's use of the Mediterranean, see Emily C. Bartels, "Malta, the Jew, and the Fictions of Difference: Colonialist Discourse in Marlowe's *The Jew of Malta*," *ELR* 20:1 (1990): 1–16; "The Double Vision of the East: Imperialist Self-Construction in Marlowe's *Tamburlaine*, Part One," *Renaissance Drama* 23 (1992): 3–24; "Marlowe, Shakespeare, and the Revision of Stereotypes," *Research Opportunities in Renaissance Drama* 32 (1993): 13–26; and *Spectacles of Strangeness: Imperialism, Alienation, and Marlowe* (Philadelphia: University of Pennsylvania Press, 1993).

45. Daniel J. Vitkus and Nabil Matar, eds., *Piracy, Slavery, and Redemption: Barbary Captivity Narratives from Early Modern England* (New York: Columbia University Press, 2001), p. 6.

46. Jonathan Bate, "Othello and the Other—Turning Turk: The Subtleties of Shakespeare's Treatment of Islam," *Times Literary Supplement* (October 19, 2001): 14.

47. For a historicized account of English captivity narratives and to Braudel's view of the politicized Christian-Islamic polemics, see Nabil Matar, "English Accounts of Captivity in North Africa and the Middle East: 1577–1625," *Renaissance Quarterly* 54: 2 (2001): 553–72, on p. 554.

CHAPTER 1

EMPLOTTING THE EARLY MODERN MEDITERRANEAN

Jonathan Burton

Traveling from London by air, passengers to Istanbul today cross the English Channel, proceed southeasterly above continental Europe before passing over the Sea of Marmara and arrive at Ataturk International Airport approximately four hours later. During this passage across eight nations' airspace, virtually all transactions are conducted in English and many relax enough to sleep away the journey, ignoring entirely the logistics of flight and weather as well as the curiosities of the countries passing below at 500 miles per hour. A traveler might easily book passage for such a trip one day in advance, choosing from as many as sixteen different departure times and six different carriers. Likewise, thirteen flights from five carriers depart from Istanbul for London in the same twenty-four hour period.

In the first decades of Anglo-Ottoman commercial and diplomatic relations, a similar trip was, of course, unthinkable. A journey to Istanbul (i.e., Constantinople) would be planned months in advance. Then a ship might sit anchored for days or even weeks awaiting a favorable wind or better visibility. Storms regularly scuttled ships or sent them northwards into the Irish Sea, so that ships often spent a month "at sea" before actually leaving British waters. A reasonable expectation would be for the ship to pass through the Straits of Gibraltar and into the Mediterranean after six weeks of travel. When another ship appeared on the horizon—whether English, French,

Spanish, Moorish, or Turkish—a captain would assess the strength of his own ship and crew, choosing either to take flight or pursue without regard for the ship's ostensible itinerary. The same crew might on one day act as pirates / privateers, and the next day flee the depredations of a stronger vessel. Once on the Mediterranean, ships made numerous landfalls, securing provisions, trading for local produce such as currants, oils, and wines, and taking aboard and disembarking passengers of various nationalities and religions. A ship heading to Constantinople might first sail as far as Iskenderun before turning back to sail up the Dardanelles. So, for example, passengers traveling from Gravesend aboard the *Hector* embarked in mid-February 1599 and sailed up the Bosporus to Constantinople in August of the same year.

In a culture of supersonic travel, scholars of the early modern Mediterranean regularly pass over this sea voyage with its impediments and contingencies to fly ahead to more captivating moments of cross-cultural exchange. This essay will not seek to fill in the lacunae of the voyage. Instead, I offer these contrasting journeys as a heuristic device. They merely gesture toward the risks we face in our own crossings, risks of effacing cultural and temporal distances as we reach back from the standpoint of early twenty-first century Western academia to the early modern world and more particularly the early modern Mediterranean. Despite the claims of publishers and theater companies, the early moderns are *not* our contemporaries. Though we may find in their writings moments that speak to our own experience, our own schematization of the past was not matched in the minds of those we examine. The early modern Mediterranean is a particularly engaging subject today because it presents a situation where Western hegemony was a fantasy and arguably the greatest regional power was an Islamic empire centered in Istanbul. Its history therefore offers a host of counternarratives to the kind of history that posits European empires as dominant or inevitable. But how do we tell the story of the early modern Mediterranean?[1] What are the sources we use? What kinds of journeying do we embark upon as we attempt to deposit ourselves in and reproduce another space and time? In our eagerness to arrive in a fresh new space of postmodern, anti-imperial history, how can we do justice to the obstacles, uncertainties, and transformations that marked early modern Mediterranean ventures?

By now it is an old saw to argue against Edward Said's contention that Orientalism can be traced back as far as the European Renaissance. A virtual army of critics indicates instead that not only were relations between "the East" and "the West" often characterized by European compromise, deference, and a desire for exchange, nothing resembling discursive coherence in regard to "the Orient" was even possible before the eighteenth century (if at all).[2] In place of Said's unilateral model (which he has gone to some lengths to correct himself), we have begun to explore models of exchange—exchanges of merchandise, of bodies, of ideologies.[3] The appeal of exchange models lies in their bi- or even multilateral nature, their admitting the possibility of agency on various sides of a given transaction. Yet exchange models do more than allow for agency. They also admit the possibility that a given discourse can be engaged and influenced by its nominal object. Thus "the East" can participate in shaping its various incarnations in Western discourse, and vice versa. Such partic- ipation is not necessarily direct, pointed, or immediately recognizable. We cannot pinpoint and track the exchange of ideas as if they were one of many commodities, and notions of a "contact zone" can obscure the ways in which discursive forces may collide and intermin- gle without the oversight of individual wills. Exchange models demand a new kind of scholarship, one that reflects the multilateral nature of foreign exchange as well as its sometimes disjointed and syn- chronic engagements. In short, any reconstruction of early modern Mediterranean exchanges calls for not just a different history, but a different kind of history.[4]

In this essay I would like to address some methodological questions related to our development of such histories. More specifi- cally, I am concerned with two particular questions: First, how do literary scholars reconstruct and theorize exchange when our archives are one-sided? Second, how can we avoid in our own histories repro- ducing the problems of emplotment that we find in early modern accounts of exchange?

My first concern with a one-sided archive derives from the fact that the libraries, databases, or microfilm sets that shape and limit our research afford us access to ample European sources, but far fewer Ottoman, East Asian, Native American, or African sources. Locating non-European sources to supplement Western archives has been a slow and complex process in many of the areas that most interest us. In my own area of interest, the most elusive are Turkish accounts of Anglo-Ottoman encounters. This deficiency has been attributed not only to a lack of Muslim interest in the English, but also to a relatively underexplored and bureaucratically vexing Turkish archive.[5] To fur- ther complicate matters, the translation of Ottoman documents requires learning Turkish, Arabic, and Persian, and deciphering no fewer than six handwriting scripts. Given the material obstacles to archival work on Ottoman culture, currently there are barely enough qualified scholars to properly catalogue, let alone translate, the sundry volumes in Turkish archives.

As a result, in seeking to contextualize the dramatization of Turkish figures on the English stage, we typically read English accounts of travelers' encounters with Turkish customs in sources like William Biddulph's *The Travels of Certain Englishmen* (1609), but rarely consider how a Turkish source might otherwise inscribe the same moment. Regardless of their provenance, texts invariably emplot their subjects in explicatory narratives—narratives designed to perform functions such as compensation, rationalization, and validation. To emplot a given moment or set of events is to endow them with meanings they lack in and of themselves; it is to crystallize *experience* into the more finite *event*, and in turn to locate such *events* in relation to a series from which other experiences have been left out. As Hayden White reminds us, "the specific chronological scale used for this ordering procedure is always culture-specific and adventitious, a purely heuristic device the validity of which depends upon the scientific aims and interests of the scientific discipline in which it is used."[6] Biddulph's supposed editor, "Theophilus Lavender," is unusually conscious of and forthcoming with his text's aims and interests. In a preface (announced by a page-sized, boldface warning urging, "Good Reader read the Preface, or else read nothing"), Lavender claims to have published the text against the will of the author in order to serve "a public good."[7] As he goes on to explain, this means that in the course of reading about Biddulph's travels in the Ottoman sultan's realm, English readers are expected to learn "to love, honor and obey their good and gracious King" (sig. A2^r). Similarly, in reading about Islamic "chicanery," they may "learn to love and reverence their pastors" (sig. A2^r), and religion. Beyond these lessons in political and religious dogma, wives may learn "to love their husbands, when they shall read in what slavery women live in other countries, and in what awe and subjection to their husbands" (sig. A2^r), while "servants may be taught to be faithful to their [comparatively merciful] masters" (sig. A2^r). Biddulph's and Lavender's text is merely one example of the various ways in which our access to moments of exchange is limited by ideological emplotment. As the preacher to the company of Englishmen resident in Aleppo, Biddulph was troubled by the abuses of Christians living in the Islamic world: "They which dwell long in wicked countries and converse with wicked men," he worried, "are somewhat tainted with their sins, if not altogether fouled with the leaven of their ungodliness" (p. 81). He observed Christian men taking and later abandoning local wives, as well as the children they had sired, and accounting it "no sin, or at least wise such a sin as may be washed away with a little holy water" (p. 81). Biddulph concluded, "these are the virtues which many Christians learn sojourning long in heathen countries" (p. 81). With the help of his god-loving (Theophilus) editor, Biddulph's account of the Ottoman world is therefore framed to fashion a conservative brand of patriarchal, Christian Englishness. Consequently, his portrait of the Ottoman world is in many ways collateral, or derivative.

We can discern Biddulph's strategic reshapings when he interrupts his account of Aleppo to explicate "Mahomet's laws and eight commandments" as practiced by the Turks. What is initially striking about this account is the notion that Islam has *eight* commandments. Muslims are, in fact, enjoined to structure their lives around *five* ritual acts ordained by the Qur'an. These are the declaration of belief (*shahada*); daily prayer (*salat*); fasting (*sawm*); almsgiving (*zakat*); and pilgrimage (*hajj*). Of these, Biddulph's commandments include the first four, omit the last and insert in its place four additional edicts: a prohibition against murder; a version of the Golden Rule ("Do unto others as thou wouldst be done unto thyself"); an obligation that all Muslim men marry; and a mandate for children's obedience to their parents. While each of these additions is certainly part of the Muslim tradition, none is considered among the five pillars of the faith.[8] Why then does Biddulph characterize them as such and what are the resultant effects?

It is only fair to point out that Biddulph was not the first to make this error. Indeed, he seems to have learned his "commandments" from *The Policie of the Turkish Empire*, published a dozen years earlier in 1597. It is possible that Biddulph even had his information corroborated by Turks, but failed to make a proper distinction between Islamic laws, customs, and the "pillars of the faith." It is also possible that Biddulph had his information corroborated by Turks who were not particularly well-versed in Islamic doctrine. All the same, preserving these additions that fabricate, or at least decontextualize Islamic doctrine provides Biddulph with a venue for musing on problems in the English community. He notes that, unlike his factious English subjects who were "most forward to offer me wrong only for doing my duty and following the order of our Church of England" (p. 62), the Turks check their murderous impulses among themselves, regardless of the severity of their conflicts. Though they may be "unjust and deceitful in their proceedings with strangers" (p. 53), Biddulph contends similarly that amongst their coreligionists, the Turks adhere to the Golden Rule. His discussion of Turkish marital customs likewise reflects poorly on the English as Biddulph concludes that "If the like order [Turkish customs] were in England, women would be more dutiful and faithful to their husbands than many of them are" (pp. 55–6). In the last case, the doctrine of filial devotion, the addition is less flattering toward the Turks but works to the same ends. Biddulph remarks, "How badly this duty is performed among them, I know by experience; for I did never read or hear of more disobedient children to their parents, either in word or in deed" (p. 53). What these four additions share in common is a concern with order and unity within a society of faith. They effectively call for a renewed sense of community under the banner of the Protestant (i.e., patriarchal) family. Thus they speak to Biddulph's experience in ten years of traveling around the Mediterranean where he claims he "never received, neither was offered wrong by any nation but mine own countrymen, and by them chiefly whom it chiefly concerned to protect me from wrongs" (p. 62). Islamic customs thus function primarily as a screen upon which English problems are projected. So as Biddulph's description of Aleppo is interrupted by his account of Islamic precepts, the Ottoman scene is effectively repopulated with English characters and themes.

Up to this point, any conclusions I have drawn regarding Biddulph's account of the "Mahometan Commandments" have been derived from exclusively internal evidence. While they indicate how moments of encounter are refracted through an ideologically skewed lens, they also represent what we might call a *formalist historicism*. By restricting its vision to the text in question, this account reproduces Biddulph's tendencies to crowd out his ostensible subject, largely writing over the possibility that Biddulph's letters might also have been shaped by local, which is to say Turkish, influences. The appropriate response would seem to be to supplement our sources with non-English texts, texts shaped no less by ideological emplotment, but at least offering competing narratives. To counter Biddulph we might consider, for example, an Ottoman traveler's account of Aleppo, or a seventeenth-century Muslim's explication of Qur'anic doctrine. But what would we learn from such a comparison and how would we choose the appropriate text(s) for comparison? For the moment I want to suspend these important questions and instead pursue the kind of comparative analysis I am describing, considering as I do so, to what extent a different kind of history is possible.

To these ends, I will first consider English treatments of the 1453 siege of Constantinople alongside Ottoman accounts. Often seen as a watershed moment in the history of Eastern Europe and the Levant, the 1453 siege of Constantinople culminated in the Ottoman conquest and transformation of the Byzantine Empire. In English accounts of this event, like the one in John Foxe's "The History of the Turks," the "loss" of Constantinople is inserted into a providential narrative concerned with the "the dissension and discord, falsehood, idleness, inconstancy, greedy avarice, lack of truth and fidelity among *christian* men."[9] For Foxe and others, the triumph of the Turks is attributable to Reformation conflicts, and the very rise of the Ottoman Empire is made contingent upon Christian error and a momentary rift in the greater (if vexed) history of Christianity. In the words of one early sixteenth-century commentator, "the begynnynge of all these warres captyvyte oppressyon and all plages whych the Turkes have brought upon Christen people maye be clerely preceyved to be in oure selfe."[10] Similarly, after attributing the rise of the Turks first and foremost to the sinfulness of Christians, Richard Knolles remarks upon the great number of Christians serving in the Turkish army at the time of the siege, and goes on to note how the miners who dug beneath the city walls were "directed by Christians skillful in that kind of work."[11] Similarly it is "a wicked Christian" that shows the Turks "a device how to bring a great part of his fleet overland into the haven and thereby to assault that part of the city by water which the citizens least feared" (p. 343). In the end the Turkish victory is figured by Knolles as God's punishment of a lapsed Christendom, as the Turks themselves are merely implements of God's justice.

Ottoman chroniclers of the siege offer skewed, providential histories of their own. Here the siege is emplotted within a lengthy history of Ottoman ascension, studded with prophesies foretelling the event and dating as far back as the seventh century. Evliya Çelebi, whose great-grandfather was a standard-bearer at the 1453 conquest, catalogues no less than ten sieges of Constantinople (beginning from AD 663), noting the slow but steady inroads made by Islam with each successive campaign. Following the 5th siege, one of the conditions of peace was that Muslims "should be allowed to settle in that city."[12] Following the 6th siege (in AD 777), Çelebi notes, three new Muslim districts as well as a mosque were added. Thus the conquest is figured as a slow and steady conversion, rather than a sudden, violent scourge. What bears consideration in this comparison is how each author's account contends with a competing tradition that denigrates his own. European versions like Foxe's seek to disavow the significance of Islam's millennium-long claims on what we call "the West."[13] Ottoman accounts, on the other hand, emphasize a heterogeneous

Constantinople whose transformation into "Islambol" ("ample in its Islam") was characterized by submission to the virtue and might of Islam. Each participates in a synchronic exchange, coeval with and shaped in part by a rival tradition, but not necessarily in direct, sequential, or reciprocal dialogue. As Walter D. Mignolo argues of a *pluritopic hermeneutics*, multiple perspectives take us beyond cultural relativism to an understanding of how the understanding subject "has to assume the existence of alternative politics of location with equal rights to claim the truth."[14] By virtue of their thematic proximity, each makes greater sense in relation to the other as, more generally, "neither the Ottoman polity nor Europe makes a lot of sense without the other" (Goffman, p. xiv).

This initial example does not offer a moment of exchange in the traditional sense. Foxe and Çelebi never met, and were almost certainly unfamiliar with each other's writings. One might argue that the only thing that draws them together is this essay. However, restricting ourselves to documented instances of direct exchange fails to account for the various avenues of informal exchange that go unrecorded. Perhaps what we can reasonably argue is that Foxe and Çelebi participated in and supplemented overlapping traditions marked by their competing claims on Mediterranean history. Of course, the danger in this kind of analysis is in overestimating the degree to which overlapping traditions engage with and absorb one another.

One recent attempt to recover the Ottoman past, particularly in relation to the West, is found in Daniel Goffman's most recent book, *The Ottoman Empire and Early Modern Europe*. Goffman begins by describing an "acute shortage of personality . . . in our sources on the early modern Ottoman world" (p. xiv). In response, he prefaces each of his book's richly researched chapters with one in a series of pseudo-biographical vignettes, featuring encounters between the fictionalized Ottoman envoy, Kubad Çavus and his European counterparts. These vignettes, Goffman explains, are designed to allow the reader "a richer and more empathetic understanding of an Ottoman world that many Westerners, inaccurately I believe, consider alien, profane, unknowable, and inconsequential" (p. xv).

While I sympathize with Goffman's desire to "flesh out and personalize the historical record" (p. xv), and to redress any dismissal of the Ottoman Empire's significance, I am troubled by the implica-tions of an empathetic reading. On one hand, an empathetic reading of the sort Goffman proposes might be seen as a kind of *strategic positivism*, highlighting the fact that ideas as well as merchandise were exchanged in the various instances of cross-cultural trafficking in the early modern world. On the other hand, as its details provide sharpness and tone to broader views, an empathetic reading can obscure the fact that while some new understandings may have developed, misapprehension often shaped the encounter. Empathy involves the imaginative putting of oneself into an "other's" place. It is grounded in a sense of clarity and absolute identification. Should the alienness of the Ottoman world for its European interlocutors be erased? To read with empathy is to allow ourselves to create from speculative materials a positivist "structure of factuality" such as often eluded the participants of cross-cultural encounters.[15] While one might argue that any history, no matter how source-based, is a rhetorical invention, pseudo-biography encourages us to find in past encounters transparency and unmitigated exchange, where we might otherwise find confusion and misunderstanding. It is clear that no history can transcend the politics of place, but an empathetic reading encourages us to feel a proximate familiarity with the past and ignore its distance and foreignness. Of course, familiarity is not a priori an evil to be avoided at all costs. As I will later indicate more fully, by eschewing familiarity entirely we run the risk of reifying difference and reconstructing superseded binary models of cultural otherness. My concern is that in an empathetic reading we tend to emplot the encounter within a teleology of secularist understanding that too easily confuses mercantile exchange with cultural exchange.

So what are some strategies that we might pursue in place of empathetic reading? In a provocative response to Peter Hulme's work on New World cannibalism, Myra Jehlen proposes that, in the absence of resistant or "other" voices to counter European narratives, we maintain a conceptual space for uncertainty and indeterminacy as grounds for denying the absolute authority of any account.[16] Given its implications for disabling the celebratory narratives of imperial progress, this can be a welcome methodology. Yet in regard to the Anglo-Ottoman encounter, where we are dealing with two highly literate cultures, it makes less sense to give up entirely on supplemental voices. Instead, I wish to propose some other alternatives that, I hope, may also be suggestive for other areas.

Ideally, our histories of the Anglo-Ottoman affairs would derive from English and Ottoman accounts of the same moment, highlighting the various and conflicting ways in which a given event is emplotted within disparate narratives, at least partially in response to potential or prior, competing narratives. This method could highlight the imposition onto a given moment of the putative certainty necessary to constructing a clear, unchallenged account such as those we manufacture in an empathetic reading. But as I have already noted, such sources are rare and difficult to locate. Thus, instead of limiting our search to sources documenting direct contact, where both sides describe the same event or object, we might turn to instances where parties from either side of a given exchange commented on the same kinds of affairs (no matter how mundane), with others or among themselves. Potentially fruitful areas for research might include the English and Turkish assessments of a given commodity, or of the role of converts or travelers. Additionally, we might consider how each approached the issue of sodomy, or described women's erotic behavior in the seraglio and at the bath? To whom did each attribute advances in navigation and gunnery? How did Turkish and English assessments differ in response to events like the Battle of Lepanto or Spanish colonial practices in the New World?[17] Or, we might compare records of English appearances at the Ottoman court with appearances of representatives from Venice, Persia, or Morocco. My concern is that we should not allow an interest in and search for instances of "exchange" to unnecessarily narrow our inquiries. Rather than seeking an archive that fits our models, we need to consider how our models might be refitted by the available archive.

Beginning in the late sixteenth century, both English and Ottoman histories remarked on the decline of the Ottoman Empire. The numerous versions of this narrative featured the image of a luxurious sultan whose epicureanism was posed against the great (or tyrannical) and war-like Sultans of the past. The English historian Richard Knolles described the Turks' "late emperors in their own persons far degenerating from their warlike progenitors" (sig.Gggggl[v]), while Fynes Moryson went on to describe "the Emperors of late being given to pleasure and nothing warlike."[18] Authors like Knolles claimed repeatedly, and with a degree of truth, to be following "the Turks' own histories" (p. 191 and passim), but what was the nature of this exchange?[19] How did "the luxurious sultan" function differently in Ottoman and European narratives? In English as well as continental narratives tales of decline functioned most often as a reassurance, encouraging the alliance of divisive Christians, or as a warning to leaders growing corrupt in their own countries' administration. But the truth is that the Ottoman Empire was changing, not declining. The long-standing and popular theory of the Sultan as a *gazi*, or holy warrior, visible on every battlefront was incompatible with the dissemination of power and growth of bureaucracy requisite to the growth of the empire.[20] Turkish accounts of a voluptuary sultan are more indicative of a nostalgia for a more visible sultan than reflective of reality; tales of the Sultan's decline were greatly exaggerated.[21]

Concomitant with stories of Ottoman luxury was the idea of the Turks as insatiable sodomites. *The Policy of the Turkish Empire* insists that "they are so given over to the abominable sin of sodomy, that it is impossible without horror to be uttered . . . the contagion of this detestable sin & enormity hath so overspread all degrees of men" (p. 46). In this case too, European authors might have based their own accounts on related charges made by Turkish authors themselves. Unlike the English who, as Alan Bray indicates, were reluctant to recognize sexual behavior at home, but quick to point it out elsewhere, the Turks regularly pointed toward the "problem" of sodomy within their own borders. Yet if we look more closely, we will find that sodomy is located elsewhere *within* the Ottoman Empire. City dwellers located sodomy in the country; Anatolian writers located sodomy at the frontiers.[22] The empire was large enough to contain its own elsewheres, thus our approach to cross-cultural exchange must account for differences within, not just between societies. As in the case of the luxurious sultan, English authors could very well have been influenced by Turkish self-representations. Emplotted within English works, however, they were unmoored from Turkish motives, engaged with English concerns, and deployed to utterly different ends. Even with the possibility of direct encounters, exchange models must account for the likelihood of distortion, reorientation, and misunderstanding.

When the English organ maker Thomas Dallam visited Constantinople in 1599, he described in his journal the formal salutation made by the English ship *Hector* to the Sultan and his court. Concerned that such a triumph was "evile bestowed, beinge done unto an infidell," Dallam nevertheless recounts the event with pride:

> This salutation was very strange and wonderful in the sight of the Great Turk and all other Turks. She was, as I have said before, new painted (upon every top an [ensign], viz., main top, fore tope, mizzen top, sprit sail top, and at every yards arm a silk penant). All her [bravery] I cannot now relate; her faightes was out, and in every top as many men, with their muskets, as could stand conveniently to discharge them. . . . All things being ready, our [gunners] gave fire, and discharged eight score great shot, and betwixt every great shot a volley of small shot; it was done with very good decorum and true time, and it might well deserve commendations.[23]

Like a sonneteer depicting his beloved, Dallam professes his inability to describe all the ship's "bravery," but proceeds to a point-by-point maritime blazon. His delight in the ship's artillery and ceremonial trim here work to compensate for the fact that the salute effectively subordinates the English to an "infidel" Sultan. The Sultan himself is figured as no less dazzled as he sends men aboard to examine the ship's battery, and two days later comes to view the "wonderful" ship up close himself. But why did the Sultan inspect the *Hector*? Was it a marvel deserving commendation? Were the Turks impressed by the English display?

Turning to an earlier Ottoman account of the arrival of an English ambassador, we find a comparable moment that may shed some light on the occasion. Selaniki Mustafa Effendi's chronicle includes the following brief and relatively unremarkable entry for October 1593:

> The Ambassador of the Vilayet of the Island of England, which lies in a sea three thousand seven hundred miles distant from the Bay of Constantinople, together with a letter from the woman who, as its ruler, rules with absolute power the hereditary kingdom, state and dominion and worships in accordance with the Lutheran community, came to the Threshold of the Refuge of Felicity [where] his worthy tributes and gifts were presented. That day, the Divan was crowded, and the ambassador was feasted and honored in accordance with the old state canon—on 22 Muharram in the year 1002.
>
> And there had never come to the Port of Istanbul such a curious example of a ship as his ship. It would make a trip of three thousand seven miles by sea and had the use of eighty-three pieces of cannon. In addition to other armaments, [there was] a flame thrower. Its external aspect was [in] the semblance of a swine. It was a wonder of the age. [The like of] it had not been seen so that it be set down [in writing].[24]

Selaniki's report begins by treating the arrival of the English ambassador as a mark of England's awe before and deference to the Ottoman Sultan. By designating it a *vilayet*, Selaniki treats England as an administrative unit of the Empire, rather than a sovereign state by itself. The ambassador is thus figured as a mere servant of the Sultan. Furthermore, whereas the ambassador has traveled a great distance in order to present his tribute, the Turks do not go out of their way for the Englishman, merely responding in accordance with canon law. In other words, a moment comparable to the one Dallam describes is inverted to signify its opposite. The ambassador's unnamed gifts seem not to impress the Turks. Indeed they pale alongside those brought to Istanbul three months later, by Ibrahim Pasha, the former *Beylerbey*, or Governor of Diyarbakir, and enumerated by Selaniki with venerative detail.[25] The English ship does impress Selaniki, but what makes it "a wonder of the age?" Is it the ship's fearsome arsenal, or is the ship "curious" because it resembles a pig, a filthy animal forbidden by Muslim dietary law? Regardless of the answer to this question, the moment is shaped by a history of military conflict in the Mediterranean and a religious ideology that sees the non-Muslim in terms of his heresy or error.

On its own, Dallam's account offers an English ship as a competing wonder in the Turks' overwhelmingly lavish court. Read together with Selaniki's chronicle, Dallam's narrative appears instead to perform a compensatory function. Examined together, these ostensibly disparate texts call attention to the continued misapprehension and cultural situatedness of accounts that obscure their own evidence-selection, crystallization of facts, and narrative emplotment in order to present moments of exchange precisely "the way they were."

Clearly, one needs to consider the emplotment of non-British as much as British texts. Selaniki, for example, was writing for the Grand Vizier, whose autonomy was the subject of a rivalry between the Grand Vizier and the Sultan. This conflict resulted from accusations that the Vizier had abused his power by pursuing his own interests in the Sultan's name.[26] When, in the entry mentioned above, Selaniki lavishes attention on Ibrahim Pasha and his gifts, he demonstrates how the wealth of entrusted officials ultimately reverts to the glory of the Sultan. The lack of detail regarding the English gifts makes the Beylerbey's gifts that much more impressive. Thus, a debate that has nothing to do with the English, and in no way involves them, indirectly shapes Ottoman representations of the English ambassador. In other words, an Ottoman account of the English (and vice versa) does not necessarily have everything to do with Anglo-Ottoman exchange. Looking only at accounts of direct contact can obscure the ways in which bilateral relations were regularly shaped by triangulating forces beyond self and other. By privileging those few relevant and accessible sources that seem to bear directly on a given moment, we can in certain cases actually distort the significance of that moment.

In our eagerness to locate instances of exchange, we must be wary of how our own cultural locations and research agendas result in further instances of emplotment. As I have done with Biddulph, Dallam, and Selaniki, we regularly identify how moments of cross-cultural exchange in early modern texts are accommodated to fill out narratives shaped by a chosen discourse such as nationalism, patriarchy, or piety. But to what extent are our own accounts of exchange emplotted within new explicatory narratives that are no less confining—narratives of mercantile growth, the rise of capitalism, the ideological origins of Empire, the Protestant Reformation, national formation, or a host of others?

Myra Jehlen has identified ways in which, in their eagerness to participate in the decolonization process, recent histories of "exploration," settlement, and colonization, "demonstrate the possibility for a radical uncertainty unanchored by material evidence to transmute . . . into an equal and opposite radical certainty" (p. 681). Similarly, any attempt to reconstruct a polyvocal, multilateral Mediterranean past cannot pose as disinterested or representative without reproducing in reverse the positivism it seeks to redress. To borrow a term from Hans Kellner, we have to "get the story crooked."[27] That is, we need to counter the idea that a story is out there; and that it can be told straight by calling attention to modes of emplotment both in early modern texts and in our own analyses. This is *not* to say that we must give up on stories or forego the pleasures of the archival hunt. Rather, we need to rematerialize the story in histories, both early modern and our own, European and otherwise. All stories are "crooked" but few call attention to the "who" or the "what" that is "crooking" them.[28] By scrupulously making the politics of each story visible, we can account for the ordering relations of a given narrative and begin to juggle the claims of positivist histories, of imbalanced archives, and more generally of our own moment.

Scholarly and popular interest in Islam has grown simultaneously with the escalating prominence of tensions between what we might call the Anglo-American Axis and numerous factions and governments in the Islamic world. One measure of this interest is the collection of nearly two hundred books on Islam currently available for order *in advance of publication* through the web-based bookseller Amazon.com. (This is fifty more than the number of books about baseball and baseball players also available for preorder.) The current environment makes the literature and scholarship on Islam not just relevant but also particularly susceptible to incorporation into highly contentious and politicized narratives. Thus, when Michael Sells's slim volume highlighting the doctrine of charity in 35 *suras* of the Qur'an was assigned to all incoming freshmen and transfer students at the University of North Carolina, Chapel Hill, in the summer of 2002, a storm of controversy arose. For those supporting the lawsuit against the University, *Approaching the Qur'an* threatened to "indoctrinate" impressionable readers into a false (i.e., overly lenient) mind-set in regard to Islam. For others, Sells's book was a timely and important publication, protecting Muslims from intolerance and bigotry.[29]

Beyond the realm of publishing companies and professional scholars, evangelical churches now regularly run seminars on Islamic error where Christians are trained to proselytize Muslims. In these seminars, we find Biddulph's intermingling of fact and polemical fiction reproduced as students are taught, for example, that Muslims are enjoined to pray daily, but that "communal prayers each Friday are 'a day of rage.' "[30] Arguably, the tendency of the American public to conflate Islam with fanaticism and Muslims with terrorists may partially account for my own attempt to emphasize misapprehension in early modern accounts of cross-cultural exchange. Similarly, the desire to challenge histories that segregate East from West, and Christian from Muslim, by positing an obstinate Muslim resistance to and disinterest in the West, seems to shape Nabil Matar's recent translation of four Arabic writers' accounts of their travels, *In the Lands of the Christians.*

For Matar, these texts are particularly helpful in filling in a history of "conflict, exchange, and two-way trade" dating back to the Crusades (p. xviii). More particularly, Arab accounts trip up the juggernaut of Orientalist thought by highlighting a history of scattered hegemonies. Yet Matar insists that throughout that history Muslim writers went to Europe "with an open mind and a clean slate" (p. xxxii) and "all wrote with precision and perspicacity" (p. xxii) about their encounters. Matar's point, here and throughout his work, seems to be that so much cross-cultural exchange occurred that it makes little sense to see Christian Europe and the Islamic Levant / North Africa in terms of a rigid self / other binary. Unfortunately, Matar often makes his argument in ways that invert rather than invalidate such binaries. In such inversions all grounds for exceptionalism and alternative histories are effaced. The works of Arab writers are offered as a corrective contrast to those of European travelers who "carried with them ideological and polemical baggage that burdened their accounts" (p. xxxi). Were Arab writers of the period somehow free of ideology? According to Matar, they "described what they saw, carefully and without projecting unfounded fantasies." Although he admits that "every once in a while, travelers resorted to a policy of using the description of Europe to serve in the glorification of the ruler" (p. xxxvi), Matar insists that "they did not invent information because most of them were writing to governmental and ecclesiastical superiors who, if not accurately apprised, could blunder in their dealings with their European counterparts" (p. xxxi). Examples like Selaniki or even Walter Raleigh, suggest instead that Muslim and Christian authors alike distorted their reports *because* they were writing to superiors. Where English

Christian travelers tended to accommodate their accounts within providentialist narratives, Ottoman Muslim writers regularly emplotted their histories in narratives reminiscent of Firdawsi's *Shahname, or Book of Kings*, or popular *gazi* and *menakib* stories featuring saints and holy warriors, pitted against infidels.[31]

Matar's insistence on objectivity, sets up Arabic travelers as extraordinary and absolutely representative, capable of "invest[ing] themselves with an exemplary self in which their 'I' was collective of their coreligionists" (p. xxxii). No consideration is made for how an individual author's investment in a certain career or sect, let alone gender or class position, might shape his account. No attention is paid to the ways in which individual wills and ideologies are transformed by their obligations to legitimating interpretive communities and the sociopolitical communities in which they are formed. By effacing the possibility of variously motivated Arab narratives, Matar does not just reinforce the idea of Arab uniformity; he presents seventeenth-century Arab authors as fully visible, open, and knowable. In effect, the early modern Mediterranean becomes a passive reflection of contemporary knowledge.

My point is not to discount the value of these remarkable accounts. Instead, I want to suggest that in our efforts to reconstruct the early modern Mediterranean, we must not allow our eagerness to balance the archive to result in our exchanging one ideology for another. Reading non-European accounts will not clarify or correct our picture so much as it offers another compelling but no less deeply emplotted perspective. Because multiple perspectives cast their shadows across the positivist histories of Mediterranean encounters and exchanges, they help us to construct a less appropriative dialogue with the past and allow us to see how narratives of Mediterranean's past obscure their own evidence-selection and emphases in contention with other, competing accounts. Multiple perspectives keep us from seeing any given history—English, Ottoman, or other—as inevitable or for that matter as uncontested. Of course, the appositions in this kind of work will invariably remain heuristic. Regardless of how many voices we include in our Mediterranean histories, we will not be any closer to "the truth" or "the way it really was." What we may gain, however, is a better sense of how and to what extent various cultures endow events with meaning in relation to the forces their narratives seek to bring to light, to contest, or to disavow. Multiple perspectives cannot (nor should they be asked to) remedy the *horror vacui* we can feel in seeking to reconstruct the past, but they may lead us to ask self-critical questions about the stories we tell and about the means by which we tell them.[32]

Notes

1. Mediterranean histories from Fernand Braudel's *The Mediterranea and the Mediterranean World in the Age of Phillip II* (trans. Sìan Reynolds, New York: Harper & Row, 1972) to Peregrine Horden and Nicholas Purcell's *The Corrupting Sea: A Study of Mediterranean History* (Malden, MA: Blackwell Publishers, 2000) remind us that the Mediterranean cannot be treated as a unity. The current essay does not attempt to tell *the* story of *the* Mediterranean. Instead it offers a historiographic corollary to Harden and Purcell's call for a treatment of Mediterranean "micro-ecologies." My treatment of Anglo-Ottoman relations is certainly *not* offered as an archetypal Mediterranean experience.

2. While this group is too large to enumerate fully, some of its more important arguments include Emily C. Bartels, "The Double Vision of the East: Imperialist Self-Construction in Marlowe's Tamburlaine, Part One," in *Renaissance Drama in an Age of Colonization*, ed. Mary Beth Rose (Evanston: Northwestern University Press, 1992), pp. 1–24; Ania Loomba, "Shakespeare and Cultural Difference," in *Alternative Shakespeares*, vol. 2, ed. Terence Hawkes (New York: Routledge, 1996), pp. 164–91; Nabil Matar, *Islam in Britain, 1558–1685* (Cambridge: Cambridge University Press, 1998); Gerald MacLean, "Ottomanism before Orientalism?" in *Travel Knowledge*, ed. Ivo Kamps and Jyotsna Singh (New York: Palgrave Macmillan, 2001), pp. 85–96; and Daniel Vitkus, *Turning Turk: English Theater and the Multicultural Mediterranean, 1570–1630* (New York: Palgrave Macmillan, 2003).

3. Noteworthy in this regard are Lisa Jardine and Jerry Brotton, *Global Interests: Renaissance Art between East and West* (Ithaca: Cornell University Press, 2000); Matar's *Islam*; and Kamps and Singh's *Travel Knowledge*.

4. See Myra Jehlen's critique of colonial histories in "History before the Fact; or, Captain John Smith's Unfinished Symphony," *Critical Inquiry* 19 (Summer 1993): 677–92.

5. The argument for a lack of Ottoman interest in Europe has been made most strenuously by Bernard Lewis, both in his *The Muslim Discovery of Europe* (New York: Norton, 1982) and *Islam and the West* (New York: Oxford University Press, 1993). Important challenges to this position may be found in Bernadette Andrea, "Columbus in Istanbul: Ottoman Mappings of the 'New World.' " *Genre: Forms of Discourse and Culture* 30 (1997): 135–65; Daniel Goffman, *The Ottoman Empire and Early Modern Europe* (New York: Cambridge University Press 2003), and Nabil Matar, *In the Lands of the Christians: Arabic*

Travel Writing in the Seventeenth Century (New York: Routledge, 2003). For a discussion of the Ottoman archive and translations of early sources, see Suraiya Faroqhi, *Approaching Ottoman History: An Introduction to the Sources* (Cambridge: Cambridge University Press, 1999); and Ehud Toledano, "What Ottoman History and Ottomanist Historiography Are—Or, Rather, Are Not," *Middle Eastern Studies* 38:3 (July 2002): 195–207. In the wake of America's war on Iraq, the looting of Iraqi libraries housing Ottoman documents has made the work of cataloguing Ottoman materials still more difficult.

6. Hayden White, *The Content of the Form: Narrative Discourse and Historical Representation* (Baltimore: The Johns Hopkins University Press, 1990), p. 34.

7. William Biddulph, *The Travels of Certaine Englishmen* (London: Th. Haueland, 1609), p. A2r.

8. The Qur'an discusses the act of murder in several passages including 4.92, 5.27–32, and 17.31–3. Parental obedience is enjoined in the Qur'an at 17.23, marriage is urged at 24.32 and 30.1, and a version of the Golden Rule may be located in the sayings of the prophet, in Hadith 40 of an Nawawi 13.

9. George Townsend, ed., *The Acts and Monuments by John Foxe*, vol. IV (New York: AMS Press, 1965), p. 23 (emphasis mine).

10. Theodor Bibliander, *A Godly Consultation unto the Brethren and Companyons of the Chrisen Religyon. By what Meanes the Cruell Power of the Turkes Bothe may and ought to be Repelled of the Christen People* (Basill [Antwerp]: Radulphe Bonifante [M. Crom], 1513), pp. viv–viir.

11. Richard Knolles, *The Generall Historie of the Turkes* (London: Adam Islip, 1603), p. A5r.

12. Evliyá Çelebi, *Narrative of Travels in Europe, Asia, and Africa in the Seventeenth Century*, trans. Joseph Von Hammer (London: The Oriental Translation Fund of Great Britain and Ireland, 1834; repr., Johnson Reprint Corporation, New York, 1968): p. 1.1.24. Admittedly, dependence on translated materials imposes limits on the conclusions we can draw, but as I argue in greater detail below, the point of including non-English sources is not to produce "the truth" about the past, but rather to disentrench the "truths" produced by an always-already limited archive.

13. Similarly, *The Policy of the Turkish Empire* (London: John Windet, 1597) begins by addressing the question of how the Turks "could attain *within the compass of so few years*, to the excessive height of their greatness" (sig. A3v, emphasis mine).

14. Walter D. Mignolo, *The Darker Side of the Renaissance: Literacy, Territoriality, & Colonization* (Ann Arbor: University of Michigan Press, 1995.), p. 15.

15. Robert Berkhoffer, "The Challenge of Poetics to (Normal) Historical Practice," in *The Postmodern History Reader*, ed. Keith Jenkins (New York: Routledge, 1997), p. 146.

16. See note 5.

17. For an exemplary treatment of the New World as approached through European and Ottoman texts, see Andrea cited in note 5.

18. Fynes Moryson, *Shakespeare's Europe: A Survey of the Condition of Europe at the End of the 16th Century* (New York: Benjamin Bloom, 1967), p. 70.

19. Although Knolles typically cites these texts in order to fashion a denigrating history of the Turks, he simultaneously argues for the importance and value (and implicitly the influence) of Turkish sources when he urges his readers not to "condemn" such accounts, "being happily taken from a more certain reporter than was that whereunto thou givest more credit" (p. A6v).

20. See, Linda T. Darling, *Revenue-Raising and Legitimacy: Tax Collection and Finance Administration in the Ottoman Empire, 1560–1660* (Leiden: Brill Academic Publishers, 1997), pp. 8–15.

21. Tales of decline might also be motivated by careerism, as in Mustafa Ali's vitriolic 1581 *Counsel for Sultans*, trans. and ed. Andreas Tietze (Wien: Verlag Der Österreichischen Akademie Der Wissenschaften, 1979). Ali's frustration with bureaucratic nepotism and venality lead his biographer Cornell Fleischer to deem the *Counsel for Sultans* "the very head of what in the seventeenth century became a peculiarly Ottoman literary genre, the literature of reform devoted to diagnosis of the causes of Ottoman decline and prescription of measures to reverse it" (p. 8).

22. See, for example, Evliya Çelebi's descriptions of Albania, Kosovo, Montenegro, and Ohrid in *Evliya Çelebi in Albania and Adjacent Regions*, trans. and ed. Robert Dankoff and Robert Elsie (Boston: Brill, 2000).

23. J. Theodore Bent, ed., *Early Voyages and Travels in the Levant* (London: Works issued by the Hakluyt Society #67) (London, 1893), p. 59.

24. William Samuel Peachey, *A Year in Selaniki's History: 1593–4*, diss. Indiana University, 1984, p. 282

25. Entry number XCVII of Selaniki's chronicle details the "Presentation of Gifts at the Sublime Divan by Ibrahim Pasha," the former Beylerbey of Diyarbakir. Ibrahim Pasha's presentation is also figured as taking place in accordance with canon law, but in this case Selaniki cannot resist itemizing the 1110 gifts. The extravagant tribute comprised among other things 3 gilded volumes, 129 gold and silver items, 918 whole cloths, many of which were gold- or silver-threaded or embroidered, 43 bolts of cloth, and 16 horses.

26. Ebru Turan, "Some Reflections on Ottoman Grand Vizierate in the Classical Age (1300–1600)," available at http://humanities.uchicago.edu/sawyer/islam/ebru.html (accessed September 20, 2003).

27. Hans Kellner, "Language and Historical Representation," in *The Postmodern History Reader*, ed. Keith Jenkins (New York: Routledge,1997), p. 127.

28. For Roland Barthes, all histories are purposeful, but some are less "mythological" than others to the extent that they call attention to their own location and process of production. For a fuller discussion, see "The Discourse of History," trans. Stephen Bann, *Comparative Criticism* 3 (1981): 7–20.

29. In the face of a lawsuit and a national debate, the University amended its requirements to allow any student opposed to reading parts of the Qur'an to choose not to read the book and to instead write a one-page essay explaining his/her decision.

30. Laurie Goodstein, "Seeing Islam as 'Evil' Faith, Evangelicals Seek Converts," *New York Times*, May 27, 2003, sec. A, pp. 1, 22.

31. Colin Imber, "Ideals and Legitimation in early Ottoman History" in *Suleyman the Magnificent and His Age*, ed. Metin Kunt and Christine Woodhead (New York: Longman, 1995) p. 141.

32. A number of colleagues were very helpful in getting me to ask self-critical questions about this piece. I am especially grateful to Emily Bartels, Jonathan Gil Harris, Jennie Evenson, John Soluri, and Valerie Traub for their questions, suggestions and generosity in reading drafts of this essay.

CHAPTER 2

POISONED FIGS, OR "THE TRAVELER'S RELIGION": TRAVEL, TRADE, AND CONVERSION IN EARLY MODERN ENGLISH CULTURE

Daniel Vitkus

In Thomas Nashe's prose tale, *The Unfortunate Traveller* (1594), the young hero, Jack Wilton, journeys to Rome, where he is accused of a double murder he did not commit. He is about to be executed when, at the last moment, he is saved by "a banished English earl," a noxiously homesick exile who warns young Jack about the dangers, follies, and temptations of travel.[1] As soon as he gets down from the gallows, Jack is eager to be gone in pursuit of a Roman Courtesan, but he is held up when the earl launches into a long and bilious tirade against travel, travelers, and anyone who is not English: "The first traveller was Cain," says the earl, "and he was called a vagabond and a runnagate on the face of the earth."[2] He goes on: "He that is a traveller must have the back of an ass to bear all, a tongue like the tail of a dog to flatter all, the mouth of a hog to eat what is set before him, the ear of a merchant to hear all and say nothing."[3] After cataloguing the immorality and folly of every other nation in Europe, the earl finally gives his opinion of English travelers in Italy: "Alas, our Englishmen are the plainest-dealing souls that God ever put life in. . . . Even as Philemon, a comic poet, died with extreme laughter at the conceit of seeing an ass eat figs, so have the Italians no such sport as to see poor

English asses, how soberly they swallow Spanish figs, devour any hook baited for them."[4] Here, the image of the "Spanish fig" suggests poisoning, but also an English appetite for exotic commodities. The Englishman abroad is an uncomprehending sucker, ready to swallow whatever poisonous foreign delicacy he is offered.

As far as Jack is concerned, the English earl is a terrible bore; but as far as Nashe's satire goes, the earl turns out to be quite right about Italy. In *The Unfortunate Traveller*, Roman Catholic Italy is Sodom at best, a kind of hell on earth where lechery, blasphemy, vengeful violence, and false forswearing are the norm. These dangers threaten to convert young English travelers such as Jack Wilton from the normal vices of youth to a much more perilous condition. There were many writers in Protestant England, contemporaries of Nashe, who cautioned against the dangers of travel to places such as Italy where young men might be seduced by other religions. Bishop Joseph Hall, in *Quo Vadis? A Just Censure of Travel as It Is Commonly Undertaken by the Gentlemen of Our Nation* (1617), railed against travel and explained in the text's dedicatory epistle that his experience accompanying the profligate young Lord Hay (the Jacobean favorite whose motto was "Spend, and God will send") on an embassy to France had moved him to publish this antitravel tract for the good of the English Protestant nation. He explains that while in France, "I bent my eyes upon others, to see what they did, what they got: my inquirie found our spirituall losse so palpable, that now at last my heart could not chuse but breake forth at my hand, and tell my Countrymen of the dangerous issue of their curiositie"[5] Other English writers joined a veritable chorus of reaction to the rise of extra-insular travel. Like Hall, Baptist Goodall condoned certain forms of travel he deemed necessary, but warned against spiritual risks in a 1630 poem called "The Tryall of Travell:"

> With piety our travailes must agree,
> Nor must our gaine religions ruin be.
> That proteus like, we as a feather change
> Nor through religions as through realmes we range.
> Love Calvin here, there Luther: Bellarmine
> And to advantage make a stall of sin
> See masse, hugg relicks, trade in Images,
> Bulles, paxes, pardons, or like trash as these.
> Nor as the preist, and giddy braine steale ore,
> To serve before their state, that Romish whore . . . .[6]

In a travel conduct book printed in 1642, James Howell writes, "It is very requisit that hee who exposeth himselfe to the hazard of Forraine

Travell, should be well grounded and settled in his Religion . . . and somwhat versed in the Controversies 'twixt us and Rome. . . ."[7] Howell goes on to describe safe travel using the following set of analogies:

> he that is well instructed in his own Religion, may passe under the torrid Zone, and not be Sun-burnt, if he carry this bon-grace about him, or like the River Danube which scornes to mingle with the muddy streame of Sava, though they both run in one Channell, or like Arethusa, which Travelleth many hundred miles through the very bowels of the Sea, yet at her journeys end issueth out fresh again, with out the least mixture of saltnesse or brackishnesse: So such a one may passe and repasse through the very midst of the Roman See, and shoot the most dangerous Gulfe thereof, and yet returne home an untainted Protestant.[8]

Howell's elemental metaphors make the process of returning home uncontaminated seem almost a divine miracle.

Another travel conduct book, published in the subsequent year, is Thomas Neale's *Treatise of Direction, How to travell safely, and profitably into Forraigne Countries*. Neale inveighs against the "many braine-sicke Travellours" who "live from day to day . . . and being over heated by a furious brain, doe skip in forraigne Countries, without method or discretion, from one place to another."[9] He particularly warns against "the heedlesse devouring of outlandish foode":

> Infinite numbers of which summer Birds, that are onely like Swallowes or Cuckowes, good for the sack and smoke in the chimnies, doe so overheate themselves with hot exotique wines and fruits, perpetually gowstering on the French or Italian delicates, that scarce one of 10 returneth home alive . . . the same fortune run many of our young lusty merchants and mariners in Java, at Bantam, at the Moluccaes, Amboina, Banda, the gulfe of Bengala, Coromandel, Pegu, Tenussery, Mocasser, Achen, Sumatra, Zeilan, and finally in all those hot Countries of China and Japon, which doe overthrow your health with the hot fruits of those Countries, and by excessive drinking of a strong wine, Called Arecca, Common throughout the east, and with the contagious women, and almost as Contagious heat of the Country.[10]

In these antitravel writings, foreign commodities are associated with both religious difference and sexual intercourse. The consumption of foreign goods (such as wine or tobacco) was thought to bring disease to the body politic of the English Protestant commonwealth. For example, John Deacon's tract, *Tobacco Tortured* (1616), is a dialogue between Hydrophorus and Capnistus, a tobacconist, in which Hydrophorus rails against "filthy pollutions" and "contagious corruptions" that arise from travel and trade. In *Tobacco Tortured*, the cultivation, importation, and sale of tobacco comes to stand for all that threatens the health and purity of the Protestant church, the English state, and the moral well-being of its Protestant subjects. The imbibing of tobacco smoke becomes an analogy for all forms of moral, political, or cultural pollution of English purity. Deacon recommends that young men should not be allowed to travel until they are "ripe" enough to be immune to the diseases they will encounter abroad. His condemnation of foreign influence leaves no neighboring nation unscathed:

> our carelesse entercourse of trafficking with the contagious corrup-tions, and customes of forreine nations . . . from whence cometh it now to passe that so many of our English-mens minds are thus terrible Turkished with Mahometan trumperies; thus ruefully Romanized with superstitious relickes; thus treacherously Italianized with sundry antichristian toyes; thus spitefully Spanished with superfluous pride; thus fearfully frenchized with filthy prostitutions; thus fantastically Flanderized with flaring net-works to catch English fooles; thus huffin-gly Hollandized with ruffian-like loome-workes, and other Ladiefied fooleries; thus greedily Germandized with a most gluttenous manner of gormandizing; thus desperately Danished with a swine-like swilling and quaffing; thus sculkingly Scotized with Machiavellian projects; thus inconstantly Englished with every newfantasticall foolerie.[11]

Note that Deacon begins his list of corrupting foreign influences with explicitly religious influences—the threat of conversion posed by Islamic and Roman Catholic powers—but the emphasis is on how religious and commercial influences are combined through the impor-tation of commodities.

Deacon, Nashe, and the other authors cited above paint a negative, frightening picture of travel, but there were others in England who believed that there was much to be gained when English subjects sailed to foreign lands. Some, usually authors who had an investment in the overseas interests of the English economy, argued that travel had great benefits. They claimed that it was not only necessary for merchants and diplomats, but also advantageous and educational for young men wishing to gain experience. By the late sixteenth century, an increasing number of Englishmen of means traveled abroad for educational purposes: to learn about other countries and their institutions, to perfect foreign language skills, and generally to become more worldly and sophisticated. In John Fletcher's *The Wild-Goose Chase* (1621), the dashing young gallant Mirabel declares, "There's nothing good or handsome bred amongst us: / Till we are travelled, and live abroad, we are coxcombs" (2.2.14–15). And Mirabel holds Italy in high esteem: he praises "Roma la Santa, Italy for my money! / Their policies, their customs, their frugalities, / Their courtesies so open, yet so reserved too, / As when you think you are known best, you're a stranger" (2.2.23–6). This was the attitude that would lead to the continental Grand Tour of the eighteenth century.

During the early modern period, English authors produced many travel conduct books and manuals as moral and practical guides for English merchants and travelers. These writers sought to condone and regulate travel. There were also travel narratives that tend to represent and promote travel as an intellectually or commercially profitable activity. On the other hand, plays and fictional texts tended to ridicule the "fantastical" behavior of those who affected foreign manners. Nashe's *Unfortunate Traveler* is typical in this regard. And through its unusual use of first-person narration, it mocks and parodies the non-fictional traveler's tale that purports to be a "true story." We know that Jack Wilton's account of his own experiences is a tall tale, but those texts that advertised themselves as "true reports" were also suspected to be fabrications. Many travel narratives begin with lengthy assurances to their readers, proclaiming the accuracy of their narrative—and insisting that their story differs from all those others that are full of false reports.

In 1599, William Parry was among those who accompanied Thomas and Robert Sherley when they embarked from Venice on their infamous voyage to Persia. Upon his return to England in 1601, Parry published a pamphlet titled *A new and large discourse of the travels of Sir Anthony Sherley . . . to the Persian empire*. It begins with these words: "It hath been, and yet is, a proverbial speech among us, that travelers may lay by authority." Parry went on to proclaim the veracity of his discourse—and to defend the very notion of travel itself. The fact that Parry and other traveler-authors of early modern England were always assuring their readers that what they had to say was true, attests to the intense anxiety about travel and travelers that existed in the culture at that time. And it was not only lies that the English feared, but also the contaminating importation of foreign goods, texts, ideas, people—even foreign languages. Parry himself associated lying travelers with merchants who returned from abroad, bringing back counterfeit goods for sale: "certain I am," he wrote, "diverse there are (entitling themselves travellers, for crossing the narrow sea to the neighbor parts of Picardie peradventure, or the Low Countries perhaps) from thence take great authority to utter lies in England (at their return) by retail, which they have coined there in gross."[12]

English worries about travel and conversion were part of a complex of anxieties brought on by England's increasing openness to foreign influences. An ancient, insular hermeneutics of suspicion was intensified by a new sense of commercial and intellectual invasion. English culture was beginning to go global, and in the process, it was being globalized. In the "Prologue" to his play, *Midas* (1587), John Lyly expostulates on the perplexing sense of change and variety produced by these exotic importations: "Traffic and travel hath woven the nature of all nations into ours, and made this land like arras, full of device, which was broadcloth, full of workmanship." In the new, global economy, solid English commodities produced by honest domestic labor were being replaced by foreign luxury goods that were pleasing, but decried as false, insubstantial, and superfluous.

It was not just travel or foreign trade that was controversial, but specifically a foreign trade that imported outlandish luxuries while exporting English domestic goods or spending silver and gold coin. In *The Canker of England's Commonwealth* (1601), the Elizabethan merchant Gerrard de Malynes deplored the "overbalancing of forraine commodities with our home commodities, which to supply or countervaile draweth away our treasure and readie monie, to the great losse of the commonwealthe": "our merchants, perceiving a small gaine and sometimes none at all to be had upon our home commodities, do buy and seek their gaines upon forraine commodities."[13] The importation of foreign words, ideas, commodities, and people caused changes in English culture, and these changes were sometimes frightening.

English subjects who left home and traveled to other countries were thought to be in danger of contamination or conversion. And when they returned, it was thought that they might carry with them the corruptive taint of contact with foreign culture that was seen as a threat to English cultural integrity. These tropes of contamination and disease caused by foreign agency participate in the "discourses of social pathology" that have been discussed by Jonathan Gil Harris in his study, *Foreign Bodies and the Body Politic.* As Harris points out, the metaphor of the body politic remains a powerful constitutive discourse in our own time. This is truer than ever for our current domestic situation, when anthrax spores circulate through the mail and in the government offices of our nation's capitol, and when fears of invasive enemies have stimulated desperate prophylactic and inoculative efforts to protect the American "homeland" from attack. Late sixteenth- and early seventeenth-century England was another time and place where a morally questionable, globalizing economy produced backlash and blow-back, and brought on an intensified fear of a religious menace that was allegedly growing both within and without the body politic.

*   *   *

In her book, *Images of the Educational Traveller in Early Modern England*, Sara Warneke shows how, as the number of travelers grew during the second half of the seventeenth century, travel became an increasingly controversial activity. Warneke claims that "The year 1570 is a key date in the development of the public criticism and negative imagery" on travel. She adds that, "Although educational travel had enjoyed a relatively favorable press before 1570, from this year the practice increasingly suffered from virulent public criticism."[14]

The intensifying debate about the status of travelers and the function of travel was similar to the debate about the status of the English language in relation to foreign tongues, and that debate intensified at just the same time. Authors argued over the benefits of incorporating imported words into English, some claiming that this was contaminating the language, while others maintained that the introduction of foreign words was producing a needed enrichment of the English tongue. C.L. Barber remarks that "before 1575, most writers agree that English is barbarous. After 1580, there is a whole chorus of voices proclaiming that English is eloquent."[15] English authors began to praise and defend their native tongue as a reaction to foreign influences and importations.

It is also around this time that the number of travel narratives and travel conduct books being printed begins to rise. What accounts for this sudden outpouring of travel tracts and conduct books? And what explains the intense anxiety that they express about travel and travelers? It is interesting to note that 1570 is the same year that the English made diplomatic contact with the Ottoman sultan, and it marks the beginning, for economic historians, of a sudden surge in overseas trade between England and the Mediterranean. This increased circulation was accompanied by the initiation of English voyaging to other faraway destinations in Asia, Africa, and the Americas.

There had always been some circulation of peoples between England and the other economies beyond England's shores, but in the last part of the sixteenth century an unprecedented burst of commercial activity abroad produced a more extensive trade diaspora emanating from England's ports, especially London. This was an "expansionary thrust" (Robert Brenner's term) that brought England (and later, Britain) into an increasingly important role in what Immanuel Wallerstein has called the "European world-economy."[16] These developments comprise a "Great Leap Outward," a revolutionary phase in England's economic and cultural development. Historians have argued that the economic changes of this period, especially in the area of international trade, "would enable England to assume primacy in the world economy that was taking shape."[17] As traffic with the Mediterranean expanded, interaction between English subjects and foreigners intensified. Contact with Roman Catholics, Muslims, Jews, Armenians, and other non-Protestants came with the territory. It is important to emphasize that this was not just an outward movement, not merely an "age of discovery": the English traveled away from England but they also returned, bringing goods and ideas with them as they went back and forth. According to economic historian Philip Curtin,

> People of a trade diaspora were not only members of an urban society, they were also members of a plural society, where two or more cultures existed side by side. Some trade diasporas tried very hard to protect the integrity of their original culture. In spite of their role as cross-cultural brokers, they developed intricate systems of social control to prevent their traveling merchants from "going native."[18]

The increased contact with foreign cultures caused by the new expansion profoundly affected urban culture in England. During the late sixteenth and early seventeenth centuries, as commodities, sailing vessels, and people moved back and forth between English ports and foreign destinations strongly affected the flow of information and commodities that ensued the English sense of place and purpose, within a global context. The increase in interaction with known civilizations outside England, along with the new contacts made with cultures that were previously unknown (primarily in Asia and the Americas), was a shock to England's cultural system. English subjects began to see themselves differently in relation to this "new world order" that began in 1492 with the linking of the hemispheres.

In this changing cultural and economic environment, English writers reacted in both xenophobic and xenophilic ways. Certain authors fell back upon the atavistic fears of cultural contamination, but these fears were given new forms and energies under the stimulation of increased circulation through trade and travel. I am concerned in this paper with merchants and travelers, not colonists—with English subjects who went East, not West, and whose journeys were undertaken, not to "plant" themselves in a new land, but to go abroad and then return wealthier or wiser. It is hard to separate commercial motives for travel from others: crusade and pilgrimage were no longer viable options for Protestants in a post–Reformation era, and even those who claimed to travel for reasons of state or self-education were often involved in commercial transactions or at least traveled side by side with those who were.

As foreign trade increased, travel became more controversial than ever before. In spite of the backlash expressed by writers like Nashe and Hall, some writers continued to defend travel as a civilizing, educational experience. In his essay "Of Travel," Francis Bacon wrote, "Travel, in the younger sort, is a part of education; in the elder, a part of experience"[19] (p. 54). As an accompaniment to his travel text, *Coryates Crudities*, Thomas Coryate included a translation of the German humanist Herman Kirchner's oration on travel that praised the virtues of a personified "Travel": "Thee, O travell, justly do we call that most renowned Schoole, wherein we are instructed in good artes, sciences, and disciplines, to true wisdome and learning; the doe we truly call the Seminary of the worthiest virtues, wherewith we attaine to the greatest happinesse and blisse."[20] English writers defended the virtue of travel in conduct books, and at the same time the authors of travel narratives often took on a defensive posture when introducing their subject. For example, William and Peter Biddulph's *Travels of Certaine Englishmen* (1609) offers a catalogue of justifications for printing the Biddulph's epistolary account of life in Aleppo and the Levant. The text's preface contains a long list of claims for the moral function and didactic value of the narrative, beginning with the following: "And who knoweth what good may redounde unto others, by reading of this discourse of other Countries? For hereby all men may see how God hath blessed our Countrie above others, and be stirred up to thankfulnesse."[21] According to the Biddulph's preface, the purpose of travel is "to get wisdome and learning."[22] Travelers are said to be brave and heroic, unlike those timid homebodies who "cannot abide to bee tossed and tumbled like tennis-bals on the turbulent and tempestuous seas . . . ."[23] Robert Dallington, in *A Method for Travel* (1605?), also sneers at those who fear to roam, declaring that only "Base and vulgar spirits hover still about home: those are more noble and divine that imitate the heavens and joy in motion."[24]

English authors advocating a sectarian purity rejected the ideal of noble travel. Perhaps the best-known supporter of the antitravel argument has already been mentioned—the Protestant divine Joseph Hall. In *Quo Vadis? A Just Censure of Travel*, Hall addresses those English subjects who "professe to seeke the glory of a perfect breeding, and the perfection of that, which we call Civilitie, in Travell."[25] Hall claims that he has "seen too many lose their hopes, and themselves in the way; returning as empty of grace, and other virtues, as full of words, vanitie, mis-dispositions."[26] Hall admits "two occasions wherein Travell may passe, Matter of trafique, and Matter of State," but he provides this warning: "let our Marchants take heed, least they go so far, that they leave God behind them; that whiles they buy all other things good cheape, they make not an ill match for their soules, least they ende their prosperous adventures in the shipwracke of a good Conscience."[27] He is particularly concerned at "how few young travellers have brought home, sound and strong, & (in a word) English bodies,"[28] and tropes of prostitution, disease and contamination predominate in his description of the Roman Catholic threat to English health and commonwealth. Roman Catholic countries are "professedly infectious, whose very goodnesse is either impietie, or superstition."[29] "Do we send our sonnes to learne to be chaste in the midst of Sodome?" demands Hall. He goes on to say, "The world is wide and open; but our ordinarie travell is southward, into the jawes of danger: for so farre hath Satan's policie prevailed, that those parts which are onely thought woth our viewing, are most contagious; and will not part with either pleasure, or information, without some tang of wickednesse."[30]

Sir Thomas Palmer, though more supportive of travel, is also concerned about the danger of religious conversion, and he is at pains to provide advice for its prevention. Travelers must "take heed in their travaile they be not corrupted with false doctrine," and they must "be well grounded in their Religion before, and consequently faithfull, secret & honest to their Countrie, having a vigilant eye, that they be not misseled by the subtilties of other Nations."[31] Palmer warns against travel to Italy, the "corrupter of men," and especially "Rome, the forge of evil."[32]

Robert Dallington's *A Method for Travel* begins with a dedicatory epistle, "To All Gentlemen that Have Travelled," that deals with "the traveler's religion" and the dangers of foreign religion and the need for strength of will to resist conversion to other religions in other lands: "as all innovation is dangerous in a state; so is this change in the little commonwealth of a man." Dallington compares steadfast religious faith to a man remaining true to a woman and draws an analogy between inconstant love and religious infidelity. He refers to the case of "a Gentleman I knew abroad, of an overt and free nature zealously forward in the religion hee carried from home while he was in France, who had not bene twentie dayes in Italy, but he was as farre gone on the contrary Byas, and since his returne is turned againe. Now what should one say of such men but as the Philosopher saith of a friend, *Amicus omnium, Amicus nullorum,* A professor of both, a believer of neither."[33] Italy, and especially Rome (home to the Pope), is constructed in many English accounts as the polar opposite of a chaste English Protestantism, a seductive whore of Babylon who leads young men astray.

*   *   *

Much of the scholarship on early modern English travel narrative, influenced by postcolonial theory, has focused on the demonization of foreign peoples and their customs, stressing an English perception of a radical difference between English subjects and foreigners. More recently, Daniel Carey and Barbara Fuchs have both emphasized, not the unknowable alienness of the "other," but the belief that the development of similarity with foreign culture would make Englishmen lose their native identity and be transformed into something un-English.[34] English writers, observes Carey, "worried about the impact of travel precisely because they accepted the commensurability of human beings, and therefore the capacity of the English to become like those they observed and with whom they lived."[35] There was, on one hand, a feeling that England was the Elect Nation, a unique bastion of true Christianity protected and favored by a providential deity; but on the other, this attitude was contradicted by the realization that it was a big world out there, and that England lagged behind the power and geographic reach exhibited by Spain. And that there were huge, highly civilized empires—the Ottoman, the Persian, the Mughal, the Chinese—that dwarfed England. There was a lot to learn, and it would be necessary to learn about other cultures in order to compete economically. This was a frightening historical moment—a small island kingdom caught between global ambition and a sense of profound isolation. This isolation was evident as soon as English travelers stepped onto foreign soil, where other languages were spoken and other faiths were practiced. As England's trade diaspora developed, pockets of expatriate Englishmen were forced to adapt to other cultures where there were no Protestant churches at all, and where, as in the case of the Levant, cultural heterogeneity and mixture surrounded and perplexed them. The general tendency toward ethnocentric reaction to foreignness remained powerful, but English writers also acknowledged that cultures such as those of the Ottoman Turks were far more prosperous, sophisticated, and powerful than theirs were. But overriding all fears and perplexities was the powerful profit motive that drove English merchants and travelers to journey forth and interact with foreigners.

The English conduct books on travel are attempts to cope with this anxious desire to know and profit from foreign peoples. English writers sought mechanisms of control, establishing long lists of do's and don'ts in travel conduct books that responded to the concerns about traveler's going "too far." And yet, for English Protestants who traveled to the Continent or the Mediterranean, the confrontation with Roman Catholicism could not be avoided. Furthermore, Islam was a powerful presence in the Levant, where English merchants carried on a trade that also brought them into contact with Mediterranean Jews, some of whom were employed by the Ottoman authorities to deal with Christian traders. Under these circumstances, the threat of conversion was ever present. Though the dual temptations of turning Turk and converting to Catholicism were real, as they were of particular importance ideologically, they figure as larger-than-life menaces in the Protestant travel narratives.

To begin with, antitravel writers claimed that contact with Continental culture, in France or Italy especially, could encourage outlandish affections, debauchery, moral corruption, religious indifference, scorn for simple English ways, and, at worst, Machiavellianism or atheism. Travelers who had first-hand experience of other cultures (or mixtures of cultures) could develop a sense of cultural relativism that was potentially destabilizing to their own faith. It was feared that Englishmen visiting foreign places would change their faith as they changed garments, "doffing their religion, as they doe their clothes," in the words of an English sermon on returned renegades.[36] Some English travelers converted to Catholicism, while others chose to join Muslim communities in North Africa or the Levant.

The idea of renegades who had converted to Islam returning to England without telling anyone of their apostasy, and simply rejoining the Protestant church, was at the extreme end of a range of fears about returned travelers polluting the Anglo-Protestant homeland. The fear of contamination caused by travelers who returned to England registered through various discourses of exchange, including the ethnographic, commercial, doctrinal, and erotic. But the primary force that motivated all of these exchanges was the expansion of international trade and the power of the joint-venture companies. The logic of risk and profit—of "venturing"—was a logic that embraced danger and prepared for violence.

The period following 1570 saw the proliferation of travel conduct books; the expansionary thrust of the English economy; renewed fears of Roman Catholic conversion by the invasion of the Armada or by secret agents infiltrating English society; and fears of English subjects turning Turk, joining the renegades of North Africa, and returning to raid England. Various changes in cultural identity and practice accompanied these events, and were to some degree caused by them. The English were "turning Turk," in a figurative sense: they were observing and then incorporating Machiavellian methods—new systems of credit and debt, a new aggressive globalism, a growing aspiration for empire, and an eager participation in the violent competition to control foreign trade and its profits. English merchants were becoming experienced in the ways of transnational competition, and by imitating Turkish and Italian ways they were becoming rich. Older notions of "adventuring" were being adapted to the new commercial context as English culture redefined itself.

I would like to conclude this essay by suggesting that in London an important medium for the representation and mediation of these changes was the theater. The playhouses were sites where foreign ventures were staged and where audiences were invited to observe and react to representations of travel and conversion. The drama of this era exhibits a strong interest in foreign trade and exotic settings because economic relations with the world outside were affecting and changing English society so profoundly, especially in London. Walter Cohen has traced the connection between England's commercial expansion and Shakespearean drama, arguing that "the plays register the rise of England's international trade, not least geographically."[37] Within English culture, the theater played a special role in adapting, articulating, and disseminating representations of foreignness. Drama was an important medium through which the different appearances, behaviors, and beliefs of other cultures were imported, distorted, and displayed. And it was not just exoticism that fascinated the English, but above all the *exchange* with or between exotic cultures (through armed conflict, trade, religious conversion, erotic encounter etc.). In a sense, the theater took on a pedagogical role, offering examples of "foreign" action and English (or Christian) reaction. This is not to say that play scripts were transcripts of social or economic reality in England or the Mediterranean; rather, they provided scripts for the practice and performance of cultural behavior, modeling both virtuous and vicious conduct.

A good example of this exotic drama of exchange is Philip Massinger's *The Renegado* (1624). The opening scene brings together erotic, commercial, and religious concerns when a Venetian gentleman, Vitelli, comes to Tunis, in Muslim North Africa, disguised as a merchant. His mission is to find and rescue his sister, Paulina, who has been captured by pirates and is being held as a sex slave by the Turkish basha Asembeg. The play highlights the dangers of trade and travel, and its story begins in the marketplace, where Christians meet Muslims and where commercial exchange leads to sexual intercourse and religious conversion. The opening dialogue between Vitelli and his servant Gazet introduces the association of cross-cultural, commercial mobility with the temptation of apostasy. Gazet is selling pornographic portraits of "bawds and common courtesans in Venice" (1.1.13) while claiming that they are pictures of noblewomen, and offering other trifles fraudulently presented as fine wares. He tells Vitelli, "I cannot find but to abuse a Turk / In the sale of our commodities must be thought / A meritorious work" (1.1.21–3), and when Vitelli asks him, "I wonder, sirrah, what's your religion?" (1.1.23–4), Gazet responds:

> I would not be confined
> In my belief: when all your sects and secretaries
> Are grown of one opinion, if I like it
> I will profess myself—in the mean time,
> Live I in England, Spain, France, Rome, Geneva:
> I'm of that country's faith. (1.1.32–7)

Gazet's attitude, though presented as laughable, encapsulates the dangerous instability of identity that was feared by the English. Vitelli, alarmed at hearing Gazet's folly go too far, replies with another scornful question: "And what in Tunis? / Will you turn Turk here?" (1.1.37–8). Here Gazet puts a limit on his convertability, one that is explained in terms that combine erotic and commercial language:

> No, so should I lose
> A collop of that part my Doll enjoined me
> To bring home as she left it: 'tis her venture,
> Nor dare I barter that commodity
> Without her special warrant. (1.1.38–42)

Circumcision is, literally and figuratively, the mark on the body politic that cannot be erased, and yet is a secret stigma that can be concealed. It is a measure of Gazet's folly that he hopes to gain wealth and preferment among the Turks of Tunis and to come home with his "commodity" uncut.

Later in the play, the analogy between sexual and commercial goods continues when Gazet offers to purchase a position as a court eunuch and comes close to being castrated. He tells Carazie, an English eunuch and renegade, "I'll be an eunuch, though I sell my shop for't / And all my wares" (3.4.50–1). Though Gazet's threatened conversion is a comic one, Vitelli faces a more serious temptation to turn—in his case, for the love of a beautiful Turkish princess, Donusa. For both Gazet and Vitelli, conversion to Islam and the rite of circumcision come to stand for the threat to a venturing Christian masculinity that sails forth, not to convert the infidel, but to exchange with them and bring back foreign goods. In the end, *The Renegado* offers a compensatory fantasy in which the Christians maintain their faith, and the Muslim princess Donusa converts to Christianity, inspired by the zeal of Vitelli. Nonetheless, Massinger's play strongly registers the potential of commercial exchange to convert and contaminate English subjects, and the need to offer an imaginative response, including the fantasy of a united Christendom, to the very real threats that English travelers confronted. The play's substitutive function bears witness to the possibility of conversion and indicates that English travelers and merchants were taking on a new identity that bore the mark of their exchange with foreign partners.

NOTES

1. Thomas Nashe, *The Unfortunate Traveller and Other Works* ed. J.B. Steane (New York: Penguin, 1972), p. 340.
2. Ibid., p. 341.
3. Ibid.
4. Ibid., pp. 342–3.
5. Joseph Hall, *Quo Vadis? A Just Censure of Travel as It Is Commonly Undertaken by the Gentlemen of Our Nation* (London, 1617), sig. A4v.
6. Baptist Goodall, *The Tryall of Travell* (London, 1630), sig. H1r.
7. James Howell, *Instructions for Forreine Travel, Shewing by what cours, and in what compasse of time, one may take an exact Survey of the Kingdomes and States of Christendome, and arrive to the practicall knowledge of the Languages, to good purpose* (London, 1642), p. 16.
8. Ibid., pp.18–19.

9. Thomas Neale, *A Treatise of Direction, How to travell safely, and profitably into Forraigne Countries* (London, 1643), p. 11.

10. Nash, *The Unfortunate*, pp. 11–13.

11. John Deacon, *Tobacco Tortured* (London, 1616), p. 10.

12. William Parry, *A New and Large Discourse of the Travels of Sir Anthony Sherley . . . to the Persian Empire* (London: V. Simmes for F. Norton, 1601), p. 98.

13. Gerard de Malynes, *A Treatise of the Canker of England's Common Wealth* (London: Richard Field for William Iohnes, 1601), sig. B1v, B2v.

14. Sarah Warneke, *Images of the Educational Traveller in Early Modern England* (Leiden and New York: Brill, 1995), p. 7.

15. Charles L. Barber, *Creating Elizabethan Tragedy* (Chicago: University of Chicago Press, 1988), p. 51.

16. See the opening chapter, "Medieval Prelude," of Immanuel Wallerstein, *The Modern World-System: Capitalist Agriculture and the Origins of the European World-Economy in the Sixteenth Century* (New York and London: Academic Press, 1974), pp. 15–63.

17. Alan K. Smith, *Creating a World Economy: Merchant Capital, Colonialism, and World Trade, 1400–1825* (Boulder: Westview Press, 1991), p. 121.

18. Philip Curtin, *Cross-Cultural Trade in World History* (Cambridge: Cambridge University Press, 1984), p. 11.

19. Sir Francis Bacon, *Essays*, ed. Michael J. Hawkins (London: J.M. Dent, 1972), p. 54.

20. Cited in Daniel Carey, "Questioning Incommensurability in Early Modern Cultural Exchange," *Common Knowledge* 6:2 (Fall 1997): 34.

21. William and Peter Biddulph, *The Travels of certaine Englishmen into Africa, Asia, Troy, Bythnia, Thracia, and to the Black Sea. And into Syria, Cilicia, Pisidia, Mesopotamia, Damascus, Canaan, Galile, Samaria, Judea, Palestina, Jerusalem, Jericho, and to the Red Sea and to sundry other places* (London, 1609), sig. P3v.

22. Ibid.

23. Ibid.

24. Robert Dallington, *A Method for Travell* (London by Thomas Creed, [1605?]), B1r.

25. Hall, *Quo Vadis?*, sig. A5r.

26. Ibid.

27. Ibid., pp. 2–3.

28. Ibid., p. 17.

29. Ibid., p. 11.

30. Ibid., pp. 11–12.

31. Sir Thomas Palmer, *An Essay of the Meanes to Make Our Travailes More Profitable* (London: H. L[ownes] for M.Lownes, 1606), p. 25.

32. Ibid., p. 44.

33. Dallington, *A Method*, sig. B1v–B2r.

34. See Daniel Carey, "Questioning Incommensurability in Early Modern Cultural Exchange" and Barbara Fuchs, *Mimesis and Empire: The New World, Islam, and European Identities* (Cambridge: Cambridge University Press, 2001).

35. Ibid., *Mimesis*, p. 40.

36. Fuchs, Henry Byam [and Edward Kellet], *A Returne from Argiere* (London, 1628), 74.

37. Walter Cohen, "The Undiscovered Country: Shakespeare and Mercantile Geography" in *Marxist Shakespeares* ed. Jean Howard and Scott Cutler Shershow (New York: Routledge, 2001), p. 132.

CHAPTER 3

CRUISING THE MEDITERRANEAN: NARRATIVES OF SEXUALITY AND GEOGRAPHIES OF THE EASTERN MEDITERRANEAN IN EARLY MODERN ENGLISH PROSE ROMANCES

Goran V. Stanivukovic

I'th'East my pleasure lies.

> —William Shakespeare, *Anthony and Cleopatra*, 2.3.38[1]

it was my intention to turn my mind to other stories I invented . . . romances taking place in lands I'd never seen, in desolate wastes and frozen forests, involving a wily merchant who wondered into them like a wolf.

> —Orhan Pamuk, *The White Castle*[2]

Like Antony in *Antony and Cleopatra*, many traveling knights, wandering noble youths, and entrepreneurial merchant-travelers in the early modern English prose romances have found pleasures in the eastern Mediterranean. And like the young Italian scholar-narrator in Pamuk's novel set in sixteenth-century Constantinople, many early modern English readers turned to romances for tales of chivalry and courtship. Self-exiled, banished, orphaned, shipwrecked, and cast off on the shores of the eastern Mediterranean, the heroes of romances get caught up in heroic and romantic adventures that subject their masculinity to compromising tests. Romances of Mediterranean crossings raise several crucial questions: Why do English heroes embark on arduous voyages in the Mediterranean in order to battle and trade, but end up being distracted by romantic plots there? How does exploring plots based on desire about heroic Englishmen in the context of eastern Mediterranean travel and geography alter our notions of masculinity, sexuality, and non-Christian "otherness"? Why are certain sexual practices and actions imagined as suitable to specific locations in the eastern Mediterranean?

Prose romances that burgeoned between the 1580s and the 1620s, on one hand, capture nostalgia for the lost heroic masculinity that had been replaced by the romantic masculinity of the 1590s. On the other, they imagine new plots for that romantic masculinity and the new individualism inspired by profitable pursuits and travels in the eastern Mediterranean. When that region became dominated by politically charged but thriving commercial networks, the relative chaos on the seas caused by piracy and conflicts with the Ottoman Empire of the early sixteenth century was replaced by more stable exchanges between the Christians and the Muslims.[3] Decades of ruthless profit-making in the late sixteenth and early seventeenth centuries replaced the era of warrior-crusaders from the West fighting religious wars with the Ottomans in the East. Contacts with and interactions between the peoples of the eastern Mediterranean started to be represented as both liberating and disorderly in travel literature, and romances registered these conflicting impulses in their narratives of sexual and gender transgressions.[4]

The connection between romances and travel literature was often made in the early modern period. Fynes Moryson tells us about a band of Turkish marauders operating in the hills and along the roads, and he does so in ways that explicitly link romances and travel literature. The Turkish robbers "were armed with Launces, Shields, and short broad Swords, so as a man would haue said, they had been the Knights of *Amadis de Gaule*" (sig. X3ᵛ). The link between the Turks and the characters that are hardly heroic in *Amadis de Gaule* originates in anti-Turkish sentiments. Given the overlapping themes in travel literature and romances, it is sometimes not easy to tell which way the influence went, from romances to travel literature or the other way round. Even the method of conceptualizing the narrative in travel literature was often modeled on "the romantic mode of viewing experience,"[5] which gives voyage accounts the status of literature. Just as romances were considered light reading in early modern England, so were proto-ethnographic texts depicting newly discovered and far-away lands "published for the entertainment of a general public which was more concerned with curiosities than with acquired systematic information."[6]

With their focus on the eastern Mediterranean, romances and travel literature complemented the growing interest in geography.[7] The rise of geography both as a university discipline and as a pragmatic skill occurred in England in the period between 1590 and 1620, when the theme of the forging of nationhood was in vogue in literature and, in the form of heroic and mercantile narratives, in travel writing as well. Growing interest in descriptive geography at that time, Leslie Cormack argues, "helped [the Renaissance's ambitious men] see the world as an endless source of wondrous tales and new goods, thereby creating a mentality that would condone and encourage the exploitation of foreign peoples and resources" (p. 162). Both geography and romances combine tales of wonder and travel with nationalistic narratives that represent the distant world and the people that inhabit it as the world of alterity. Often marked by fictions of sexual or gender aberration, these texts embody what one might call erotic ethnography.

In addition to travel and geography, the classical erotic fictions set in the Hellenic Mediterranean, as well as nostalgia for the loss of the world of early Christianity to the Turks, contribute to the conceptual framework of the romances. The latter theme is the reason why in romances the eastern Mediterranean is represented as a region where English heroes fight the infidels. It is also the reason why a heroic evocation of the allegorical Christian reclaiming of the eastern Mediterranean from the Turks is a prominent motif in romances: Iohn Rhodes, for example, in his play, *The Spy. Discovering the Dangers of Arminian Heresie and Spanish Trecherie* (1628) laments, "how we [Christians] lost all those countries of the East"; the reminders of that loss are the "rubbish towers" (sig. C2ᵛ) of Carthage.[8] Because of such associations with the loss of the Christian world's link with antiquity, the culturally complex world of the eastern Mediterranean provided the English romance imagination with fantasies of "the idealized world of soldiery"[9] at a time when " 'romantic fiction' [emerged as] a direct consequence of literature's increasing devotion to the representation of *masculine* social agency as 'civil' rather than martial."[10]

Through their overlapping discourses of empire and sexuality, romances capture the paradox of conquest: that which is deprecated because of its difference is at the same time the locus of erotic fulfillment. Because romances depend on a high level of fantasy and are typically set in the lands well beyond England (and Western Christianity in

general), they are suitable for the representation of nonnormative sexualities, otherwise kept in check by the strict protocols of Protestant
English morality. What I will argue in this essay is that romances, geographical writing, and travel literature represent the non-Christian
body of the eastern Mediterranean as at once horrifying and titillating.
The effect of this double perspective is that in these texts the English
attitude toward the eastern Mediterranean oscillates between suspicion and attraction. What interests me about male sexuality in prose
romances is how a historical, complex, and ambiguous notion of
male-male desire in romances echoes tensions between the prescrip-
tive norms of sexual conduct and erotic transgressions in romance
tales and creates fresh digression from the otherwise repetitive heroic
and romantic conventions. As Adam Phillips puts it, "What is so
striking about the notion of the forbidden—about the idea of
transgression—is that it always invites us to imagine the thing we must
not do."[11] Prose romances work within this proto-psychology of
transgression in that their narratives often take pleasure in imagining
the culturally forbidden and unsanctified within the normative
narratives of romantic courtship.

English prose romances emerged at the time when the utility of
geographical knowledge became "attractive to men with aspirations
to serving the commonwealth and achieving status within the
networks of power."[12] Together, geography and romances create a
network of texts that privilege male alliances within the homosocial
cultures of universities, merchant-adventurer overseas ventures, and a
growing male readership of romances. Just as geography provided
early modern young men with opportunities to test their masculinity
and fulfill their heroic ambitions, so did romances provide those
young men, pillars of the commonwealth, with discursive strategies to
imagine further mercantile and political potential for such efforts.[13]
Rather than simply mirroring discourses of travel or geographical
mapping, romances became agents in the production of knowledge
about new and distant lands and their inhabitants and in the shaping
of discourses about sexuality. The eastern Mediterranean of romances
thus becomes an arena for the spectacles of pleasure enjoyed by the
traveling young knights. It also becomes the "Ethnicke world," as
Thomas Coryate calls the multicultural non-Christian eastern
Mediterranean. It becomes a space in which expanding geographical
frontiers mean erasing sexual boundaries. On one hand, within this
circuit of ambition and fantasy, mobility and homoerotic desire often
feature as markers of a radical difference from the "ethnicke world."
On the other, the Western men's amorous conquest of women from

the eastern Mediterranean is similar to encounters between English men and Ottoman women in plays that dramatize the multicultural Mediterranean.[14]

Specific regions of the eastern Mediterranean that feature as setting in romances include the lands of antiquity in Asia Minor, such as Phrygia (Troy), Galatia, Bithynia, Lydia, Lycia, and Cappadochia, all listed in the short entry on Natolia (Asia Minor) in Abraham Ortelius's *Theatrvm Orbis Terrarum* (1570). In the 1606 English translation of Ortelius, William Bedwell, an orientalist and "the father of Arabic studies in England,"[15] expands the original Latin entry in *Theatrvm Orbis Terrarvm* by adding his impression of the lands of Asia Minor. Here he refers to "the miserable estate and condition of [the Natolian] countries, [and] the maner of life and customes which the people there do now at this day vse."[16] Then Bedwell draws his readers' attention to "the mines of Copper and Brasse" of Paphlagonia and to Paphlagonian wealth accumulated through high taxes collected in gold by the country's King Ismael. On one hand, Bedwell's account reflects the idea of alterity based on religion and status, common in early modern England. On the other, his description of some parts of Natolia as poor and some others as resourceful and wealthy expands Ortelius's Latin original in ways which imply that because they are poor, those lands are inferior to England; but because they are rich in metals, they are attractive to colonial enterprises.

In romances, however, Bedwell's Natolia becomes not only a land of mercantile opportunity, but also an arena of sexual pleasure. In the English translation of Diego Ortuñes Calahorra's romance *Espejo cavalleros*, rendered as *Myrrour of Knighthood* (Book 1, Part II, 1585), Rosicler, an English knight, nicknamed the King of the Sun, is about to defend the Natolian princess Claridiana from the giants Crudamante and Rocardo.[17] On his way to Natolia, ambiguously located on the border between Macedonia and Greece, he encounters a procession of twenty young women dressed lavishly, each with "verie faire and gallant bunch of feathers," riding on unicorns "all betrapped with cloth of gold"[18] and pulling a chariot on twelve wheels made of ivory. A richly adorned tent on top of the chariot is divided into a chamber and a closet. In the chamber sits a beautiful lady and in the closet a melancholy knight of "good and gentle proportion" (sig. Ll^r) dressed in an exquisite armor covered with the scales of Atlantic fish, gold, and precious stones. The knight's sword is of fine gold; he carries a scepter made of emerald, and on his head he wears a hat made of green silk covered in rubies. Rosicler ignores the lady in the front chamber but fixes his gaze on the knight, the sight of whom makes him feel "within himself a great weakness" (sig. K8ʳ). When he reaches the princess Claridiana at night, he greets her briefly but rushes to join his three friends, Brandizel, Claueryondo, and Floriandus in their tent. The four friends spend the whole night embracing. The happy reunion of separated friends, a prolonged celebration of male friendship, is occasionally interrupted by Rosicler's description of the gaudy knight in the closet. The erasure of women from the romance's erotic narrative and the substitution of a fiction of homosocial male bonding suggest that in this romance, marriage is not the only end to courtship. *Myrrour's* exotic pageant becomes a spectacle for and about men, and the desire it inscribes in the narrative of male friendship helps to consolidate power in the world of heroic men.[19]

In Richard Johnson's romance *The Seuen Champions of Christendome* (1608), at the moment of parting from Rosalinde, with whom St. Antony of Italy had spent a whole season in amorous play, the young Italian knight justifies forsaking his beloved with the following words:

> Ile stand as Champion again all knights in the world: But to impare the honour of my knighthood, and to lieu like a carpet dancer in the laps of Ladies I will not: though I can tune a Lute in a Princess Chamber, I can sound as well a fierce alarum in the filde: honour calls me fourth, dear Rosalinde, and fame intends to buckle on my armour, which now lies rusting in the old Court of Thrace.[20]

Rosalinde protests, reminding him of the tragic outcome of Alcyone's parting from Ceux in Book 11 of Ovid's *Metamorphoses*. She suggests that, cross-dressed as a page, she accompany him on his "longer trauell" to Natolia. But Rosalinde as page is represented ironically: "Her rapier was a Turkish blade, and her poniard of the finest fashion, the which shee wore at her backe tyed with an Orange tawny coloured scarfe, beautified with tassels of unwoven silke, her buskins of the smoothest kiddes skinnes, her spurres of the purest Lidian steele."[21] Buried in the page's fashionable silk robes, the Turkish blade looks like a sword of gold carried by the Melancholy knight in the marvelous procession in the *Myrrour* romance; it is a mock blade, more a fashion accessory than a soldier's weapon. It ironically deflates the militant traits of Turkish power meant to signify the page's heroic characteristic. The irony attached to the female figure in this instance cuts both ways: the costume invites mockery of a woman fantasizing a heroic posture, ironically undercutting the heroic male's comportment. Yet more is at stake in this example of "romance transvestism."[22]

Johnson sets this part of his narrative in Troy, evoking heroism ruined by Helen of Troy's destructive beauty. By implication, Troy subverts the heroic motif in his fiction. His ironic undercutting of the page's heroic stance and her master's heroic plans are not markers of the period's anxiety over cross-dressing. Rather, this episode inscribes the fiction with nonnormative desire, represented not in Rosalinde cross-dressed as a page but in her comparison to Ganymede, Jupiter's cupbearer, associated in the early modern period with homoeroticism. An emasculated hero becomes a synecdoche for deprecating Turkey. In the Troy of a seventeenth-century romance, as a "carpet dancer" (pawn, or a silly knight), a Christian knight's power is destabilized once luxury and desire overtake him, however much he is determined to recover his rusty armor from Trace, a region inhabited by the Turks at that point in history. The politics of this geographical space in this romance pits romantic against chivalric masculinity, and it enables the circulation of nonnormative desire within a heroic narrative.

At a time when England was engaged in difficult diplomacy with the Ottoman Empire over commercial routes and the political domination of the eastern Mediterranean, making the Ottoman Mediterranean a home of sexual vices and transgressions became one of the most common ways in which early modern English writers defamed the Ottomans. In the late sixteenth and early seventeenth centuries, during a series of Ottoman financial crises, when the empire felt particularly vulnerable to English political interests, there was hardly a Western traveler to the Levant who did not associate Turkey, especially its emperors, with sodomy. That association became a shortcut for the West's obsessive denunciation of the Ottomans, an attitude based on religious difference, and political and economic interests. Turkish sodomy was routinely interpreted as one of the most abhorred sexual sins practiced by the infidels. For example, Robert Couverte, a traveler in the eastern Mediterranean and the Far East, observes that Persians "are common Buggerers, as the Turks are."[23] Associating it with rape, Henry Timberlake considers sodomy a transgressive and violent misogynistic behavior. He says that the Turks "vse the sinne of Sodom and Gomorah very much . . . whereby the poor Christians that inhabit therein, are glad to marry their daughters at twelve yeares of age vnto Christians, least the Turks should rauish them."[24] Similarly, Fynes Moryson reports that after the Turkish sultan Amuranth died, his son sent out of the court all of his father's "sodomiettical boyes."[25] Yet rather than just a pejorative jibe at the Turks, Moryson's observation implies that the Turks themselves dealt with sodomy harshly and did not indulge in it freely, as many other

English accounts suggest. Another issue is their own special interest in sodomy as a topic. The emphasis on sodomy, then, says more about the English attitude to sodomy in general than about Turkish sexual practices specifically. Such discursive practice allows sodomy to circulate in texts for English readers, making those texts outlets for pleasures proscribed in England. English prejudice about the salacious nature of the Islamic Mediterranean shared by the Christian West of the early modern period is best demonstrated in the chapter called "The oriental Peregrination" in Nicholas de Nicolay's travelogue on the Mediterranean. Nicolay says that "the Ilands and Coastes of the Sea Mediterane, [are] giuen all to whoredome, sodometrie, theft, and all other most detestable vices, lyuing onely of routings, fpoyles, & pilings at the Seas, and the Ilande, beyonde them."[26] The Ottoman Mediterranean of Nicholay's narrative is a region sunken in decay and debauchery at the time when the West was conscious of the region's political decline after the Battle of Lepanto in 1571.[27] My point here is that early modern Europe (and Protestant England) saw and described in its narratives of the East what it desired to find there: the useful metals of Bedwell's account and the erotic bodies of romances. Romances and travel writing need to make those unruly bodies one of the ethnic traits found in the eastern Mediterranean in order not only to set them off from Christian sexual normativity, but also to elide the possibility for such erotic unruliness in England. Once the transgressive male desire is made into a foreign sin, Ottoman, Spanish, Italian, Jewish, or Catholic, the implication is that the sin cannot be English. Thus it is the rhetorical game of representation that at the same time displaces the sin beyond the boundary of the national and the familiar and gives that representation a form that makes the foreign sin potentially also a domestic one.

In another romance the discourse of a (multi) culturally shared sin is even more apparent. The story comes from Laurence Twine's *The Patterne of Painefull Adventures* (1594), a pastiche of romance and travel narrative. The episode involves the events that befell Apollonius, a bridegroom on his way to marry Lucina. Shipwrecked in Turkey and stranded in an unfamiliar town, Apollonius contemplates how to "sustaine his life."[28] He is deep in thoughts when suddenly he spots "a boy running naked through the street" (fol. 19), with only a towel wrapped around his waist and his head shining with oil. The boy yells at top of his voice, inviting everyone, citizens and strangers, masters and servants, to follow him if they want to "exercise" and "wash" (fol. 19). Thinking that this might provide a way out of his misery, Appolonius obliges, following the boy to a "Bania" where he takes off his clothes and lets the boy wash and anoint him with scented oils. Satisfied and scented but bored, Appolonius spots Alistrates, "king of the whole land" (fol. 19), playing tennis with his men and joins them. He turns out to be a good tennis player, a fact that wins him the King's favor. After the game that ends as soon as the King has developed a liking for Appolonius, he and the King together jump into one of the "banias," where Appolonius "washed the king very reuerently" (fol. 20), so much so that the King says gleefully: "I sweare unto you of truth as I am a Prince, I was neuer exercised nor washed better than this day" (fol. 20). After the stray Christian bridegroom has finished playing an "oriental" boy to the King, the men part company. It is in this substitution of an Ottoman for a Christian that Twine's homosocial fiction, in which the Ottoman and Christian bodies come into contact within a private space of pleasure, inscribes homoerotic intimacy in the narrative. This episode is not about heroic power or public honor but about men's play. It is the playfulness and privacy of this narrative that imply homoeroticism.

The episode from Twine also draws on the motif of the shipwrecked youth, found in the Hellenic romances (e.g., Longus's *Daphnis and Chloe*), early modern romances (e.g., Philip Sidney's *Arcadia*), and romantic comedies (Shakespeare's *Twelfth Night*). In early modern literature, Bruce Smith has shown, the motif—he calls it a myth—of the shipwrecked youth is most often associated with homoerotic seduction, even in a less transparent cultural scenario than the one involving the boy, the baths, and the frolicking king.[29] The shipwrecked body of a wandering male youth has had a particular attraction for the erotic fictions, not just in pagan but also in the early Christian culture that preceded early modern romances, but that is a deep cultural subtext to them. As Peter Brown suggests, "The idea of the wandering stranger, his continent body charged with the power to shake the kingdoms of the earth, had lost none of its appeal in the Christian Near East."[30] The liberated Christian body of Twine's Mediterranean fiction is not far from the renounced erotic desire of the early Christian body in the eastern Mediterranean. Yet a detour from the narrative of romantic, heteroerotic courtship to a digression of pleasurable play with another man not only complicates Appolonius's heteroerotic masculinity but marriage as well. Privileging for a moment sensual homosocial dalliance over companionate marriage, Twine's fiction plays with the idea that courtship does not directly lead to marriage. The ambiguity of the episode of the King and Appolonius and the irony embedded in it are only some of the ways in which romances reflect playfully upon their own ideological and narrative conventions. What is compelling about these examples in romances and travel literature is that the writer-observers continually turn motifs of sexual transgression and corporeal practices in their fictions of Turkey into forms of cultural difference, making a body from the eastern Mediterranean the violator of sexual norms.

Yet what further interests me about Twine's narrative is how the illusion of a record that it projects depends on the intertextual relationship between this and similar texts involving female-female sexuality. These texts create a network of orientalizing tales in which same-sex desire is represented as pleasurable if it concerns men, but disturbing if it involves women. Thus George Sandys, a seventeenth-century translator of Ovid's *Metamorphoses*, visited the public baths in Constantinople and observed, "Much vnnatural and filthie lusts is said to be committed daily in the remote closets of these darksome *Bannias*: yea women with women; a thing incredible, if former times had not giuen thereunto both detection and punishment."[31] As Sandys suggests, male same-sex desire is a matter of suggestion, which allows the reader to take pleasure in it; female same-sex desire is represented directly, and is therefore condemned in this masculinist perspective on same-sex desire. Yet Sandys's account occludes the possibility that pleasure may be involved despite the scandalized condemnation by male readers of those Eastern women. Valerie Traub has recently written about how exactly the same topic of women washing one another in Turkish baths crops up in both Nicholas de Nicolay's *The Navigations, Peregrinations, and Voyages, Made into Turkie* (1585) and Thomas Glover's account of Turkish baths published in the second volume of Samuel Purchas's collection *Purchas His Pilgrimes* that appeared in 1615, the same year as Sandys's account.[32] The association of the Turkish baths with illicit sexuality, then, is a cultural trope rendered as a rhetorical formula that is frequently repeated in early modern English travel accounts of Turkey. Yet what is symptomatic about different versions of the account of women's baths lies precisely in what they are silent about: the possibility that men's baths may involve "unnaturall and filthie" lust, which is what Twine's narrative gestures toward. It is through this occlusion that misogyny is ensured: it locates women in the context of "filthie" desire, of female-female eroticism, leaving men safely out of the realm of same-sex pleasure in the accounts by Glover and Sandys. Twine's narrative of pleasure relegates male-male pleasure outside the boundaries of Christianity, but it makes the Mediterranean location the center of pleasure, which it associates with the infidel's body as a seducer.

Both Twine's fiction and Johnson's romance, as well as the travel narratives of Turkish *bannias*, show how fiction and travel literature enable "cultural observation as a means of self-knowledge" that is also "an element of imperial strategy" in the early modern period.[33] Turning a Turkish emperor into a seducer of a traveling youth is only a version, less horrifying but no less titillating, of turning a non-Christian prince into a sodomite. By targeting an upwardly mobile male youth, often a main character in romances, Twine's and Johnson's works can be said to be both warnings to that youth to beware the emasculating allure of the East and an invitation to the same. In both Twine and Johnson, there is an invitation to identify with the participants in the episodes implying homoeroticism. That appeal is present even if there is a counterappeal of the implicit homophobic discourse in these two episodes.

Although we lose sight of Appolonius in Twine's narrative, we know what befalls men in Johnson's romance. For example, St. George's masculinity is soon recuperated in ways that link sexuality to the larger concepts of politics, geography, and nationalism. After this English champion has saved the Egyptian princess Sabra from being raped by the giant Osmond, St. George marries her, takes over the governments of Egypt and Persia, "there established good and Christian lawes" (sig. Ee2^r), and "surnames" other champions his viceroys and "pettie kings" of Egypt, Persia, and Morocco. This marriage comes late in the narrative, after St. George has exhausted his victories on the battlefield and is prepared to "tie himselfe to the troublesome state of marriage" (sig. C4^v). The imperialist signification of this marriage and the ensuing appointments come as a resolution after the narrator's lament that the champions have wasted too much time on amorous pleasures in Asia: "Come they from Europe to fight in cotes of steele, and will they lye distraught in tents of loue? Come they to Asia to purchase kingdoms, and by bludy war to ruinate countries, and will they yeeld their victories to so foule disgrace? O shame and great dishonour to Christendome! O spot to knighthood and true Chivalrie" (sig. Dd3^v). By the time Johnson's romance was published, St. George had already acquired the image of a transgressor and heretic. Thus in Johnson's romance, St. George's excessive heroism turns him into a parody of heroic masculinity. He is embodied as a voice of the English imperial power, for what matters to him more than marriage is "purchasing kingdoms," conquest, and profit. Marrying an eastern Mediterranean princess, Sabra, is, then, directly connected to the extension of Christian political power over territory and religion. In line with the conventions of romance, that marriage is also related to the expansion of property, signified through the subjugation of a non-Christian female body to that of a Christian man. At the end of Johnson's romance, St. George,

Tamburlaine-like, "in Princely manner marches . . . with his warlike troups through the territories of Affrica and Asia in greater royalty, then Darius with his Persian souldiers toward the campe of time-wandering Alexander" (sig. Ee2ᵛ). Persia and Arabia were considered in the early modern period "the traditional *termini* or the edge-lands of the *orbis terrarum*—theater of the world,"³⁴ in which Arabia was often represented in the geographical account as the southeast corner of the globe. The imaginative conquest of the Mediterranean Middle East in Johnson's romance is thus linked with the fantasy of extending power through oriental women to the outermost margins of the world. The intent of this fiction, in which empire and eroticism intricately mesh in a political allegory of heroic and religious triumph, is to imagine chivalric Englishmen as conquering heroes of the lands that have not been obtained by conquest but by the myth of empire: material possession and religious subordination.

Since lust is continually associated in these literary and nonliterary texts with traveling, the period created an allegory of lust as a traveler starting off in the eastern Mediterranean. In the anonymous treatise *Pathomachia*, made up of dialogues between allegorized concepts, Virtue tells a story of the origin of Lust. It says that once Lust "came from the dead Sea . . . she came afterwards to Aegypt; some say she was in Babylon, and Sardis of Lydia . . . She past thence into Europe, and kept Open House at Corinth."³⁵ Lust advances with almost colonizing strides toward Europe, stopping along the way in some of the same places of the eastern Mediterranean in which men of romances face challenges to their temperance. The author of *Pathomachia* imagines the Levant as the cradle of lust, and the islands and towns of the eastern Mediterranean as its hotbed, embodying the region as one of excessive sensuality and provocative danger.

Some of the fears surrounding lust may be culturally and historically specific. The last pages of Johnson's romance echo in fiction the anxieties about James I's expansion of the English kingdom and about his power over the non-Christian cultures of Asia Minor and Africa. The Levantine realms in the romance, as the champions' reports to the King of England suggest, are gifts to "the omnipotent God of New Jerusalem" (sig. Ee2ᵛ), to King James in the City of London. Like travel accounts, maps, and geography, romances are conceits for Western dominance over the eastern Mediterranean, over a space in which the power of Christian chivalric norms does not cancel the circulation of transgressive desire. The significance of upholding those norms and desire in the fictions of travel opens up the possibility for readers to identify with the narratives of sexuality as not negative.

Although at first glance the celebration of erotic liberties in the geographical romances might appear to be a version of "the socially orderly homoerotic desire,"[36]—of homoerotic desire that does not subvert the established political order (as, for example, in Christopher Marlowe's play *Edward II*)—that celebration, in fact, suggests that in romances transgressive desire interrupts the conventional narrative of courtship and combat.

Although my readings of the cultural texts in this essay might be said to exhibit what Dominic LaCapra describes as "extravagant tendencies in reading and interpretation" of history as a literary narrative,[37] my primary task has been to suggest a close relationship between fictional and historiographic narratives about the East-West exchanges. In so doing, I imply that reading of romances and travel literature as narratives that belong to a related sphere of interest in overseas travel and the eastern Mediterranean, not only reshape our attitude toward literature and history as separate spheres in early modern England, but change our perception of how the meaning of both the erotic and the ethnic are imagined in early modern culture. What appears to be an erotic disorder in the texts I have analyzed represents in fact a Western projection of its own desire fueled by the Western writers' imagining of the threat the Ottomans posed to Europe. The fear of Ottoman's threat to the order of Western states, however, was unfounded, given a principled internal organization of the Ottoman Empire and its communities.[38]

Prose romances produce narratives of English dominance over the power and exotic eroticism of the eastern Mediterranean. Homoeroticism and other forms of sexual transgression counter prevailing discourses of marriage and courtship that romances are meant to promote. In doing so, romances also enable the circulation of alternative kinds of desire among male readers. Both the genre of romance, a genre dependent upon a high level of fantasy, and the eastern Mediterranean, imagined by the early moderns as a space in which illicit desire abounds, work together as a conduit for nonnormative desires within the culture of rigid morality in early modern England. As agents of normative and nonnormative sexual ideologies, romances thus recover for their readers passions both outside England and beyond the Christian rigor of the body.

NOTES

1. William Shakespeare, *Anthony and Cleopatra*, ed. Michael Neill (Oxford: Oxford University Press, 2000).

2. Orhan Pamuk, *The White Castle*, trans. Victoria Holbrook (London: Faber and Faber, 1990), p. 131.

3. For the changing politics in the eastern Mediterranean in the seventeenth century, see Molly Greene, "Beyond the Northern Invasion: The Mediterranean in the Seventeenth Century," *Past and Present* 174 (February 2002): 42–71, esp. 43–47.

4. Valerie Traub has argued "Since at least the late sixteenth century, travel narratives had included tales of gender disorder." See Traub, "Mapping the Global Body," in *Early Modern Visual Culture: Representation, Race, and Empire in Renaissance England*, ed. Peter Erickson and Clark Hulse (Philadelphia: University of Pennsylvania Press, 2000), pp. 44–97, on p. 80.

5. W.T. Jewkes, "The Literature of Travel and the Mode of Romance in the Renaissance," *Bulletin of the New York Public Library* 67 (1963): 219–36, on 233.

6. John Howland Rowe, "Ethnography and Ethnology in the Sixteenth Century," *Kroeber Anthropological Society Papers* 30 (1964): 1–19, on p. 2.

7. That interest was manifested in the translations of Flemish and Italian geographical maps and atlases and in the establishment of geography as a discipline at the universities.

8. Iohn Rhodes, *The Spy.Discovering the Dangers of Arminian Heresie and Spanish Trecherie* (Strasburgh: [n.p.], 1628), sig. C2v. In the early modern period, the eastern Mediterranean was considered to be closer to England than it actually was, because of the different perception of geographical boundaries, defined more by religion than by territory. Conceptually, the eastern Mediterranean also incorporated Syria and Armenia.

9. Nabil Matar, *Turks*, p. 55.

10. Lorna Hutson, *The Usurer's Daughter: Male Friendship and Fictions of Women in Sixteenth-Century England* (London and New York: Routledge, 1994), p. 97. Hutson's emphasis.

11. Adam Phillips, *Equals* (New York: Perseus Books, 2002), p. 57.

12. Leslie B. Cormack, *Charting and Empire: Geography and the English Universities, 1580–1620* (Chicago and London: University of Chicago Press, 1997), p. 50.

13. Naomi Miller argues that the early modern science of mapmaking could be subordinated "to a desire to convey ideas no less dear [than the science of mapmaking] to [a] particular ideology or politics." Naomi Miller, *Mapping the City: The Language and Culture of Cartography in the Renaissance* (London and New York: Continuum, 2003), p. 156.

14. For the theater of the multicultural Mediterranean, see Daniel Vitkus, *Turning Turk: English Theater and the Multicultural Mediterranean, 1570–1630* (New York: Palgrave, 2003).

15. Cormack, *Charting the Empire*, p. 77.

16. William Bedwell, *Theatrvm Orbis Terrarvm*, trans. Abraham Ortelius (London: Iohn Norton, 1606), fol. 112.

17. The translation has been ascribed to Robert Parry, a writer of a solo romance *Moderatus* (1595), but that attribution has recently been disputed in favor of Richard Parke, an Elizabethan translator of Spanish. See *Moderatus* by Robert Parry, ed. John Simons (Aldershot: Ashgate, 2002), pp. 4–5.

18. Myrror of Knighthood. *The Second Part of the First Booke of the Myrrour of Knightood*, trans. R[obert] P[arry] (London: Thomas Este, 1585), sig. L1r.

19. Jeffrey Masten, *Textual Intercourse: Collaboration, Authorship, and Sexualities in Renaissance Drama* (Cambridge: Cambridge University Press, 1997), p. 28 passim.

20. Richard Johnson, *The most famovs history of the seuen Champions of Christendome* (London: Elizabeth Burbie, 1608), sig. J1r.

21. Ibid., sig. J1v–2v.

22. I borrow this term from Barbara Fuchs, who uses it in her book *Passing for Spain: Cervantes and the Fictions of Identity* (Urbana and Chicago: University of Illinois Press, 2003), p. 35.

23. Robert Couverte, *A trve and almost incredible report of an Englishman, that (being cast away in the good Ship called the Assention in Cambaya the farthest part of the East Indies) Trauelled by Land through many vnknowne Kingdomes, and great Cities* (London: William Hall for Thomas Archer and Richard Redmer, 1612), sig. I1r.

24. Henry Timberlake, *A trve and strange discourse of the trauailes of two English Pilgrimes* (London: Thomas Archer, 1608), sig. E4r.

25. Fynes Moryson, *An Itinerary Written By Fynes Moryson Gent. First in the Latine Tongue, and then Translated By him into English. Containing his Ten Yeeres Travell Through The Twelve Dominions of Germany, Bohemia, Sweitzerland, Netherland, Denmarke, Poland, Italy, Turkey, France, England, Scotland, and Ireland* (London: John Beale, 1617), sig. X2v.

26. Nicholas Nicolay, *The Nauigations, peregrination and voyages, made into Turkie by Nicholas Nicholay Daulphinois, Lord of Arseulle, Chamerlaine and Geographer ordinarie to the King of Fraunce: conteining sundry singularities which the Author hath there seene and obserued*, trans. T. Washington (London: Thomas Dawson), sig. B4r.

27. See Andrew C. Hess, "The Battle of Lepanto and Its Place in Mediterranean History," *Past and Present* 57 (1972): 53–73.

28. Laurence Twine, *The Patterne of Painefull Aduentures* (London: Valentine Simmes for the Widow Newman, 1594), fol. 19.

29. Bruce R. Smith, *Homosexual Desire in Shakespeare's England: A Cultural Poetics* (Chicago and London: University of Chicago Press, 1994), pp. 12–57.

30. Peter Brown, *The Body and Society: Men, Women, and Sexual Renunciation in Early Christianity* (New York: Columbia University

Press, 1988), p. 197. It is precisely the Christian Near East of the eastern Mediterranean that early modern English prose romances and geographies are concerned with.

31. George Sandys, *A Relation of a Journey begun An: Dom: 1610... Containing a description of the Turkish Empire, of Egypt, of the Holy Land, of the remote parts of Italy, and island adioyning* (London: for W. Barrett, 1615), sig. G5r.

32. Valerie Traub, *The Renaissance of Lesbianism in Early Modern England* (Cambridge: Cambridge University Press, 2002), pp. 200–1.

33. Stuart B. Schwartz, ed., *Introduction, Implicit Understanding: Observing, Reporting, and Reflecting on the Encounters Between Europeans and Other Peoples in the Early Modern Era* (Cambridge: Cambridge University Press, 1994), p. 7.

34. John Gillies, *Shakespeare and the Geography of Difference* (Cambridge: Cambridge University Press, 1994), p. 67.

35. Anon., *Pathomachia: Or, the Battell of Affections* (London: Thomas and Richard Coats for Francis Constable, 1630), sig. F3v.

36. Mario DiGangi, *The Homoerotics of Early Modern Drama* (Cambridge: Cambridge University Press, 1997), p. 141.

37. Dominic LaCapra, *History and Reading: Tocqueville, Foucault, French Studies* (Toronto: University of Toronto Press, 2000), p. 37.

38. Christine Woodhead, " 'The Present Terrour of the World'? Contemporary Views of the Ottoman Empire c. 1600," *History* 72:234 (February 1987), 20–37, on p. 36.

CHAPTER 4

IMPERIAL LEXICOGRAPHY AND THE ANGLO-SPANISH WAR

Edmund Valentine Campos

A translator travaileth not to his own private commodity, but to the benefit and public use of his country.[1]

—Nicholas Udall

In the sixteenth century, English translators applied themselves to making literature in foreign languages available to their countrymen. This bloom in translation activity stemmed in part from a national crisis over the uncertain status of the English vernacular. Throughout the period, English intellectuals doubted whether or not their native tongue compared favorably with the emergent national languages of their Continental neighbors to the south. The mid-century scholar Andrew Boorde, for example, lamented the low estimation of English relative to other Continental languages; "The speche of Englande," he complains, "is a base speeche to other noble speches, as Italion, Castylion, and Frenche."[2] Translation offered a means to remedy this cultural inferiority complex; for it was generally believed that translations from Greek and Latin would imbue the vernacular with classical eloquence while the domestication of contemporary foreign texts would render the tongue worldlier.[3] Among the spokesmen for this project was Thomas Hoby whose work imported Italian literature and courtly customs. In the dedicatory epistle of his landmark translation of Baldassare Castiglione's *The Courtier* (1561), he implores others to follow his example:

> As I therefore haue to my smal skil bestowed some labour about this piece of woorke, even so coulde I wishe with al my hart, profounde learned men in the Greeke and Latin shoulde make the lyke proofe, and euerye manne store the tunge accordinge to hys knowledge and delite above other men, in some piece of learnynge, that we alone of the worlde maye not bee styil counted barbarous in oure tunge, as in time out of minde we have bene in maners. And so shall we perchaunce in time become as famous in Englande, as the learned men of other nations have ben and presently are.[4]

The task of the translator then was a patriotic act that could put the nation on par with its neighbors. But the virtue of translation went beyond the kind of state service envisioned by Hoby and others. By the last quarter of the sixteenth century, vernacular translation was allied not only to the consolidation of the state, but also to the expansion of the state. In other words, the need to compete with their Continental neighbors was as much a vernacular concern as it was an expansionist one. This double function of translation prompted F.O. Matthiessen in 1931 to compare English translators to questing conquistadors:

> The nation had grown conscious of its cultural inferiority to the Continent, and suddenly burned with the desire to excel its rivals in letters, as well as in ships and gold. The translator's work was an act of patriotism. He, too, as well as the voyager and merchant, could do some good for his country: he believed that foreign books were just as important for England's destiny as the discoveries of her seamen, and he brought them home with all of the enthusiasm of a conquest.[5]

Hence, the early modern concern for imperial expansion through exploration, discovery, and global trade coincided with a rush of Elizabethan translator activity at a time when England was growing increasingly aware of its lack of overseas territory.

Essential to the success of translation as a practical, political, and ideological movement was the compilation of bilingual dictionaries and interlingual manuals for foreign language learning. The promise of global communication offered by these texts, suggests Jonathan Goldberg, was nothing less than a fantasy of extended reach and imperial access.[6] My concern in this essay is precisely this. Consider, for example, the powerful claims made by John Florio in his popular English-Italian dictionary, *Queene Anna's New World of Words* (1611). In the dedicatory epistle to his royal patron, Florio calls his book a brainchild who, "with a travellers minde, as erst Columbus at command of glorious Isabella . . . hath (at home) discovered halfe a new world."[7] Translation's imperial power, then, resides in its ability to mimic the primary act of the discoverer by rendering other worlds knowable, translatable, transferable, and ultimately bestowable through lexicography.

This striking image of Florio's book purveying new words, and hence new worlds, to Queen Anna is underscored by the dedicatory poem written by John Thorius, a fellow linguist who Englished a French-Spanish primer in 1590:

> Florio, eres fruto, y no flor,
> Pues nos tanto aprovechays,
> Y al mundo dos mundos days.
>
> [Florio, you are a fruit, and not a flower,
> because you profit us so,
> and to the world, two worlds give.]

The appearance of Thorius's Spanish verse in the preliminaries to an Italian-English dictionary is a noteworthy occurrence, for it is rare to find a dedicatory poem in a Renaissance bilingual dictionary that is not in Greek, Latin, or in one of the vernaculars treated by the particular lexicon. Thorius's conspicuous language choice not only complements the Spanish model of lexicographical conquest raised in Florio's dedication, but also foregrounds the importance of the Spanish language in matters of imperial acquisition generally.

In Stephen Greenblatt's seminal essay "Learning to Curse," we were introduced to the notion of linguistic colonialism, or the imposition of a national vernacular upon cultural *others* as a form of territorial control and expansion.[8] In this essay, I will be addressing a concurrent form of expansionist linguistic pedagogy whereby foreign language acquisition by a would-be imperial power constitutes a form of imperial practice. By the end of the century, it was clear to the English that they needed to learn Spanish to facilitate their nascent dreams of empire. Spanish, after all, was the lingua franca of conquest and dominion in both the New and Old Worlds. In Thorius's Spanish primer of 1590, for example, the English printer promotes the book by pointing out Spanish's global profile:

> Considerando en quanta estima sean en este tiempo los que hablan diversos lenguages: y en quan diversas regiones del orbe se estiende el

uso de la lengua Española: procuré que estos tratadicos Españoles, se imprimiessen con nuestros caracteres.

[Considering the esteem in which we hold those who speak diverse languages, and in what diverse regions of the globe is spread the use of the Spanish tongue, I have seen to the printing of this Spanish treatise in our English tongue.][9]

English translators interested in seeing their country become an imperial power took the adage of Queen Isabella's grammarian, Antonio Nebrija, to heart. If indeed "language has always been the companion of empire" then English scholars saw it necessary to make the Spanish tongue their imperial companion in the early stages of their expansionist efforts.

Despite the unions between Henry VIII and Catherine of Aragon in 1509, and Mary Tudor with Philip II of Spain in 1554, knowledge of Spanish among the Tudors remained limited to a small number of courtiers, scholars, and diplomats.[10] But by the final quarter of the century, the war between England and Spain intensified the need for a broader set of the population to speak with the enemy, especially in contested regions of Spanish imperial activity overseas. Thus, Spanish's status as the widespread vernacular of dominion made it an essential acquisition to the growing number of English subjects with overseas interests, a group that included colonial propagandists, merchants, and privateers. Spanish skills were particularly important for this last group. England relied upon its privateers, many of whom were merchants turned pirates, to exploit widespread Spanish economies. Such predation comprised not only a compensatory imperial practice in the absence of grand-scale territorial conquest, but also the form of England's wartime offensive.

Privateers returned home with much more than Spanish loot. They also captured Spanish texts, including cartographical and ethnographical communiqués, as well as testimonies extracted from seized Spaniards. Before these texts could be exploited to their full potential, they needed to be translated for the consumption of English readers. One of the most practiced at such hack translation was the imperial ideologue Richard Hakluyt. In the third volume of the second edition of *The Principal Navigations* (1600) devoted to New World travel narratives, he aligns English translation activity with wartime privateering:

Moreover, because since our warres with Spaine, by taking of their ships, and sacking of their townes and cities, the secrets of the

West Indies, and every part thereof are fallen into our peoples hands (which in former time were for the most part unknowen to us,) I have used the uttermost of my best endevour to get, and having gotten, to translate out of the Spanish, and here in this present volume to publish such secrets of theirs, as may any way availe us or annoy them.[11]

A raid upon the Spanish treasure fleet was a raid upon the Spanish colonial archive that demanded quick and ready dissemination via translation.[12] In light of this information, Matthiessen's earlier comparison between translators and conquerors should perhaps be emended to reflect the true and limited extent of English imperial activity during this period. As Hakluyt suggests, the act of translation should be linked to predacious and entrepreneurial theft rather than to conquistadorial conquest.

But how did the English learn to speak to their Spanish rivals? And how was the acquisition of Spanish as a foreign language tantamount to various forms of imperial acquisition, both real and symbolic? These questions are at the heart of my exploration that takes as its historical focus, the Spanish Armada invasion of 1588. At first glance, the connections between lexicography and the Armada battle are not self-evident. But the Armada brings home the nature of the faraway overseas war that characterized Elizabeth's imperial struggle with Spain. The Armada confrontation and the representational texts it generates, therefore, offer a rich field for investigating the relationship between imperial ideology and lexicography. In what follows, I address the cultural work of Renaissance English-Spanish dictionaries, and the specific wartime event that enabled their production.

* * *

The most celebrated event of the defense of the realm was the capture of the *Nuestra Señora del Rosario* by Francis Drake. The rhymer Thomas Deloney composed a ballad celebrating this high point of the battle as proof of God's Protestantism:

> This great Galleazzo which was so huge and high,
> That, like a bulwark in the sea did seem to each man's eye.
> There was it taken, unto our great relief,
> And divers nobles, in which train Don Pietro was the chief.
> Strong was she stuffed with cannons great and small,
> And other instruments of war, which we obtained all.
> A certain sign of good success we trust:
> That God will overthrow the rest, as he hath done the first.[13]

The *Nuestra Señora Rosario* was the vice-flagship of the Andalusian squadron. In the course of battle, it ran afoul of another ship and lost her foremast. The supreme commander of the Armada, the Duke of Medina Sidonia, abandoned the *Rosario* and fled the scene. English forces were ordered to pursue the Duke and his fleeing ships. But the hapless *Rosario* presented too great a temptation for Francis Drake who, in defiance of orders, detached himself from the English fleet to come aboard and seize the vessel. Upon learning that his aggressor was England's "dragon," Pedro de Valdéz, the ship's commander, gracefully surrendered himself, his ship, and one-third of the Armada's treasure (50,000 escudos) that had been entrusted to his care.[14] I will return to Don Pedro and the instrumental role he played in Anglo-Spanish lexicography later in this essay. For the moment, however, I wish to focus on the material consequences of the seizure.

Some historians of the Armada have voiced surprise at Drake's profit-minded insubordination. Richard Corbett, in *Drake and the Tudor Navy*, writes:

> it seemed the act of an incorrigible pirate . . ., and from sheer greed of plunder the great vice-admiral had sacrificed the chance of dealing their enemy a deadly blow . . . . Indeed that a man of his wealth and position at the zenith of his ambition would turn aside at such a moment from the heels of his life-long enemy for the chance of plunder and ransom is quite incredible.[15]

Corbett seems to forget that Drake *was* an incorrigible pirate. He was behaving true to form by pursuing plunder and ransom. Garrett Mattingly, in contrast, rightly contextualizes Drake's action by linking it to his career as a successful corsair:

> Francis Drake was famous all over the seven seas for the craft or instinct which led him to the exact spot in a vast expanse of water where he could find a specially desirable prize, and such the *Nuestra Señora del Rosario* certainly was, by far the richest as it turned out to be taken in the entire campaign. . . . This was exactly what made excuses unnecessary. No one was prepared to blame a feat which everyone frankly envied. Conduct which in any modern regular navy would have resulted in court martial and disgrace just brought Sir Francis added fame and a tidy packet of prize money. His contemporaries never blamed him; why should we?[16]

Indeed, the only contemporary to voice an objection was Martin Frobisher; but his murmur was a bitter complaint for having been left out of a share of the *Rosario*'s spoils.

As Mattingly's justification suggests, Drake's actions are reminiscent of his privateering exploits overseas. The Armada battle was the natural climax of a diffuse and prolonged naval struggle between English marauders and Spanish galleons in foreign waters. Indeed, in some respects the engagement of 1588 was like a massive scene of privateering enacted on a domestic stage.[17] It is not surprising then, that popular political memorabilia (like the Deloney ballad offered above) often celebrate the material gains of the Channel confrontation. This emphasis on loot is graphically underscored by an eighteenth-century illustration by John Pine etched in imitation of an Elizabethan original by Robert Adams. The work is a commemorative diptych representing aerial vistas of the opposing navies (figure 4.1). The eighteenth-century framing device, however, is entirely Pine's own. The lower border of the work depicts Drake on the shores of England: in the background, English soldiers lead the Spanish crew of the *Rosario* into custody, while in the foreground Drake claims the loot from a clutch of large treasure chests won from the galleon (figure 4.2). It is in this economic setting that Drake's capture of the ship should be understood: the engraving celebrates booty.

While privateering was conveniently framed as a political act of "singeing the King of Spain's beard," it was nevertheless at its core a profit-seeking activity. The achievements of Drake and his ilk inspired merchants and tradesman to follow his example. For instance, many members of the Spanish Company for the trade in wool turned to privateering following the impasse of the Spanish trade embargo of 1585.[18] In the years between 1589 and 1591, over 200 private reprisal voyages shipped out to prowl the Spanish waters in search of profit.[19] One contemporary commonplace book explains that Drake's example "inflamed the whole country with a desire to venture unto the seas, in hope of the like good success, [so] that a great number prepared ships, mariners and soldiers and travelled any place where profit may be had."[20] The Venetian ambassador to England attributes the economic well-being of the nation to the popularity of piracy: "Nothing is thought to have enriched the English more or done so much to allow many individuals to amass the wealth they are known to possess as the wars with the Spaniards in the time of Queen Elizabeth. All were permitted to go privateering and they plundered not only Spaniards but all others indifferently so that they were enriched by a constant stream of booty."[21]

Privateering was a joint-stock affair that owed its success to the merchant classes responsible for their practical organization. Hence, it relied on the pooled resources of private individuals for the outfitting

Figure 4.1 John Pine's reproduction of Robert Adam's Armada scene, courtesy of Duke University Library.

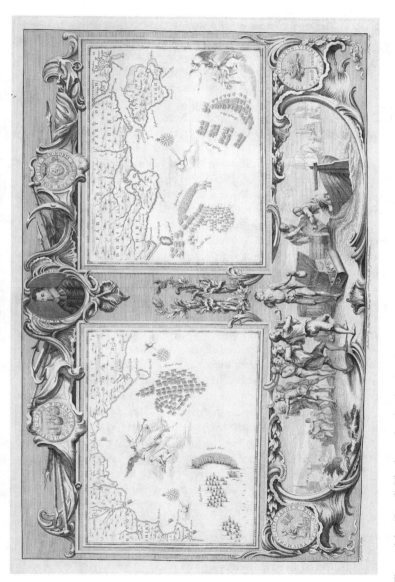

Figure 4.2 (Detail) The lower border showing Francis Drake on the Dartmouth shore taking charge of the spoils from the *Nuestra Señora del Rosario*, courtesy of Duke University Library.

of ships with each subscriber receiving a dividend share of the captured spoils.[22] By the 1580's the gentry—even the Queen herself—
took an interest in pledging their name and money to such mercantile
enterprises. This promotion by the upper classes endowed such ventures with national importance. From this state-sanctioned piracy arose
national cults of heroism centered on Drake and his kind, thereby
focusing the anti-Spanish sentiment present in all classes of society and
transforming privateering into an empire-building activity underwrit-
ten by mercantile interests. In this light, the line dividing merchant
and state-sanctioned pirate was hazy at best.

The imperial economics that characterized English foreign policy
toward Spain are dramatized in a postinvasion play that bluntly juxtaposes the emergent mercantile strategies of London with the defeat of
the Spanish Armada. Thomas Heywood's *If You Know Not Me, You
Know No Bodie* (1605 / 1606) is a two-part history play chronicling
the reign of Queen Elizabeth. Part I, subtitled *The troubles of Queene
Elizabeth*, concerns the passing of Philip and Mary and the triumph of
Protestantism on Elizabeth's accession. Part II, however, seems to
lose sight of its royal subject by presenting the story of the famous
London merchant Thomas Gresham. The subtitle to this sequel, *With
the building of the Royall Exchange: and the famous Victorie of Queene
Elizabeth, in the Yeare 1588*, hints at the connections I am attempting
to make between mercantilism and foreign politics.

The Gresham plot concerns itself with the mercantile transactions
of London merchants culminating in Gresham's founding of the
Royal Exchange, a place where merchants of the realm could conduct
business with each other and with foreign agents especially. But the
play forgets Gresham at its end, and finishes with an unforeseen coda
relating the routing of the Spanish Armada. The addition of this non
sequitur presents a puzzle for textual historians. Madeleine Doran
offers one plausible theory to account for this mystery. Doran suspects
that the Armada ending was originally intended as the epilogue to
Part 1, *The Troubles of Queene Elizabeth*, where it would make narrative sense as the crowning achievement of Elizabeth's reign. The
chronology of its composition might go something like this: shortly
after completing the first play about Elizabeth, Heywood composed a
play devoted to the life of Thomas Gresham; later in 1605, both plays
were amalgamated and entered into the Stationer's Register by
Nathaniel Butter as the two-part play we know today with the Armada
scenes excised from Part I and appended to the end of Part II as a
vague gesture of continuity.[23]

The explanation offered by Doran could imply that the Armada ending of Part II is a gratuitous addition of dubious relevance to the rest of the play. Be that as it may, this reconstruction does not account for the contemporary popularity of the play in performance, nor for the fact that when Heywood revised the series in 1633 he did not see fit to relocate the Armada scenes. In fact, he went so far as to expand them as more historical information about the war became available to him in print in the intervening years. Thus, Heywood and his audience must have perceived the intuitive logic that yoked the mercantile and martial despite the fact that the coda appears to us as an out-of-place misfit originally intended for Part I.[24] Economic analyses of the play appear to bear this point out, even though such analyses tend to stop short of the anomalous Armada coda.

I find Theodora Jankowski's reading of the play particularly insightful in this regard because she links the merchant plot of the play to emerging ideas of imperialism and capitalism. What Heywood is doing in this tale of industrious merchants, she suggests, is visualizing an internal empire of trade in which merchants are celebrated for extending commerce and capital beyond the bounds of the insular kingdom.[25] Mercantile expansion in this way transforms the nation's venturing capitalists into an army of commercial "conquistadors" in quest of foreign markets rather than foreign territory. She explores this idea on two fronts: one, the merchant factor stationed abroad as a trade representative—a concern taken up in the play's comic subplot, and two, in the attraction of foreign agents to London—a concern reflected in the erection of the Royal Exchange. In general, the play labors to show the mutually beneficial relationship between the Crown and its entrepreneurial subjects.

The connection between the monarch and merchants is most evident in the opening of the London bourse, Gresham's greatest achievement. Lest we forget that this play is ostensibly about Elizabeth's reign, the Queen makes a cameo appearance at this highpoint of the Gresham storyline to commend the good work of her subject and to christen the bourse "The Royal Exchange," thereby articulating the connection between the state and its budding capitalists. The Queen, moreover, dubs Gresham a knight, thereby fulfilling her obligation in the symbiotic relationship between Crown and merchant. Notably, the historical Gresham was knighted twelve years before the royal visit.[26] Heywood's decision to make these two events coincide reflects his modification of the history play—normally an elite genre—to accommodate and valorize the increasingly important trading classes.[27]

The abrupt transition from Gresham's story to the defeat of the Armada marks the entrance of the history play genre into the traditional elite subject matter. The final scenes are dominated by Elizabeth who waits at Tilbury receiving regular progress reports of the battle occurring just offstage apparently. These posts update the monarch on the feats of the English captains Francis Drake and Martin Frobisher until at last the two heroes appear on stage whereupon Drake relates the final moments of battle himself. While nothing in the Gresham storyline anticipates these Armada scenes, certainly one aspect that unites the play's disparate parts is the emphasis put on the relationship between the Queen and her agents. In other words, the royal valorization of merchants as servants of the state finds its parallel in the Queen's praise of her Armada champions.

The implicit analogy between merchants and war heroes is strengthened when we recall that the English navy was composed of a commercial fleet made combat-ready by the addition of armaments.[28] Indeed the militarization of this mercantile play by the addition of the Armada epilogue only underscores the ambiguity between merchant and patriot. Furthermore, if, as I argued earlier, the privateering spirit characterizes the actions of England's naval defense, then the merchants in the first part of the play share implicitly in the naval victory of Elizabeth's favorites whose fame derives in large part from their willingness to take to the seas in search of profit for the nation. The play acknowledges this by locating the origins of the invasion in Drake's lucrative privateering raids on the West Indies (sc. xvii.2550–6). Thus in some ways, the play understands the victory as the continuation of an imperial agenda meant to baffle Spain's expansionist efforts. To this end, not only had the English navy prevented the Armada generals from conquering and rechristening England as "New Spaine" (sc.xviii.2682), but they had also drained the Spanish treasury by "Burying at once more wealth within the Sea / Then th'Indies can in many yeeres restore" (sc.xx.2880–1).

The play concludes with a tally of the spoils of war. When the victorious Drake and Frobisher enter bearing Spanish standards, the Queen is prompted to ask, "What means those Spanish Ensigns in the hands / of English subjects?" (sc.xx.2858–60), and Drake answers "They shew that Spaniards lives are in the hands of *Englands* Soveraigne" (sc.xx.2862–3). Drake then provides the final account of the battle with mention of his famous seizure of Don Pedro de Valdéz. As for the Spanish standards, the Queen orders them displayed in St. Paul's Cathedral as trophies of war. While this final Armada scene does not mention the economic gains celebrated in other Armada propaganda, it nevertheless celebrates the taking of Spanish ships and the symbolic capital represented by the Spanish standards and, most importantly, human booty brought back from the war.

*   *   *

Drake's capture of Don Pedro was bruited about far and wide. When a Continental rumor held that Drake had been taken prisoner in the course of the Armada campaign, the Crown issued a public statement addressed to Bernadino de Mendoza, Philip's ambassador to France, to refute this misinformation:

> But the truth is, Sir Frances Drake was so far off to be a prisoner, that he was the taker: for he tooke Pedro de Valdez and 400. more Spanish prisoners at one time. And to prove this to be true Mendoza shall have if he require it, Pedro de Valdez own hand to shewe that he is a prisoner to Sir Frances Drake and 400. more taken with him, and not one English Man taken in that service.[29]

The proffered letter of confirmation from Don Pedro's "own hand" was never sent. Instead Don Pedro's hand was put to work contributing to the first serious work of Anglo-Spanish lexicography, Richard Percivale's *Bibliotheca Hispanica* (1591).

Valdéz's presence in England seems to have made him the subject of topical interest. Not only does he appear in post–Armada propaganda such as Robert Greene's *The Spanish Masquerado*, and the Deloney Ballad quoted earlier, but literary works too seem to have acknowledged his presence, if only archly. Gustave Ungerer, for instance, sees him behind the pirate Valdes, Marina's captor in Shakespeare's *Pericles*, and as the inspiration for Valdes, Doctor Faustus's colleague in Marlowe's play[30], especially since he voices a magical fantasy of conquest modeled after Spain:

> Faustus, these books, thy wit, and our experience
> Shall make all nations to canonize us.
> As Indian Moors obey their Spanish lords,
> So shall the subjects of every element
> Be always serviceable to us three. (1.1.120–4)[31]

If these characters are truly Don Pedro's namesakes, then his literary associations with piracy, kidnapping, and American conquest suggest he was a focus for English New World fantasies.

Generally speaking, Valdéz was more than a living trophy brought back from the war, for his capture represents one of the most famous examples of English exploitation of unwilling Spanish informants. Such exploitation usually occurred at sea in the context of English privateering. The pages of Hakluyt's *The Principal Navigations*, for example, abound with ethnographical, topographical, and cartographical information extracted from Iberian captives. Privateering then, not only provided material booty but also informational prizes in the form of texts and hostages that proved equally essential to English overseas efforts.

The employment of Drake's prisoner by Percivale is in keeping with the intelligence-gathering aspect of English wartime efforts to which Percivale himself contributed according to his abilities.[32] Percivale belonged to an informal group of translators that the state relied upon to keep tabs on Philip's movements and to circulate anti-Spanish propaganda.[33] This style of ad hoc intelligencing was an embryonic form of imperial lexicography, but it did not result in a thorough text that could school the servants of the state until Percivale published his 1591 dictionary.[34] Although Percivale was competent enough to decipher the Spanish documents confirming the imminent arrival of the Spanish fleet, he was by no means bilingual, and so his first attempts at lexicographical compilation were amateurish and halting. Having access to Don Pedro as a native informant at the final stages of his efforts must have surely proved useful. Although it is impossible to measure with certainty the extent of Valdéz's contribution, Percivale briefly acknowledges him in his address to the reader explaining that he "ranne it [i.e. the dictionary] over with Don Pedro de Valdes, . . . to whom I had accesse, by the favour of my worshipfull friend Maister Richard Drake."[35]

Percivale's close professional involvement with the circle of state agents and intelligencers under Lord Burghley seems to have politicized the work, turning it into a kind of weapon of the state. Furthermore, the dictionary relied heavily upon the unfinished work of Thomas Doyle, an English physician stationed in the Netherlands—that other front of the Anglo-Spanish war.[36] Percivale's dictionary then springs directly from international territorial conflict.[37] The book's wartime utility is underscored in the dedication to Robert Devereux the earl of Essex, where the compiler recalls the earl's military service in Flanders and his raids against the Iberian coast:

> . . . and remembering that having emploied yourself so honorablie against the Spaniard in Flanders, Spayne & Portugal; you had gained an

immortall memorie withe all posterite, & might encounter with them
againe upon like occasion. (Percivale, sig. A2ᵛ)

Like most wartime initiatives, however, the *Bibliotheca* betrays its
parallel concern in the dedicatory poem written by Thomas Doyle,
whose Latin verses reveal an economic interest in Spain's lucrative
colonial activity. The English translation reads:

> What riches the New World brings forth,
> What fruits the Indies offer,
> What pearls, the ocean;
> What gold mines, the earth;
> All these things, the Spaniard has.
> The wealth of Jason's Golden Fleece is his.
> It is desirable to speak to the Golden People.
> The Spaniard seeks to conquer Flanders,
> To depose the King of France by force.
> He seeks the fall of England.
> What will he not do, to be Monarch of the World?
> It is desirable to speak to those with whom
> We desire War, Commerce or Peace.
> Percivale's book provides a quick and easy way
> To speak to the Spanish people. (Percivale, sig. A3ᵛ)[38]

The links between Anglo-Spanish lexicography, war and profit
becomes clearer in the subsequent version of Percivale's dictionary
updated by the language teacher John Minsheu. Minsheu expanded
the work of his predecessor by adding a *Spanish Grammar* and a
separate Spanish primer called *Delightful Dialogues in Spanish
and English*. In the grammar manual, a dedicatory sonnet likens the
book to a labor of Hercules. Minsheu (i.e., Hercules) penetrates the
guarded orchard of Atalanta (i.e., Spain) to steal the golden apples of
Hesperus for his countrymen. Thus the lexicographer laboring at
home becomes analogous to the privateer working abroad to enrich
the nation. The English raid on Cadiz in 1596 may have helped
inspire Minsheu's metaphor of theft since, according to Gustave
Ungerer, the *Pleasant and Delightful Dialogues* was probably corrected by a Spanish noble hostage brought back from the assault and
housed in the house of Minsheu's friend Edward Hoby.[39]

Minsheu's efforts, more so than Percivale's, appeal openly to those
interested in commerce with the Spaniard. The updated dictionary
comes appended with practical vocabulary lists useful for roving
merchants: "implements, ships at sea, officers in war, trades and

occupations." In the *Pleasant and Delightful Dialogues*, Minsheu makes a move that resonates with the tenor of Heywood's Armada play by staging a conversation between two Spaniards and two bilingual English merchants in the London Royal Exchange. After a lengthy exchange of pleasantries, the Spaniard, Alonso, points out England's shortcoming: owing to its cold climate, the island is not self-sufficient and must import foreign commodities. Spain, in contrast, with its access to the spiceries, has all it could ask for. He goes on to say that the English are virtuous in all respects except that they display "an infatigueable covetousness." Like Heywood's Gresham play, this dialogue of casual merchant banter reminds its readers that the flourishing of England relies on international commerce. In Minsheu's view, such merchants need to be proficient in Spanish to gain access to foreign markets. Despite the emphasis on legitimate trade, the dialogue still retains an element of political hostility toward Spain. In another example, two profit-minded English soldiers discuss the rumor of a second Spanish Armada:

> *Corporal:* . . . the rumor goeth that the king of Spaine makes preparation to come against England.
> *Sergeant:* Let him come, if he bring good store of crownes to leave us.
> *Corporal:* I would content myself with a chaine of golde, that were worth a hundred pound. But in faith, the Spaniards are not wont to sell them very cheape.
> *Sergeant:* And I hope to buy one with an ounce of lead [i.e., a bullet].[40]

Together these dialogues show how war with Spain is always perceived as a lightening of Philip's purse through international commerce, licit or otherwise. To rehearse these language lessons is to rehearse an economic political agenda.

* * *

After the 1599 revision of Percivale's dictionary, Minsheu began compiling his most ambitious work, the *Ductor in Linguas, The Guide into Tongues* (1617), a polyglot etymological dictionary that promises to lead its readers to the mastery of eleven languages, and in later additions, thirteen.[41] Although the book advertises English as a keystone language providing access to all of the other tongues, the dictionary's usefulness actually depends on a basic reading knowledge of Spanish. The configuration of the entries indicates that the volume was founded on Minsheu's revision of Percivale's English-Spanish dictionary. Indeed, most surviving copies of *The Guide* are bound together with this earlier lexicon, which in turn is specially cross-referenced to be used in tandem with *The Guide*. As a result, full practical use of *The Guide* rests on whether one could navigate the English-Spanish portion to discriminate meaning between an entry and its multiple glosses.[42]

The cost of printing this colossal project proved initially prohibitive. In a bold move reminiscent of the mercantile investment practices of the day, Minsheu resorted to selling subscriptions in order to fund the enterprise.[43] More than half of the surviving copies include a *Catalogue of Names of such Persons which . . . have received the Etymologicall Dictionarie* consisting of a single folio leaf listing the names of subscribers. The nearly 400 names include noblemen, intellectuals such as Francis Bacon and William Camden, professional men, clerks, and a liberal sprinkling of merchants. As Franklin Williams explains, this ingenious form of advertising could be distributed as a handbill, inserted into the dictionary, or posted before a bookstall.[44] Prospective investors could be assured that they were buying into illustrious company and that their names might well appear in the next printing of the *Catalogue*. So, like most foreign economic ventures, this text relies upon the participation of merchant classes and endorsement by the gentry to insure its success. In essence, this was a kind of joint-stock investment in words whose dividend returns were certainly intellectual, and potentially economic, if such knowledge were applied to foreign trade.

The mercantile nature of the text is reinforced in the preliminary material where the author expresses gratitude to the merchants who helped him during the compilation of the volume. And though not a merchant himself, Minsheu portrays himself as a commercial adventurer recently returned from foreign lands to offer his wares for the good of the commonwealth:

> What use merchants may make of this booke, especially those that are to trafficke in person to foreign countries and tongues, I need not set down. . . . And seeing I have made so dangerous a voyage, and adventure, in so many tempests in an ocean of travails, troubles and hard sufferings, and wants, . . . to bring this tossd barke unwrecked which here unloads and layes in order to your viewes the commodoties that are in the same. I shall be right glad and comforted that Merchants . . . might make great use of my paynes.

Despite *The Guide's* origins in Elizabethan Anglo-Spanish lexicography— a practice that aligns the privateer and the lexicographer in a discourse of maritime conflict and theft—*The Guide's* promise of polyglot communication reflects a Jacobean concern with establishing conventional international trade relationships. James's peace with Spain put an end to the glory days of corsairs such as Francis Drake and John Hawkins—days when the acquisition of Spanish as a foreign language was symbolically linked to imperial forms of gain, and England's lexicographers, like its naval heroes, could turn a profit for the nation.

Notes

1. *The Paraphrase of Erasmus upon the newe Testament* (1548), quoted in *An Elizabethan Art*, trans. F.O. Matthiessen (Cambridge: University of Cambridge Press, 1931), p. 25.
2. Andrew Boorde, *The fyrst boke of the introduction of knowledge* (London: William Copland, 1555), STC (2nd ed.) 3383, sig. B2r.
3. On the relationship between the vernacular and widespread translation, see C.H. Conley, *The First English Translators of the Classics* (New Haven: Yale University Press, 1927) and Richard Foster Jones, *The Triumph of the English Language: A Survey of Opinions Concerning the Vernacular from the Introduction of Printing to the Restoration* (Stanford: Stanford University Press, 1953).
4. Thomas Hoby, *The courtyer of Count Baldessar Castilio diuided into foure bookes*, (London: William Seres, 1561), STC (2nd ed.) 4778, sig. B1r.
5. Matthiessen, *Translation*, p. 1.
6. Jonathan Goldberg, *Writing Matter From the Hands of the English Renaissance* (Stanford: Stanford University Press, 1990), p. 204.
7. John Florio, *Queen Anna's new world of words, or dictionarie of the Italian and English tongues* (London: M. Bradwood and W. Barret, 1611), STC (2nd ed.) 11099, sig. A2v.
8. See Stephen Greenblatt, "Learning to Curse: Aspects of Linguistic Colonialism in the Sixteenth Century," *Learning to Curse: Essays in Early Modern Culture* (New York and London: Routledge, 1990), pp. 16–39.
9. Antonio del Corro, *Reglas gramaticales para aprender la lengua española y francesa, confiriendo la una con la otra, segun el orden de las partes de la oration latinas* (Oxford: Joseph Barnes, 1586), STC (2nd ed.) 5789.
10. For a good survey of Elizabethan courtiers proficient in practical Spanish, see Gustav Ungerer, *Anglo-Spanish Relations in Tudor Literature* (Madrid: Artes Gráficas Clavileño, 1956), pp. 43–67.
11. Richard Hakluyt, *The Principal Navigations Voyages Traffiques and Discoveries of the English Nation*, 12 vols. (New York: Augustus M. Kelley, 1969), vol. 1, p. lxxxvii.
12. The consummate spy, Hakluyt often understands his American information as second-hand intelligence wrested from Spanish texts and

Spanish mouths. His collection abounds with entries that boldly announce the hijacked character of English New World intelligence. Here is just one typical example: "A letter intercepted of Bartholomew del Cano, written from Mexico the 30 of May 1590, to Francis Hernandez of Sevil, concerning the speedy building of two strong forts in S. Juan de Ullua," Hakluyt, vol. 9, p. vi.

13. Thomas Deloney, *A joyful new ballad, declaring the happie obtaining of the great galleazo, wherein Don Pietro de Valdez was the chiefe, through the mightie providence of God, being a special token of his gracious and fatherly goodness towards us, to the great encouragement of all those that willingly fight in the defense if his gospel and our good Queene of England* (London: John Wolfe, 1588), STC (2nd ed.) 6557.

14. For a thorough microhistorical study on the fate of the *Nuestra Señora del Rosario* and her crew, see Paula Martin, *Spanish Armada Prisoners* (Exeter: Exeter University Publications, 1988).

15. Julian Corbett, *Drake and the Tudor Navy*, vol. II (London, New York: Longmans, Green, and Co., 1899), p. 230.

16. Garrett Mattingly, *The Defeat of the Spanish Armada* (Oxford: Alden Press, 1959), p. 253.

17. The formal characteristics of England's defense mirrored their privateering tactics in Spanish shipping lanes. Lord Howard Effingham's description of the Channel battle corresponds to New World engagement tactics with Spaniards defending large convoys of merchantmen galleons while the English harassed them from the rear. He writes, "Their force is wonderful great and strong; and yet we pluck their feathers by little and little." See *State Papers relating to the Defeat of the Spanish Armada*, 2 vols., ed. J.K. Laughton (Navy Records Society, 1894) p. 341.

18. Simon Adams, "The Outbreak of the Elizabethan Naval War Against the Spanish Empire: The Embargo of May 1585 and Sir Francis Drake's West Indian Voyage," *England, Spain and the Gran Armada, 1585–1604: Essays from the Anglo-Spanish Conferences London and Madrid 1988*, ed. M.J. Rodriguez-Salgado and Simon Adams (Edinburgh: John Donald, 1991), p. 45.

19. Kenneth Andrews, *English Privateering During the Spanish War 1585–1603* (Cambridge: Cambridge University Press, 1964), p. 4.

20. Quoted in ibid., p. 128.

21. *C.S.P. Venetian*, 1617–19, p. 146.

22. See Theodore K. Rabb, *Enterprise and Empire: Merchant and Gentry Investment in the Expansion of England 1575–1630* (Cambridge: Harvard University Press, 1967), p. 29.

23. Rabb emphasizes that the merchants in such arrangements were motivated by trade, whereas the gentry were motivated by the kind of fame extolled in pamphlets such as *The Trumpet of Fame* (1595), a tribute to Drake and Hawkins. See Madeleine Doran's introduction in Thomas Heywood, *If You Know Not Me, You Know Nobodie, Part II* (Oxford: Oxford University Press, 1934/35), pp. xvii–xix. See also

Theodore B. Leinwand whose discussion of credit in this work extends to both sections of the play.

24. Theodore B. Leinwand, *Theatre, Finance and Society in Early Modern England* (Cambridge: Cambridge University Press, 1999), p. 28.

25. Theodora Jankowski, "Historicizing and Legitimating Capitalism: Thomas Heywood's *Edward IV and If You Know Not Me, You Know Nobodie*," *Medieval and Renaissance Drama in England*, vol. VII, ed. Leeds Barroll (London: Associated University Press, 1995), p. 308.

26. *The Dictionary of National Biography*, vol. 23, p. 146.

27. Jankowski, "Historicizing," p. 308.

28. Ibid., p. 326.

29. Anon., *A packe of Spanish lyes sent abroad in the vvorld: first printed in Spaine in the Spanish tongue, and translated out of the originall. Now ripped vp, vnfolded, and by iust examination condemned, as conteyning false, corrupt, and detestable wares, worthy o be damned and burned* (London: Christopher Barker, 1588), STC, 23011, p. 3, sig. A2v.

30. Gustav Ungerer, *Anglo-Spanish Relations in Tudor Literature*, pp. 163–6.

31. Christopher Marlowe, *Doctor Faustus*, ed. Michael Keefer (Peteborough: Broadview Press, 1991).

32. Valdéz was not the only Spanish captive to be exploited in this way. Sir Edward Hoby's Spanish studies were overseen by two noble hostages brought back from Cadiz: Archdeacon Don Payo Patiño and Alonso de Baeza, Treasurer of the King's Customs. Gustav Ungerer, "The Printing of Spanish Books in Elizabethan England," *The Library*, fifth series, vol. XX, no. 3, 1965, pp. 177–229.

33. Ungerer, "The Printing," p. 180.

34. Sir Edward Hoby claims that the *Bibliotheca Hispanica* gave him such an excellent command of the language that he was later able to translate a military treatise by Don Bernardino de Mendoza. See Ungerer, "The Printing," p. 203.

35. Richard Percivale, *Bibliotheca Hispanica* (London: John Jackson, 1591), STC(2nd ed.) 19619, Sig. A3r.

36. For a full account of Doyle's sources see Roger Steiner, *Two Centuries of Spanish and English Bilingual Lexicography (1590–1800)* (The Hague: Mouton, 1970), pp. 17–35.

37. Steiner, *Two Centuries*, p. 26. Among the additions Percivale made to Doyle's lexicon are words connected to military and warfare.

38. I am grateful to Valentina Ricci and Meg Worley for their help with this translation.

39. Ungerer, *Anglo-Spanish Relations*, p. 64.

40. John Minsheu, *Pleasant and delightful dialogues in Spanish and English* (London: Edmund Bolifant, 1599), sig. P1r.

41. Minsheu's reputation as a competent lexicographer comes under fire in an essay by Jürgen Schäfer who observes that many of his etymologies are taken from other sources or simply incorrect. Nevertheless,

my concern here is not with Minsheu's accuracy but rather with the way he positions himself and his work within the culture. See, Jürgen Schäfer, "John Minsheu: Scholar or Charlatan?" *Renaissance Quarterly* 26, no.1, (Spring 1973), pp. 23–35.

42. Steiner, *Two Centuries*, p. 53.
43. On Minsheu's contribution to this method of subscription publication see Franklin B. Williams Jr., "Scholarly Publication in Shakespeare's Day: A Leading Case." *Joseph Quincy Adams Memorial Studies*, James McManaway, Giles Dawson, and Edwin Willoughby, eds. (Washington: The Folger Shakespeare Library, 1948), p. 771.
44. Williams, "Scholarly Publication," p. 755.

CHAPTER 5

THE BATTLE OF ALCAZAR, THE MEDITERRANEAN, AND THE MOOR

Emily C. Bartels

In the summer of 1578, in the North African town of El-Ksar el-Kebir, two Moors and their factions fought for rule over the Moroccan domains of Marrakech and Fez.[1] Abd el-Malek, the ruler at that time was the legitimate head of state, next in line after his brother. Abd el-Malek was challenged, however, by his brother's son, Mulai Mohammed el-Meslokh, who had usurped power in 1574 and been ousted in 1576. As the conflict unfolded, Abd el-Malek enlisted the support of the Turks, while Mulai Mohammed sought aid from the Portuguese king, Don Sebastian, who was backed also by Spain, Rome, and a wayward Englishman, Thomas Stukeley. The final battle—what the Renaissance would know and critics come to know as "the battle of Alcazar"—restored the legitimate line. Abd el-Malek died from illness during the conflict, but his brother, Ahmed el-Mansur, succeeded and ruled from 1578 to 1603. Sebastian and Stukeley were killed, and the dispossessed Mulai Mohammed drowned on the battlefield, his recovered body was flayed, stuffed, and displayed as part of the triumphant progress of the restored regime.[2]

In England, Alcazar was news from almost the moment it happened. Anonymous tracts, "A Dolorous Discourse of a most terrible and bloudy Battel fought in Barbarie" (1579) and "Strange newes out of Affrick" (ca.1586), sensationalized the event, drawing on eyewitness accounts of Portuguese and Spanish survivors.[3]

George Whetstone's *English Myrror* (1586) and John Polemon's *Second part of the booke of Battailes* (1587) wrote Alcazar into history—in Whetstone's case, exemplary English history. Montaigne's "Against Idlenesse, or Doing Nothing" (1600) sanctified Abd el-Malek as a moral hero, who "stoutly" and "vigorously" made "use" of his "undanted [*sic*] courage" and who "caused himselfe to be carried and haled, where-ever neede called for him," while he "was even dying," "lest the souldiers hearing of his death, might fall into dispaire."[4] In 1633, the English would still be reading his story, in John Harrison's *Tragicall Life and Death of Muley Abdala Melek.*[5]

Importantly, too, the events at Alcazar prompted the very first representation of Moors on the English Renaissance stage. As best we can tell, in 1588–89—just after Marlowe had astounded audiences with his inimitable Scythian conqueror, Tamburlaine—George Peele produced *The Battle of Alcazar*, featuring the conflict between Muly Mahamet, the "barbarous" "negro" Moor, and Abdelmelec, the "brave Barbarian lord" (1 Pro. 6–7, 12).[6] Clearly influential, the play provided the dramatic precursors for Moors who would follow in fairly regular succession: Aaron of *Titus Andronicus* (1594), Eleazar of *Lust's Dominion* (ca. 1599), and Othello (1604).[7] Alcazar appeared as well in *The Famous History of Captain Thomas Stukeley* (1605). And in the second part of *If You Know Not Me, You Know Nobody* (ca.1606), Thomas Heywood actually interrupts two focal points of nationalist action—the building of the Royal Exchange and Elizabeth's defeat of the Spanish Armada—to announce the results of "that renowned battell / Swift fame desires to carry through the world" (293).[8]

The obvious question is *why?* Why would the early modern world *desire* to hear about a "civill mutinie" between two Moors over the disposition of Moroccan rule?[9] Why would Heywood interrupt representations of foundational moments in the evolution of English nationhood to direct attention to Alcazar? And why would the events at Alcazar prompt Renaissance dramatists to embrace a new dramatic subject, the Moor? What was Alcazar to England, or England to Alcazar?

We may find the clearest answers if we look to Peele's *Alcazar* that marketed its novel topic as important to English audiences. The play starts as a provincial history of a Moroccan civil war, dogged by a dramatically archaic backstory of revenge. First, a dumb show reveals Muly Mahamet murdering his younger brothers and his uncle. The staged action begins thereafter, with Abdelmelec taking arms against the "traitor-king" and calling for "showers of sharp revenge"

(1.1.87–8). Abdelmelec triumphs, and Muly retreats to a "blasted grove" (1.2.81), only to be haunted by requisite ghosts who echo the stock refrain "*Vindicta!*" (S.D. 2 Pro. 8). It is not until Muly comes out of exile and begins the challenge that will end at Alcazar that a new history, what the choric Presenter calls a "modern matter" of a "true and tragic war," unfolds (1.1.49–50).

Although the play starts thus, with a local history conveyed through soon-to-be outmoded dramatic conventions, scene by scene its cultural and historical vision expands into what George Hunter has called "the tangled web of Realpolitik."[10] In Peele, Morocco provides a space where the Turks, Spanish, Portuguese, the Pope, and an Englishman can "perform, in view of all the world" (1.1.27)—a phrase, "all the world" that becomes pronounced on the stage at just this moment, I think not coincidentally, within plays featuring Moors. Historically, Morocco was central to the Mediterranean economy and it served as England's vital link to the markets of that region.[11] Queen Elizabeth sustained important trades with Mulai Mohammed as well as with Abd el-Malek and Ahmed el-Mansur, even though her practice of trading arms (for salt peter, a prime ingredient in gunpowder) with "infidel" rulers violated a papal ban and strained her relations with Europe's Catholic states.[12] Moving beyond a revenge plot, *Alcazar* emphasizes what is already the way of the world, already "modern" or commonplace, in the Mediterranean: an accommodating realpolitik that allows for multiple, sometimes conflicting alliances of just the sort Elizabeth made with the contending Moors. Peele sets this improvisational politics beside the nationalist impulses, which propagandists such as Richard Hakluyt were articulating to advance England's standing worldwide and through which playwrights such as Heywood were reading the story of Alcazar.[13] In staging this confluence of political options, *The Battle of Alcazar* challenges the boundaries of geography and nation, recognizing instead the reality, if not also the advantage, of a world order grounded in flexible exchange, contingent on political expediency and the inevitable, if unpredictable, cultural intermixing already in place by necessity.

* * *

In Hakluyt's *Principal Navigations* (1589–1600), an account of Portuguese involvement at Alcazar ends with the assertion that "divers . . . English gentlemen were in this battell, whereof the most part were slaine" (VI:294).[14] The account names an English survivor, "M. Christopher Lyster," who was "taken captive" and "long detained in miserable servitude" at "the cruel hands of the Moores" (VI:294). Nonetheless, from the Renaissance onward, commentaries on *Alcazar* and on the histories behind it have been preoccupied with one and only one Englishman, Thomas Stukeley. A known Catholic, Stukeley spent much of his career as an expatriot in alliance with Catholic leaders such as Shane O'Neill, a powerful Irish nationalist, Philip II of Spain, and Pope Gregory XIII.[15] Under the auspices of the Pope, Stukeley set out on a mission to invade Ireland, but was waylaid in Portugal and was either coerced or convinced by the crusading king, Sebastian, to fight for Mulai Mohammed. In England, Queen Elizabeth sometimes embraced and sometimes spurned, even imprisoned, Stukeley; in the end she feared that he would steer the Portuguese to Ireland (rather than be steered by them to Morocco) as a first step to invading England.[16] Ultimately, his contributions to the Moroccan war were negligible: Mulai's faction was defeated, and Stukeley seems to have been dishonored and killed by his own men. Nonetheless, shortly after, Stukeley was featured in a pamphlet *Newe Newes contayning A Shorte rehersall of the late enterprise of certain fugytive Rebelles: fyrst pretended by Captaine Stukeley* (1579).[17] The title to an early quarto of *Alcazar* spotlights "the death of Captaine Stukeley"; Anthony Munday's *The English Romayne Lyfe* (1582) later reframes his life.[18] In the seventeenth century, *The Famous History* brought Stukeley's domestic and political fortunes to the center stage, tracing his moves across the globe, from England to Ireland, Calais, Spain, Rome, Portugal, and finally to Morocco. Stukeley also earned a ballad, "The famous life and death of the renowned *English* gallant, *Thomas Stukley*" (1612?), and a chapbook, *The Famous History of Stout Stukley: or, His valiant Life and Death* (1638).

Literary critics have absorbed this fixation and have routinely ascribed England's interest in Alcazar to Stukeley's presence there. Thorleif Larsen's exploration of "the historical and legendary background" of Peele's *Alcazar*, for example, centers on Stukeley and has set the terms for the criticism to follow, from 1939 on.[19] As late as 1987, Joseph Candido proposed the play, and Stukeley, as the starting point for "Tudor biographical drama."[20] In these influential studies, the events at Alcazar provide only the "panoramic backdrop against which the life of the central character [Stukeley] is brought into relief."[21]

But why? Stukeley's oft-noted appeal as both a historical and a dramatic figure has derived from his "dare-devil courage," "boundless energy," and "charismatic and controversial" persona—which, since early times, has received both praise and blame, admiration and disdain.[22] Heywood unequivocally celebrates Stukeley as "that renowned Englishman, / That had a spirit equal with a king" and "in warlike strife, / Honord his country, and concluded life" (*If You Know Not Me*, 293), while the contemporaneous *Famous History* introduces him rather as a "lewd misordred villaine" (279) badly in need of reformation (which comes). Years later, in 1662, Stukeley survives in Thomas Fuller's *History of the Worthies of England* as a "bubble of emptiness, and meteor of ostentation."[23] Notably, however, despite the shifts in Stukeley's own national and religious allegiances, representations such as these share a telling emphasis on his status as a representative "Englishman." *The Famous History* goes out of its way to stress Stukeley's connection to England. In the opening act, Stukeley competes for a wife against a rival, Vernon, in order to gain access, everyone rightly fears, to her father's wealth. The plot works toward the redemption of this economically shifty Englishman by inserting his English compatriot, Vernon, signally into the story. Although Vernon leaves England to escape his rival, he runs into Stukeley everywhere he goes, and the unhappy (though comic) coincidence predicates a moral resolution. On the fields of Alcazar, Stukeley and Vernon join in a ritual of forgiveness, with Stukeley declaring them both of "one selfe heart" and "one country" (2938–9). Their "English bloud," he insists, will be the last of its kind spent in Barbary, even as it gets mingled, if they're lucky, with "the bloud of kings" (2944–6). Stukeley's men finally kill him; but at its end, the play emphasizes rather the intervention of the righteous Vernon, who sacrifices himself in an attempt to save Stukeley, and whose death, along with Stukeley's, becomes a sign of English solidarity.

In Peele, the depiction of Stukeley is at once more vexed and more complex. For if Stukeley is a hero in *Alcazar*, he is by no means a *national* hero.[24] Although the play underlines Stukeley's Englishness, it does not promote Englishness as a political ideal. Instead, Peele suggests, within the unpredictable context of Euro-Mediterranean exchange, nationalism is not only *not* equivalent to heroism, but it also appears inherently conflicted and potentially coercive as political theory and discourse.

From the start Stukeley's campaign is marked by split loyalties. When he first appears, he is accompanied by an Irish bishop and "Italian" followers (S.D.5.1.108), headed to Ireland but grounded in Portugal because of "foul weather" (2.2.19). Their mission, as the Bishop explains to the Portuguese, is to "conquer" Ireland "for his Holiness / And so restore it to the Roman faith" (2.2.15–16).

The announcement of this crusade immediately causes a clash between national and religious allegiance that together might otherwise complement a Christian, imperialist cause. The Governor of Lisbon, Diego Lopez, embraces Stukeley and his men as at once "valiant Catholics" and "brave Englishmen" (2.2.1–2), but he aggressively supports the claim of nation over the assertion of faith. "Are ye not all Englishmen," he asks Stukeley, "And longs not Ireland to that kingdom?" (2.2.20–1). Assuming both answers are yes, he declares the expedition therefore "unhonourable," a "scandal to the holy see of Rome" (2.2.23–4), despite the fact that Stukeley is authorized by the Pope and accompanied by "voluntary men" from Rome (2.4.158). Their loyalty is to the Church, and when Sebastian, the "most Christian king of Portugal," pressures them to join him in aiding Muly Mahamet, they are reluctant to act " 'gainst [their] vows" (2.4.21, 149). These men later turn on Stukeley, the "ambitious Englishman," because he has aborted the "famous expedition" to Ireland, betrayed them and "his Holiness," and supported "our heathen foe" (5.1.109, 112–15). Lopez explains that, in condemning Stukeley's mission, he is merely "speak[ing] [his] conscience" (2.2.22). But even if his privileging of English nationhood over Catholic supremacy would have played well with English Protestants, these words come from a Catholic leader. At best, Lopez's nationalist argument naively undermines the religious loyalties of his state; at worst, it furthers Portugal's nationalist cause by encouraging Stukeley to abandon the Irish project and assist in the Portuguese invasion of Morocco. Either way, the exchange emphasizes that the representative Englishman is nonrepresentatively Catholic.

Moreover, Peele exposes as troubling the nationalist and imperialist edges of the Portuguese mission Stukeley ultimately joins. Sebastian markets his campaign in Morocco as a "holy Christian war," designed "to plant the Christian faith in Africa" (2.4.66, 165). Yet attached to that agenda is his hope to "propagate the fame" of Portugal (3.1.7) and make the enemy "tremble at [his] strength" (2.4.48–9). Sebastian is lured into the Moroccan conflict by Muly's (false) promise to "surrender up the kingdom of Moroccus" to Portugal and render the "realm of Fess" "contributary" to the Portuguese king (2.4.14–17). Similarly, when Sebastian turns to King Philip of Spain for additional troops, he is coaxed into trusting the Spanish king by promises of the king's daughter *and* "the Islands of Moluccus" that Philip "commands" (3.1.26–7). Although the historical Philip did send token troops to Alcazar, despite serious reservations about the mission, Peele changes the facts to incriminate the king (who neither appears nor sends aid) for "disguising with a double face" and "flatter[ing] [Sebastian's] youth and forwardness" (3.1.50–1). Yet it is Sebastian's vulnerability to promises of tribute and territory that do him in. Even the choric Presenter, who repeatedly defends Sebastian's honor, questions the Portuguese king's misguided ambitions. Anticipating that neither "aid of arms or marriage" will follow Spain's promises, he warns: " 'ware ambitious wiles and poison'd eyes!" (3 Pro. 21); although "honour was object of [Sebastian's] thoughts," the Presenter qualifies, "ambition was his ground" (4 Pro. 13).

Within this context, Peele includes an extended glorification of the English state, of the sort we would expect to find (and question) in an English history play. Articulated by the Portuguese Sebastian, its function is to dissuade Stukeley from the Irish mission and engage him in the Moroccan war. In Sebastian's idealization, Elizabeth's "seat" is "sacred, imperial, and holy," "shining with wisdom, love, and mightiness," and everything works to "bless and serve her royal majesty" (2.4.109–10, 16). Further, Sebastian's England is surrounded on every side by natural defenses—by "wallowing oceans" and "raging floods" that "swallow up her foes," by "the narrow Britain-sea," "where Neptune sits in triumph to direct / Their course to hell that aim at her disgrace," and so on (2.4.117–18, 123–5). According to the king, "danger, death, and hell" await "all" who "seek to danger" this blessed island or blessed queen (2.4.132–3). We are to take no more comfort in Sebastian's argument, I think, than in John of Gaunt's moving but vacantly nostalgic idealization of the "sceptred isle" (2.1.40) in Shakespeare's *Richard II* (1595).[25] For Sebastian's ideological sanctification of the state is linked to an exaggerated estimation of the practical implication: that no one, not even Stukeley, could stage a successful invasion of English territory (which includes Ireland). Insisting that Stukeley's forces "are far too weak to violate the Queen of Ireland's right," Sebastian argues:

> Were every ship ten thousand on the seas,
> Mann'd with the strength of all the eastern kings,
> Conveying all the monarchs of the world,
> T'invade the island where her highness reigns,
> 'Twere all in vain, for heavens and destinies
> Attend and wait upon her majesty. (2.4.100–8)

The hyperbole, manifest in a cascade of "every" and "all," "kings," "monarchs," and "majesty," "heavens and destinies," argues obviously against realizable or verifiable truth. Moreover, Peele magnifies the historical Stukeley's force from roughly six hundred men and three or fewer ships to six thousand men, seven ships, and two pinnaces, making Sebastian's negative estimation of Stukeley's chances in Ireland somewhat less credible than they might actually have been.[26] Even with Stukeley leading only the six hundred, the Queen *was* worried that he might threaten England, albeit with Portugal's help.

Sebastian's appropriation of English nationalism appears thus as just that: an appropriation that works strategically not in England's but in Portugal's behalf. If we confidently embrace Stukeley as England's national hero and the play as a celebration of English nationhood, we endorse terms Peele has rendered suspect. The characterization of Stukeley suggests a different model of identity and subjectivity—one that hovers irreverently outside the bounds of both hero and nation. For even as Stukeley presents himself as a representative Englishman he simultaneously declares national origins an arbitrary and inadequate determinant of political allegiance or action. In responding to the Portuguese governor's pointed greeting, Stukeley advises Lopez to "understand":

> As we are Englishmen, so are we men,
> To follow rule, honour, and empery,
> Not to be bent so strictly to the place
> Wherein at first I blew the fire of life,
> But that I may at liberty make choice
> Of all the continents that bounds [sic] the world. (2.2.26–33)

In Stukeley's formulation, "to be begot or born in any place" is "a thing of pleasure and of ease / That might have been perform'd elsewhere as well" (2.2.34–7). This is not the breaking apart of an English "fantasy of ethnic coherence," though, as John Drakakis has suggested, that would happen elsewhere.[27] Birth is not irrelevant; it is random, at least as far as politics are concerned.

Candido has declared Stukeley, at this moment, an enlightened "citizen of the world."[28] Crucially at stake for Candido is the development of a newly compelling stage personality, one rife with "innate tensions and contradictions" and with an "expansiveness of spirit that typifies the Marlovian hero at his overweening best."[29] Candido's model (and Peele's) is Tamburlaine, an "established stage type" onto which, Candido argues, Peele "graft[s] popular," individuating details.[30] Yet there is more in this intertextual transaction than a cult of personality, set against a " 'history' " that is simply and solely "the scenery in the portrait" and "never the main subject of the play."[31] History makes an important difference and dissonance here. Unlike Stukeley, Tamburlaine begins as a Scythian shepherd, whose political ambitions focus on the conquest of "the East"; although he hopes to be "monarch of the Earth" (*Tamb. II*: 5.3.217), he never steps foot on English ground, and his hyperbolic fantasies stop at England's shores.[32] For Peele to "graft" Stukeley, the self-proclaimed Englishman, onto Tamburlaine, the Scythian shepherd turned Emperor of the East, requires a preposterous leap of political faith within a world defined by insular nations and nationhood. And yet it is precisely that kind of leap that *Alcazar* and *Tamburlaine* encourage.

Much like Tamburlaine, Stukeley is driven obsessively by the desire to hold a crown, any crown. In an early aside, he admits, with Tamburlainean extravagance:

> There shall no action pass my hand or sword,
> That cannot make a step to gain a crown;
> No word shall pass the office of my tongue,
> That sounds not of affection to a crown. (2.2.69–73)

If the overreaching, overconfident mode of this articulation makes obvious the provocative overlap between English rover and Eastern conqueror, the content–that, as obviously, mirrors Tamburlaine's lust for "the sweet fruition of an earthly crown" (*Tamb. I* 2.7.29)— manifests the problem of their similarity and the disturbing implications of their difference. Tamburlaine's monarchical ambitions, which are only a small starting point for him, are not as directly treasonous: Tamburlaine has no designs on Scythia, and when he usurps the Persian crown, his first, he acts in collusion with and rebellion against the Persian king's brother, Cosroe, who is the instigator of the usurpation. Stukeley's actions, however, are dangerously close to treason and dangerously close to home. Initially, he intends to be "King of Ireland" (2.2.79)—a place Willy Maley has described as a "repository for expatriate Englishness, nascent Britishness and colonial otherness" and a place only one short step from England.[33]

But if these ambitions border on treason in the play, the political philosophy that grounds them is less easy to judge. In Peele's play, Stukeley is neither a traitor nor a heroic nationalist; he is driven by personal and political expediency rather than by any set loyalty or ideology for or against England. Even as he imagines ruling Ireland, he privileges position over place, asserting: "King of a mole-hill had I rather be, / Than the richest subject of a monarchy" (2.2.80–1).

His whole history, which he recounts on Alcazar's fields, consists of political improvisation. According to Stukeley, he "touch'd the height of Fortune's wheel" during his early years in London but was driven by "a discontented humour" "to Ireland, then to Spain" (5.1.139, 142–3). Though he received great favor and fortune "in King Philip's court," he explains, he was finally banished because of an altercation with a bishop and "a bishop's man" (5.1.148, 151). He then moved to Rome, where he was created "Marquis of Ireland" and "made lieutenant-general" of the Irish campaign (5.1.157, 160). Therefore, as he tells it, "in fatal hour" he landed in Lisbon, was "dared to the field" and "driven, to fight or else to die" in Morocco (5.1.166–7). His explanation for his and Sebastian's defeat is finally destiny: Stukeley insists that "from our cradles we were marked all / And destinate to die in Africa" (5.1.171–2). The play is too invested in the implications of political choice, I think, to endorse such fatalism. For the self-promoting Stukeley, destiny may be little more than a convenient rationalization for failure. Be that as may, on display is a career of spectacular successes and defeats, all unpredictably contingent on circumstance. That career cannot be contained or explained by any set terms of Englishness, nation, or religion any more than the simultaneous attraction and detraction prompted by Stukeley's charismatic narcissism can be wiped off by easy judgments of good or bad.

In fact, Stukeley's most subversive statement of his political aims— his insistence that he would rather be "king of a mole-hill" than "the richest subject" to someone else's rule—survives as an apocryphal sign of his outspoken intimacy with the English queen. In *The History of the Worthies of England*, Fuller writes that Stukeley was "so confident" in "his ambition,"

> that he blushed not to tell queen Elizabeth, "that *he preferred rather to be sovereign of a mole-hill, than the highest subject to the greatest king in Chistendom [sic];*" adding, moreover, "that he was assured he should be a prince before his death." "I hope," said queen Elizabeth, "I shall hear from you, when you are stated in your principality." "I will write unto you," quoth Stukeley. "In what language?" said the queen. He returned, "In the style of princes; To our dear Sister."[34]

In Fuller, the "mole-hill" is not Ireland but Florida. Yet that the line would carry thus from Peele or his sources to Fuller, asserting an English connection Peele's Stukeley seems to flout, only underscores the complicated conflation of Stukeley the representative Englishman with Stukeley the worldly rover. Stukeley stands out in Alcazar as a figure who can negotiate for gain in "all the continents that bound the world." But he is nonetheless connected to the English queen, who would bargain with Moors on both sides of the conflict and risk alienating European rivals in order to secure England's place in that world—an English queen whom he therefore resembles or who, therefore, resembles him.

*   *   *

If *Alcazar* thus challenges the apparent single-mindedness of nationalist ideology, it also complicates the characterization of the Moor, using that figure to produce a historical alternative to the construct of a national—and we would say, ethnically coherent—self.[35] Despite all of Stukeley's roving, he *is* a representative of the English people or race at the moment he claims Englishness as his birthright, though not, as I have argued, as his politics. He must deflect that birthright, with its assumed purity of blood, in order to profess and achieve his "liberty" in the world, since that identity compels conscription to national service: if England is solely for the English, the English must be wholly for England. As a supplement to this kind of ideology, in certain pockets of English discourse, the Moor would become the representative of an ethnically indeterminate but distinctively color-coded race. At the turn of the century, Queen Elizabeth herself confused Moors with west Africans in her now-often-cited orders to deport certain "Negars and Blackamoors" from England, officially separating this new category of blacks from her "own liege people."[36] Yet in Peele, in the first play on the English popular stage to feature the subject, Moors appear diverse and divided in their characterizing allegiances, actions, and "race."

In recovering Alcazar's history, Peele's play presents two competing models of the Moor: on the one side is the "brave Barbarian," Abdelmelec, and on the other, the "black" and "barbarous" Muly Mahamet (1 Pro.12, 6, 16). There is a striking—but, in early discriminatory discourse, familiar—nonequivalence in these descriptive markers: where the noble Moor has a named ethnicity ("Barbarian"), the ignoble Moor receives only the denigrating behavior ("barbarous") derived from that name, and he alone has color.[37] That color registers an incriminating morality: "the negro Muly Hamet" proves to be as "bloody in his deeds" as he is "black in his look" (1 Pro.7, 16). But if the moral or behavioral difference is unmistakable, there is less distinctiveness surrounding racial lineage. Both the "Barbarian" and the barbarian share the bloodline of their "grandsire Muly Xarif," whom the Presenter introduces as "th' Arabian Moor" (1 Pro.65, 15), and who was actually the Turk, Moulay Mohammed el-Kaim bi amer Allah.[38] This is not the only place in Renaissance texts or Mediterranean history where distinctions between Moors, Arabians, and Turks seem to blur: before his suicide, Othello imagines his tears as the "medicinable gum" of "Arabian trees" (5.2.350–1) and scripts himself simultaneously as a Turk who killed a Venetian and a Moor who killed the Turk. Peele's slippage may be testimony to the legacy of Ottoman history in Mediterranean domains where, as a result of sustained contact and the shifting overlap of rule, Turks and Moors and Arabs might well share a race. But whatever Peele understands about the social consequences of the long history of conquest and collaboration in the western Mediterranean, he understands the Moor as a subject not of a race but of *mixed* races.

These complicating intersections of race do not undermine the distinction—between Abdelmelec the brave and Muly the barbarous—that defines the Moroccan conflict; nor do they undo the color coding that is layered on top and begins even here to establish an equivalence (which will become ingrained) between race and blackness. They do, however, set the stage for a reading of difference that pivots on the integration or collaboration, rather than the bounding or segregation, of otherwise culturally marked peoples. For as the initial conflict unfolds, Abdelmelec's alliance with the Turks gives him a singular edge over Muly as an ethical and political leader. Having served militarily under the "colours" of the Sultan Solimon (1 Pro.46), when Abdelmelec first appears, he pays homage to "the sacred name" of Solimon's son, "Amurath the Great" (1.1.11), historically the sultan Muran III (1574–95). In the face of Muly's insurgence, Amurath's Bassa has come to Morocco "to gratify and remunerate" (1.1.24) Abdelmelec's service to the Turk,

> to perform, in view of all the world,
> The true office of right and royalty;
> To see thee in thy kingly chair enthroned,
> To settle and to seat thee in the same,
> To make thee Emperor of this Barbary. (1.1.27–31)

If that performance advances Turkish power, it also restores Abdelmelec's rule and contributes to an extended chain of reciprocity and remuneration: Abdelmelec offers Amurath's envoy "the noblest ladies of the land," while the Turk leaves the "chosen guard of Amurath's janizaries" to "honour and attend" on the Moor (2.1.26, 48–9). Even if the presence of the janizzaries (elite, converted Christian soldiers whom the Turks usually acquired as tribute) shadow the scene with the suggestion that the Turks are keeping guard over Morocco, there is no sign of impending Turkish domination of the sort that taxes the Christian government of Malta in Marlowe's *Jew of Malta*.[39] Abdelmelec does gives the Turk his "due," but the Moor rules Morocco without interference, "in eye of all the world" (3.4.42), and "intitle[s]" his brother, Muly Mahamet Seth (Ahmed el-Mansur), "true heir unto the crown" (2.1.17–19).

Editors and critics of the play have tended to take a darker view of the interaction here between Moor and Turk, portraying Amurath as a "cruel voluptuary" and Abdelmelec's relation to him as "slavish deference."[40] To be sure, Amurath's reputation would come under fire in the 1590s as he waged what Leeds Barroll has called "a major land offensive in central Europe."[41] In 1590–91, Shakespeare's *Henry IV Part 2* presents Amurath as the Turkish antithesis to the English king, drawing on the allegations that the historical figure killed his brothers in order to secure his reign.[42] Hal assures his brothers: "This is the English, not the Turkish court, / Not Amurath an Amurath succeeds, / But Harry Harry" (5.2.46–8). Yet in this period, impressions of the Turk were always highly mixed; in the years before *Alcazar*, Queen Elizabeth had, after all, negotiated with the "great Turke" "Murad Can" to secure authorization for trade in the Levant.[43] Moreover, the historical Abd el-Malek enlisted the support of the Turks, offering in exchange an ultimately unfulfilled promise to join them against Spain.[44] In Peele, it is only the discredited Muly and his son who fear that the Turk will, like "Tamburlaine," "invade," "chastise," and "menace" Africa's "lawful kings" and "right and royal realm" (1.2.22, 33–4). Even so, they recognize the advantage of Abdelmelec's connection to "that brave guard of sturdy janizaries / That Amurath to Abdelmelec gave / And bade him boldly be with them as safe / As if he slept within a walled town"—a guard that now advances on Muly "threatening revenge, / Bloody revenge, bloody revengeful war" in Abdelmelec's behalf (1.2.40–5).

In contrast to Abdelmelec, Muly at first stands alone; and the more isolated he becomes from the dramatic fiction, the more stereotyped he appears as a dramatic character.[45] In his initial attempt to get the throne, Muly imagines that his gold will provide "the glue, sinews, and strength of war" (1.2.8) and surrounds himself only with his immediate family (his wife Calipolis and his son) and his guard. There is an imminent threat of the annihilation of both character and characterization. Overthrown, "the Moor" retreats to the "shade / Of some unhaunted place, some blasted grove, / Of deadly yew or dismal cypress tree," where he means to "pine with thought and terror of mishaps" (1.2.80–2, 86). There, in a space of "cursed solitaries" (2.3.38), the objective correlative of his despair, Muly "lives"—and imagines he will always live—"forlorn among the mountain-shrubs / And makes his food the flesh of savage beasts" (2 Pro.34–5), with the Furies seeking revenge against him. His only recourse and discourse consists of "huge exclaims" and lamentations (2.3.16), which his starving wife underscores as pointless. Only when he sends word to Sebastian, "the good and harmless King of Portugal," promising "to resign the royalty / And kingdom of Morocco to his hands" in exchange for military aid, can Muly's small cadre of supporters grasp "the slenderest hair" of opportunity and see an end to "this miserable life" (2.2.48–50, 55–6).

Muly does in fact come out of hiding to join with Sebastian and challenge the restored Abdelmelec. As the dramatic events progress toward the battle at Alcazar, the play's focus shifts from the local to the global, from the Moroccan civil war to the network of alliances that surrounds it. But if the configuration of factions at Alcazar becomes the evolving center of interest, of history and the *realpolitik*, Muly's ambitions remain trapped and caricatured within the regressive revenge plot, which recedes with him into the background. The Presenter predicts that "war and weapons, and blood and death, / Wait on the counsels of this cursed king," "this Moor, this murderer of his progeny" (4 Pro. 3–5); yet Muly rarely appears. When he does, he calls on Nemesis to "sprinkle gore amongst these men of war," all "eager of revenge" (4.2.81–2), to "descend and take to thy tormenting hell, / The mangled body of that traitor-king," Abdelmelec (4.2.85–6), and "for revenge, for deep revenge," to "let him be, damn'd, and condemn'd to bear / All torment, tortures, plagues, and pains of hell" (4.2.94, 96–7). In the final act, when Muly's defeat is imminent, he can only imagine retreating once again to "some unfrequented place, / Some uncouth walk, where I may curse my fill" (5.1.75–6). The last time he appears alive, he stands before the river that will drown him, calling for revenge and "a horse, a horse . . . a horse" (5.1.96). Shakespeare subsequently echoes that line to mark the desperation of Richard III, whose unmitigated obsession with vengeance leads, like Muly's to self-annihilation and erases the more complex and provocative interiors that Shakespeare would soon prefer.

To be sure, Muly's characterization plays in counterpoint to Sebastian's, though the two figures are presumably allied.[46] As the Presenter tells it, Muly's "wily trains" and "smoothest course of

speech" mislead Sebastian into "dangerous war" (5 Pro. 3–5), partially excusing, or at least explaining, Sebastian's own "deceiving
hope" and imperialist designs (3.2.1). On the fields of Alcazar, the
hapless Portuguese prince is able to "see [his] oversight": he confronts
the "treachery" of the "false-hearted Mahamet" and remembers
warnings he had ignored "to beware / a face so full of fraud and
villainy" (5.1.67–70). Yet the potential catharsis of this tragic recognition is diminished significantly by the displacement of Sebastian's
death (which happens offstage) and his body (which is lost).

Ultimately, it is not Sebastian who frames Morocco's story, but
Morocco which frames Sebastian's, and not the revenge play that pre-
vails but the political history. At the end, Abdelmelec dies, and Muly
Mahamet Seth claims victory in his stead. Newly instated, Muly Seth
sends Portuguese prisoners to recover Sebastian's body, and with that
body before him, he seizes the moment to honor the "earth and clay /
Of him that erst was mighty King of Portugal" (5.1.222–3). His
eulogy anticipates Marc Antony's public adulation of Brutus, the
"noblest Roman of them all" (*Julius Caesar* 5.5.68), and Fortinbras's
reconstruction of Hamlet as one who would "have prov'd most royal"
"had he been put on" (*Hamlet* 5.2.397–8)—gestures that happen
only after these rivals are dead and unable to flex their political mus-
cles. In Shakespeare, the opportunism is glaring. In Peele, however,
Muly Seth's appropriation of Sebastian's body accommodates rather
than annuls the opposition. While displaying his power over "the
mighty King of Portugal," Muly Seth allows the Portuguese
prisoners-of-war to "return from hence to Christendom" (5.1.225);
he further orders his lords to "tread a solemn march, / Trailing their
pikes and ensigns on the ground / So to perform the . . . funerals" of
"this Christian king" (5.1.256, 258–69). The Moroccan king thus
absorbs and allows Christian ritual, giving it its place and its due
without losing or compromising his ground.

Muly Mahamet's final fate is set against these tributes (his body is
found at the same time as Sebastian's) and so, against the inclusive
politics that define the triumphing regime. Pronouncing that death by
drowning is "too good for such a damned wretch," Muly Seth calls
for a spectacle of retaliation that will answer and embody the "rage
and rigour of revenge" (5.1.246–7) appropriate to Muly's story. He
orders that Muly's skin "be parted from his flesh," "stiffen'd out and
stuff'd with straw," "that all the world may learn by him t'avoid / To
hale on princes to injurious war" (5.1.249–52). *Othello* may actually
be invoking this moment at its outset, when Iago introduces that
play's Moor as a general "horribly stuff'd with epithites of war"

(1.1.14). But what is a figurative beginning in Shakespeare is a literal dead end in *Alcazar*, where the characterization of Muly turns into a spectacular caricature of itself. Stuffed and stiffened, Muly's body becomes an unforgettable warning to "all the world" against self-enclosed and self-destructive politics such as his: the fault Muly Seth emphasizes is not that the "damned wretch" usurped the Moroccan throne but that he abused a foreign prince and prompted Sebastian into an "injurious war."[47] Muly Seth's political actions stand in contrast: instead of closing Morocco's borders or invading Portugal's, he accommodates the enemy in a mutually beneficial display.

Historically, representations of the battle of Alcazar stressed the extraordinary outcome: the "death of three Kings," Abd el-Malek, Mulai Mohammed, and Sebastian.[48] Within that billing, as in Peele's play, station trumps nation. Granted, Alcazar would also be remembered for enabling, with the death of Sebastian, the "transmission of so great a Kingdome [Portugal] to the crowne of *Castile*."[49] Yet even that admission underscores the permeability of national bounds and national histories, during what we might consider an era of high nationalism. *Alcazar*'s representation of Morocco and the Moor clearly invokes an ideological climate where terms of nation and race serve political needs. Yet in Peele, realities of Mediterranean exchange provide and demand something more—the integration and accommodation of cultural, religious, political, and racial differences. *The Battle of Alcazar* does create a "barbarous" black Moor who would become an subtext for stereotype. But it presents that figure, in counterpoint, as part of a race that includes a "brave" Arabian Moor, whose nobility and success hinge on a sustaining connection to the Turks.

Alcazar thus offers an alternative to plays such as *The Famous History* or Heywood's *If You Know Not Me* that promote England through some form of nationalist politics. But Peele's vision may, in fact, be closer to home—to an English Queen who secured her nation's military and economic strength by aligning herself, as needed, with Moors who had clear ties to the Turks as well as to the Spanish and Portuguese. *Alcazar* brings "all the world" to England's popular stage as a "modern matter"; but notably that matter is neither exclusively of England nor exclusively of Europe. If Peele's play is any indication, at the turn of the century, the matter of the emerging "world" lies in the Mediterranean, in Morocco, where cross-cultural exchange, accommodation, and improvisation provide the order of the day.[50]

NOTES

1. This history is from E. W. Bovill, *The Battle of Alcazar: An Account of the Defeat of Don Sebastian of Portugal at El-Ksar el-Kebir* (London: Batchworth Press, 1952).

2. On this spectacle, see ibid., p. 159.

3. On the "Alcazar" literature, see *The Dramatic Works of George Peele*, vol. 2, ed. John Yoklavich (New Haven: Yale University Press, 1961), pp. 226–36, and pp. 369–73.

4. *Montaigne's Essayes*, 3 vols. trans. John Florio, intro. L.C. Harmer (London: J.M.Dent, 1965), II: 405–6.

5. Cited in Nabil Matar, *Islam in Britain 1558–1685* (Cambridge: Cambridge University Press, 1998), p. 36.

6. George Peele, *The Battle of Alcazar* in *The Works of George Peele*, vol. 1, ed. A.H. Bullen (1888; Port Washington, NY: Kennikat Press, 1966); all citations come from this edition. There remain some questions about date and authorship; see Yoklavich, *The Dramatic Works*, 221–3, and Eldred Jones, *Othello's Countrymen: Africans in English Renaissance Drama* (Oxford: Oxford University Press, 1965), p. 42.

7. Shakespeare may actually have collaborated with Peele on *Titus*; see, for example, Brian Vickers, *Shakespeare, Co-Author: A Historical Study of Five Collaborative Plays* (Oxford: Oxford University Press, 2002), pp. 148–243.

8. Thomas Heywood, *If You Know Not Me, You Know Nobodie, in The Dramatic Works of Thomas Heywood*, 6 vols. (New York: Russell and Russell, 1964), vol. 1, cited here by page numbers. On Heywood's nationalism and its expression in his *Apology for Actors*, see Crystal Bartolovich, "Shakespeare's Globe?" in *Marxist Shakespeares*, ed. Jean E. Howard and Scott Cutler Shershow (London: Routledge, 2001), pp. 178–205, esp. pp. 182–3.

9. *The Famous History of Captain Thomas Stukeley* (1970; Oxford: Oxford University Press, 1975), 1585. This text is marked only by line numbers.

10. *English Drama, 1586–1642: The Age of Shakespeare* (Oxford: Clarendon Press, 1997), 79. Compare Jones, who argues that *The Battle* "starts as a revenge play" that is then "blurred into chronicle"; *Othello's Countrymen*, p. 44.

11. For a comprehensive Mediterranean history, see Fernand Braudel, *The Mediterranean and the Mediterranean World in the Age of Philip II*, 2 vols., trans. Siân Reynolds (New York: Harper and Row, 1972). On England's place in the world, see Walter Cohen, "The Undiscovered Country: Shakespeare and Mercantile Geography," in *Marxist Shakespeares*, ed. Jean E. Howard and Scott Cutler Shershow, pp. 128–58.

12. See Bovill, *The Battle*, pp. 43–52.

13. The pivotal study of England's early nationalism is Richard Helgerson, *Forms of Nationhood: The Elizabethan Writing of England* (Chicago: University of Chicago Press, 1992). On nationalist tropes in early modern drama, see also *Shakespeare and National Culture*, ed. John J. Joughin (Manchester: Manchester University Press, 1997), Walter Cohen, *Drama of a Nation: Public Theater in Renaissance England and Spain* (Ithaca: Cornell University Press, 1985), and Jean E. Howard and Phyllis Rackin, *Engendering a Nation: A Feminist Account of Shakespeare's English Histories* (London: Routledge, 1997).

14. Richard Hakluyt, *The Principal Navigations, Voyages, Traffiques and Discoveries of the English Nation*, 12 vols. (Glasgow: James MacLehose and Sons, 1904).

15. On Stukeley's history, see Yoklavich, *The Dramatic Works*, pp. 247–51, and Bovill, *The Battle*, pp. 79–81.

16. Bovill, *The Battle*, pp. 79–81.

17. For a survey of the popular literature on Stukeley, see Yoklavich, *The Dramatic Works*, 247–73, and Thorlief Larsen, "The Historical and Legendary Background of Peele's 'Battle of Alcazar,' " *Proceedings of the Royal Society of Canada* (1939), pp. 185–97, on p. 192n23.

18. The subtitle to the 1594 quarto reads: *The Battell of Alcazar, fought in Barbarie, betweene Sebastion king of Portugall, and Abdelmelec king of Marocco. With the death of Captaine Stukeley* (quoted in Yoklavich, *The Dramatic Works*, 218).

19. From the title to Larsen's essay, cited in note 17.

20. Joseph Candido, "Captain Thomas Stukeley: The Man, the Theatrical Record, and the Origins of Tudor 'Biographical Drama,' " *Anglia-Zeitchrift für Engische Philologie* 105 (1987): 50–68, on 50.

21. Ibid., p. 51.

22. Ibid., p. 54; Larsen, "The Historical and Legendary," p. 193.

23. Thomas Fuller, *The History of the Worthies of England*, 3 vols., ed. P. Austin Nuttall (New York: AMS press, 1965), I: 415.

24. Compare Leeds Barroll's essay in this collection, "Mythologizing the Ottoman: *The Jew of Malta and The Battle of Alcazar*," pp. 159–79.

25. From *The Riverside Shakespeare*, ed. G. Blakemore Evans and J.J.M. Tobin (Boston: Houghton Mifflin, 1972).

26. Yoklavich, *The Dramatic Works*, p. 251.

27. John Drakakis, "Afterword" in *Shakespeare and National Culture*, ed. John J. Joughin (Manchester: Manchester University Press, 1997), p. 336. See also Graham Holderness and Andrew Murphy, "Shakespeare's England: Britain's Shakespeare," pp. 19–41, in the same collection.

28. Candido, "Captain Thomas Stukeley," p. 55.

29. Ibid., pp. 55, 57.

30. Ibid., p. 56.

31. Ibid., p. 51.

32. All quotations from Marlowe are from Christopher Marlowe, *The Complete Plays*, ed. J.B. Steane (1969; London: Penguin, 1986). Mary Floyd-Wilson has argued that Scythians were merged with Britons within the category of "northerners"; *English Ethnicity and Race in Early Modern Drama* (Cambridge: Cambridge University Press, 2003), p. 15, see also p. 28. Even so, there remains an important difference between these groups and figures.

33. Willy Maley, " 'This sceptred isle': Shakespeare and the British Problem" in *Shakespeare and National Culture*, ed. John J. Joughin (Manchester: Manchester University Press, 1997), p. 89; see also pp. 83–108.

34. Fuller, *The History of the Worthies*, I: 414; emphasis added.

35. Compare Anthony Gerard Barthelemy, *Black Face, Maligned Race: The Representation of Blacks in English Drama from Shakespeare to Southern* (Baton Rouge: Louisiana State University Press, 1987), who reads the clash between the ruling Moors in terms of "the classical confrontation between good and evil," p. 78; and G.K. Hunter, "Othello and Colour Prejudice," in *Interpretations of Shakespeare*, ed. Kenneth Muir (Oxford: Clarendon Press, 1985), pp. 188–91.

36. From Elizabeth's public letter of 1601, quoted in Jones, *The Elizabethan Image of Africa* (Charlottesville: University of Virginia Press, 1971), p. 20. See my essay, "Too Many Blackamoors: Deportation, Discrimination, and Elizabeth I," *SEL*, 46:2(Spring 2006):305–22.

37. Michael Neill, " 'Mulattoes,' 'Blacks,' and 'Indian Moors': *Othello* and Early Modern Constructions of Difference," *Shakespeare Quarterly* 49: 4 (1998): 361–74, identifies this kind of nonequivalence.

38. On Abd el-Malek's history, see Bovill, *The Battle*, pp. 36–9.

39. On janizzaries, see Matar, *Islam in Britain 1558–1685* (Cambridge: Cambridge University Press, 1998), p. 22. See my own discussion of the edgy imperialist dynamics in *The Jew of Malta*, in *Spectacles of Strangeness: Imperialism, Alienation, and Marlowe* (Philadelphia: University of Pennsylvania Press, 1993), pp. 82–108.

40. Yoklavich, *The Dramatic Works*, p. 350; Jack D'Amico, *The Moor in English Renaissance Drama* (Tampa: University of Southern Florida, 1991), p. 82.

41. Leeds Barroll, *Medieval and Renaissance Drama*, p. 444.

42. I am grateful to Linda Woodbridge for calling my attention to this reference. On Amuranth. See the note to line 5.2.48 in the Riverside edition of the play.

43. See the Levant Company's charter of 1580, in Hakluyt, V: 178–91.

44. Bovill, *The Battle*, p. 22.

45. Compare Hunter, who reads this isolation instead as "a total freedom in villainy that gave Peele's image of Muly Mahamet its contemporary reputation" (p. 80).

46. Compare Barroll, who argues that "*Alcazar* idealizes the Portuguese king chiefly by casting his Negro 'puppet-king' as villain," p. 440.

47. Within three years after Sebastian's death, the crown belonged to Philip, Portugal to Spain. For fuller summary, see Yoklavich, *The Dramatic Works*, p. 226, and Bovill, *The Battle*, pp. 148–57.

48. *Montaigne's Essayes*, II: 403. Compare Larsen, who argues that "what had impressed the popular imagination apparently was the ghastly slaughter which took place at the battle, and the fact that no fewer than three kings had there lost their lives" (p. 186).

49. Ibid., II: 405. Bovill remarks, the "turnover of Portugal to Spain" meant the turnover of "the richest parts of Asia, the minerals of the West, and the spices of the East" (p. 151).

50. I want to add a note of special thanks to the members of the Medieval / Renaissance seminar at the University of Pennsylvania. Their comments on another of my essays significantly changed the shape of this one.

CHAPTER 6

MYTHOLOGIZING THE OTTOMAN:
THE JEW OF MALTA AND *THE BATTLE OF ALCAZAR*

Leeds Barroll

At the close of the fifteenth century, just as Christopher Columbus was initiating European colonization into a new world, the Muslim presence remained a significant factor in the old. Indeed, we know that a new wave of Islamic expansion was then rising in Anatolia, the southwestern and anciently civilized section of Turkey where, from 1300 on, the beginnings of an Ottoman empire had gradually been coming into play. Progressing from the status of a local Anatolian grouping to a state comprising a number of Anatolian cities, the Ottoman surge had grown to a cosmopolitan power.[1] Significantly, its polity did not embrace that three hundred-year-old *pax Islamica* that had governed the Mediterranean since the twelfth century. Instead, the new Ottoman entity has been described by historians as dynamic and aggressive, penetrated from its very origins with a sense of what warlike *jihad* that had characterized the Islamic outreach of the eight century, seven hundred years previously.[2] The purpose of this essay is to deepen our understanding of how the development of Ottoman influence in the Mediterranean helped to configure the cultural history of early modern England as manifested in several "alien" plays (my term) of the 1590s. Because there is no simple cause / effect relationship that yokes English affairs with those of the Mediterranean, I wish to approach this issue by isolating several events that may provide a suitable framework for analysis.

Just prior to 1485, the year in which Henry VII established the
Tudor dynasty, Mehmet II, "The Conqueror" (of Byzantium), had
become master of the Mediterranean coast of southeastern Europe, as
well as of Greece and Albania in the environs of the Adriatic and the
Aegean. He now planned to move against the east coast of Renaissance
Italy. In 1481, the Ottomans captured the port of Otranto, on the heel
of Italy's east coast, and also Apulia, a move described by Guicciardini.
But at this point, fortunately for Europe, Mehmet died suddenly and
was succeeded, after a considerable political struggle, by his son
Bayezit II. The conflict over the succession precipitated such a crisis in
the Ottoman Empire that their military forces were obliged to with-
draw over the western back to Albania. That this situation represented
a narrow escape for western Europe is emphasized by Bernard Lewis,
who notes the ease with which, only fifteen years after this voluntary
Ottoman withdrawal, French forces moved down through Italy, conquering with little trouble the Italian states, one after another
(pp. 31–2). Given this weakness of the Italian states, persistence by
vastly superior Ottoman forces in the same regions could have accomplished much more, configuring a situation quite different from that
now termed "The Italian Renaissance." Indeed, the rest of Europe
might have found itself associated in the fifteenth century with an
Italian peninsula, where, in the words of the anonymous Ottoman historian who chronicled the earlier capture of Otranto, "The [Italian] temples of idols became mosques of Islam and the five-fold prayer which is
the watch call of Muhammed, upon him be peace, was sounded."[3]

Notwithstanding this lost opportunity, the Ottoman Empire
attained the peak of its power over the Mediterranean during the lifetimes of Shakespeare's and Marlowe's parents, and its status as an early
modern superpower continued even well beyond the lifetimes of the
playwrights. As is well known, the Ottoman apogee occurred under
Suleyman the Magnificent, who had inherited the throne from his
father Selim I in 1520 and ruled until 1566, through the early years of
the reign of Elizabeth I. Indeed, Elizabeth's long monarchy witnessed
four successive Sultanates: that of the legendary Suleyman, of his son
Selim II (1566–74), of Murad III, also known as Amurath
(1574–95), and of Mehmet III, often called Mohamet (1595–1603).
During her reign, the dominating Ottomans even indirectly empow-
ered Muslim (non-Ottoman) naval forces from North Africa to penetrate into the Atlantic where their ships conducted raids close to the
British Isles. Indeed as late as 1627, eleven years after Shakespeare's
death, Muslim corsairs would raid Iceland, taking several hundred

Christian prisoners and offering them for sale in the slave markets of Algiers.

We are accustomed to think of the seventy or so years before Marlowe and Shakespeare wrote their plays as a time of expansion for the Atlantic states of western Europe, and for their programs of Christianizing and exploiting the Atlantic colonies of the Americas. But Selim I and his famous offspring held a very different view of global configuration. To them western *Europe* was the colonial frontier, an area which they and indeed many other Muslim powers regarded in much the same way as Europeans were to view the Americas. From the Ottoman viewpoint, rich and barbarous lands lay beyond their northern and western frontiers, and it was *their* sacred mission to bring religion, civilization, order, and peace to these alien peoples—while, of course, reaping the customary rewards of the pioneer and the frontiersman (Lewis, p. 29). In the end, the Ottomans coexisted with early modern Europe as, so to speak, a form of antimatter. The empire was, in Braudel's observation, a huge anti-Europe, a counter-Christendom.[4] Indeed, as Elizabethan dramatists were growing into their early teens, the playing out of the conflict between these irreconcilable cultures can be seen in the European response to Ottoman expansionism.

An important goal of the Ottomans was the capture of Malta. Crucial because of its location, standing just south of Sicily and dominating the narrowing waters separating southern Europe from North Africa, the island of Malta geographically effected a strategic (naval) division between the "western" and "eastern" Mediterranean. Because Suleyman already possessed Tunis and North Africa, his capture of Malta would have established his domination over the seaways of the middle Mediterranean.[5] Consequently, the fleets of Suleyman Malta in 1565 (Marlowe and Shakespeare both being one-year old). But Suleyman's attempt was unsuccessful, and Malta became—and remained—a symbol of Euro-Christian success. It never came under Ottoman domination, a circumstance of some importance considering Marlowe's use of the island as the locale of *The Jew of Malta*, one of the most popular plays on the early London stage.

The ambitions of Selim II, son of Suleyman, for his own empire included an effort to recapture Cyprus, the fictional locale of *Othello*. Just forty miles away from the Ottoman homeland, the island had been occupied by the Venetian Republic since 1488. In Shakespeare's play, during a debate in the Venetian Senate about whether the Turk is heading for Rhodes or Cyprus, one of the senators remarks,

> When we consider
> The importancy of Cyprus to the Turk
> And let ourselves again but understand
> That as it more concerns the Turk than Rhodes . . .
> We must not think the Turk is so unskilful
> To leave that latest that concerns him first. (1.3.20–3; 28–9)[6]

Indeed, in 1570, just five years after Suleyman's failure at Malta, Selim II successfully seized Cyprus, establishing an extremely important strategic base for Ottoman naval control of the eastern Mediterranean, the waters around Turkey and Crete, and ports leading to the on-land spice routes to India.[7] And just as Malta, contrary to impressions given by Marlowe's play, never fell to the Ottomans, Cyprus, contrary to the scenario painted in *Othello*, had been in Ottoman hands since 1570 and was not retaken in Shakespeare's lifetime—not, indeed, until the nineteenth century.

The immediate reaction of the West to the loss of Cyprus—particularly that of Spain which seems, *faut de mieux*, to have borne the main burden of resisting Ottoman expansion in the Mediterranean—urges the importance that Europeans attached to controlling an island in such close proximity to Turkey.[8] Entrusting the military logistics to his half-brother, Don John of Austria, Philip II exerted Spanish imperial power to recapture Cyprus by organizing a naval force that included ships from Venice and other Italian city states. But the combined European force encountered the Ottoman fleet much sooner than planned—at a point far from Cyprus, near the Gulf of Corinth that separates the Peloponnesus from Northern Greece, in a body of water then known as the Gulf of Lepanto.[9] There, on October 7, 1571 (Marlowe and Shakespeare now being seventeen), Don John, despite the unexpectedness of the encounter, inflicted a crushing naval defeat on the Ottoman naval forces. The news of the Ottoman defeat was apparently such a relief to western Europe that church bells in all those cities that in 1565 had rung to celebrate the successful defense of Malta now all resounded for Lepanto.

The victory, in fact, became legendary. Such was the sense of triumph in the West that paintings were rendered by Titian, Veronese, and Tintoretto, and chapels were built within many cathedrals to thank God for this destruction of the pagans. Fourteen years later, King James VI of Scotland, who had been four years of age at the time of Lepanto, considered the event significant enough to write an epic poem on the subject, a poem that celebrated the Venetians and the city of Venice as the victors.

These celebrations, however, were premature, and off the point politically. The original *casus belli*, Cyprus, of course remained "Turk": Don John's combined naval force, in the end, had not really accomplished its goal. Instead, whether from the attrition of the naval battle, or for other reasons, the Western fleet seems to have been in a limbo for two years until Philip II approved Don John's recommended shift in strategic planning for the Mediterranean to a secondary target: the strengthening of the European position in *western* Mediterranean waters, specifically, through the taking of Tunis. This change of plan took several important English interests into account.

In the 1500s, sea battles were fought within sight of land. We recall that in Shakespeare's *Antony and Cleopatra*, Enobarbus watches the Battle of Actium from the vantage point of some cliff, a detail with a contemporary resonance to Shakespeare's audience. As Guilmartin notes, military success at sea was dependent on proximity to the shore because—at least in Mediterranean combat—oared galleys served essentially as troop carriers, rowing to close with enemy ships in order to enable soldiers to board and fight hand to hand with their adversaries.[10] The scarred soldier pleads with Antony:

> O noble emperor, do not fight by sea
> Trust not to rotten planks. Do you misdoubt
> This sword and these my wounds? Let the Egyptians
> And the Phonecians go a-ducking: we
> Have used to conquer, standing on the earth
> And fighting foot to foot. (3.7.61–6)

It was, then, crucial that the coast near the fighting fleets be held by the would-be victor so that reinforcements would be available from shore.

Although Europe held the key sites of Malta and Sicily in the western Mediterranean, the Ottomans dominated (through local Muslim rulers) most of the Maghrib—the North African principalities of Morocco, Tunis, Algiers, and Tripoli, known to the English as "Barbary." The most important of these locations, from the European point of view, was Tunis (the land once ruled by Marlowe's Dido, Queen of Carthage, and the state from which the wedding party of Shakespeare's *The Tempest* is returning), because the naval approaches to this city formed a triangle completed by Malta and Sicily. The Christian capture of Tunis would thus allow domination of that narrowest part of the Mediterranean that had made Malta so desirable to the Ottomans even offer access to the Maghrib. In 1573, with Don John of Austria again in command, the allied Christian fleet succeeded in taking the city, placing the Mediterranean "straits" wholly in European lands.

But the same kind of alarm that had sounded through Christian Europe when the Ottomans took Cyprus from Venice must now have electrified Istanbul, as the Ottomans grasped at once the naval implications of a *Christian* Tunis. At the same time, unlike their European counterparts, the Ottomans had huge resources, despite the total destruction of their fleet at Lepanto, and were capable of quickly reconstituting an entirely new fleet. Already, after Lepanto, Mehmet Sokollu, Grand Vizier of Selim II, had begun rebuilding the naval force, and is reputed to have observed: "The might of the empire is such that if it were desired to equip the entire fleet with silver anchors, silken rigging and satin sails, we could do it."[11]

If the boast was idle in fact, it was not in spirit. For in 1574, just nine months after Don John had captured Tunis, a completely new Ottoman fleet suddenly materialized before that city to recapture it in a now obscure naval action that proved ultimately of far greater significance than the much-touted Battle of Lepanto. This is because the Ottoman victory at Tunis served to redefine the balance of naval power in the Mediterranean until well into the seventeenth century (including, of course, the rest of Shakespeare's lifetime).[12] That is, both Philip II and Selim II, unwilling to pursue their former ambitions, participated in an unspoken naval truce. As if by mutual consent, a long frontier in the Mediterranean was established after 1574, a zone of division determined not by battle lines, but at the point beyond which the Ottomans and the western European states neither could nor would try to impose their own institutions upon each other.[13]

The wisdom for the West of this restraint was emphasized, if negatively, by a disastrous military expedition by the Portuguese in 1578— an action that, it turned out, would greatly interest London theatergoers of the 1590s. The young King Sebastian, described in the year of the expedition by Matteo Ricci, the Jesuit missionary, as twenty-five years old, with blue eyes, long blonde hair, and burning with fervor, was apparently obsessed with the fact that his country had once led the West in exploration. Notwithstanding its having circumnavigated Africa, established trade empires in the Indian Ocean and in the Americas, and inspired its great epic poet Camões to write the *Lusiads* in praise of these achievements, Portugal was no longer the leader in global expansionism. But now, captivated by the concept of a new Portuguese Empire stretching from India to Brazil,[14] Sebastian determined to gain for Portugal and for the Jesuits the section of Barbary known as Morocco.[15] Because most of the coastline of Morocco fronted the Atlantic instead of the Mediterranean, and paralleled Portuguese trade routes to some parts of Africa, its acquisition promised to consolidate Portuguese naval power in the area.

As Emily Bartels reminds us, however, his expedition was a disaster. In this definitive rout, as E. W. Bovill has pointed out, somewhere between ten and twenty thousand Portuguese nobles, mercenaries, and conscripts were taken prisoner and held for ransom, a great prize for the Muslim defenders. Indeed, Morocco became the richest state in Barbary from the consequent revenues. In order to get back its ruling class, Portugal was forced to send all its available coinage, as well as jewels and precious stones, as ransom to Morocco and Algiers.[16] Thus Morocco's new ruler, Ahmad (brother of the slain Sharif Abd-al-Malik) was not only called al-Mansur (the victorious) but in testimony to his colossal ransom, "al-Dahibi" (the golden). Twenty years later, Shakespeare would interestingly characterize Portia's suitor, a Prince of Morocco, through the ambience of gold.[17]

However, the most significant consequence of the Alcazarquivir debacle was the death of King Sebastian. Because Sebastian was unmarried and heirless, the Portuguese crown, together with the domination of its far-flung colonies, eventually fell to Philip II, who, by outstripping other foreign claimants, was able to annex Portugal to the Spanish Empire. Braudel sums up the situation in 1580 (when Christopher Marlowe and Shakespeare were sixteen) as follows:

> The day Philip II took up residence in Lisbon he placed the center of his composite empire on the shore of the Atlantic . . . The Hispanic bloc and the Ottoman bloc, so long locked together in a struggle for the Mediterranean . . . at long last disengaged their forces. (pp. 1184–5)

In the end, it was the Atlantic coast of Spain that was greatly extended by Sebastian's adventurism, introducing a powerful new presence in those Mediterranean and ocean stretches that had served as the mercantile and military pathways of the northern European and mostly anti-Catholic states. Given Spain's détente with the Ottomans, Philip II was now in an ideal position to concentrate his country's imperial ambitions on the New World and its gold, thereby setting the foundation for the inevitable conflict of interests with the emerging sea power of England.

Theatrical productions of the Elizabethan public theater were variously configured by the situations reviewed here. There were few famous victories on which to base chauvinistic stage celebrations. Moreover, Muslims had been villains at least since the time of Chaucer's "Man of Law's Tale," and continued to be treated as such by dramatists who dealt with the subject (although Fulke Greville's closet plays *Alaham* and *Mustapha*, are obvious exceptions). Yet Marlowe's *The Jew of Malta*, c. 1588, and the anonymous *Battle of Alcazar*, c. 1592, two very popular plays concerned with the Mediterranean scene, seem actually to repress the powerful reality of the Ottoman Empire and its implications. Although Marlowe's play does paint conflict between Christian and Ottoman, it curiously, and significantly, suggests that the Ottomans generally had the upper hand on Malta.

As previously noted, Malta had permanently repelled Ottoman capture in 1565, a year before the death of Suleyman. The Knights of Malta, the famous martial religious order and protectors of the island, whose bitter and unflagging defense saved it for Christendom, had constructed an almost impregnable series of fortresses. Thus throughout Marlowe's lifetime, Malta never became subject to Ottoman rule. Indeed, it might be thought of as standing as a symbol of Christian strength, the rock, as it were, that was St. Peter and the Church set firm against the forces of Satan.

Yet Marlowe's play begins with the Knights of Malta talking to an Ottoman ruler, "Selim," who can only be construed as Selim II, destined to succeed to the Sultanate in 1566. Selim begins the political plot by reproving the Knights for being ten years late with their tribute saying that this money is instantly required to *placate* the Sultan (Suleyman?) who, one is led to assume, will otherwise occupy the island. Barabas, his Jewishness and his wealth thus play themselves out against this antiquated—and gloriously inaccurate—political backdrop, compounded further when Barabas later betrays Malta and the Ottomans, who bombard it into ruins. When Barabas invents a plot to kill the Ottoman occupiers, the Knights of Malta hear of it and honourably tell Selim, who has Barabas executed. Thanking the Christians, "Selim Calymath" prepares to return to Turkey to intercede with his father to forgive the Maltese their tribute, only to find that his own forces have been overthrown by the Knights, and that he himself is now a hostage. He will be held on Malta until his father not only repairs the island but also liberates it from Ottoman hegemony.

The final lines of the play, spoken by the Christian leader, are, at least historically accurate, if boastful and hyperbolic:

> for come all the world
> To rescue thee, so will we guard us now,
> As sooner shall they drink the ocean dry,
> Than conquer Malta, or endanger us. (5.5.118–21)[18]

In this rendition of events, Marlowe has in effect trivialized the Ottoman Empire, de-historicizing its power and position and suggesting that the heir apparent to the Sultanate of the Ottoman Empire can be easily captured and held hostage by the champions of Christianity.

The second play with a Mediterranean scenario, in that it concerns Sebastian's invasion of Morocco, as Bartels has noted elsewhere in this volume, was *The Battle of Alcazar*, performed fourteen times during the six months of play available in the London playhouses between February 1592 and January 1593, prior to the onset of plague.[19]

The representation of the Moroccans in *Alcazar* is interestingly double-edged. There is, fist, the perspective of the prologue or presenter, who describes "The barbarous Moor, the Negro Muly Hamet" as follows:

> . . . this tyrant king,
> Of whome we treat sprong from the Arabian moore
> Blacke in his looke, and bloudie in his deeds,
> And in his shirt staind with a cloud of gore,
> Presents himselfe with naked sword in hand,
> Accompanied as now you may behold,
> With deuils coted in the shapes of men. (sig. A2ʳ)

Later, Abdelmelec castigates King Sebastian as one who "hether bends, / In hope to helpe Mahamet to a crowne / And chase vs hence, and plant this Negro moore" (sig. D3ʳ), a disparaging term he uses several times in reference to his competitor. Since he does not hesitate to address his own Moroccan troops as Moors ("Forward . . . ye manly moors" [sig. D3ᵛ]), Abdelmelec seems here to be isolating the *Negro* Moor, as did the presenter, as villainous.[20] Further, the audience is informed at the end of *Alcazar* that the entire Portuguese debacle was caused by Muly Mahamet, who, mounted upon a hot Barbarian horse, fled to his drowning. So notoriously evil is this "damned wretch," that the newly established Moroccan king (another brother of Abdelmelec) plans to ensure an appropriate after-life as a kind of evil trophy:

> A death too good for such a damned wretch,
> But sith our rage and rigor of reuenge,
> By violence of his end preuented is,
> That all the world may learne by him to auoide,
> The hall on princes to iniurious warre,
> His skin we will be parted from his flesh,
> And being stifened out and stuft with strawe,
> So to deterre and feare the lookers on
> From anie such foule fact or bad attempt,
> Awaie with him. (sig. G1^v)

It may be of more than passing interest that in one brief period prior to the onset of the plague of 1592–94, there were five instances in Henslowe's *Diary* in which a performance of *The Jew of Malta* is noted on the day before or the day after a performance of *Mully Mulloco*, as if performing the two plays in tandem was thought of as a way of profiting from public interest in Ottoman history. Ironically, however, as I have suggested, what Marlowe's *Jew* and *Alcazar* actually have in common is a *misrepresentation* of the Ottoman presence in the Mediterranean, presumably for the purpose of demonization: in the fist instance, of the Jew, and in the second, of the Negro. It is interesting to speculate as to why Ottoman "paganism" would serve as the framework for these demonizations, as well as why historical events of the preceding decades would be so radically skewed. It is, of course, possible that neither Marlowe nor the author of *Alcazar* was aware of distorting history. But it hardly seems likely that Marlowe, a person active in Elizabeth's service, would be ignorant of the fact that the Ottomans never held Malta. The same unlikelihood might also be argued in the case of *Othello*: would Shakespeare—or the courtly audience for his play—be unaware that although Othello is sent by the Venetian Senate to protect Cyprus from the Turks, the Ottomans had owned the island since 1570? My own speculation is that representations of the Ottomans on the English stage, especially before 1595, involved a kind of double demonization that was at the same time a displacement. That is, the situating of Barabas in a country presumably controlled by the major ideological enemy of Christianity—the Muslim, the anti-Christ—intensifies his alien status as Jew; and of course, *all* the Moroccans, as the presenter suggests, whether Negro / Moor, or Moor of another color, are by the same token infidels, at least from the English perspective. There is, then, a kind of dramatic convenience in conflating Turk, Muslim, Moroccan, Negro, and Moor under the undifferentiated umbrella of "barbarian," even though such simplification inevitably leads to inconsistencies, as seen in the shifting designations from "moor" and "negro" in *Alcazar*. I would argue further that in the hands of a skilled dramatist such inconsistencies can become a mode of *exploring* racial, religious, and cultural stereotypes, as Shakespeare seems to be doing in *Othello*, and to a lesser extent, Marlowe in *Jew*.[21]

Still, the convenience of conflation does not quite satisfy as the whole answer to the rewriting of history, to what I earlier called the trivializing of the Ottoman threat in Marlowe's play, and the caricaturing of the Moroccan factions in *Alcazar* (factions tolerated, we recall, by the regime of Amuranth). In my view, what might be called the scapegoating of the Jew and the Negro in these plays serves to evade the central, irrevocable, and implacable problem of the Ottomans themselves, whose formidable power seemed to mock the concept of Christian supremacy, and even the validity of the Christian god. The issue then is not so much what Marlowe, Shakespeare, and other playwrights of the period might or might not have known about sixteenth-century Ottoman history, as it is what the playgoing public would want to believe about the Ottoman Empire.

There is little doubt that the English people were fascinated with the exotica and sensationalism of contemporary legends about the Turk. These appetites are suggested by two other plays of the period, both produced prior to 1595, and both dealing with the lives and reigns of world-renowned Sultans. The first of these plays, published in 1594 and entitled *The First Part of the Tragical Reign of Selimus*, was produced in c. 1591. Its plot concerns Selim I (the Grim), father of Suleyman the Magnificent, who, in accordance with Ottoman royal practice, killed all the other sons of his various wives in order to ensure Suleyman's undisputed accession to the throne. *Selimus* ends by promising a part two that either has disappeared or was never written: presumably, this anticipated play would have focused on Suleyman. Another play, entitled *Mahomet*, was produced in 1594, although its text is not extant. According to Henslowe, *Mahomet* was performed on August 11, 1594, when the theaters had reopened after the plague (the *Diary* does not make clear whether at this time the play was new or revived); there is evidence of eight performances in 1594, and of a revival in 1601 (see Foakes, p. 178). Since "Mahomet" was a frequently used variant for "Mehmet," it seems likely that this play was also about a Sultan, Mehmet II (1444–46, 1451–81), the conqueror of Constantinople and the progenitor of the famous sultans of the Henrician and Elizabethan reigns.

Although the exploitation of sensational subject matter was hardly new on the Elizabethan stage, it seems to me that this particular kind of escapism was of a piece with the tactics of evasion described earlier. That is, the English playgoing public wanted a version of the Ottomans in which their adversaries pretended to a power they could never quite achieve, or hold onto; and in which Ottomans were done in, predictably and with regularity, by their own barbarism. In this self-congratulating scenario, the Ottoman Empire would inevitably fall by itself: as the early modern representation of anti-Christ, failure was its only conceivable fate.

Moreover, in the 1590s, there were new and compelling reasons for repressing the reality of the Ottoman menace. In 1593, under Amuranth, and more than a decade after the détente in the Mediterranean, the Ottomans began a major land offensive in central Europe. By 1594, they were threatening the Christian stronghold of Vienna, and though the Turks never succeeded in taking the city, their conflict with the Habsburgs was to go on till 1606. This means that during the heights of the popularity of English plays that trivialized, patronized, and brutalized the Turk, there was a great fear, at least among the ruling hierarchies of Europe, if not generally among their populations, that a Christian metropolis, a symbolic beacon of the true faith, would fall to the infidel. Interestingly, this *contemporary* subject matter was not dramatized on the English stage, as were the events in Malta and Morocco, except perhaps, as I have argued elsewhere, indirectly—in a spate of plays about Timor Khan between 1594 and 1595 (including a revival of both parts of Marlowe's own great play, *Tamburlaine*).[22]

But the enormously popular *The Jew of Malta* and *Alcazar*, as well as *Captain Thomas Stukeley*, a play discussed by Emily Bartels in some detail in this volume, provide more direct evidence of *Alcazar*'s popularity together with a sense of the English "take" on the Ottomans. If one assumes that the dramatizing of history in early modern England represents a mode of mythologizing, then all the plays speak to a need for cultural repression of a nonetheless persistent awareness—of Ottoman global supremacy—as well as a growing fear of this dangerously alien civilization. To recognize openly that this particular alien might be powerful enough to subjugate major strongholds of Christian Europe was, however, anathema. Instead, the English theater dramatized European victories, real and invented, over the "barbarian" that Christianity could not, at that time, quell.

NOTES

1. See M.F. Koprulu, *The Origins of the Ottoman Empire*, trans. Gary Leiser (Stony Brook, New York: SUNY Press, 1992), chapters 1 and 2; and Cemal Kafadar, *Between Two Worlds: The Construction of the Ottoman State* (Berkeley: University of California Press, 1999), esp. chapter 1; and for a more recent view by Halil Inalcik, *An Economic and Social History of the Ottoman Empire, 1300–1600* (Cambridge: The Cambridge University Press, 1997).

2. See Bernard Lewis, *The Muslim Discovery of Europe* (New York and London: Norton, 1982), chapter 1, esp. pp. 22–38.

3. Beg Tursun, *The History of Mehmet the Conqueror*, ed. and trans. H. Inalcik and R. Murphy (Minneapolis and Chicago: University of Minnesota Press, 1978), fols. 156a–156b, quoted in Lewis, p. 31.

4. See Fernand Braudel, *The Mediterranean and the Mediterranean World in the Age of Philip II*, 2 vols., trans. Sîan Reynolds (Berkeley: University of California Press, 1988), vol. 1, p. 467.

5. See Stanford J. Chaw, *History of the Ottoman Empire*, vol. 6 (Cambridge: The Cambridge University Press, 1976), pp. 309–14 for a detailed view of the scholarship describing and documenting Suleyman's Mediterranean activities.

6. All quotations from Shakespeare's works are from *The Riverside Shakespeare*, ed. G. Blackmore Evans (Boston: Houghton Mifflin, 1974).

7. For Cyprus, see *The New Cambridge Modern History*, vol. III, ed. R.B. Wernham (Cambridge: The Cambridge University Press, 1968), pp. 352–4.

8. For recent observation on the role of Spain vis-à-vis the Ottomans, see John Lynch, *Spain: 1516–1598* (Oxford: Blackwell, 1991), pp. 321–9.

9. See Andrew C. Hess, "The Battle of Lepanto and its Place in Mediterranean History," *Past and Present* 57 (1972): 53–73; and *The Forgotten Frontier: A History of the Sixteenth-Century Ibero-African Frontier* (Chicago: The University of Chicago Press, 1978).

10. See J. Guilmartin, *Gunpowder and Galleys* (Cambridge: The Cambridge University Press, 1974), chapter 1.

11. *Tahiri-i-Peçevi* (Istanbul, 1283 A.H.), 1, quoted in Lewis, p. 44.

12. See Hess, "The Battle of Lepanto."

13. See Braudel, *The Mediterranean*, pp. 1184–5.

14. For the foundations of this policy, see Rhoads Murphey, "Suleyman's Eastern Policy," in *Suleyman the Second and His Time*, ed. Halil Inalcik and Camel Kafadar (Istanbul: Isis Press, 1993), pp. 229–48.

15. See Jonathan D. Spence, *The Memory Palace of Matteo Ricci* (New York: Viking Penguin, 1984), pp. 36–8; 277nn. 29–30.

16. See Bovill, *The Battle*, pp. 89–157.

17. It is also noteworthy that the Prince takes pains to disassociate himself from the Ottomans, claiming that his "scimitar" has won "three fields of Sultan Solyman" (2.1.26).

18. Christopher Marlowe, *The Jew of Malta*, ed. James R. Siemon (London: A & C Black and New York: WW Norton, 1994).

19. See *Henslowe's Diary*, ed. R.A. Foakes, 2nd ed. (Cambridge: The Cambridge University Press, 2002), pp. 19–22.

20. In this context it may be significant that in the surviving "plat" of *Tamar Cham*, "Nagars" are distinguished from "olive-collored moores." For the plat, see W.W. Greg, *Dramatic Documents from Elizabethan Playhouses* (Oxford: The Oxford University Press, 1931), vol. 1, pp. 27–8.

21. For a classic study of Marlowe's use and subversion of stereotypes of the alien, see Emily C. Bartels, *Spectacles of Strangeness: Imperialism, Alienation, and Marlowe* (Philadelphia: University of Pennsylvania Press, 1993).

22. Timur the Lame or Timur Khan was the ruler of Transoxania, with his capital in Samarkand. Conqueror of vast regions in the fourteenth century, including lands held by the Ottomans, he claimed to be descendent of the legendary twelfth-century Mongol, Ghengis Kahn.

CHAPTER 7

ANOTHER COUNTRY: MARLOWE
AND THE GO-BETWEEN

Richard Wilson

In *The White Castle*, Orhan Pamuk's novel about Renaissance go-betweens, the Turkish writer has the scientist from Florence and magician from Istanbul change identities, when their combined genius fails to provide the Sultan with the "incredible weapon" he needs to storm the ultimate fortress of the title.[1] They spend the remainder of their lives inside each other's customs, clothes and minds; both blaming their double for the futile obsession with those illusory weapons of mass destruction, on which they together wasted all the reason of the West and wisdom of the Orient. Back in Florence, the Muslim taken for the Christian, and author of "a stack of books describing his unbelievable adventures among the Turks" (p. 140), might have been "the Leonardo of the seventeenth century" (p. 142), it is often said, if he had not fallen into slavery at the primitive and superstitious hands of Islam. But in Istanbul the real Florentine—who ends the book installed as the Imperial Astrologer—is haunted by the recognition that:

> I loved Him. I loved Him the way I loved that helpless, wretched ghost of my own self I saw in dreams, as if choking on the shame, rage, sinfulness and melancholy of that ghost, as if overcome with shame at the sight of the selfishness of a son of my own. And perhaps most of all, I loved Him with the stupid revulsion of knowing myself: my love for

Him resembled the way I had become used to the insect-like movements
of my own arms and hands. (p. 144)

"The past is another country," in the words of *The Go-Between*;[2] yet
they do things similarly there. Thus, on April 7, 1589 an English merchant named John Lucas appeared before the Maltese Inquisition
charged with passing defense secrets to the Turks through his business
contacts. According to Genoese sources, he was a "malicious and
perverse enemy of Catholics," and a member of an English spy ring
centered on Istanbul[3]; but asked whether he had ever written to that
city, "Never in my life," he protested. On being warned by the Grand
Inquisitor, however, that his letters were all on file in Rome, Lucas
confessed that he had "stayed here in Malta, in the middle of the
world," to report shipping movements, but no other matters: "May I
be struck dead if it is otherwise." Unimpressed, the Inquisition sent
him to Rome, where the Tribunal of the Holy Office tried him in
December 1590.[4] At that instant, the Venetian ambassador in Turkey
was relaying news of the great game in which Lucas was a pawn: an
unholy league between Protestants and Muslims to seize Malta from
its Spanish overlords. "Daily consultations take place between the
English ambassador and the Grand Vizier," the Doge was notified,
while "in a secret chamber they are preparing models of Malta for the
Sultan."[5] Their plot hinged on intelligence supplied by traders such as
Lucas; but ever-present with "information about all Christendom"
was a Jewish-Italian arbitrageur named David Passi, "a man of natural
ability and sufficient knowledge, able to do both great good or
harm." "This David, for one truth tells a hundred lies," the dispatches
cautioned: "He would betray us all if he could. He is agent for Don
Antonio of Portugal, yet in the confidence of the King of Spain. He is
a warm supporter of Venice, yet the trusty spy of the Sultan."[6] Now,
it was rumored all around Istanbul, he was also the English agent.
"The Sultan said that slaves like the Vizier he had in abundance, but
never a one like David."[7] Yet on February 2, 1591, when the fleet was
about to set sail for Malta, "David Passi is at this moment secretly
writing to King Philip to give him warning," the Venetian noted, "and
offering to avert the expedition for money."[8] Evidently, the trick
worked, because on March 16, the ambassador wrote that the armada
was aborted:

> The models of Malta, which were entrusted to Christian slaves to con-
> struct, have resulted in a failure. The main reason why matters are not
> proceeding is the fact that David Passi is suddenly in disgrace. The

Grand Vizier hoped to secure his drowning. The Sultan's secretary said to me that the Republic of Venice ought to consider Passi's liquidation worth a million in gold. But seeing he is supported by people in the highest authority, who assure the Sultan that he is the only truthful and informed spy against Christian powers, I will watch the issue of events and see your Serenity's interests are not affected. The Sultan shows more thirst for gold than for Christian blood.[9]

In Marlowe's *The Jew of Malta*, Machevill dates the play from the assassination of the Duke of Guise on December 23, 1588; and the audience at the first recorded performance in February 1592 doubtless viewed its action within a perspective of Machiavellian politics current at that time. But perhaps only the elite would recognize the extent to which Marlowe's Barabas represents the identification of England's global strategy with international Jewish finance. The historian Fernand Braudel reminds us, however, that in the reign of Philip II, Mediterranean power was always reliant on data transmitted by Jewish trading agents, "born interpreters of all speech," whose *diaspora* "forced them willingly or unwillingly into the role of brokers of cultural exchange." It was no accident, Braudel observes, that the Jews, who had been the go-betweens "through whom the West received Arab thought and science" so rapidly developed a preeminence in printing.[10] For while Catholicism and Islam consolidated territorial empires by conquest, stateless Israel chose a different destiny, but its theater was a worldwide web, spanning oceans and seas, new nations and ancient civilizations, as "an entire intelligence network, with direct links between Spain and the Indies" (p. 573), was circuited out through "Jewish intermediaries, agents for trading houses" (p. 402). Jewish traders formed the key commercial network of this first age of globalization because they had representatives everywhere, "though their numbers might be very small: there were only 1424 Jews in Venice in 1586; barely a hundred in Hamburg; 400 in Antwerp" (p. 575); for to flourish, as Braudel notes, "capitalism presupposes the organisation of mutual confidence and cooperation throughout the world," which "had been true for centuries of Jewish merchants" (p. 579). And it was this covert yet universal dominion that clearly fascinated Marlowe, whose Jew of Valetta controls a multinational corporation with its offices "In Florence, Venice, Antwerp, London, Seville, Frankfort, Lubeck, Moscow, and where not" along early modern trade routes (4.1.71–3), and defines his worldwide hegemony precisely in terms of the *longue durée* so beloved of the *Annales* school. Thus, the Jew is the true hero of the story told by Braudel and Marlowe, because what impresses both the historian and the dramatist is the resilience of the long-term economic *structure* he represents beneath any temporary political *conjuncture*:

> They say we are a scattered nation:
> I cannot tell, but we have scrambled up
> More wealth by far than those that brag of faith.
> There's Kirriah Jairim, the great Jew of Greece,
> Obed in Bairseth, Nones in Portugal,
> Myself in Malta, some in Italy,
> Many in France, and wealthy every one:
> Ay, wealthier far than any Christian.
> I must confess, we come not to be kings:
> That's not our fault: alas, our number's few,
> And crowns come either by succession
> Or urged by force; and nothing violent,
> Oft have I heard tell, can be permanent.
> Give us a peaceful rule. Make Christians kings,
> That thirst so much for principality. (1.1.123–37)

"Nothing violent . . . can be permanent": one civilisation against the rest, in Braudel's phrase, Barabas's Jewry will constitute the advance guard of capitalism not with armaments and fortification, but by means of the informational revolution of the "long sixteenth century." In this sense, Marlowe's merchant is more Machiavellian than his Machevill, who misquotes *The Prince* when he maintains that "a strong built citadel," such as Malta, "Commands more than letters can import" (*Pro*, 22–3). In fact, what Machiavelli wrote about fortresses was the exact reverse of this obsolete realpolitik, when he theorized that "the Prince who fears foreign invasion should forget about them. In our own time there is not a single instance of a fortress proving its worth to any ruler."[11] It was by his "constant questioning" and "patient listening" (p. 119) for information, rather than by brute force, that Machiavelli's Prince triumphed. And in the play, power likewise belongs to those who engineer not the "lofty turrets that command the town"—which are "rent in sunder" by the "bombards" shot and basilisks' of enemy artillery (5.3.3–5)—but the interchange of communications. Marjorie Garber has noticed how Marlowe's plots all privilege writing over speech, as this heroes' "high astounding terms" (*1Tamb*, Pro, 5) are cut short by written texts: Tamburlaine's Koran; Edward's death sentence; above all, Faustus' "deed of gift" of body and soul (*Faustus*, 2.1.59).[12] In *The Jew of Malta* this mercantile confidence in writing propels the entire action, which is nothing but a struggle for control of script. Whether the love letter and challenge faked by Barabas to snare Christians; Abigail's confession accusing him of murder; Bellamira's billet-doux to Ithamore; the slave's own blackmail notes to his master; the Maltese subscription for the Jew; or Barabas's invitation to trap Calymath, which rebounds against its sender, the messages which activate this tragedy are signals that in this hermeneutic system, it is letters which "command" a surplus meaning more than any citadel can "import," because (as the merchant teaches his agent) whatever is written in them, "The meaning has a meaning" (5.1.75).

The meaning of meaning in Marlowe's Malta is the supplement accrued from the boundless world of negotiable paper. Jean-Christophe Agnew describes the semiotic upheaval caused by multilateral trade cycles, when "Carried along on a tide of commercial paper that spoke voicelessly the utterances of the absent, commerce now filled the intervals between fairs and interstices between markets."[13] Likewise, Braudel records how in "The Reign of Paper" (which he dates from the 1560s) a proliferation of bills of exchange and promissory notes broke the age-old concept of plain dealing through face-to-face negotiation, provoking an astonished new awareness that "money could lead an existence apart from commodities," and that accounts could be settled in the clearing house "by juggling with a set of figures."[14] Sixteenth-century observers, such as Philip II, confessed themselves bewildered by the new credit machinery; but Barabas, who has debts owed him in all of Europe's financial centres, "and in most of these, / Great sums of money lying in the banco" (4.1.73–4), is a magus of the futures markets, and conjures an interest rate of "A hundred for hundred" (54). No wonder he gave up a career as an engineer "in the wars 'twixt France and Germany" (2.3.191). Though he imagines entrepreneurialism as war (1.2.206), and debts as wounds (2.1.10), this modern Midas knows that his "kingly kind of trade" will sooner "purchase towns" (5.5.48) than the profession of arms. As "a merchant and a moneyed man," (1.2.54) he is the first to admit, "we are not soldiers" (1.2.51), but calculates that the Jews' secret services to the enemy insure his ship: "I know her and her strength" (1.1.83). With his risk spread from London to Teheran, the merchant of Malta can thus discount a default of even "a hundred tun of wine: I weigh it thus much; I have wealth enough" (2.3.248–9). For the virtual reality of paper transactions secures investments across the globe regardless of the actual physical presence of their agent. Faustus will dream of such a universal magic; but to Barabas, god-like qualities of invisibility and ubiquity are the rational techniques of paper finance:

> Go bid them come ashore,
> And bring with them their bills of entry:
> I hope our credit in the custom house
> Will serve as well as I were present there.
> Go send 'em threescore camels, thirty mules,
> And twenty wagons to bring up the ware.
> But art thou master in a ship of mine,
> And is my credit not enough for that . . .
> Go tell 'em the Jew of Malta sent thee, man:
> Tush, who amongst 'em knows not Barabas? (1.1.56–68)

In 1593, Jewish brokers had fantastic hopes of installing Don Antonio, the half-Jewish Portuguese Pretender, on the throne of India, "where they would receive him as coming from heaven."[15] But Marlowe's Jew knows that in the "Reign of Paper" the go-between is king, not because of his presence, but because he was *nowhere and everywhere* at once. So, if meaning begets meaning in Barabas's book, that is because he makes his paper money "increase and multiply" immaculately, like those holy nuns who, he jokes, "do no man good . . . / but in time reap fruit" (2.3.87–91). As the governor moralizes, the Jew's invisible overseas earnings make a mockery of Christian doctrine that "Of nothing is nothing made," since "From nought at first thou cam'st to little wealth, / From little unto more, from more to most" (1.2.108–9). Barabas's question when his capital is confiscated, "How can I multiply?" (1.2.104), seems disingenuous, then, because he knows as well as Shylock how to make gold and silver "breed as fast" as ewes.[16] Marc Shell argues that Shakespeare was uniquely alive to this illicit productivity of money and meaning[17]; yet Marlowe is equally aware of the increments that accrue *ex nihilo* when representations circulate, characterizing his merchant as one who acquires "a kingdom of gold," as Ithamore exclaims, with "a ream of paper" (4.2.113). And it is just this capacity to reap an exponential profit from surplus signification, in deals loaded with insinuation that makes this Jew a perfect double agent. Much has been written about the Jesuit casuistry of "lying like truth"[18]; but *The Jew of Malta* may be the first play to highlight "equivocation" as negotiable currency in modern markets. When Ithamore asks whether a letter is poisoned, "it might be done that way" (2.3.377), Barabas laughs; for his writing is indeed "the poison of the city" (2.3.54): a *pharmakon* as ambiguous as that "precious powder" bought from the Borgias with which he murders nuns (3.4.68). This is the lethal indeterminacy of "Pen and ink" (4.2.66) his clerk attempts to mimic, blackmailing him to "send three hundred by this bearer, and this shall be your warrant; if you do not, no more but so: I'll confess all" (4.2.77). But when Barabas "talked of diamonds" (2.1.61) with his victims, or "About the borrowing of a book or two," his double agency, he quips, could not have been more sharply "pointed" (2.1.61).

The center of operations in Marlowe's Mediterranean is that "little room" where the merchant drives a perpetual motion machine linking the goldmines of the Andes (3.5.6) to "the Eastern rocks" (1.1.21), or Spice Islands of the Pacific. Braudel again puts this achievement into scale, when he remarks that the value of letters in the sixteenth century was in relation to the time taken to traverse such vast distances. News was a luxury commodity of the superrich, like the Fuggers, in an era when the Mediterranean was sixty days long, and for envoys and bankers "the arrival of the mails became an obsession."[19] If the littered desk of the bureaucratic king, Philip II, symbolizes the inability of lumbering political empires to shift the paperwork of the new global economy, Barabas's counting house seems designed to expedite the transmission of bills and bullion on which European power was now coming to depend. Its impresario, who translates his business opportunistically into French, Italian, Spanish, or Latin, is the supreme huckster of this carnival of convertible exchange rates, whose bargaining in the slave market—where "Every one's price is written on his back" (2.3.3.)—seems metonymic of his genius for manipulating human beings as mere signifiers of a trade in which, as he smiles, "It is not necessary I be seen" (1.2.312). If his Catholic adversaries also "love not to be seen" (316), and have nuns who have not appeared in public for "thirty winters long" (317), their secrecy is no match for the absent presence of this "usurer, / Who with extorting, cozening, forfeiting, / And tricks belonging unto brokery" (2.3.193–5), can torment his enemies "with interest" (2.3.202). His demonic powers are functions, that is to say, of "the rise of factorage" in the sixteenth-century global market, where ever-extending lines of credit and communication were only made possible by devolution of agency, such as he masters, to more and more levered go-betweens: in the terms of the Turkey Company's patent, to "the Merchants of London," but also "their executors and administrators, servants, factors and deputies, and all such as shall be so appointed, nominated or admitted parteners or adventurers."[20] A mere courier in this highly geared symbolic system of middlemen, proxies, brokers, and agents, Ithamore none the less doubts if there was "ever seen such villainy" (3.3.1) as that which "the devil invented, my master writ, and

I carried" (3.3.19). But as we are told, such representational sleight of hand has exact technical precedents, in the invoices and ledgers of long-distance Renaissance trading houses:

> Give me the merchants of the Indian mines,
> That trade in metal of the purest mould;
> The wealthy Moor, that in the Eastern rocks
> Without control can pick his riches up,
> And in his house heap pearl like pebble-stones,
> Receive them free, and sell them by the weight. . .
> This is the ware wherein consists my wealth:
> And thus methinks should men of judgement frame
> Their means of traffic from the vulgar trade,
> And as their wealth increaseth, so inclose
> Infinite riches in a little room. (1.1.19–37)

"Pen and ink: I'll write unto him, we'll have money straight. . . . And if he ask why I demand so much" (4.2.69, p.119), parrots Ithamore, "tell him I scorn to write a line under a hundred crowns" (119–20). This sorcerer's apprentice sees his master as a new type of "rich poet" (121) whose representational power works at a remove, picking his profit up "without control," as if by trope (119). Barabas seems to predict a new commercial imperialism dependent, then, not on violent physical presence, but remote textual control. And it is this difference from the "vulgar trade" (1.1.35) that associates Marlowe's merchant with the ambitions of David Passi, John Lucas, and their London paymasters in the audience at the Rose theatre. For the opening of *The Jew of Malta* places the plot within a very specific strategic context that has less to do with the setting of the Siege of Malta in 1565 than with the English promotion of Eastern trade between 1589 and 1592. As Barabas declares, in his mouthwatering prospectus, the real profits in the last years of the sixteenth century were no longer reaped with "Spanish oils and wines of Greece" (1.1.5), imported through "those Samnites" (4) or Italians who had once monopolized world trade. "Paltry silverlings" (6) earned in this traffic were now eclipsed by the colossal potential of the circuit that shipped American "wedge of gold" (9) and "metal of the purest mould" (20), in return for the argosies "from Alexandria, / Loaden with spice and silks" (44–5), that Barabas envisions "smoothly gliding down by Candy shore / To Malta, through our Mediterranean sea" (46–7). Though his stock includes "Cellars of wine, and sollars full of wheat" (4.1.63), it is his "Warehouse stuffed with spices and with drugs" (64), bought with "chests of gold, in bullion and in coin, (65) that explains why he can guarantee that when he has "but two ships" (69) sail to the East, "Their voyage will be worth ten thousand crowns" (70). The first words of the play state that Barabas's riches are based in this way on luxury commodities imported from the Far East in "Persian ships," in exchange for "gold . . . gotten in the Western Ind" (3.5.6); but in fact his whole career can be viewed as a fulfillment of Faustus's fantasy of dragging the "huge argosies" of the East in return for "the golden fleece / That yearly stuffs old Philip's treasury" from America (*Faustus*, 1.1.129–31) and so as prophetic of the one trader he says that he admires, and who would indeed come to bestride the globe: the great East Indian.

In the 1590s, writes Robert Brenner in his study, *Merchants and Revolution*, the City of London was still dominated by the Merchant Adventurers, the traditional exporters of wool to European markets through Antwerp and Italy. But by the eve of the Civil War, a different group of merchants who had invested in trade with the Levant and the East Indies, had replaced the Merchant Adventurers at the top of London's mercantile community: "In the space of a few decades, the Merchant Adventurers saw their export markets cut in half. Meanwhile, the new trades of the Near and Far East experienced golden growth . . . By 1640, representatives of the Levant-East India combine had come to constitute the core of a recomposed merchant elite."[21] For Brenner, it is this volte-face—from a staple, export-driven economy to one fueled by luxury imports—that accounts for the radicalism of the City in the English Revolution; and his analysis explains why Marlowe began his play with such a detailed contrast between the "men of judgement" and "the vulgar trade" (1.1.34–5), and why Barabas should be so positive that the wind stands "to the East? Yes . . . East and by South" (40–1). *The Jew of Malta* accurately foresees that the vessels, which rotted at their moorings while the English commandeered the cargoes of the Levant, would be Italian ships.[22] What is striking, however, is that Marlowe should identify opportunities that were to make the East Indies trade so lucrative as the new multilateral system of deferred expenditure and delayed profit was in every sense speculative when his play was written. In fact, when Barabas's ships from Alexandria via Crete anchor "in Malta road" (1.150), pending payment of a Spanish custom duty which "comes to more / Than many merchants in the town are worth" (64–6), the text touches a raw nerve of the City of London, with an allusion to the impasse that blocked English penetration of the Mediterranean in the 1580s, and that had been the occasion of the downfall of John Lucas, the factor of the Turkey Company, and David Passi, one of the actual Jews involved in the Elizabethan politics "of Malta."

The prediction, in *Dido, Queen of Carthage*, that "No bounds but heaven shall bound his empery" and that the East's "azur'd gates" will open up and "make the morning haste . . . To feast her eyes" upon the mariner (1.1.100–3), is a repeated theme of Marlowe's plays, where the London stage records the increasingly urgent Elizabethan search for some sea route into Asia, and what the historian of Europe's first encounters with Japan, Derek Massarella, sees as the identity crisis of the "English inability to decide which way to sail to the Indies, either East or West, by a northwest, northeast or southwest route, every direction, that is, except the proven one, round Africa."[23] Whether "slicing the sea with sable-colour'd ships" (4.3.8), westward toward the goldmines of "Hesperia" like Aeneas (35); marching eastwards "toward Persia, / Along Armenia" and the spice roads of the Caspian, like Tamburlaine (*2 Tamb*, 5.3.126–7); or "whirling round . . . within the concave compass of the pole, / From East to west" like Faustus (*Faustus*, 3.1.11–13), Marlowe's heroes are obsessed with thrashing a passage out of Europe; but it is an indication of English priorities that the threshold of their ambitions should be the straits between Italy and Africa, where the Trojan admiral is "wracked and welter'd" (*Dido*, 1.1.223) to "trace the Libyan deserts all despis'd" (228); the Tartar emperor is required to clear "the Terrene sea" (*1Tamb*, 3.3.50) of the "cruel pirates of Argier, / That damned train, the scum of Africa" (57); and even Faustus is brought down to earth, overawed by the treasure "Julius Caesar brought from Africa" (*Faustus*, 3.2.56). Turning its back on the Barbary corsairs, Aeneas's fleet sails for Italy, and the coast where English traders established their free port at Livorno; but it is suggestive that Barabas's cargo has no forward destination after Malta. As Lucas had been taught when he first approached the island in 1582, on "a very rich English ship" called the *Reynolds*, bound for London from Crete, the central paradox of the Mediterranean in the age of Philip II was that Ottomon defeats had resulted not in the freedom of the seas, but in a Spanish stranglehold on the lifelines of Europe. In the words of one of the captains of Malta's Knights of St. John:

> Four galleys of our Order were returning from Barbary. As we approached Malta we spotted a ship eight miles distant. The General of the Galleys ordered us to give chase and prepare for combat. When we came near, we signalled to her and the English fired a volley to which we answered. Immediately the English prepared a skiff with a merchant aboard to talk with us. When we ordered the English to lower their flag, they at first refused; but when we opened fire on them they submitted and their ship was towed into Malta.[24]

News of the highjack of the *Reynolds* reached London within two weeks, on May 24, in the post of the financier, Horatio Pallavicino, who reported to Walsingham that questions were being asked in Rome about the motives of the English, "which makes me think there is suspicion about which my correspondent cannot speak, but which I greatly desire to know."[25] In fact, when the crew were interrogated they learned they were detained, along with the crew of another English vessel, the *Roe*, on espionage charges. One of the passengers on the *Roe*, a courier for the earl of Leicester named Thomas Angliobin, had been betrayed by a companion called F in the transcript, as an agent sent from London to spy on Maltese defenses, "since one day Malta would be an English possession." F alleged Angliobin

> wanted me to go to Venice, where he would send me plans of the fortress for the Queen's Privy Council. He told me that on the pretext of obtaining stores, from each ship passing Malta a number of persons would disembark, so that when the time came, there would be a good number of Englishmen on the island . . . With English ships in the straits, Malta would not be able to receive aid, and the Turkish fleet would attack the island assisted by Englishmen within and without.

F topped his testimony with warnings that "Captain Hawkins had passed the Straits of Gibraltar with a number of armed ships and orders to strike Malta," and that "there was a treaty between the Queen and the Great Turk that whatever was captured was to be shared between them."[26] After such sensational disclosures, it was not surprising that the prisoners from the *Roe* were hauled to Rome, where they were either roasted alive or condemned to the galleys. French arbitration eventually secured the release of the other crew; but whether or not the Knights were plotting with Spain to wage war on England, as agents claimed, for the rest of the century, the sea around Malta would be an exclusion zone for English shipping.

If Shakespeare's *The Merchant of Venice* voices some of the deep anxieties ("Your mind is tossing on the ocean, / There where your argosies . . . Do overpeer the petty traffickers") of international finance about its Eastern exposure in the closing years of the sixteenth century, his queasiness that "all my fortunes are at sea" is more likely to have been prompted by the galleys of the Holy Catholic League than danger from the Turks.[27] In 1571, the bells of London rang out for Lepanto; but twenty years later, the resolve of the Knights, reaffirmed at the end of Marlowe's text, that "sooner shall they drink the ocean dry, / Than conquer Malta" (5.5.125–6), had a bitter taste for

London merchants. As Stephen Greenblatt has noticed, the silent presence of the Spaniard Del Bosco, "Vice-Admiral unto the Catholic king" (2.2.7), gives "a powerfully ironic" ending to a drama that "depicts Renaissance international relations as glorified gangsterism, a vast protection racket."[28] But for original audiences, the irony would have been compounded by the fact that whereas one of Elizabeth's first acts had been to forbid her subjects from joining or assisting the Maltese Order, English traders were now affiliated instead with the likes of Barabas, their secret agents in a Christendom under siege from Islam, and were grateful to "call a knave like Passi friend."[29] The jugular of the global trade cycle, bisecting the Mediterranean at the point of interchange in traffic between North and South, East and West Indies, Africa and Europe, Indian Ocean and Atlantic, or Christianity and Islam, Malta was exactly located to subvert the dichotomies of Renaissance ideology. And it was this liminality that made it the laboratory in Marlowe's geopolitics for both a modern intelligence system, and the doctrine, avowed by Barabas, that since "he from whom my most advantage comes, / Shall be my friend" (5.3.115–6), my enemy's enemy is my friend.

When the Spanish slaver warns the (historically, mainly French) Knights that Philip II "has title to this isle, / And he means quickly to expel you hence" (2.2.37), editors alter "you" to "them," assuming the only "Others" must be Turks.[30] Yet Marlowe here makes no mistake, and seems intent on puncturing the very prejudices the editors betray. The subversiveness of *The Jew of Malta* begins, indeed, with its title, for though there had been a prosperous Jewish community on the island from Roman days, there were no Jews *of* Malta after their expulsion from Aragon and its dependencies in 1492. The play starts by recapitulating that calamity, when the Knights order every Jew to "pay one half of his estate" (1.2.73) and appropriate all Barabas's wealth; just as the Spanish had confiscated everything, bar "a mattress, a pair of worn sheets, and a coin," from each of the Maltese Jews as they embarked for exile in the Levant.[31] Barabas's hatred of the Knights seems, therefore, in tune with the anathema pronounced on the island by sixteenth-century rabbis: "May its name be wiped out." As Jewish historians observe, the very notion of a "Jew of Malta" was a contradiction in terms, because "the island occupied a disproportionate importance in Jewish eyes as a symbol for all that was cruel and hateful in the Christian world"; whilst Messianic prophecies detailed how "the Redemption would begin with the fall of the four kingdoms of unrighteousness, the first of which would be Malta."[32] Moreover, if there ever were Jews on Renaissance Malta, it was in circumstances like those that carried English merchants to the dreaded island, when the Knights kidnapped them. Jewish chronicles are punctuated with such episodes, like those that occurred in 1567, when large numbers of refugees from persecution in Italy were held hostage; and in 1620, when a party of pilgrims was highjacked on their way to Palestine. Jews were the most lucrative victims, in other words, of the slave traffic that made Malta infamous until the Knights were evicted by Napoleon. Thus, "the monks of Malta are exceedingly evil to the Jews," it was reported in 1600: "They sail in Italian seas to prey on seafarers, and sell them for slaves, both men and women, unless they can pay ransom."[33] So it is telling that Barabas is known to the slave traders as one who would "give present money for all" their captives (2.3.6), since the role in which Mediterranean Jews were indispensable to England was as go-betweens and ransomers for the prisoners of Malta.[34]

Del Bosco's raid ("The captain's slain, the rest remain our slaves, / Of whom we would make sale in Malta here" (2.2.10) on Turkish shipping "upon the coast of Corsica" (17) is a reminder that the chief meaning of Malta for Marlowe's audience was as the lair of Spanish slavers, like those who had intercepted a Turkey Company convoy in 1586, and were only beaten off, Hakluyt records, with help from the Pasha of Algiers. Richard Hasleton, a galley slave who escaped to Barbary in 1592, considered ten years' captivity had taught him how much more cruel Christians were than Turks.[35] Historians confirm that it was as common victims of Catholic slave traders that Muslims and Protestants were first brought together.[36] When English warships did first pass through the Straits of Gibraltar, in 1620, it was part of a campaign to release English slaves, to which the Levant Company contributed £1,800.[37] But it was Jewish brokers who took the lead in founding fraternities for "Redemption of Captives," and it was under the auspices of these that a few Jews were allowed into Malta in the 1580s, as middlemen charged with negotiating freedom for captives on commission, "normally 15 per cent of the ransom."[38] This Jewish ransom network "rested on a great web of credit, and although well organized, was prone to disaster," being dependent on mutual trust.[39] When Marlowe set a key scene of The Jew of Malta in the slave market of Valetta, and had Barabas, a Jew who claims to come from Florence, "redeem" (2.3.23) Ithamore, a Muslim born "In Thrace; brought up in Arabia" (133), he was not only glancing at the fate of Londoners like Lucas. He was dramatizing a situation which disrupted all the traditional polarities between friend and foe, or the Crescent and the Cross, in a place where, as English witnesses reported, "the victims are persons of any race, age or sex, who happen to be sailing in captured ships," and "Jews, Moors, Turks and Christians are enslaved and sold together."[40] It was the Spanish slave trade that cut the road to riches for London merchants, and made Jews and Turks their allies. But the fact that in this scene the Quarto printer automatically set the word "Spanish" for the slaves, when they are, of course, Turkish, underlines the extent of the cultural reversal that formed the central paradox of Marlowe's plot. This was an irony, however, that spoke directly to Londoners' experience, which in the Mediterranean of Philip II self-interest ensured that it was a stranger like Barabas who was the Englishman's best friend:

> The surest lodging for a Christian there is in a Jew's house, for if he have any hurt, the Jew and his goods shall make it good, so the Jew taketh great care of the Christian and his goods that lieth in his house.[41]

When Barabas says, "But that was in another country, / And besides the wench is dead" (4.1.43–4), it is his cultural relativism that marks him as "not of the tribe of Levi . . . / That can so soon forget an injury" (2.3.18–19) as to assimilate in any one community. In fact, his medical studies in Florence, where he "began / To practice first upon the Italian," and so "enrich'd the priests with burials" (186–8), affiliates this Jew with the network of Jewish doctors and bankers "stretching from London to Constantinople via the Low Countries and Iberia," whose English figurehead would soon become notorious as a traitor and poisoner: the Queen's physician, Roderigo Lopez.[42] These were Marranos, or crypto-Jews of Sephardic descent, expelled from Portugal despite forced conversion to Catholicism; whose readiness to turn Protestant "facilitated their movement among the elite of Elizabethan England," and into the service, beside Marlowe, of the spymaster Walsingham.[43] The life of these *conversos* has been compared with that of "church papists" for its duplicity.[44] So, nothing identifies Barabas as such a "New Christian" more than his pretence to "turn Christian" (4.1.51) and "To fast, to pray, wear a shirt of hair" (61), and leave his fortune "To some religious house / So I may be baptised and live therein" (75–6); nor separates him from the ghettoized Ashkenazi Jew of medieval stereotype more than his disavowal of those "zealous in the Jewish faith" (51). As Emily Bartels writes, "Barabas's career is a series of performances in which he plays the Jew others want to see," and it is because he is "always acting, always disguised," that he is the ideal intermediary: a cipher, like Malta itself, without identity, but "endlessly cosmopolitan . . . cross-cultural" and relativizing.[45]

"An hebrew born [who] would become a Christian" (19), with a hat "from the Great Cham" of China (4.4.65), manners made in Italy, and a wife dead "in another country," Marlowe's Jew seems, therefore, a perfect role model for an author who thought Catholicism "a good religion" for show; "Protestants hypocritical asses"; and the crucifixion proof that "the Jews knew best."[46] English Puritans would encourage Jewish migration in the belief that "the conversion of the Jews" would usher in the Millennium.[47] But Marlowe's go-between suggests that Anglo-Jewish cooperation was based on an even deeper heresy, explored in his play, that in the world of trade, religion will only ever "count . . . as but a childish toy" (*Pro*, 14).

Liberated from religion, Marrano Jews ran an intelligence operation connecting the Sultan with the King of Spain via the Knights of Malta and the Queen of England. As Philip II was told, it was because Jews "report everything that passes at Madrid," that Walsingham received advance notice of the Armada, rushed to his dinner table by another Marrano doctor, Hector Nunez. But David Katz notes that, though this coup proved "what a diplomatic asset the Marrano community could be, the question remained, for which side they would work."[48] So, when he double-crosses the Turks, the pieces of silver Barabas is paid are pounds sterling, and although he expects a low return on English currency, "I'll satisfy myself with that," he shrugs, as he banks £100,000 (5.5.21–3). The episode is a tart exposé of the source of much of the money that funded the great game, which hinged, as Edward Barton, the Turkey Company agent, wrote from Istanbul in 1589, on bribes: "It would cost no more than the setting forth of three of Her Majesty's ships, for all are well-affectioned here and could easily be bought. The sum need not be so great nor so openly spent as to allow the Papists to accuse Her Majesty of hiring the Turk to endamage Christendom."[49] The state papers covering this Anglo-Ottoman conspiracy were only fully published in 2000; but they reveal the cash nexus connecting the Turkish military, via "the very knave" Passi, with ministers in London.[50] As Barton admitted in 1590, Passi was in competition as purveyor of advice to the Turks on the West with Alvaro Mendez, agent for the richest of all the Marrano families, but "if the Queen would put him in hope of reward he would be useful" to incite the attack on Malta.[51] In March 1591, the envoy warned that "rumours of preparations were bringing a Spanish agent to Constantinople, whose prodigality might dash Her Majesty's credit": a hint of Passi being paid on both sides. But on April 24, he was still hoping that £5000 would "procure a fleet from Turkey. It would be a saving, not a charge, to Her Majesty, would redound to the benefit of Christendom, and force the King of Spain to accept any terms." With £20000, which he would "distribute so secretly no suspicion would be aroused," he promised to "do Her Majesty more good and Spain more harm than she could with infinite expense, and save many an English life."[52] No wonder the Turkish generals complained that, "this expedition, to send the monks of Malta to the Seraglio, is calculated more by a merchant than by a prince."[53] For from the "barrels of gold" reportedly shipped in the bark *Elizabeth* "to procure these great preparations" in Istanbul, Barton himself creamed off four percent.[54]

The perfumed language ("Izhabella, the model of all ladies honoured in the Messiah's regions—may her last moments be concluded with good!") of the "noble, exalted, world-conquering sultanic sign" issued by Murad III, permitting English traders "to come and go from their part of the world to our dominions," gave the lie to the Queen's "desire to hold a Christian-like fame with all Christian princes, and not to employ the aid of infidels, especially the Grand Turk, whose powers are so invincible that wherever he should turn, there were small hope of resistance."[55] As the records of the Turkey Company reveal, the bulk of the English exports for which the Sultan commanded safe passage "by land, sea, and in all ports," consisted of arms. Thus, by 1582 the Spanish ambassador in London was minuting that "Two years ago the English opened an extremely profitable trade to the Levant, taking quantities of lead and tin, which the Turk buys for their weight in gold, tin being vital for guns and lead for bullets."[56] The circulation of social energy was nothing if not material in Marlowe's Europe; and those "field-pieces, bombards, barrels full of gunpowder" (3.2.25), and "brass bullets" (5.5.28) with which Barabas plots nemesis in Malta, had a reality all too visible to its defenders. Likewise, London audiences knew all about the vulnerability of the Mediterranean fortress to weapons of mass destruction, since they had supplied them to the Turks themselves. In any event, on February 26, 1592—the very day Marlowe's play was first acted by Lord Strange's Men—the Grand Master recalled all the Knights to garrison their island. It was easy in these circumstances, as Hakluyt smiled, for "our foolish neighbours to find fault with this new league and traffic" between England and Turkey, since there was no doubting the size of the military colossus that English manufacturers were arming. In 1588 one ship, the *Hercules*, sold arms and gunmetal for goods valued at £70000. Thus, at the very time when the state where "Amurath an Amurath succeeds" came to seem synonymous in Christian eyes with oriental despotism,[57] market logic was generating the converse paradigm, proclaimed by Barabas when he asserts that "in extremity / We ought to make a bar of no policy" (1.2.277):

> Thus have we viewed the city, seen the sack,
> And caused the ruins to be new repaired,
> Which with our bombards' shot and basilisks,
> We rent in sunder at our entry:
> Two lofty turrets that command the town.
> And now I see the situation,
> And how secure this conquered island stands
> Environed with the Mediterranean Sea,
> Strong countermured with other petty isles;
> And toward Calabria backed by Sicily. (5.3.1–10)

It was in the London office of Marlowe's patron, Walsingham, that Braudel's "great enemy of distance" was vanquished by the English, when the correspondence from consular agents in Aleppo, Algiers, Tripoli and Istanbul was organized in the 1580s into a system for processing what Lisa Jardine, in her essay on *The Jew of Malta*, calls "alien intelligence": the networking and information gathering that included not just inside knowledge about trade or currency movements, but about courts, war, policy, diplomacy, science, or academic gossip.[58] Perhaps Marlowe was present in the map room, because like the models made by David Passi for the Sultan, his war game details the logistics of the grand design being plotted in Istanbul and London, and every aspect that made it irresistible to London spectators. It was a theater of war that depended, in a novel sense, on audience participation. For *The Jew of Malta* dates from the months after April 1589 when Maltese affairs were subject to intense speculation in the City, with proposals for a conglomerate combining the Venice and Turkey merchants into one consolidated Levant Company. In effect a takeover by the Turkey Company, this merger laid the foundation for the mighty East India combination of 1599; but in 1589 it was still contingent on raising capital. As the historian of the Levant Company relates, "merchants used their best efforts to set out the advantages to the realm they had been instrumental in obtaining. In letters to Burghley they urged how their agents had frustrated the designs of Spain in the Straits [of Malta]. They begged, therefore, 'to have an end to this tedious suit by granting us our privileges.' " Burghley convened a general meeting of investors in 1591 and it recommended "a company of as many merchants as possible; for many merchants mean many ships and in dangerous times it is advisable to have numbers to defend themselves." When launched in January 1592, the Levant

Company remained, Brenner notes, "a highly ramified network of interlocking families," dominated by Walsingham, who together "drove a trade worth more than £100,000 a year," a colossal return. But the web of speculation was now expanded to seventy-three shareholders, whose shares were divided and then subdivided, in the widest flotation until then seen in London. Like the complex chain of go-betweens in Marlowe's play, the new type of paper scrip had made his audience into secret sharers of the very meaning of his surplus meaning.[59]

"The English ship entered the harbour on Good Friday," a scandalized Venetian envoy posted, when William Harborne sailed into Istanbul as Elizabeth's first "true and undoubted Orator, Messenger, Deputy, and Agent,"[60] bearing presents worth £1000 for the Sultan, as tokens that "We are praying the Good and Great God may keep your Most Invincible Majesty in all things truly happy and fortunate."[61] Marlowe's irreligion must have struck a chord in an office like Walsingham's, where Allah could be so easily identified with the Protestant God. And since it is his Machevill who explodes all religion as "a childish toy" (*Pro*, 14), he could take heart from this irruption, planned, the Doge was told, expressly to cause maximum "grief and pain" to Catholics "as they were celebrating Divine Office, singing melodies suitable to the Passion of the Cross." For suddenly "a great noise of artillery was heard, accompanied by continual music of trumpets and drums. People were so shocked those who call themselves Christians act in such a way, so contrary to the usage of the Church, at such an hour, and to the dishonour of so solemn a festival, that when the English agent went from his ship, he was escorted by no Christians, but only Turks." The Sultan had joked that Anglicans "wanted only circumcision to make themselves Muslims," and to Catholics it did indeed appear that they were tempting judgment, since "That evening, they had fireworks and salvoes of cannon, with music and a great uproar. But they nearly paid the penalty for sin, for one of their rockets fell close to their powder magazine and very nearly set the ship on fire, and only with great difficulty were the flames put out."[62] The incident might be read as a metaphor of the dangers of those exchange relations that were relativizing all religious pieties; and the Sultan, for one, requested no more gun salutes. But it was such pyrotechnics, Thomas Nashe rejoiced, which explained why in Istanbul "not an infant of the curtailed skin-clipping pagans but talks of London as often as of their prophet's tomb in Mecca, as if it were but one sun shin'd over us all"[63]; and the display of English military exports offers an exact context for Marlowe's unethical foreign policy and theological fireworks.

Barabas's strategy to "Make a profit from policy" by "loving neither" Muslim not Catholic, but scheming "to live by both" (5.3.113–14), repeats almost word for word the instructions given by Walsingham to agents, "for procuring the Grand Signor to divert his forces against Spain, by some incursion from the coast of Africa."[64] C.A. Patrides observed that Marlowe's vision of the conqueror as a scourge of God was adapted from Protestant theologians who interpreted the rise of Turkish power as "a scourge sent for the sins of Christians."[65] But Barabas's double-dealing has a more exact discursive context, in Walsingham's secret memoranda on commerce with "a malignant and a turban'd Turk."[66] For it was there that trade with Islam was justified according to the same mercantilist doctrine as that of Marlowe's Jew: that " 'Twere slender policy for Barabas / To dispossess himself of such a place" (5.2.65–6) where "I have got my goods / And in this city still have had success" (5.2.69–70). Walsingham's dictum that "profit and surety" were the only "two things to be considered" in economic relations is the "firm policy" of Barabas (37), who might be speaking for the City of London when he trumpets: "What more may heaven do for earthly men / Than thus pour plenty in their laps . . . Making the sea their servant, and the winds / To drive their substance with successful blasts?" (1.1.109–13). Though James Shapiro may well be right to claim that Marlowe's play incited hostility on the streets of London to the "machiavellian merchant" who "like the Jews," eats his competitors, he overlooks how much Barabas figures English mercantile policy and its determination to crush artisanal objections to global trade.[67] Going through point by point, this trading factor realizes the City's blueprint for Mediterranean traffic, starting with the convoy system for "aid or conduct of their ships" (97) devised "to withstand the force" of Spain. So in a global market powered by "The wind that bloweth all the world besides, / Desire of gold" (3.5.3), he seems to represent English as much as Jewish strategy, which had the official stamp of Sir Francis Walsingham when it rationalized, as he does, that whatever the expedience, "Christians do the like" (5.2.118):

If any man take exception against our new trade with Turks and misbelievers, he shall show himself a man of small experience in old and new histories. . . . For who knoweth not that King Solomon of old entered into league with Hiram the King of Tyrus, a Gentile? Or who is ignorant that the French, Florentines, Venetians, and Polonians are at this day in league with the Grand Signor, and have been these many years, and use trade and traffic in his dominions? And who doth not acknowledge, that have traveled the remote parts of the world, or read the Histories of this later age, that the Spaniards and Portuguese in Barbary and the Indies have confederacy with the Moors and many kinds of Pagans. . . . Why then should it be blamed in us, which is usual and common to the most part of other Christian nations?[68]

"These ships spared not the discharge of ordnance" as they docked in Turkey, exulted Hakluyt, "expressing gladness that, grounding themselves on the promise of God, they should pass the Island of Malta without acknowledgment to the Spanish King."[69] The god of English convoys was the same antipapist deity, clearly, as Elizabeth prayed to shine on "the monarch of the East": "Hermes, prolocutor of the Gods" (*1Tamb*, 1.2.210) in Marlowe's text: "He that sits on high and never sleeps, / Nor in one place is circumscriptible," (*2Tamb*, 2.2.49–50) but bids "Cynthia make a passage" (47) across "every continent" (51). For Greenblatt, it is by erecting desire of gold as such a god that Marlowe stigmatizes the Jew as one whose "avarice, egotism and murderous cunning" makes him, in Marx's phrase, "a universal anti-social element."[70] Yet this is to read *The Jew of Malta*, as we must, with the hindsight of both Marxism and modern anti-semitism. To return the play to its Renaissance context, however, is to restore a Jew who, far from being demonised for usury, personifies the genius for communication Londoners adored. When the number of English Jews was minute, it was their *absence*, Puritans argued, that cut the City out of global markets. So it was no accident that the first project for Jewish admission came from Sir Thomas Shirley, one of a family of Catholic Levant traders who, in the panic after the Gunpowder Plot, disavowed his faith by petitioning James I that "if Eastern Jews find a liking of our country, many of Portugal (which call themselves *Morani*) will come fleeing and the trade of Brazil will be converted here."[71] In an age when Jews and Turks were foes of Spain, philo-Semitism was the surest sign of antipopery. Likewise, Katz relates, the lobby for Jewish entry was fired by a Puritan cult of the cabbala as a key to "the secrets of the universe." Thus, Cromwell's 1655 Whitehall Conference welcomed the Jews, not as economic but as *intellectual* migrants, because the mystical "blessings promised to the Jews," of which Barabas boasts (1.1.107), would "benefit our nation."[72] A culture like that of Protestant England that had identified Adam's language with Hebrew, could "make account" of this Jew, as he does the Turk, as its "own fellow" (2.3.218): despised, persecuted, yet "chosen" to be providentially dispersed. Marlowe's Machevill begs us not to be prejudiced against Barabas: "And let him not be entertain'd the worse / Because he favours me" [*Pro*, 34–5]. But in the trading places of *The Jew of Malta* it is self-interest which dictates that the Other is "he who knows I love him as myself" (4.3.48). As William Empson remarked, Marlowe's plays make the forbidden "*the proper thing to do*"[73]; and in this play, this means we need to understand just how much the dramatist must himself have *loved* his Barabas: *as the image of himself.*

The Jew of Malta takes on surplus meaning in the light of the identification of English and Jewish destinies claimed by Marlowe's contemporaries. Thus, "as Moses was sent from the omnipotent God to persuade the Sultan Pharaoh to let the children of Israel free," so the English were sent to Turkey, boasted Nashe, "to free their captives and open the passage into the Red Sea."[74] And certainly, by 1700, "the English were everywhere in the Mediterranean," Braudel concludes: "they had conquered the sea, port by port," until "that paradox, an English Mediterranean, came to pass." Theirs was an empire, moreover, "not based on force," as with "two strings to their bow," Islam and Christendom, "they had triumphed by subtlety and guile." For above all, Braudel confirms, the English imitated the Jews, with "an intelligence network covering every sector of the sea."[75] Though dispatches from Istanbul were punctuated by the agent's complaints that he was "an ill pen-man with none to help,"[76] the dramatist was right to predict that in this paper war, letters would triumph over swords. Malta would indeed fall to English trade; and Barabas's plot to sodomize the citadel through its sewer, by violating "the dark entry where they take it in," and "Where they must neither see the messenger, / Nor make inquiry who hath sent it them" (3.4.80–1), seems to trope the English national desire to penetrate the enemy through its back passage. Like the character, however, the actual "Jew of Malta" would be destroyed by his own stratagem, when, having fleeced both the Turks and the English, his Spanish bribes were exposed. Though the courier ate his letters from Madrid, and died "before he could name the signatories," under torture he incriminated David Passi as a treble or quadruple agent.[77] In his last days in Istanbul, "the great wicked man" had duped the English, as well as the Poles, into funding an impostor named "Aaron, King of Bugdania, who would not repay what he owed."[78] But this farce had its Marlovian denouement when Passi was condemned to exile, "with a chain round his neck" and "terror in his face," the Venetian envoy reported: "for it is thought that as soon as the boat is out of the harbour he will be thrown into the sea."[79] To humiliate him, the Queen wrote to his rival, Mendez, "who carried her letters up and down, showing them in every tavern, and interpreting them at his pleasure."[80] English power would indeed, as Braudel says, be built on control of texts, for the plot claimed one last victim, with the trial of Lopez, after messages to Spain were intercepted. Like Marlowe's Jew, the Queen's doctor protested that he had only "talked of diamonds" in a commercial code, and seeing him as a tragic model for both Barabas and Shylock, critics have assumed his innocence.[81] But Barton attested that the intercepted letters "sufficiently proved" treason, and the evidence does indeed confirm that "Lopez's secret contacts with the Spanish Crown were more than enough to hang him many times."[82] The go-between went to the scaffold, as Marlowe had foretold, because his meaning had a meaning.

NOTES

1. Orhan Pamuk, *The White Castle*, trans. Victoria Holbrook (London: Faber & Faber, 1991), pp. 98, 142–4.

2. L.P. Hartley, *The Go-Between* (Harmondsworth: Penguin, 1964), p. 1.

3. Andrew Vella, *An Elizabethan-Ottoman Conspiracy* (Malta: Royal University of Malta Press, 1972), p. 72; and see also "A Sixteenth-Century Elizabethan Merchant in Malta," *Melita Historica*, 5:3 (1970), pp. 198–238.

4. Vella, *An Elizabethan-Ottoman*, pp. 73–6.

5. *Calendar of State Papers Venetian, 1581–91* (henceforth *CSPV*), pp. 513, 525.

6. Ibid., pp. 519, 514 and 525; see also pp. 125–6, 128, 474, 524, and 529.

7. Ibid., p. 514.

8. Ibid., p. 521.

9. Ibid., p. 533.

10. Fernand Braudel, *The Mediterranean and the Mediterranean World in the Age of Philip II*, rev. ed., trans. Siân Reynolds, abr. Richard Ollard (London: Harper Collins, 1992), p. 572.

11. Niccolo Machiavelli, *The Prince*, trans. George Bull (Harmondsworth: Penguin, 1961), pp. 118–19.

12. Marjorie Garber, " 'Here's Nothing Writ': Scribe, Script, and Circumscription in Marlowe's Plays," in *Christopher Marlowe*, ed. Richard Wilson (Harlow: Longman, 1999), pp. 30–53.

13. Jean-Christophe Agnew, *Worlds Apart: The Market and the Theater in Anglo-American Thought, 1550–1750* (Cambridge: Cambridge University Press, 1986), p. 50.

14. Braudel, *The Mediterranean*, p. 360.

15. *Calendar of State Papers Foreign* (henceforth *CSPF*), *July 1593–December 1594*, p. 497.

16. William Shakespeare, *The Merchant of Venice*, ed. John Russell Brown (London: Routledge, 1955), 1.3.93.

17. Marc Shell, *Money, Language, and Thought: Literary and Philosophic Economies from the Medieval to the Modern Era* (Baltimore: Johns Hopkins University Press, 1982), pp. 48–9.

18. Steven Mullaney, *The Place of the Stage: License, Play, and Power in Renaissance England* (Chicago: Chicago University Press, 1988), pp. 121–33.

19. Braudel, *The Mediterranean*, p. 262.

20. Richard Hakluyt, *The Principal Navigations, Voyages, Traffics and Discoveries of the English Nation*, 9 vols., ed. John Masefield (London: J.M.Dent, 1907), vol. 3, pp. 65–6. For the rise of the trading factor, see T.S. Willan, *Studies in Elizabethan Foreign Trade* (Manchester: Manchester University Press, 1959), pp. 1–33.

21. Robert Brenner, *Merchants and Revolution: Commercial Change, Political Conflict, and London's Overseas Traders, 1550–1653* (Princeton: Princeton University Press, 1993), pp. 3–4. See also B.E. Supple, *Commercial Crisis and Change in England, 1600–1642* (Cambridge: Cambridge University Press, 1959), pp. 258–9.

22. See Ralph Davis, "England and the Mediterranean," *Essays in the Economic and Social History of Tudor and Stuart England*, ed. F. J. Fisher (Cambridge: Cambridge University Press, 1961), pp. 117–37.

23. Derek Massarella, *A World Elsewhere: Europe's Encounter with Japan in the Sixteenth and Seventeenth Centuries* (New Haven: Yale University Press, 1990), p. 54. For the foundations of the East India Company, see also William Foster, *England's Quest of Eastern Trade* (London: A.C. Black, 1933), pp. 144–54.

24. *CSPF, May–December 1582*, p. 153.

25. Ibid., p. 42.

26. Quoted in Vella, *An Elizabethan-Ottoman*, p. 55.

27. *The Merchant of Venice*, 1.1.8–187.

28. Stephen Greenblatt, "Marlowe, Marx and Anti-Semitism," in *Christopher Marlowe*, ed. Richard Wilson (Harlow: Longman, 1999), p. 147.

29. D.F. Allen, "Attempts to Revive the Order of Malta in Stuart England," *Historical Journal*, 33 (1990): 939–52, esp. 941; *CSPF, August 1589–June 1590*, p. 451.

30. Christopher Marlowe, *The Jew of Malta*, ed. T.W. Craik (London: Ernest Benn, 1966), p. 37; Emily C. Bartels, *Spectacles of Strangeness: Imperialism, Alienation, and Marlowe* (Philadelphia: University of Pennsylvania Press, 1993), p. 90.

31. Cecil Roth, "The Jews of Malta," *Transactions of the Jewish Historical Society of England*, 1929, pp. 187–251, esp. pp. 187 and 210.

32. Ibid., pp. 216–17.

33. Ibid. pp. 215 and 218. For the Maltese slave trade, see especially Braudel, *The Mediterranean*, p. 628; and Peter Earle, *Corsairs of Malta and Barbary* (London: Sidgwick & Jackson, 1970), chapter 5.

34. Braudel, *The Mediterranean*, p. 648.

35. Quoted in Stephen Clissold, *The Barbary Slaves* (New York: Barnes & Noble, 1977), p. 132.

36. Braudel, *The Mediterranean*, p. 629.

37. Clissold, *The Barbary*, pp. 135–8.

38. Earle, *Corsairs*, pp. 75–6 and 87. For Jews as agents of slave redemption, see Earle, *Corsairs*, p. 172; Clissold, *The Barbary*, p 105–6; Ellen Friedman, *Spanish Captives in North Africa in the Early Modern Age* (Madison: University of Wisconsin Press, 1983), p. 59; and Christopher Lloyd, *English Corsairs on the Barbary Coast* (London: Collins, 1981), pp. 116–17.

39. Earle, *Corsairs*, p. 89.

40. Ibid., pp. 145–6.

41. Hakluyt, *The Principal*, p. 122.

42. Frederick Boas, *Christopher Marlowe: A Biographical and Critical Study* (Oxford: Clarendon Press, 1940), p. 132; Cecil Roth, *A History of the Jews in England* (Oxford: Clarendon Press, 1964), pp. 135–9; David Katz, *The Jews in the History of England* (Oxford: Clarendon Press, 1994), p. 65. For the representation of the specifically Portuguese Jew on the Elizabethan stage, see also Ton Hoenselaars, *Images of Englishmen and Foreigners in the Drama of Shakespeare and his Contemporaries* (London: Associated University Presses, 1992), pp. 54–5.

43. Ibid.

44. Harold Pollins, *Economic History of the Jews in England* (Madison: Fairleigh Dickinson Press, 1982), p. 25.

45. Emily C. Bartels, *Spectacles of Strangeness: Imperialism, Alienation, and Marlowe* (Philadelphia: University of Pennsylvania Press, 1993), pp. 98, 100 and 106; Harry Levin, *The Overreacher: A Study of Christopher Marlowe* (Cambridge, MA: Harvard University Press, 1952), p. 73.

46. Richard Baines, "Concerning his [Marlowe's] Damnable Judgement of Religion and Scorn of God's Word," rept. A.D. Wraight, *In Search of Christopher Marlowe: A Pictorial Biography* (London: Macdonald, 1965), pp. 308–9. For a commentary, see Jonathan Goldberg, "Sodomy and Society: The Case of Christopher Marlowe," in *Christopher Marlowe*, ed. Wilson, pp. 54–61, esp. p. 57.

47. Andrew Marvell, "To His Coy Mistress," *The Metaphysical Poets*, ed. Helen Gardner (Harmondsworth: Penguin, 1957), p. 251; Katz, *The Jews*, pp. 112–14.

48. Katz, *The Jews*, p. 57.

49. *CSPF, January–July 1589*, p. 348.

50. *CSPF, July 1590–May 1591*, p. 459

51. Ibid., p. 460.
52. Ibid., pp. 469–70.
53. *CSPV*, pp. 528–9.
54. *CSPF, July 1590–May 1591*, p. 463; *CSPF, June 1591–April 1592*, p. 499.
55. *CSPV*, p. 51; *CSPF, July 1593–December 1594*, p. 496. For the background to the Anglo-Ottomon treaty, see Brandon Beck, *From the Rising of the Sun: English Images of the Ottomon Empire to 1715* (New York: Peter Lang, 1987), pp. 30–1; Lansing Collins, "Barton's Audience in Istanbul," *History Today* 25 (1975): 262–70; A.L. Horniker, "William Harborne and the Beginning of Anglo-Turkish Diplomatic and Commercial Relations," *Journal of Modern History*, 14 (1942): 301; H.G. Rawlinson, "The Embassy of William Harborne to Constantinople," *Transactions of the Royal Historical Society*, 4th series, 5 (1922): pp. 1–27; S.A. Skilliter, *William Harborne and the Trade with Turkey, 1578–1582* (Oxford: Clarendon Press, 1977), pp. 23–75; and Dorothy Vaughan, *Europe and the Turk: A Pattern of Alliances, 1350–1700* (Liverpool: Liverpool University Press, 1954), pp. 167–9.
56. *CSPF, 1580–1586*, p. 366; *CSPF, January–December 1596* (London: HMSO, 2000), p. 275; Hakluyt, *The Principal*, pp. 369–70.
57. Hakluyt, *The Principal*, pp. 369–70. William Shakespeare, *Henry IV, Part Two*, ed. A.R. Humphreys (London: Routledge, 1966), 5.2.48. For the development of the stereotype, see Lucette Valensi, "The Making of a Political Paradigm: The Ottomon State and Oriental Despotism," in *The Transmission of Culture in Early Modern Europe*, ed. Anthony Grafton and Anne Blair (Philadelphia: University of Pennsylvania Press, 1990), pp. 173–203.
58. Braudel, *The Mediterranean*, p. 261; Lisa Jardine, "Alien Intelligence: Mercantile Exchange and Knowledge Transactions in Marlowe's *The Jew of Malta*," *Reading Shakespeare Historically* (London: Routledge, 1996), p. 101.
59. Brenner, *Merchants*, pp. 62, 64–5 and 73; M. Epstein, *The Early History of the Levant Company* (London: Routledge, 1908), pp. 28–33; A.C. Wood, *A History of the Levant Company* (London: Frederick Cass, 1935), pp. 22–3; T.S. Willan, "Some Aspects of English Trade with the Levant in the Sixteenth Century," *English Historical Review* 70 (1955): 399–410.
60. *CSPV*, p. xxxii.
61. Beck, *From the Rising*, p. 31.
62. *CSPV*, p. xxxiii; *CSPF, January–June 1583*, p. 360; *Calendar of State Papers Spanish, 1580–1586*, p. 414.
63. Thomas Nashe, "The Praise of the Red Herring," *The Works of Thomas Nashe*, ed. Ronald McKerrow, 4 vols. (Oxford: Basil Blackwell, 1966), vol. 3, p. 173.
64. Repr. in Conyers Read, *Mr Secretary Walsingham and the Policy of Queen Elizabeth*, 3 vols. (Oxford: Clarendon Press, 1925), vol. 3, pp. 226–8.

65. C.A. Patrides, " 'The Bloody and Cruel Turk': the Background of a Renaissance Commonplace," *Studies in the Renaissance* 10 (1963): 126–35, esp. 130. See also Norman Daniel, *Islam and the West: the Making of an Image* (Edinburgh: Edinburgh University Press, 1958), chapter 10.

66. Shakespeare, *Othello*, ed. M.R. Ridley (London: Routledge, 1958), 5.2.354.

67. James Shapiro, *Shakespeare and the Jews* (New York: Columbia, 1996), pp. 184–5.

68. "A consideration of the advantages to be gained by opening a direct trade with Turkey, by Sir Francis Walsingham," *Calendar of State Papers Domestic, 1547–1580*, p. 691, CXLIV, 70; see Epstein, *The Early History*, pp. 245–7; and Read, *Mr Secretary*, p. 373.

69. Hakluyt, *The Principal*, vol. 3, pp. 85–9.

70. Greenblatt, "Marlowe," p. 146.

71. *Historic Manuscripts Commission: 9: Salisbury MSS*, 19, pp. 473–4; rpt. in Edgar Samuel, " 'Sir Thomas Shirley's Project of the Jews'— The Earliest Known Proposal for the Resettlement," *Transactions of the Jewish Historical Society of England* 24 (1974): 195–7. See also David Katz, *Philo-Semitism and the Readmission of the Jews to England, 1603–1655* (Oxford: Clarendon Press, 1982), pp. 164–5.

72. Katz, *The Jews*, pp. 110–14.

73. William Empson, "Two Proper Crimes," *The Nation* 163 (1946): 444–5.

74. Nashe, "The Praise," p. 173.

75. Braudel, *The Mediterranean*, pp. 445–6.

76. *CSPF, July 1590–May 1591*, p. 458; *May 1592–June 1593*, p. 398.

77. *CSPF, July 1593–December 1594*, pp. 500, 511.

78. Ibid., pp. 498, 512.

79. *CSPV*, pp. 550, 552. In fact, Passi returned to Malta unscathed two months later from Rhodes (p. 556).

80. *CSPF, May 1592–June 1593*: "and boasting that he had banqueted Burghley and all the nobility, that Burghley often visited him at his house, that he and all his train used publicly the Jews' rites in praying, accompanied with divers secret Jews resident in London, and that he had had frequent private and public conference with Her Majesty" (p. 397).

81. *CSPF, June 1591–April 1592*, pp. 503–4. For the background to the Lopez prosecution, see P.M. Handover, *The Second Cecil: The Rise to Power of Sir Robert Cecil, 1563–1604* (London: Eyre & Spottiswoode, 1959), pp. 111–20.

82. *CSPF, June 1591–April 1592*, p. 504; Katz, *The Jews*, p. 106.

CHAPTER 8

"COME FROM TURKIE":
MEDITERRANEAN TRADE IN LATE
ELIZABETHAN LONDON

Alan Stewart

Much of the critical attention given to Robert Wilson's play
*A Right excellent and famous Comedy, called The Three Ladies of
London* (c. 1581) has focused on its possible influence on William
Shakespeare's *The Merchant of Venice*, first performed some fifteen
years later.[1] Among the many subplots of Wilson's play is an
encounter between the Italian merchant Mercadorus and the Jewish
moneylender Gerontus, to whom Mercadorus is indebted. Two years
previously, Mercadorus had borrowed from Gerontus two thousand
ducats for five weeks, soon adding another one thousand ducats, and
lengthening the payment period to three months; by the day the
money finally falls due, Mercardorus has "fled the countrey"
(sig. D.iij.ᵛ, E.iiijᵛ). After Mercadorus fails to honour yet another
chance given him by Gerontus, the Jew runs out of patience and in an
effort to force the merchant to pay, threatens to get him arrested by,
appealing to the legal authorities in Turkey. Faced with the power of the
law, Mercadorus threatens that he will renounce his Christian faith in
favor of Islam, in order to take advantage of the Turkish court's protection
of Muslims in financial dealings with non-Muslims. When Gerontus
finally takes his case before "the Iudge of Turkie," with Mercadorus
dressed "in Turkish weedes" and prepared to reject his faith, he proposes
a compromise that Mercadorus need only pay the principal of the debt,

but the merchant refuses to pay anything. Gerontus lowers the stakes, suggesting he will accept half, but Mercadorus is still adamant: "No point da halfe, no point denere [denier], me will be a Turke I say, / Me be wearie of my Christian religion, and for dat me come away." Finally, appalled at the possibility that because of his demands Mercadorus will forsake him, Gerontus frees Mercadorus of his debt, protesting he will never "demaund peny nor halfepeny." Mercadorus's acceptance is hilariously prompt: "O Sir Gerontus, me take a your proffer, and tanke you most hartily." When the judge protests, "But seneor Mercadorus, I trow [believe] ye will be a Turke for [despite] all this," Mercadorus retorts righteously, "Seneor no, not for all da good in da world, me forsake a my Christ." "Why then," says the judge, as light dawns, "it is as sir Gerontus saide, you did more for the greedines of the mony, / Then for any zeale or good will you bare to Turky" (sig. F.^{r}). But as Gerontus leaves the stage, reluctantly accepting the merchant's thanks, Mercadorus lets us in on his real objective: "You say vel Sir: it dus me good, dat me haue cooseend de Iewe, . . . me did da scall Iewe beguile. Cosening the Jew, beguiling the scald Jew" (sig. F.^{v}).

   It was Sidney Lee who, while deploring "this tedious production," first noticed "similarities between the dialogue of Mercatore and Gerontus and that of Antonio and Shylock."[2] Following Lee, F.J. Furnivall observed that in *Three Ladies* "a Jew attacks his Christian debtor much in the way that Shylock attacks Antonio."[3] More recently, M. Lindsay Kaplan has argued that while Shakespeare "almost certainly knew" Wilson's play, and its staging of "a conflict between an Italian debtor and a Jewish creditor," there is a "striking contrast" between the plays: here, "the Jewish moneylender shows himself merciful in forgiving a loan rather than forcing the debtor into apostasy, while the Italian borrower is a fraudulent, greedy opportunist."[4] Certainly, Gerontus uses Mercadorus's lack of commercial trust to attack Christians:

> Surely if we that be Iewes should deale so one with an other,
> We should not be trusted againe of our owne brother:
> But many of you Christians make no conscience to falsifie your fayth
> and breake your day. (sig. D.iij.^{v})

The moral of the story for the judge is the odd Christianity of the Jew: "One may iudge and speake truth, as appeeres by this, Iewes seeke to excell in Christianitie, and the Christians in Iewisnes" (sig. F.^{v}). This paradox draws on an established tradition in which the contemporary evils of Christians are shockingly described as being worse than those of the Jews: Thomas Wilson, for example, in his 1572 *A Discourse on Usury* wished that "all these Englishemen . . . that lende their money or their goods whatsoever for gayne" should be banished from the realm, "for I take them to be no better then Iewes. Nay, shall I saye: they are worse then Iewes. For go whither you wil through out Christendom, and deale with them, and you shall haue vnder tenne in the hundred, yea sometimes for sixe at their handes, whereas englishe usurers exceed all goddes mercye. . . ."[5] Of course, just as this move appears to exonerate the Jews, it reinscribes their a priori evil—and thus Christian and Jew remain opposed.

In a recent article, Lloyd Kermode argues that the play's supposed collapsing of the opposition of Christian and Jew is emphasized by the "the effect of distance" in Mercadorus's journey across geographical divide between "the core team of London characters" and "Turky": "the geographically separated Jew in the Moslem country effectively exposes the hypocrisies and evils of the Christians in England and those in transit."[6] I shall argue by contrast that Wilson shows that while the "Jew in the Moslem country" may be "geographically separated" from London, he is in truth intricately and inexorably involved with the English capital—and with English capital. The play's central concern is the economic position of London, and by extension, England; but its analysis of that economy inevitably leads us into foreign trade. Building on the economic historical work of Robert Brenner,[7] recent literary critical work has called for a reevaluation of early modern London's place as a centre of "global" trade.[8] Here I shall suggest further that for an understanding of *The Three Ladies of London*, at least, we need to add a more specific focus: the ethnic, religious, political, and commercial mix of the Mediterranean.[9]

*   *   *

The Three Ladies of London explores new dangers to the prosperity of the English commonwealth, all done for love of "Lady Lucar [Lucre]." Lady Lucar's right hand man is a foreign merchant, Mercadorus, who follows her orders to export from England her staple "good commodities" and import instead "slight, prettie and pleasant" "trifles." At first glance, this plot device merely follows a firmly established satirical tradition of representing threats to England through figures of foreign infiltration via overseas trade.[10] As early as the fourteenth century, Ranulph Higden was complaining that the English were "full curious to knowe straunge thynges by experience, depravenge theire awne thynges [they] commende other straunge, unnethe other never contente of the state of theire degre, transfigurenge to theyme that is congruente to an other man."[11] It is precisely in "economic" terms that this anxiety is couched—Higden's very concept of "straunge thynges" is premised on their opposition to the English people's "awne thynges"— commodities and concepts produced by "strangers," that is, people from overseas, in explicit competition with homegrown domestic goods. A similar concern for import-export imbalance is the driving force behind the anonymous *Libelle of Englyshe Polycye*, usually dated 1436.[12]

Into this established tradition, however, *The Three Ladies of London* introduces a very particular context: London's relation with the Mediterranean. Mercadorus is an Italian merchant, "come from Turkie", who turns to a Jewish moneylender in Turkey to provide him with the "trifles" needed to bankrupt England—all done for love of "Lady Lucar." As Love introduces her, Lucar draws to England men "come from Italy, Barbary, Turky, From Iury," that is, men arriving in England from Mediterranean locations defined in terms both geographical and ethnoreligious. The latter possibility is stressed as Love explains how:

> the Pagan himselfe,
> Indaungers his bodie to gape for her pelfe.
> They forsake mother, Prince, Countrey, Religion, kiffe and kinne,
> Nay men care not what they forsake, so Lady Lucar they winne.
> (sig. A.ii.ᵛ)

Mercadorus epitomizes the flexibility of Mediterranean trade as "an Italian" who arrives in England not from Italy, but "come from Turkie" (sig. B.ii.ᵛ): he is also the only character for whom there is textual evidence of his portrayal as non-English: he speaks in a supposed dialect (substituting "me" for "I," and adding "-a" onto many of his words) still recognizable and current as cod-Italian. Challenged by Lucar as to whether he dare "vndertake / Secretlie to conuey good commodities out of this countrey for my sake?" (sig. B.ii.ᵛ), Mercadorus assures her that he would do anything for Lucar:

> Me will a forsake a my Fader, Moder, King, Countrey & more den dat.
> Me will lie and forsweare me selfe for a quarter so much as my hat.
> What is dat for loue of Lucar me dare or will not doe:
> Me care not for all the world, the great Deuill, nay make my God angry for you. (sig. B.ii.ᵛ)

Love of lucre thus frees the merchant from ties of filial and patriotic duty, but his declaration betrays how this love undoes him: he would "forsweare me selfe," and "make my God angry for you," in terms that foreshadow his threatened conversion to Islam.

Once this is established, a well-pleased Lucar gives Mercadorus instructions, and here we suddenly shift to a highly specific pro-gramme of import-export:

> Thou must carry ouer Wheate, Pease, Barly, Oates, and Fitches [vetches] and all kinde of graine,
> Whiche is well sould beyond sea, and bring suche Merchauntes great gaine.
> Then thou must carie beside Leather, Tallow, Beefe, Bacon, Belmettell and euery thing. (sig. B.ii.ᵛ)

These, and the "Brasse, Copper, Pewter" mentioned later (sig. C.iii.ᵛ), are defined as "these good commodities" against which Mercadorus must bring in such "trifles" "As Bugles [glass beads] to make bables, coloured bones, glasse, beades, to make bracelettes withall . . . Amber, Ieat, Corall, Christall, and euery such bable, / That is slight, prettie and pleasant"(sig. B.ii.ᵛ–B.iii.ʳ).

This notion of good exports being swapped for bad imports is a famil-iar trope in late sixteenth-century England. In his *Description of Britaine* (1577), William Harrison complains that "for desire of novelty we oft exchange our finest cloth, corn, tin and wools for halfpenny cockhorses for children, dogs of wax or of cheese, twopenny tabors, leaden swords, painted feathers, gewgaws for fools, dogtricks for dizzards, hawkshoods, and suchlike trumpery."[13] While Harrison sees these trinkets as fodder for children and fools, Wilson's play, however, consistently genders their target market as female. Later in the play, Lucar sends Mercadorus "to search for some new toyes in Barbary or Turky / Such trifles as you thinke will please wantons best: / For you know in this Countrey tis their chiefest request" (sig. C.iiii.ʳ); as Mercadorus claims, "Indeede de Gentlewomans here [in London] buy so much vaine toyes, / Dat me straungers laugh a to tinke wherein day haue their Ioyes" (sig. C.iiii.ʳ). When Gerontus asks whether he's looking to buy "such necessaries as they lacke" in England, Mercadorus laughingly responds, "O no lack, some prettie fine toy or some fantastike new knack, / For da Gentlewomans in England buy much tinges for fantasie" (sig. D.iiij.ʳ). Gerontus in Turkey knows exactly what is called for to fulfill "that coun-try gentlewomans Ioyes": "Muske, Amber, sweet Powders, fine Oders, pleasaunt perfumes, and many such toys . . . Diamondes, Rubyes, Emerodes, Safiors, Smaradines [smargadines], Opalles, Onacles [onyx-stone], Iasinkes, Aggattes, Turkasir, and almost of all kinde of precious stones"—all "fit thinges to sucke away mony from such greene headed wantons" (sig. D.iiij.^r).

The export of staple goods was a constant cause of concern in London. Merchants knew that there were greater profits to be made by exporting certain commodities to markets where they were rare, than by selling them locally, where there was a surplus. As a result, there were strict limitations on who might legally export certain goods, and licenses to export were highly prized: in the play *A Knacke to Knowe a Knaue* (c.1592), when the courtier Perin asks a poor farmer what he could best do for him, the Farmer asks for "Nothing but procure me the Kings letter to conuey corn beyond seas, for in England it is so good cheap, that a man can make no liuing by selling thereof."[14] Mercadorus "and my cuntrimans" have long been engaging in the kind of trade proposed by Lucar, and the only thing that worries him is that "some skall [scald, skurvy] knaue will put a bill in da Parlament / For dat such a tinge shall not be brought here" (sig. B.iij.^r). Here *Three Ladies* is highly topical. Since 1565, some commodities, such as wool, wool-fells, hides and leather, were subject to the "great custom," a substantial export duty, in order to hinder their exodus from England[15]; and the short sittings of Elizabeth's fourth parliament of the 1570s saw a further string of measures proposed to aid England's overseas trading relations.[16] In May 1572, for example, a bill was introduced to prosecute "the transporters of lether over the sea," with guilty parties facing not only the forfeiture of the leather, but also "to be set upon the pillory for the first offence, and for the second offence to suffer as in case of fellony."[17] Lucar dismisses Mercadorus's fears: even if such a bill is introduced in parliament, "there is some other will flatter and say, / They do no hurt to the cuntry, and with a sleight fetch that bill away" (sig. B.iij.^r). And indeed, the debates in the House of Commons heard the airing of vested interests. Such a law would be "very perilous," asserted Ralph Seckerston, MP for Liverpool, and a prominent draper.[18] It hit hard at merchants, who were not themselves responsible for "the dearth of shooes," a direct result of the leather shortage. He argued rather that the fault lay with the gentlemen who "sell the hides so deere at first," and suggested that the gentlemen "might be hanged." Even in principle, export licences were "very hurtful" since "under colour of every licence a great many more" commodities left the country than the licence allowed for. John Marshe, MP for London, a mercer and merchant-adventurer and a founder member of the Spanish Company and Muscovy Company, disagreed. It was the merchants provoking "the carriage over sea" who caused the dearth, and who consequently forced the gentlemen to "sell it so deare." For Marsh, it was a simple case of the commonwealth versus private wealth: "No merchaunte should seeke his living to the spoile of his country. . . . Licences cannot do so much hurt as the carrying of everybody. The licences although they be hurtful cannot be denied to the Prince; but he wisheth it were well looked to, such persons as have licences did not so deceive the Queen and the realm."[19] This echoes Thomas Wilson's *Discourse on Usury* where the Preacher compares England unfavourably with other nations: "This must I say of other nations, they are more unwillinge to offende in those thinges that hurte a common weale then we are. As looke, what generallye is noysome to the state, noe man wyll seeke to get by licence, nor otherwise by dealynge against the common welfare, because they preferred the wealth of theire countrey before their owne commoditie."[20] When the bill returned from the Lords, Seckerston kept up his offensive. Surely it was "more beneficiall to the common wealth" that there was a dearth of these commodities in the realm due to export, rather than they were cheap because of a glut, as was the case with wool. Yes, leather might be leaving English shores, but the foreign markets "have it not for nothing. Good mony is returned for the same." But Seckerston lost his cause; after a third reading, the bill was passed on June 10, 1572.[21]

There were also attempts during this session of the parliament to "restraine the bringing in of any forraigne wares from any country where and during the tyme that our wares are forbidden in the same country."[22] The treasurer reasoned that while "the King of Spaine taketh all our goodes which he can catch," English merchants were in fact aiding his cause: "Our men conveye away our goodes thither to the relief of our enemy, and yet hee restraineth our wares." It stood to reason therefore that Elizabeth should "doe the like, and to encourage such merchauntes as trade to such places with whom the Queene is in amytie."[23] The debates again revealed deep-rooted oppositions. This bill was "altogether for [the] benefit of the City," opined Seckerston, meaning London, as opposed to his constituency, Liverpool. Despite its best intentions, the bill left a loophole: although English merchants might not trade with countries that restrain English wares (Spain, France, and Flanders), they could simply go to other markets, and "bring from Handborough [Hamburg] what they will," including Spanish goods. After all, there were some Spanish wares they could not go without, such as "iron and oyle." While Seckerston attacked this privileging of Hamburg merchants, Robert Apley, MP for Barnstaple in Devon, complained Hamburg was "to farr a passadg" for his fellow Devon men, and they were therefore "of necessity compelled to buy Spanish wares in Fraunce." John Marshe pointed out that Spain and Flanders had no such loophole: English wares found there would be "confiscate,"even if "the goods came from Rome." Robert Snage, MP for Lostwithiel, allowed that it was right that no merchant should be allowed to "fetch any wares out of Spaine," but thought they should not be prohibited from bringing "Spanish wares out of other countries with which we are in amity," and suggested an amendment to allow this. Eventually it was moved that "the bill may be stayed and not put to the question."[24]

The debates here are highly revealing. The second one in particular betrays the extent to which parliament is helpless in the face of international trade: no matter what it decides, and even if it can successfully impose its will, it cannot control the machinations of foreign merchants. Lucar is well aware of this: in her attack on the three ladies. Even if Parliament does pass such an act, she tells Mercadorus,

> I know you Merchants haue many a sleight and subtill cast.
> So that you will by stealth bring ouer great store:
> And say it was in the Realme a long time before.
> For beeing so many of these trifles heere as there are at this day,
> You may increase them at pleasure, when you send ouer sea.
> And do but giue the searcher [customs house officer] an odde bribe in his hand,
> I warrant you he will let you scape roundly with such things in and out the land. (sig. B.iij.ʳ)

Lucar's cynical confidence points to the ultimate ineffectiveness of parliamentary impositions on trade, thanks to the subterfuges endemic among traders: crafty merchants will lie—and customs officials can be bribed. But significantly also, neither of these parliamentary debates is between gentlemen and merchants: both are between individual merchants with differing interests—some seeking to protect a particular provincial market, others heavily invested in overseas trade. Their arguments on the floor of the Commons point to the range of opinion within "the merchant community," and remind us that, then as now, there was no agreement on how commerce should be conducted—its proper relation to private and common wealth.

*   *   *

Much has been made of the xenophobic actions of the English in the crisis years of the 1590s, when a series of perceived threats to social stability—Spanish invasion, creeping Catholic incursions, bad harvests, and alleged attempts on the Queen's life—led to an outpouring of antiforeign discourses, both legal and literary, and even to riots. But several aspects of that xenophobia are found in *The Three Ladies of London*, written and performed a decade earlier, even if the causes are notably different. The London of *The Three Ladies* is decidedly cosmopolitan, filled with merchants and artisans from across the Channel. To Lucar, these "strangers," as early modern London referred to those coming from overseas, are simply another source of easy income. As Mercadorus suggests, they "are content / To dwell in a little roome, and to pay muche rent," especially "da French mans and fleminges," who will willingly share a single lodging between ten families, and pay "fiftie or three score pound a yeare" for the privilege, while "da English mans" would balk at a rent of "twenty marke" (sig. C.iii.^{v}). Lucar does not need to be advised: she already has a whole network of overpriced leasing: "infinite numbers in London that my want doth supply," as well as willing tenants in "Bristow, Northampton, Norwich, Weschester [i.e., Chester], Caunterbury, / Douer, Sandwich, Rie, Porchmouth [i.e., Portsmouth], Plimmoth, and many moe" (sig. C.iiii.^{r}).[25] Here is a rare moment that looks beyond the London of the play's title to acknowledge an impact beyond the capital.

But to Artifex, representing English artisanal skill, this mass immigration of foreign workers poses a threat to his livelihood: he complains to Dissimulation that he is "almost qvite vndoone" despite his conscientious hard work. He identifies the problem as a skilled immigrant workforce, indulged by a foolish English marketplace:

> For there be such a sort of straungers in this cuntry,
> That worke fine to please the eie, though it be deceitfully,
> And that which is slight, and seemes to the eie well,
> Shall sooner then a peece of good worke be proffered to sell.
> And our english men be growne so foolish and nice,
> That they will not giue a peny aboue the ordinary price. (sig. B.iij.^{v})

The complaint was familiar. In his 1592 *A Direction for Trauailers*, Sir John Stradling remarked it was human nature "[(]especially of vs English) that, as we admire and entertaine strange artificers before our owne, so wee wonder at, and more willingly intreate of learning with the learned forrainer, then with our own natiue countrey man."[26] But Artifex's anxiety gestures toward the pitched battles fought throughout the late sixteenth century between self-described London artisans and merchants, and their immigrant competition.

Social historians have explored the vexed status of "strangers" within the City of London, and of attempts to clamp down on immigrant workers and their offspring.[27] Steve Rappaport, for example, cites the City's Court of Common Council who complained in 1574 of "great numbers" of strangers flooding in, and provided a narrative that spoke not only of current discomfort but future problems. Children of strangers born within the realm "are by law accounted English," but "experience has well proved that children born of such strangers have and do retain an inclination and kind affection to the countries of their parents. Partly for that natural disposition and partly by the examples of their fathers whose steps they follow," they will abuse the privilege of their Englishness by abetting the illicit trade of further strangers; "Being made apprentices and so attaining the liberties of the city of London, they [become] common colourers of strangers' goods." The situation will deteriorate inexorably, as more strangers become freemen of the City, and make "apprentices of their own countrymen's children, they . . . are like to fill and pester [the city] with freemen of the same kind." The Common Council's remedy was to forbid any citizen of the city from taking as an apprentice "any person whose father is not the child of an Englishman born," effectively giving the truly English citizens breathing space for one more generation.[28]

Significantly, it is precisely on physical commodities, "objects of trade," that anxiety focuses. The practice by which strangers' children will abuse their adopted city is detailed: "Being made apprentices and so attaining the liberties of the city of London, they [become] common colourers of strangers' goods." "Colouring strangers' goods" was the practice whereby a freeman of a city would pass off the goods of a stranger as his own in order to evade the higher customs duties levied on goods belonging to strangers—in return for a cut of the monies saved by the stranger. The practice was as old as customs duties and treated with great extremity by merchant organizations. In Bristol, for example, the oath taken by each new burgess [freeman] contained the solemn promise that "You shall not colour the goods of any Forreigner, or Stranger."[29] In 1478, Bristol traders in Toulouse complained to the Mayor, Sheriff, and Common Council of "the moost pituouse fallinge and decayeng of merchaundyse" through "entercomenyg of Straungers and senestre colouryng of their goodis." It was ordered that in future every shipment's "Carte of Warrantise" had to be examined by the mayor and three aldermen "for the more perfait knowleche to be hadd of colouryng of enny straungers goods in the same."[30] In 1500, Bristol's Common Council attempted a reformation of "dyvers colourable and crafty delyng" by burgesses who "colored" goods of strangers and foreigners by buying and selling them as their agents, and the subject was returned to in charters of 1508, 1520 and 1527.[31] Examples could be multiplied ad infinitum: "colouring strangers' goods" was endemic to import trade as practised in sixteenth-century England.

The parliamentary debates on "strangers" were therefore not simply xenophobic in motivation or execution; nor were they an attack on a particular nationality, ethnic grouping, or perceived "race": rather, they responded very precisely to challenges to the monopolies enjoyed by the guild organizations of London. Once again, in its representation of English and non-English, Christian, Muslim and Jew, *The Three Ladies of London* lays bare the complex—and often contradictory—mechanisms of trade in the early modern capital.

*   *   *

Kermode is of course correct in pointing out that *Three Ladies of London* moves between London and only one other geographical site, Turkey. The shift to Turkey is central to the furtherance of Lucar's plans to capture London's economy, and it is telling that Mercadorus, although emphatically and comically Italian, is at pains from the outset to tell Lucar that he has "come from Turkie"—his homeland allegiance is less important than the site of his most recent travel, since "com[ing] from Turkie," evidently denotes a certain level of commercial skill. And indeed, once Mercadorus has proved his ability to export vital English commodities and import foreign trifles, Lucar sets him another challenge that explicitly involves the region: "senior Mercadore, dare you to trauell vndertake: / And goe amongest the Moores, Turkes, and Pagans for my sake?" Mercadorus accepts with alacrity: "Madona, me dare a goe to de Turkes, Moores, Paganes and more too," commenting with what turns out to be foresight, "What doe me care and me goe to da great deuill for you." Lucar sends him to search for "trifles" for England's "wantons," "some new toyes in Barbary or Turky" (sig. C.iiii.ʳ).

While "Turky" remains nonspecific, it is represented as being under Islamic law while remaining multicultural, religiously diverse, and commercially vibrant. Those familiar with the Mediterranean would have assumed that Wilson was portraying Constantinople (Istanbul): Nabil Matar has argued that Britons knew only a peculiarly Mediterranean Islam, centered on Constantinople, Aleppo, Beirut, Jerusalem, Cairo, Algiers, and Fez[32]; and as Fernand Braudel points out, Constantinople "was cast in the image of the immense Turkish empire," and epitomized it for the West.[33] A vast city by contemporary standards, its late sixteenth-century population estimated at 700,000, Constantinople was, as the play suggests, also predominantly Islamic, but not overwhelmingly so: Muslims made up some 58 percent of the population, with significant visible populations of Greeks, Jews, Armenians, and Tziganes.[34] As William Biddulph noted in 1609, from the time Mahomet II seized the city in 1453, foreigners were "permitted there to live there according to the institutions and precepts of such Religion as it pleased them to obserue, and to exercise with all safety, their handicrafts and merchandises; which ministered an occasion vnto an infinite multitude of *Iewes* and *Marannes*, driuen out of *Spaine*, for to come and dwell there: By meanes whereof, in very short time the City began to increase in trafficke, riches, and abundance of people."[35] So, in *Three Ladies*, going to "Turky" leads Mercardorus quite naturally into the path of "Gerontus a Iewe" (sig. D.iij.ᵛ), a member of one of the four thousand Jewish households (most of Iberian origin) estimated to be in Constantinople in 1550 by Sinan Paşa's personal physician, Cristobal de Villalon.[36]

But I would argue that events between 1578 and 1582 lent a new significance to merchants coming to London from Turkey. While a few English merchant travelers had been given passports to travel through and privileges to trade in the Ottoman Empire, it was not until the late 1570s that such arrangements were formalized. William Harborne was sent to the Sublime Porte, the Ottoman court at Constantinople, in 1578; from early 1579, negotiations by letter were in hand between Sultan Murad III and Elizabeth leading to Murad's grant securing English rights in May 1580; Harborne was appointed as England's first ambassador to the Porte and took up his position in March 1582. *The Three Ladies of London*, probably written in 1581, was therefore composed when these negotiations were at their height.[37]

Recently critical interest has focused on the notion of "turning Turk," a persistent trope in early seventeenth-century English travel writings and drama,[38] and of course *Three Ladies of London* exploits contemporary anxieties about conversion to Islam to comic effect in Mercadorus's threat to renounce his Christianity. But less attention has been paid to the economic underpinning of this concern. Anglo-Turkish trade had been regular for some time, to the dismay of England's competitors, especially Spain. As the Spanish ambassador in London Bernardino de Mendoza reported to his king in November 1579, England had been exporting tin to the Turks "for the last few years," and that sole commodity was enough to "maintain the trade with the Levant."[39] Tin and lead were "extremely profitable" for the English: as Mendoza noted in May 1582, the Turk "buys of them almost for its weight in gold, the tin being vitally necessary for the casting of guns and the lead for purposes of war," [40] especially after their efforts against Cyprus, their defeat at Lepanto, and with the ongoing war with Persia.[41] The Pope prohibited the selling of materials for weapons to infidels: but following his excommunication of Elizabeth in 1570, English merchants were no longer subject to his edict.[42] Mendoza's dispatches testify to a steady trade in these illicit commodities [43]; and in May 1580, the French ambassador at Constantinople attributed Harborne's diplomatic success at the Sublime Porte directly to his steady supply of tin.[44]

"Belmettell" is among the "good commodities" that Lucar urges Mercadorus to export. An alloy of copper and tin, bell metal is, as S.A. Skilliter notes, a particularly intriguing export from a Protestant to an Islamic state that forbade bells because of their Christian associations: "broken ones such as these, to be made into cannon for use against blasphemers, would seem to be the ideal export from one idol-destroyer to another."[45] But the role of Mercadorus, as a non-English and non-Turkish merchant, is also significant here. When English policymakers were assessing the pros and cons of direct English trade with what after all remained an infidel force, it was noted that one positive effect would be the eradication of such foreign middlemen. In a 1578 position paper entitled "A consideration of the trade into Turky," Principal Secretary, Sir Francis Walsingham pointed out to the English merchant community that "You shall vent your owne Commodities with most proffitte which beffore did fall into strangers handes"—that is, no Mercadorus—and "You shall furnishe not onlie this Realme but also the most parte of the hyther parte of Ewrope with suche Commodyties as are transported owt of the said Turkes dominions, to the great enrichinge of this realme"—it would be England that controlled the trade in eastern commodities throughout Western Europe.[46]

The Three Ladies of London thus hints at London's burgeoning trade with Turkey, and presents that trade in all its alarming complexity: vulnerable to the machinations of foreign middlemen, whose own trade might well be kept afloat by interest-heavy loans from yet another set of parasites, the moneylenders—and all of these relations giving rise to a worrying slippage in national and religious interests. In *Three Ladies*, the financial success of English Protestant London depends on the services of Catholic non-English merchants, themselves dependent on maintenance by offshore Jewish loans, upheld by Islamic law centered in the Ottoman Empire. It is a play in which trade leads slipperily to conversion: where Catholics become Turks, and Jews (as the judge puts it) become Christians.

*   *   *

Can we therefore argue, with Lloyd Kermode, that "the geographically separated Jew in the Moslem country effectively exposes the hypocrisies and evils of the Christians in England and those in transit"?[47] Certainly, the play allows for a rhetorical and paradoxical mirroring of Christian and Jew, in the behavior of Mercadorus and Gerontus. Moreover, unlike *The Merchant of Venice*, *The Three Ladies of London* refuses to allow the stereotypical collapsing of Jew and usurer. Gerontus is the first extant representation of a Jew in sixteenth-century English drama. In 1579, Stephen Gosson reports approvingly a play entitled *The Jew*, played at the Bull theatre, "representing the greedinesse of worldly chusers, and bloody mindes of Usurers,"[48] but this play is now lost. Reading back through the prism of *The Merchant of Venice*, it seems fair to conclude that Gosson's eponymous *Jew* would be the bloody-minded usurer, but Wilson's play refuses such an easy assumption. In *The Three Ladies of London*, Usurie is completely separate from the moneylender Gerontus, and definitely resident in England. He is central to the designs of Lady Lucar who decrees he shall "be my Secretariy, / To deale amongest Merchantes, to bargen and exchaunge money" (sig. B^v), but his reported actvities include seizing properties and letting them out at exortionate rents. Usurie is bloody-minded, violent, and malevolent, and specializes in the vein of black humour mined by Shylock: when he threatens Hospitalitie that he will "cut thy throat," and Hospitalitie querulously asks, "What will you kill me?" Usurie responds with a sick equivocation that foreshadows Shakespeare's creation: "No, Ile do nothing but cut thy throat" (sig. D.ij.^{v}). But Usurie is not the Jew in this play: and Gerontus, although clearly a moneylender, is revealed to be the more humane character in relation to Mercadorus: thus, as the judge points out, "Iewes seeke to excell in Christianitie" (sig. F^r).

Despite this, Wilson refuses to allow the apparent geographical separations of the play to become absolute. Protestant, Catholic, Muslim, and Jew are seen to be mutually interdependent; London is an integral part of Mediterranean trade, its staple export fulfilling a function for overseas markets, just as its trifling imports make money for them. And while *Three Ladies of London* may keep Usurie discrete from the

Jewish character of Gerontus, the play's sequel, *The Three Lordes and Three Ladies of London*, insists on Usurie's Jewish heritage, even as it points out his native Englishness. Fraud reminds Usurie, "thy parentes were both Jewes, though thou wert borne in *London*."[49] This revelation leads us to a different understanding of the complex ethnic, geographical, national, and religious mix of *Three Ladies*. Here, even supposedly established Londoners are revealed to be second generation immigrants of non-Christian heritage.

During the fourth parliament of Elizabeth's reign, the question of the status of children born on English soil whose parents were both born "strangers" was raised continually. On February 21, 1576, it was proposed that such children "should pay subsidies and customes and in all other respects to be as straungers"; not coincidentally, on the same day, a bill was proposed for the "manumising" of the mirror image—children of Englishmen who by accident happened to be "borne beyond the seas."[50] The attempt to penalise strangers' English-born children was intriguingly unpopular: it was rejected on March 3, 1576,[51] only to be reintroduced in a very stark form—"that the childrene of strangers should not be accompted English"—on January 24, 1581.[52] This bill argued that all strangers' children born since the first year of the present queen's reign—children who would now be over twenty years old—should be "deemed as aliens." The debate that followed was lively. The bill was "impugned" as "being against charitie, against the lawe [of] nature, an imposition for the fathers' no offence." Interestingly, it was pointed out that the bill was "very perilous to all," since who was wholly English? It was "a thing that might be obiected to our children after two or three discentes [i.e., generations] and call every man's enheritance in question." Most significantly, however, it could have detrimental commercial effects: "under pretense/ of providing for the Queene's custome it would doe much harme."[53] The bill was sent to a committee, and returned with a different caveat: that Englishness would remain only as long as the children remained "dwelling in England and continue their sole obedience to the Queene of England" (ultimately the bill was quashed in the Lords).[54]

Late Elizabethan drama started to take stock of this challenge: in William Haughton's play *Englishmen For My Money Or A Woman Will Have Her Will* (c. 1598),[55] a usurer named "*Pisaro*, a Portingale [Portuguese]" (sig. A^v) attempts to deflect his daughters Laurentia, Marina, and Mathea from marrying their English gentlemen true loves, Harvie, Heigham, and Walgrave. Drawing on banal stereotypes, Haughton has Pisaro ply "the sweete loude trade of *Vsurie*" (sig. A2^r), and describe his modus operandi with the indebted prospective sons-in-law: "though I guild my Temples with a smile, / It is but *Iudas*-like, to worke their endes." He is Judas, the eponym of anti-Christian Jewry. He is "Signior Bottle-nose," whose "snoute" is "Able to shaddow *Powles*, it is so great," overshadowing the legendarily visible beacon of London's Christianity, St Paul's Cathedral.

Pisaro's opening speech describes his journey to his present state in life, how "euery Soyle to mee is naturall":

> Indeed by birth, I am a *Portingale*,
> Who driuen by Westerne winds on *English* shore,
> Heere liking of the soyle, I maried,
> And haue Three Daughters: But impartiall Death
> Long since, depriude mee of her dearest life:
> Since whose discease, in *London* I haue dwelt. (sig. A2^r)

But while Pisaro is the essence of diaspora—a seed that takes root anywhere—the play's comedy relies on the daughters being English rather than Portuguese. In his survey of "Elizabethans and Foreigners," G.K. Hunter sniffed that the "three daughters are (illogically enough) totally English in outlook."[56] But this is precisely what happens when the windblown seed takes root in London. Daughter Mathea makes this very clear, as she berates whom she thinks is her French suitor:

> Heare you *Frenchman*, packe to your Whores in *Fraunce*;
> Though I am *Portingale* by the Fathers side,
> And therefore should be lustfull, wanton, light;
> Yet goodman Goosecap, I will let you know,
> That I haue so much *English* by the Mother,
> That no bace slauering *French* shall make me stoope: (sig. G4^v)

English-born and resolutely "English" characters such as Usurie and Pisaro's daughters, second generation immigrants of Jewish heritage, reflected a particular and recognizable constituency in London life. Pisaro and his daughters are specifically described by Heigham as living in the street "Croched-Fryers" (sig. B^r), a detail that may have had significant import to the play's original audience. When Thomas Coryate visited Constantinople in April 1613, he was invited to witness a Jewish ritual circumcision in a private house in Galata. This, he explains, is "the house of a certaine English Jew, called Amis, borne in the Crootched Friers in London, who hath two sisters more of his owne Jewish Religion, Comorant in Galata, who were likewise borne in the same place." Coryate claims that Amis was, in 1613, sixty years old (making his birth date c. 1552–3), and had lived in England "till hee was thirtie yeeres of age" (until c. 1583).[57] These London-born expatriate English siblings have been identified as Jacob, Rachel, and Elizabeth Añes, three children of Dunstan Añes.[58] "Dunstan Ames," as he was most commonly known, rose to become a Freeman of the Grocers' Company in 1557, to be appointed "Purveyor and Merchant for the Queen's Majestie's Grocery," and to receive a coat of arms in 1568. On his death in 1594, he was buried in the north quire of his local church, St Olave's in Hart Street.[59] And yet this pillar of London guild and Anglican parish life was in fact born Gonsalvo Añes in Valladolid; he commonly used his Hebraic name of Benjamin, and gave five of his children Jewish names.[60] And, as Coryate testifies, at least three of his children at some stage of their lives decided to give up their identity as London Protestants and live and worship openly as Jews in a city that permitted such "apostasy."

The children of Dunstan Añes, Pisaro's daughters, and Robert Wilson's Usurie, point to the fluidity of commercial, ethnic, religious, and national affiliations in late Elizabethan London. The life stories of the Añes children suggest not only something of the capital's true cosmopolitanism, but also of the tensions and contradictions that cosmopolitanism failed to contain. In order to be a successful player in a global trade still centered on the great ports of the Mediterranean, London had to deal with overseas traders most of whom were not Protestant, and many of whom were non-Christian. Moreover, despite its best efforts, London could no longer see itself as somehow remote from and untainted by this Mediterranean world. Those elements that made London economically great—its immigrant artisans and its global merchants—were precisely the elements of which it could be least sure.

NOTES

1. Robert Wilson, *A right excellent and famous Comœdy, called the three Ladies of London* (London: Roger Warde, 1584).

2. Sidney L. Lee, "Elizabethan England and the Jews," *Transactions of the New Shakspere Society 1887–92*, 143–66 at pp. 144, 145.

3. F.J. Furnivall, "Introduction" to *The Century Shakspere* (1908) as quoted in Jacob Lopes Cardozo, *The Contemporary Jew in the Elizabethan Drama* (Amsterdam: H.J. Paris, 1925), p. 94.

4. M. Lindsay Kaplan, *William Shakespeare: The Merchant of Venice: Texts and Contexts* (Boston and New York: Bedford / St Martin's, 2002), p. 154.

5. Thomas Wilson, *A Discourse on Usury [1572]*, ed. R.H. Tawney (London: G. Bell, 1925), p. 232.

6. Lloyd Edward Kermode, "The Playwright's Prophecy: Robert Wilson's *Three Ladies of London* and the 'Alienation' of the English," *Medieval and Renaissance Drama in England* 11 (1999): 60–87 at p. 63.

7. Robert Brenner, *Merchants and Revolution: Commercial Change, Political Conflict, and London's Overseas Traders, 1550–1653* (Princeton: Princeton University Press, 1993).

8. Crystal Bartolovich, " 'Baseless Fabric': London as a 'World City' " in *"The Tempest" and its Travels*, ed. Peter Hulme and William Sherman (London: Reaktion, 2002), 13–26; and Phyllis Rackin, "The Impact of Global Trade in *The Merchant of Venice*," *Shakespeare Jahrbuch* 138 (2002): 73–88.

9. See Goran V. Stanivukovic, "Recent Studies of English Renaissance Literature of the Mediterranean," *English Literary Renaissance* 32:1 (Winter 2002): 168–86.

10. Sara Warneke, "A Taste for Newfangledness: The Destructive Potential of Novelty in Early Modern England," *Sixteenth Century Journal* 26 (1995): 881–96.

11. Ranulph Higden, *Polychronicon*, 9 vols., ed. Joseph Lumby Rawson (London: Longman et al., 1865–1886), 2:173.

12. Sir George Warner ed., *The Libelle of Englyshe Polycye: A Poem on the Use of Sea-Power 1436* (Oxford: Clarendon Press, 1926). I am grateful to Derrick Higginbotham for bringing this text to my attention.

13. William Harrison, *The Description of England*, ed. Georges Edelen (Ithaca: Cornell University Press / Folger Shakespeare Library, 1968), p. 359.

14. *A most pleasant and merie new Comedie, Intituled A Knacke to knowe a Knaue* (London: Richard Iones, 1594), sig. D4v.

15. Neville Williams, "The London Port Books," *Transactions of the London and Middlesex Archaeological Society* 18 (1955): 13–26 at p. 17.

16. The following discussion is based on the account in Thomas Cromwell's journal, printed in *Proceedings in the Parliaments of Elizabeth I vol.1 1558–1581*, ed. T.E. Hartley (Leicester: Leicester University Press, 1981). Simonds D'Ewes, *The Journals of All the Parliaments during the Reign of Queen Elizabeth*, rev. Paul Bowes (London: John Shirley, 1682); *Journals of the House of Commons* vol. 1 (n.p., n.d.); and entries in *The House of Commons 1558–1603*, 3 vols., ed. P.W. Hasler (London: HMSO / History of Parliament Trust, 1981), 1: 346–7, 3: 20–2 and 364–5.

17. Hartley, *Proceedings*, 1: 381, 385, 388, 397, 402. In 1576, a similar bill was introduced (1: 488, 489).

18. On Sekerston, see Hasler, *House of Commons 1558–1603*, 3: 364–5.

19. Hartley, *Proceedings*, 1: 386.

20. Wilson, *Discourse upon Usury*, 204.

21. Hartley, *Proceedings*, 1: 402.
22. Ibid., 1: 385, 387, 390, June 3 and 4, 1572.
23. Ibid., 1: 387, June 4, 1572.
24. Ibid., 1: 390, June 6, 1576, debates.
25. Kermode notes that measures in 1580 and 1592 aimed to stem immigration into London's suburbs by banning new house building within three miles of the city walls. Kermode, "The Playwright's Prophecy," p. 74.
26. Justus Lipsius, *A Direction for Trauilers*, trans. John Stradling (London: Cutbert Burbie, 1592), sig. B3r cited in Warneke, "A Taste for Newfangledness," p. 895.
27. Irene Scouloudi, *Returns of Strangers in the Metropolis 1593, 1627, 1635, 1639. A Study of an Active Minority* (London: Huguenot Society of London, 1985), passim; Steve Rappaport, *Worlds Within Worlds: Structures of Life in Sixteenth-Century London* (Cambridge: Cambridge University Press, 1989), pp. 54–60; Ian W. Archer, *The Pursuit of Stability: Social Relations in Elizabethan London* (Cambridge: Cambridge University Press, 1991), pp. 131–9.
28. Corporation of London Records Office, Journals of the Court of Common Council, 20: 176v–177v, discussed in Rappaport, *Worlds Within Worlds*, p. 55.
29. Cited in Patrick McGrath, ed., *Merchants and Merchandise in Seventeenth-Century Bristol* (Bristol: Bristol Record Society, 1955), p. 26.
30. Cited in David Harris Sacks, *Trade, Society and Politics in Bristol 1500–1640*, 2 vols. (New York and London: Garland Publishing, 1985), 1: 114–15.
31. Sacks, *Trade, Society and Politics*, 2: 570, 574.
32. Nabil Matar, *Islam in Britain 1558–1685* (Cambridge: Cambridge University Press, 1998), pp. 2–3.
33. Fernand Braudel, *The Mediterranean and the Mediterranean World in the Age of Philip II*, vol. 1 [1966], trans. Siân Reynolds [1972] (Berkeley: University of California Press, 1995), p. 347.
34. Robert Mantran, *İstanbul dans la seconde moitié du XVIIe siècle: Étude d'histoire institutionelle, économique et sociale* (Paris: Adrien Maisonneuve, 1962), pp. 44–5, cited in Braudel, *Mediterranean*, 1: 347–9.
35. William Biddulph, *The Travels of certaine Englishmen into Africa, Asia, Troy, Bythinia, Thracia, and to the Blacke Sea* (London: W. Aspley, 1609), sig. E4r, quoted in Kermode, "The Playwright's Prophecy," pp. 65–6.
36. Mantran, *İstanbul*, p. 44, pp. 57–63. On the Jewish community in early modern Constantinople, see also Avram Galante (Abraham Galanté), *Histoire des Juifs de Turquie* 9 vols. İstanbul: Editions Isis, [1985]); Avigdor Levy, *The Sephardim in the Ottoman Empire* (Princeton: Darwin Press, 1992).

37. See S.A. Skilliter, *William Harborne and the Trade with Turkey 1578–1582: A documentary study of the first Anglo-Ottoman relations* (Oxford: Oxford 0University Press for the British Academy, 1977), passim.

38. See, for example, Daniel J. Vitkus, "Turning Turk in *Othello*: The Conversion and Damnation of the Moor," *Shakespeare Quarterly* 48 (1997): 145–76; Matar, *Islam in Britain*, passim.

39. Bernardino de Mendoza to Philip II, November 28, 1579, cited in Skilliter, *Harborne*, p. 22.

40. Mendoza to Philip II, May 15, 1582, cited in Skilliter, *Harborne*, p. 24.

41. Skilliter, *Harborne*, p. 23.

42. "It is of double important to the Turk now, in consequence of the excommunication pronounced *ipse facto* by the Pope upon any person who provides or sells to infidels such materials as these." Mendoza to Philip II, May 15, 1582, cited in Skilliter, *Harborne*, p. 24.

43. See Mendoza to Philip II, November 28, 1579, December 28, 1579, January 9, 1581, cited in Skilliter, *Harborne*, pp. 24, 25.

44. Jacques de Germigny to Henri III, May 1580. E. Charrière, *Négociations de la France dans le Levant*, 4 vols. (Paris, 1848–1860) 3: 907n, quoted in Skilliter, *Harborne*, p. 25.

45. Skilliter, *Harborne*, p. 75.

46. "A consideration of *the* trade into Turky. 1580. By mr Sec. Walsingham. BL Cotton MS Nero B. xi. ff. pp. 280–1, published in Skilliter, *Harborne*, pp. 28–30 at p. 28, and dated at ca. 1578.

47. Kermode, "The Playwright's Prophecy," p. 63.

48. Stephen Gosson, *The Schoole of Abuse* (London: Thomas Woodcocke, 1579) sig. C6v.

49. Robert Wilson, *The pleasant and stately morall, of the three lordes and three ladies of London* (London: Richard Jhones, 1590), sig. F4r.

50. Hartley, *Proccedings*, 1: 481–2, February 21, 1576.

51. Ibid., 1: 486. *The Commons' Journal* (1: 110) suggests it was "committeed" rather than "rejected."

52. Ibid., *ccc*1: 527.

53. Ibid., 1: 528, January 27, 1581.

54. Ibid., 1: 531, 532, 533, 537; *CJ* 1: 127, February 3, 4, 8 and 17, 1581.

55. William Haughton, *English-men For my Money: or, A pleasant Comedy, called, A Woman will haue her Will* (London: W. White, 1616). See also Edmund Campos, "Jews, Spaniards and Portingales: Ambiguous Identities of Portuguese Marranos," *ELH* 69 (2002): 599–616; Alan Stewart, "Portingale Women and Politics in Late Elizabethan London" in *Rethinking Women and Politics in Early Modern England, 1450–1700*, ed. James Daybell (Basingstoke: Ashgate, 2004), pp. 83–98.

56. G.K. Hunter, "Elizabethans and Foreigners," in *Shakespeare in His Own Age*, ed. Allardyce Nicoll, *Shakespeare Survey* 17 (1964): 37–52 at p. 43.

57. "Master Coryats Constantinopolitan Observations Abridged" in *Hakluytus Posthumus or Purchas His Pilgrimes: Contayning a History of the World in Sea Voyages and Lande Travells by Englishmen and others*, vol. 10, ed. Samuel Purchas (Glasgow: James MacLehose and Sons, 1905), pp. 427–8.

58. Identified in Lucien Wolf, "Jews in Elizabethan England," *The Jewish Historical Society of England. Transactions Sessions* 11 (1928): 1–91 at pp. 14–16; and E.R. Samuel, "Portuguese Jews in Jacobean London," *TJHSE* 18 (1958): 171–230 at p. 179 and 179n.1.

59. Anes's own burial is not in the register, but other entries refer to the location of his tomb. *The Registers of St. Olave, Hart Street, London. 1563–1700*, ed. W. Bruce Bannerman (London: Harleian Society, 1916), pp. 128, 131, 132.

60. See Edgar Samuel, "Anes, Dunstan," in *Oxford Dictionary of National Biography* (Oxford: Oxford University Press, 2004), available at http://www.oxforddnb.com (accessed September 4, 2006).

CHAPTER 9

BARNABY RICHE'S APPROPRIATION
OF IRELAND AND THE
MEDITERRANEAN WORLD,
OR HOW IRISH IS "THE TURK"?

Constance C. Relihan

Barnaby Riche was a prolific early modern writer who, as Eugene Flanagan puts it, is distinctive for having demonstrated "resilience in the shadow of [his] own marginality."[1] Riche (or Rich) is best known, perhaps, for his *Riche His Farewell to Militarie Profession* (1581), a collection of eight Boccaccian *novelle* and a major source for Shakespeare's *Twelfth Night*. He is also the author of an additional twenty-five works published between 1574 and 1617. Included among these texts are prose romances, *The Straunge and Wonderfull Aduentures of Don Simonides* (tome 1, 1581 / tome 2, 1584) and *The Aduentures of Brusanus, Prince of Hungaria* (1592) which, like most of the chivalric romances of the period, set their title characters ranging over wide expanses of geographic space, and engage in the fictional representation of imagined locations and cultures. Riche also produced texts, such as *A Short Survey of Ireland* (1609), *A New Description of Ireland* (1610), and *The Irish Hubbub; or, the English Hue and Crie* (1619), which grew out of his lengthy military service in Ireland,[2] and which engage in a less fictional way with the representations of cultural differences than do his romances and *novelle*. The three texts on Ireland named above are all texts of social criticism in which Riche attacks elements of English and Irish culture directly rather than, as might be expected at least from the *Short Survey* and *New Description*, works of ostensibly objective geographical and cultural description. As Riche explains early in the *New Description*, "My meaning is not to make any Cosmographicall description of *Ireland*, I haue nothing to do with Longitude, with Latitude, nor with Altitude: I will not speake of the Countrey how it stretcheth it selfe towards the East, or towardes the west, nor how it is deuided into Prouinces, into Shires, nor into Countries."[3] The representation and critique of various social practices these works contain, from religious rituals to burial customs and work habits, provides Riche with opportunities to educate his readers about both England and Ireland. These three Irish texts, in other words, engage in cultural didacticism directly, informing Riche's English readers of the nature of the Irish people and their cultural practices; Riche's prose fiction, in contract, participates in such didactic practices more obliquely, constructing representations of peoples and cultures under the veil of the traditional exoticism of romance conventions.

Understanding the relationship between historical and ostensibly fictional cultural representation and didacticism in Riche's work may, like comparisons between Edmund Spenser's representations of Ireland in *A View of the State of Ireland* (1598) and *The Faerie Queene* (1596), permit us to understand more thoroughly the relationship between early modern English nationalism, the growth of the British empire, and the ways in which English culture constituted and promulgated its national identity. In many ways Riche, as a perhaps less remarkable writer than Spenser, provides us with a better means of understanding the interrelation between fictional and nonfictional geographic representation during the period as it was understood by a broad swath of nonaristocratic members of early modern English culture as a whole. Moreover, analyzing the geographic discourse of these two pairs of texts by Riche can help us to understand fully the complex relationship between early modern romance and fictional histories and the construction of cultural difference. Because fictional narratives must be located in a specific setting, they require their authors to engage in geographic and ethnographic discourse, even if only in a limited way. Early modern fictional narratives directed at English readers who were unlikely to have visited the cultures in which they were set, provided their readers with knowledge of foreign cultures and attitudes toward cultural difference.[4] Put more reductively and polemically, placing the geographic discourse in these four texts in conversation with each other can help us examine the relationship between two of the cultures marked as "Other" to early modern England and answer the question: "Is 'the Great Turk' Irish?"

RICHE IN IRELAND

Barnaby Riche was a soldier as well as a writer and social critic.[5] He lacked a university degree and seems to have had recurrent financial problems, both during the years he spent stationed in Ireland, and during his time in England and the Low Countries. Much of the ideological impulse that seems to drive his writing can be found expressed in the prefatory epistle "To the Noble Soldiers of England and Ireland" appended to his *Farewell to Militarie Profession*, which begins:

> There is an old proverb, noble soldiers, and thus it followeth: "it is better to be happy than wise." But what it is to be happy how should I decipher, who never in my life could yet attain to any hap at all that was good. And yet I have had soldier's luck and speed as well as the rest of my profession. And with wisdom I will not meddle—I never came where it grew—but this I dare boldly affirm, and the experience of the present time doth make daily proof, that wit stands by in a threadbare coat where folly sometimes sits in a velvet gown. And how often is it seen that vice shall be advanced where virtue is little or naught at all regarded; small desert shall highly be preferred, where well-doing shall go unrewarded; and flattery shall be welcomed for a guest of great account where plain Tom-tell-troth shall be thrust out of doors by the shoulders: and to speak a plain truth indeed, do ye not see pipers, parasites, fiddlers, dancers, players, jesters, and such others, better esteemed and made of, and greater benevolence used toward them, than to any others that endeavor themselves to the most commendable qualities?[6]

It is a lengthy quotation but it sums up Riche's abiding concerns: the merits of a life based on male, military values and the decay of cultural values made obvious by England's rejection of individuals possessing "commendable qualities" in preference for those he refers to in *Brusanus* as "carpet knight[s]."[7] Riche's texts on Ireland amplify and repeat these concerns, and, in fact, they often do so in ways that erase the literal geography of Ireland, replacing it with an ideologically based abstract construction that permits Riche to articulate his social criticism: Ireland as a physical, geographic location is almost entirely absent from these texts. While there is a token gesture at the beginning of the *New Description* to physical description, it is largely contained within a prefatory epistle Riche dedicates to Sir William

Cokayne; in *A Short Survey of Ireland*;[8] however, Riche almost entirely avoids geographic information, erasing any of the implications of physical space the term "survey" might seem to suggest. Instead, the text presents an almost unrelenting ideological attack on Catholicism. The *Survey's* first chapter, "A description of the Countrey, with the maners, customes and dispositions of the people" (sig. B[r]), for instance, informs us that Ireland enjoys a temperate climate, has no snakes, and engages in "strange" (sig. B[v]) burial customs, but those bits of information are throwaway lines, tangential to the main subject of the text that Riche articulates toward the end of the chapter:

> *Ireland* hath euermore striued to runne into all lawlesse and irregular courses, whereby they are growne into such a habite of sauage tyranny, that nothing is more pleasing to the greatest number of them, then ciuill warres, murthers and massacres, whereunto as they are commonly inclined, so there wants not those amongst the[m] to pricke them forward, and to stirre them vp to Treason and rebellion against their Prince, that are still co[n]spiring, still practising, and still indeuouring to draw them into that mortall plague of rebellion, which is not to be cured but by the sword, by common slaughters and spilling of blood. (sig. B2[r])

The cause of this corruption is, not surprisingly, the Catholic Church, and the remainder of the text is devoted to explaining how we may know that the Pope is the Antichrist.

In the context of the social and religious polemic that dominates Riche's *Short Survey*, Ireland itself—and in fact any concrete representations of place or cultural practice—dwindles to insignificance. The cultures that are more important to the text are those of the Turks and the Jews, because Riche needs to distinguish the Pope from other contenders for the title of "Antichrist." For Riche in this text, the Antichrist must be an individual and he must be a deceiver. The Jews, in Riche's argument, were misguided by a misinterpretation of scripture, and were not motivated by malice; besides Judaism has neither a centralized hierarchy nor, analogous to the Pope a single figure, who could rise to the stature of "Antichrist." Riche's focus for comparison, then, becomes the Turk: the Pope in his guise as Antichrist, Riche argues, "must neither shew himselfe to be an open enemie to Christ, as was *Mahomet*, and as the *Turke* is, neither must he take vpon him to bee Christ, for then euery man would be warie enough of him" (sig. C[r]).[9] Catholicism becomes in this formulation a pernicious disguise the Turk wears; the Turk becomes what the Pope wishes he could be. Riche expands upon this connection in *A New Description*:

> [*There are many Sorcerers*] and the Countrey doth no lesse abound with *Witches*, and no marvel that it should so do, for the Deuill hath euer bin most frequent and conuersant amongst Infidels, Turks, Papistes, & such other, that doe neither know nor loue god, then he can be amongst those that are the true professors of the Gospell of Christ.[10]

"Infidels, Turks, Papistes"—the three are easily and unhesitatingly linked in Riche's ideology. Slightly later in the same work he rephrases the same conflation in slightly different terms:

> The wilde vnciuill *Scythians*, doe forbeare to be cruell the one against the other. The *Canibals*, deuourers of mens flesh, doe leaue to bee fierce amongst themselues, but the Irish, without all respect, are euermost cruel to their very next neighbours.[11]

"Scythians," "Canibals," and "the Irish" are easy substitutes in Riche's writing for Turks, infidels, and papists, emphasizing the lack of civilization in Ireland and the quiet linking Riche makes between Ireland and "the Turk."

The Irish Hubbub (1619), like the other two Irish texts discussed here, is also intriguingly devoid of specific details about Ireland and the Irish.[12] In this text Riche defines the term of his title (as the shout the Irish give "when any Rebels or Theeues came to doe any robbery in the Countrey" [p. 1]) and a related term, "to weep Irish" ("to weepe at pleasure, without either cause or greefe" [p. 2]), and then describes for his readers a number of practices, not necessarily occurring in Ireland, that merit the raising of the "hubbub."[13] Riche attacks male fashions, female vices, drunkenness, the use of tobacco, promiscuity, blasphemy—objects of Riche's contempt in many of his nonfictional works. Ireland itself is irrelevant to his discussion and, in fact, his relationship to Irish culture is variously and ambiguously defined. The distance from and contempt for Irish culture that clearly dominates *A Short Survey of Ireland* occasionally in this text gives way to identification with the Irish, and Riche's voice even grudgingly raises the possibility that Irish culture has suffered primarily as a result of England's interference with it:

> I might speake of some other vices, rather exceeding amongst the *Irish*, by the ill example of the *English*: And although the *Irish* haue vices enow of their owne, they need no incouragement to sin, yet *Ireland* for

these many yeares hath bin the receptacle for our *English* runnagates, that for their mis-led liues in *England*, do come running ouer into *Ireland*, some for murther, some for theft, some that haue spent themselues in ryot & excesse, are driuen ouer for debt, some come running ouer with other mens goods, some with other mens wiues, but a great number now lately, that are more hurtfull then all the rest, and those be Recusants. (p. 51)

Once again, his focus returns to Catholicism that remains for Riche the defining quality of Irish culture and the Irish landscape. And again Irish Catholicism and the Turk are linked, in this case through Riche's brief reference to "*English* runnagates." "Runnagate" is a form of "renegade" or "renegado," a term most often applied in the period to Christians who had renounced their Christianity and "turned Turk."

Such language provides Riche with a subtle context into which he may drop quick references to Mediterranean and North African cultures and peoples in order to amplify the taxonomies of cultural difference he is creating between English / Christian and Irish / Antichrist culture. These brief references provide a means of characterizing and stigmatizing cultural practices. For example, the Irish practice of keening is linked to the East, being "fitter for Infidels and Barbarians, then to bee in vse and custome among Christians" (p. 2).[14] Similarly, English women who use cosmetics "do paint with *Indian* excrements, and besmeare themselues with *Iewish spittle*" (p. 15); tobacco is described as originating "from a people that are Infidells and Aliens to God, truely reputed to bee the verie refuse of the world" (p. 44). In addition, Riche uses cultural difference to try to shame his readers, noting that "The Turkes and Infidells are more respectiue to obserue an oath that they doe make in the name of their *Mahomet*, then we that be Christians, when wee sweare by the name of the liuing God" (p. 30). Even a catalogue of laws developed by past rulers throughout the world becomes a subtle means for reinforcing distaste for the Mediterranean world:

There is not a more dangerous thing then to put an office into his hand that is both wise and wicked, or to arme him with power & authority that is of a couetous disposition; the eye of wisdom, that in former ages would looke into these enormities, was very vigilant and carefull to preuent them, and pro[vided] Lawes, whereby to bridle (not onely these) but diuers [other] abuses, which from time to time were hatched vp. Lycurgus made a law against drunkennesse, *Augustus Caesar* against pompous buildings, the *Lucanes* against prodigality, the *Lacedemonians* against excesse in apparell, the *Aegyptians* against whoredome, the *Thebanes* against negligent Parents, that brought vp their children in idlenesse and insolency. (p. 33)

The Mediterranean world, in other words, provides Riche with examples that both shame English and Irish practice, and that link sexual crimes to the North African Egyptians while linking other crimes (of duty, proportion, and responsibility) to classical cultures; moreover, the implications of Riche's text and its title is that all of these vices are to be found among the Irish.

THE ROMANCE WORLD OF RICHE

While Ireland and its people are a perpetual concern for Riche's non-fiction, they hardly appear at all in his fictional works. *The Straunge and Wonderfull Aduentures of Don Simonides* (tome 1, 1581 / tome 2, 1584) and *The Aduentures of Brusanus, Prince of Hungaria* (1592) contain no references to Ireland.[15] Only in the prefatory material to his *Farewell to Militarie Profession* does Riche name Ireland, as the place where he was living when he wrote the stories the *Farewell* contains and as the home of some of the "Ladies" to whom he directs his text. Despite this difference, Riche's fiction often serves largely to provide a platform from which Riche's characters and narrators may decry the social ills of contemporary culture, the kind of ills articulated in the *Farewell's* preface to soldiers quoted early in this essay, and to subtly amplify the taxonomies of cultural difference his nonfiction texts define. The hero in *Don Simonides*, for example, as a knight from Seville—or as it is typically spelled "Ciuile"—travels widely through the European and Mediterranean world, and the result of his travels is that he "found women inconstaunt, the world vnstable, pleasure still [f]adyng, hope vncertaine, expence remedilesse, lost tyme vnrecouerable" (p. 6). And Riche's narrator refuses to let the reader miss the didactic point, noting that the "mischeef" Don Simonides encounters "maie as well raigne in *England* as in *Spayne*" (p. 6).

The relationship between the travels of Don Simonides—from Spain to, among other places, Rome, Ferrara, Pavia, Venice, Genoa, Naples, and Athens—and the kind of cultural discourse found in Riche's Irish texts is yoked through a similarity of language that links the romance's implicit cultural criticism with the critique of Irish culture found elsewhere. In the second tome of *Don Simonides*, for example, the narrator provides the following list of good laws enacted by various cultures:

> There is no vice but Lawe bridleth it, yea, whatsoeuer past from the verie *Ethnycke*, did alwaies abate the power of excesse. *Dionisious* of *Siracusa*, though otherwise a Tirant, yet in this made a wise Lawe, that those whiche excessiuely gaue them selues to banquetyng should be

> punished very asperly. *Licurgus*, made Lawes against Dronkennesse, the
> *Romaines* against wicked and vngodly Whorehunting, the *Grecians*,
> against incest, the *Lacedemonians* against excesse in apparell. *Augustus
> Ceaser*, against pompious buildynges, the *Lucans*, against prodigalitie,
> ye *Ægiptians*, against Usurie, the *Thebans*, against iniurious Parentes,
> the *Romaines*, against cruell and hard harted Maisters. (p. 18)

Some of this language is adapted later, as we have seen, when Riche
writes the *The Irish Hubbub*, but in this case, sexual crimes are ascribed
to the Romans and Greeks (cultures I would argue that Riche often
sees as having been lost to Christianity and fallen away from their classical grandeur), and the Egyptians are linked to a crime typically, in
the period, associated with Judaism. The search that the Sevillian Don
Simonides makes for civility forces him to engage with the same language that gets used in the context of defining Irish culture. The ways
in which cultural difference is created in *Don Simonides*, in other
words, mirrors his discursive strategies in attacking the Irish in his
nonfiction texts.

A discursive link between the Mediterranean world and Riche's
nonfiction is also established in *The Adventures of Brusanus, Prince of
Hungaria*, but in a different fashion. This romance, like *Don
Simonides* recounts the adventures of a young prince as he matures
into adulthood from inauspicious beginnings:

> But in the quality of his minde, hee was so spotted with voluptuous-
> nesse so nusled in wantonnes, so giuen ouer to licentiousnesse, so
> linked to wilfulnesse, and so caried away with all kind of wickednesse,
> that neither feare of god, the displeasure of his parents, the sundry
> admonitions of his carefull and louing friendes, nor the regard of his
> owne honour could make him desiste or driue him from this detestable
> kind of life (p. 6).

Brusanus's growth and education lead him to bring his home kingdom
of Hungaria and its allies to the brink of war before he is able to complete his education in civility, justice, and love, and he and his compan-
ions travel throughout Asia Minor, Italy, central Europe, and Greece.
The romance begins, however, by reference to cultural difference:

> At that time when the most renowned Liberius gouerned the empire of
> Constantinople holding the parts of Cayre Soria, Calypha, and all
> Grecia in the most christian & catholicke faith, at that very instant ther
> raigned likewise in Hungaria [th]e noble king Myletto. . . . (p. 5)

Probably the reference is to the fourth century Pope Liberius (352–66), but the time of Christian unity and supremacy that Riche here describes in the romance's opening line is an idealized, fairytale impossibility that has been replaced by difference and schism. The use of the hendiadys "catholycke & christian" makes that clear. *Brusanus*, and in fact all of Riche's fictions, are located a world that has fallen away from the idyllic unity that "catholycke & christian" suggests. "Catholycke" for Riche has become the Papist idolatry rampant in Ireland and threatening to overwhelm the "christian" English, turning them into "runnagates" corrupted by Irish culture.

> At the conclusion of *A New Description of Ireland*, Riche writes: to this ende and porpose I have written this Booke, not against any Papist in particular, but against Popery in generall; for Popery in Ireland is the original of a number of imperfections, that otherwise would bee reformed, and it is Popery onely that hath secluded the *English* and the *Irish* from that perfect loue and amity, which else would be imbraced on both partes aswell to the glory of God as to the great benefit of this Countrey.

> God bring it once to passe, that wee might all ioyne together as well *English* as *Irish*, in the true acknowledgement of one God, of one Religion, of one King, of one Law, and of one loue, this is all that I wish for, and this is all that I haue indeuoured.[16]

Riche, in other words, desires a world in which English Protestantism has colonized all forms of cultural difference—"Infidels, Turks, Papistes"; "Scythians," "Canibals," and "the Irish"—all should become converted to a singular king, law, and religion based on the virtues that English Protestantism embodies and opposes those unruly traits Irish culture represents. It is of course too reductive and facile to say that for Riche "the Turke" is an Irishman, but it is perhaps less glib to say that Riche's Irishman is "the Turke." The discourse Riche uses in his anti-Irish texts mimics and echoes that of his romances, leading us to see these two very different kinds of discourse as engaged in the same colonizing project.

NOTES

1. Eugene Flanagan, "The Anatomy of Jacobean Ireland: Captain Barnaby Rich, Sir John Davies and the Failure of Reform, 1609–22," in *Political Ideology in Ireland, 1541–1641*, ed. Hiram Morgan (Dublin: Four Courts Press, 1999), p. 158.

2. Riche was first sent to Ireland in 1570. Although he did not remain there permanently, he spent substantial portions of his life there, serving, as Donald Beecher puts it, as James I's "chief ferret in Ireland" (Beecher, "Introduction," *Barnabe Riche His Farewell to Military Profession* [Ottawa: Dovehouse, 1992], p. 25). He died in Ireland in 1617.

3. *A New Description of Ireland: Wherein is described the disposition of the Irish whereunto they are inclined*, STC 20992. (Ann Arbor: Early English Books microfilm, reel #728), p. 4.

4. I pursue this subject at much greater length in *Cosmographical Glasses: Geographic Discourse, Gender, and Elizabethan Fiction* (Kent, OH: Kent State University Press, 2004).

5. See the introduction to Barnabe Riche, *His Farewell*, ed. Beecher, pp. 13–27.

6. Riche, *His Farewell*, p. 127.

7. *The Adventures of Brusanus* (London, 1592). Early English Prose Fiction Full-Text Database (Cambridge: Chadwick-Healey, 1997), p. 127, 130. All citations to this text are from this edition.

8. The full title is *A Svrvey of Ireland. Trvely Discovering Who It Is That Hath so armed the hearts of that people with disobedience to their Prince. With a description of the Countrey, and the condition of the people. No lesse necessarie and needful to be respected by the English, then requisite and behoouefull to be reformed in the Irish*. The title page of the Huntington Library edition included in the Early English Books microfilm series misprints the date of publication as "1069."

9. Riche makes the same point at sig. D3r-v.

10. *A New Description of Ireland*, p. 9.

11. Ibid., p. 18.

12. The full title is *The Irish Hubbub or The English Hue and Crie. Briefly Pursuing the base conditions, and most notorious offences of this vaile, vaine, and wicked AGE* (London, 1619), STC 20990 (Ann Arbor: Early English Books Microfilm, reel #635). References are to this edition by page number.

13. A similar description of both the hubbab and "to weep Irish" is contained in *A New Description of Ireland*.

14. For a discussion of English responses to the practice, see Bruce R. Smith, *The Acoustic World of Early Modern England: Attending to the O-Factor* (Chicago: University of Chicago Press, 1999), pp. 303–8.

15. The complete titles of these texts are *The Straunge and Wonderfull Aduentures of Don Simonides, a gentilman Spaniarde: Conteinyng verie pleasaunte discourse: Gathered for the recreation as well of our noble yong gentilmen, as our honourable courtly Ladies: by Barnabe Riche ge[n]tilman (1581); The Second tome of the Trauailes and aduentures of Don Simonides, enterlaced with varietie of Historie, wherein the curteous and not curious Reader, maine finde matters so leueled, as maie suffice to please all humours. For malancholie men, they shall not neede to saile to Anticera, for here they shall finde pleasaunt*

expulsiues. For merrie myndes, sober discourses to preuent excesse. For deuoute, wholesome lessons to confirme their contemplatio[n]. For al sortes, such delightes as neither alow this is of daliaunce, nor discommende honest pleasure. Written by Barnabe Riche, Gentleman (1584); and, The Aduentures of Brusanus, Prince of Hungaria, Pleasant for all to read, and profitable for some to follow. Written by Barnaby Riche, seauen or eight yeares sithence, and now published by the great intreaty of diuers of his freendes (1592).

16. See Regina Schneider, "Late Tudor Narrative Voice(s): Philip Sidney and Barnaby Rich," in *The Anatomy of Tudor Literature*, ed. Mike Pincombe (Aldershot: Ashgate, 1999), pp. 90–153.

CHAPTER 10

THEATERS OF EMPIRE IN
MILTON'S EPICS

Elizabeth Sauer

Empires of the ancient world and the Ottoman and Catholic Empires of the early modern period occupied a significant place in England's conception of its cultural, religious, geographical, and imperial identity. In the early modern era, the Mediterranean world became the seat of the Ottoman Empire that claimed Roman succession on the basis of Mehmed II's conquest of Constantinople in 1453. This empire was the direct geographical heir to the Byzantine Empire, expanding in the sixteenth century into the Mediterranean seas. Christian Europe defined itself in opposition to the Muslims, who spread through much of eastern Asia and the Barbary Coast, the southeastern part of Europe, and the regions stretching from Arabia to Egypt, Mesopotamia (modern Iraq), the Crimea, and Hungary.

Emerging as an imperial nation whose identity had been mediated by the Reformation, England viewed its role as a defender of Protestantism from papacy; yet the nation's battle against Islam was one it shared with Catholics—a commonality the English did not advertise. Catholic European nations in turn had forged many of their social aspirations and characteristics in their long holy war with the Muslim world.[1]

As empires are discursively produced, literature furthered the development of England's national identity, to which the poet and polemicist John Milton, a champion apologist for seventeenth-century England, contributed substantially. The epic in particular served Milton as an ideal genre, its encyclopedic scope enabling a sweeping surveillance and "the classification of space under the commanding eye of English standards.[2] The revelation of postlapsarian history in the prophetic books of Milton's *Paradise Lost*, a focal point for this chapter, begins with Michael guiding Adam to the highest hill of Paradise to present a geographic "prospect" of "the Seat[s] / Of Mightiest Empire" (11.386–87). This panorama anticipates the temptation of empires (of Eastern Europe, the Mediterranean, the Barbary Coast, Asia, and the Near and Far East) to which Satan subjects the Son in *Paradise Regained* (3.252ff).[3] On one hand, Milton resolutely attacks imperialist ideologies and practices, including the proposition that commerce is innocent of imperial aims. Thus he portrays Satan as a despotic Sultan in *Paradise Lost* and also freights his voyage with images of the spice trade. Further, he reproaches the domination of one people by another that begins with Nimrod who "arrogate[s] Dominion undeserv'd / Over his brethren" (12.27–28). On the other, Milton's deployment of the language of orientalism and English dominion implicates him in acts of imperialism.[4] Milton in fact works out his response to imperialism on both sides of the divide.

This chapter thus investigates how Milton's representations of the Mediterranean index his complex views on empire, whether ancient or modern, foreign or British. Though he conceives of them as distinct, Milton in key passages in his epics surveys and catalogues the various empires that border on the Mediterranean—the regions west of Eden. The map included as part of the front matter in one of Milton's sources, George Sandys's *Relation of a Journey*, charts what once were "the most renowned countries and kingdoms: once the seats of most glorious and triumphant Empires; the theaters of valor and heroicall actions" and identifies the Mediterranean around which the empires are situated as the "Mid-Land Sea."[5] Indeed the Mediterranean is a meeting point or cross section for various continents and cultures. For Protestant Europeans, ancient Romans (-turned- Papist), Babylonians, and Turks represent Satanic forces that pose a constant threat.[6] A providential reading of history through "the imperial oversight of a geographic eye" provides a lens for interpreting the age-old contest between imperial powers. Bruce McLeod is more than justified in declaring that Milton "view[ed] geography as prophetic."[7] The result is a complication of interests that pitted the imperial English nation against the ancient worlds and modern Islamic and Catholic empires, as Milton's epics reveal.

The catalogues of empires in *Paradise Lost* and *Paradise Regained* extend the boundaries of maps of Britain as found in such works as

The Theatre of the Empire of Great Britaine (1611), the term "Theatre" being derived from the 1606 English edition of Ortelius's *Theatrum orbis terrarum*.[8] What such geographical representations display and omit is furnished by the cultural and literary imagination, geography being as much concerned with "relations of Manners, Religion, Government and such like" as with "Longitudes and Latitudes."[9] Milton's descriptive geography as conveyed in his literary works reveals an indebtedness to early modern maps and travel narratives and compendiums. His use of such sources as John Speed, George Sandys, Samuel Purchas, and Peter Heylyn, to which the first section of this chapter is devoted, betrays his (and England's) fascination with a globe-consuming vision that complicates the process of national self-definition as well as of self-fashioning. This chapter thus builds on previous studies of Milton's imperialism, first by examining the Mediterranean as a site of convergence of different manifestations of empire—classical and contemporary—and then by demonstrating that the engagement with geographical, cultural, and imperial otherness is ultimately transferred to the interior landscape, the mental landscape.[10] In effect, Milton historicizes and rehearses the plot of Shakespearean tragedy of Othello, who defeats the Turkish fleet early in Act II of the play, a victory that would have reminded London audiences of the demise of the Catholic Spanish Armada nearly two decades earlier. Thereupon, however, Othello falls prey to the poisonous rhetoric of Iago and to his own internal conflicts that are coded Moorish, Turkish, and barbaric.[11] The English-Mediterranean journey that Milton undertakes likewise leads to what constitutes in *Paradise Regained* the ultimate temptation—the empire of the mind (*PR* 4. 223–33).

*   *   *

The forms of nationhood[12] through which the Europeans surveyed and classified the world generally and the Mediterranean in particular included chorographical works as maps and travel literature. Among the travel books available to Milton was the above-mentioned *Relation of a Journey* by George Sandys, which, by lending a sense of contemporaneity to classical geography, anticipated Milton's own treatment of geographical coordinates and place names.[13] Another contemporary source, the popular geographical history compiled by the Essex minister, Samuel Purchas, drew on seven hundred authors who grew to thirteen hundred by the time of the final edition. Following the death in 1616 of Hakluyt, author of *Principal Navigations* (final edition 1598–1600), Purchas secured many of Hakluyt's materials in preparing the 1625 *Hakluytus Posthumus or Purchas His Pilgrimes*. Purchas's various editions of the *Pilgrimes* presented geographies and natural histories of non-European regions. The contents alone do not tell the full story: one must also consider the politics, polemics, and perspectives through which such narratives are presented. Purchas in fact furnished the English colonial movement with a "philosophical statement of purpose,"[14] supplying information and the impetus that fueled imperial ambitions. As suggested from the "Epistle Dedicatorie" where he declares his intent to "shew the Paganisme of Antichristian Poperie" [n.p.] right through to his condemnation of Spanish atrocities in the New World recounted in the final chapter of the *Pilgrimes*, Purchas was convinced that Christianity was under siege both by the Catholic and Islamic powers.[15] Lesley B. Cormack acknowledges, "What Purchas contributed to English descriptive geography was a growing Protestant bias and an increasing belief in the ability and need of the English to achieve a Protestant hegemony over the pagan and Catholic world."[16] While Purchas's geography was for Milton considerably less authoritative than Peter Heylyn's,[17] Milton was certainly familiar with the work and quoted it in his commonplace book; occasional passages from the *Pilgrimes* also informed his poetry. The descriptive accounts of Eden in *Paradise Lost* and the Book 11 catalogue of empires, as well as the Book 3 lists of Parthian equipment in *Paradise Regained* (3.311 ff), replete with place names, raise the ghost of Purchas.

Though unmistakably royalist, Peter Heylyn's compendium had the greatest influence on Milton's geographical surveying, both in terms of the information it supplied and the philosophy that underlay it. The impressive publication history of *Cosmographie in Four Books* included six editions between 1652 and 1670. Passages were probably read to Milton in the period of his blindness, and, having judged the *Cosmographie* as authoritative and compendious, he was prepared to see the world through Heylyn's eyes. Moreover, the book provides a model for reading the relationship of history, cosmography, religion, and moral decline, thus exposing the "causes of that desolation which hath hapned in the Civill State of those mighty Empires" which "were grown a scandall unto *Christianity*."[18] Heylyn explains in his Introduction that the "intermixing" of History and Geography produces a "universal Comprehension of *Naturall* and *Civill* story, which by a proper and distinct name may be termed *Cosmography*" (1:28). For the purposes of this chapter, it is also noteworthy that each of the four books in Heylyn's work touches on Mediterranean sites, including Spain, Italy and France in Book 1, Greece and the Greek Islands in Book 2, Turcomania, Syria, and Palestine in Book 3, and the Barbary Coast, Libya, and Egypt in Book 4. The Mediterranean thus serves as a focus for various nations that Heylyn brings into Milton's "amplest reach" (PL 11.380). Ultimately, it also offers a language for describing the inward landscape and mental journey to which the national, imperial conflicts—and epic battles—are ultimately transferred.

*   *   *

Since the early stages of his literary and political career, Milton specifically associated Turkish culture with Catholic repression and despotism. He compared, for example, the English Parliament's introduction of the 1643 Licensing Order not only with the Popish Inquisition but also with the Muslim's slavish adherence to the Qur'an—"that policie wherewith the Turk upholds his *Alcoran* by prohibition of Printing."[19] These related censorship practices all denied civil liberties and retarded the advancement of Truth and of the Reformation. Most frequently, the Turk is associated with monarchical corruption and imperialism. Milton's commissioned work, *Observations on the Articles of Peace*, for example, attacks the earl of Ormond's proposed style of government which, Milton claims, is modeled on that of the Turks: "He [Ormond] passes on in his groundless conjectures, that the aime of this Parliament may be perhaps to set up first and elective Kingdome, and after that a perfect Turkish tyranny" (CPW 3:312). Milton connects Ormond's political machinations to those of "the late King himself, with *Strafford*, and that arch Prelat of *Canterbury*, his chief Instruments; whose designes God hath dissipated. Neither is it any new project of the Monarchs, and their Courtiers in these dayes, though Christians they would be thought, to endeavour the introducing of a plain Turkish Tyranny" (CPW 3:313). These comparisons in *Observations* are then extended to include Italian-bred French conspiracies to "set up in *France*" "the Turkish Tyranny," which Milton associates with the "Monarchicall designe" (CPW 3:314). What all of these quotations reveal is an identification of deviant or malicious English and British traits with crudeness and tyranny coded at once Turkish and popish.

Milton's other parliament-sponsored treatise of 1649, *Eikonoklastes*, features a concentration of references to Turkish politics and reinforces the connection between (English) kingship and Turkish tyranny. In one especially relevant example, Milton invites a comparison between

English and Greek liberation from monarchical oppression and foreign occupation, respectively, through his allusion to bringing "the *Turk* out of *Morea*, and set[ting] free all the Greeks" (CPW 3:448).[20] The domination of Greece by the Turks, who at this time wreaked havoc on the mainland and the Greek islands that they occupied, anticipated Milton's correspondence with the Athenian-born politician and scholar, Leonard Philaras in June 1652, when he confessed his desire to use his eloquence to secure the release of the enslaved Greek nation. Specifically, Milton hoped to persuade his countrymen to deliver Greece, the land of eloquence, from "the Ottoman tyrant" (CPW 4:853). However, he followed up this statement by reminding Philaras of his own duty as a greek and as spokesperson of the Greeks to "ignite the ancient courage, diligence, and endurance in the soul of the Greeks by singing of that byegone zeal"; indeed the liberation of the people from what Milton characterized in *Eikonoklastes* as Turkish, heathen self-enslavement (CPW 3:215) is a precondition for their attainment of outward freedom. As will be in the case in his Restoration epics, Milton here unsettles the conventionally oppositional relationship between the self and the degenerate, imperial other.

In composing *Paradise Lost*, Milton chose a genre that claimed an ancestral authority, one that extended into contemporary preoccupations.[21] In the epic, in which each of the sites that Milton displays reinforces the privileged perspective (the Pisgahsight) afforded to the elect, the poet associates the Ottoman Empire with the barbaric, pagan worlds. Satan appears early in the poem as the "great Sultan waving to direct / Their [the rebel angels'] course" with his "uplifted Spear" (1.348–9, 347). Both the word "Sultan" and a preceding term, "General" ("to their Generals Voyce they soon obeyd" [1.337]), suggest tyranny, as do "Emperour" ("At thir great Emperors call" [1.378]) and "barbarous" ("barbarous Sons" [1.353]). The catalogues of the devils that follow in the poem are heavily steeped in classical references and geographical place names, including the Middle East (Palestine and Syria) and the Barbary coast.[22]

Following his successful attempts to seduce the New World's inhabitants, Satan returns from his adventures abroad as a victorious imperialist. The "*Stygian* throng" (10.453) awaits the triumphant return of "their mighty Chief" (10.455):

> As when the *Tartar* from his *Russian* Foe
> By *Astracan* over the Snowy Plains
> Retires, or *Bactrian* Sophi, from the horns

Of *Turkish* Crescent, leaves all waste beyond
The Realm of *Aladule*, in his retreat
To *Taurus* or *Casbeen*: So these the late
Heav'n-banisht Host . . .
        Reduc'd in careful Watch
Round this Metropolis, and now expecting
Each hour their great adventurer from the search
Of Foreign Worlds.   (10.431–41)

The epic simile opens with an anachronistic identification of the
Satanic legions both with the invading Tartars, tribes neighboring
Russian provinces, which, "in the Year 1571 . . . broke into *Russia*,
burnt *Mosco* to the ground" (CPW 8:515), and with the assault of the
army of Bactrian Sophi (the Persian Shah), before being driven back
by the Turks and retreating to "*Tauris* and *Casbeen*" (Tabriz and
Teheran in modern-day Iran).[23] "The horns / Of *Turkish* Crescent"
(PL 10:433–34) represent the Turkish emblem, as glossed by Heylyn:
the "ensign of this Empire (or armes of it) is the *Croissant*, or half
moon" (3.157), suggestive of military might. When he appears, Satan
is portrayed as a Turkish Sultan, who "Ascended on his high Throne,
which under state / Of richest texture spread" (10.445–46). The
"state" refers to the canopy over the throne, and recalls Satan's earlier
ascent to "a Throne of Royal State."[24] The despot reports to "the
great consulting Peers, / Rais'd from this Dark *Divan*," that is, to the
Turkish Council of State I10.456–57) on the corruption of God's
"new created World" (10.481) and its newly colonized inhabitants.
Satan's victory speech concludes with the involuntary metamorphosis
of the devils into serpents, but the path for future acts of imperialism,
marked Turkish, barbaric, and demonic, has been paved.
    Idolatry, paganism, and imperialism assume another form in the
final prophetic books of *Paradise Lost* that recount a historical struggle between saintly and satanic forces. The catalogues of empires in
book 11 (ll. 385–411) and in the corresponding scenes in books 3
and 4 of *Paradise Regained* present an anti-Christian world through
the Eurocentric "Visions of God" (11.377), for which the epic
prophecy of the Roman empire in Virgil serves as a classical model. As
a prelude to the revelation of postlapsarian history in Book 11 of
Paradise Lost, Michael leads Adam to the highest hill in Paradise to
show him a geographic "prospect" of "the Seat[s] / Of mightiest
Empire[s]" (11.386–87). Milton's retelling of Mosaic history in the
final Books of *Paradise Lost* reflects his political and theological
principles in the Restoration era: he reads the empires in terms of the

millennium-long cycles of moral depravity and political upheaval to which their history is subject. Michael ascends with Adam to the top of Mount Paradise where he displays the earthly kingdoms and rulers, from "*Cambalu*, seat of *Cathaian Can*" (north China) to India and Malaya, Persia, and Russia, to the Mediterranean regions of Turkey where "the Sultan [sat] in Bizance" (395),[25] Abyssinia (empire of Negus), eastern Africa (Ercoco, Sofala), North Africa, and a Rome-dominated Europe, and finally to the New World already occupied and exploited by Spaniards. In mapping out the world in this way, Milton walks in the footsteps of Leo Africanus,[26] as well as of Sandys who outline the succession of empires from the Romans to the Greeks to the Turks.[27] Milton's wide prospect is, however, most reminiscent of Heylyn's in which the reader is invited to ascend to the great heights of Mount Atlas—a system of mountains in northwestern Africa: "On our way from *Barbarie* to Libya *Interior*, we must pass over *Mount Atlas*, a ridge of hills, of exceeding great height, and of no small length. So high that the top or *Summit* of it is above the clouds, at least so high the eye of man is not able to discern the topic of it" (1652, Part 4.1.48). Heylyn's geographical account is interspersed with quotations from Herodotus and Virgil, enabling the historian also to take into his scope the Greek mythological figure of Atlas, who "was said to have been a man of such wondrous height, that the Heavens rested on his shoulders."[28] The reference to the Greek giant also recalls the book in which this episode is presented—the *Cosmographie* that supports a globe-encompassing vision.

The Miltonic prophet and his privileged readers and spectators are likewise awarded the right to interpretation, though the sights they take in are deliberately selective. The *Paradise Lost* account of the panorama that Michael offers from the top of the Hill of Paradise excludes Europe, with the exception of Rome, which is absorbed into the imperial landscape as a nation that "was to sway / The World" (11.405–6). Rome functions throughout Milton's epic as an image of a pagan, papist Babylonian empire on which all corrupt structures—from Pandemonium in Book 1 to Nimrod's tower of Babel in Book 12—are (anachronistically) modeled.[29]

In his visionary global journey, Michael, as mentioned above, then moves westward to the New World, though the Mediterranean empires are never left behind. Thus, for example, imperial Spain is implicated in the description of Guiana: "he [Adam] also saw / ... / ... / ... / *Guiana*, whose great City *Geryon's* Sons / Call *El Dorado*" (11.406–11). "*Geryons* Sons" are the Spanish oppressors, named after the monster of Greek mythology that lived an island off the Spanish coast and was slain by Hercules. It was a bedazzled Spaniard, Juan Martinez, who, according to Walter Raleigh, after witnessing scenes of debauchery representative of the Spaniards' "solemne feast," christened the mythical New World city "the gilded man"—"El Dorado"—"for the abundance of golde which he saw in the city, the images of golde in their temples, the plates, the armours, and shield of gold which they use in the warres."[30] With the invocation of El Dorado in *Paradise Lost* (11.411), Milton completes the survey, thus linking the worldly empires of the far reaches of the east with those of the west. The monumental and lavish display of absolutist power compounds the effects of the original sin, striking Adam with near blindness (11:411–14).

*   *   *

The account of the worldly kingdoms in the brief epic, *Paradise Regained*, which was printed after the 1667 ten-book edition of *Paradise Lost* but before the first twelve-book edition (1674), complements those in the major epic while more directly critiquing the forms of language that the subjects of epic and empire have assumed. In a parallel / parallax vision that constitutes the temptation scene of Book 3 in *Paradise Regained*, Satan presents to the Son of God (second Adam) the ancient empires "in a moment of time" (Luke 4:5). In conjunction with Stephan Greenblatt's identification of "wonder" as the primary and quintessential human reaction to first encounters,[31] Satan invites the Son to survey the wide prospect: "here thou beholdest," he motions to Jesus, directing his gaze to the empires (3:269), and then again: "Turning with easy eye thou may'st behold" (3:293). The descriptions of empires identified in succession—Assyria, Babylon, Persia, Emathia or Macedonia, and Parthia—call forth their common associations with effeteness and decadence—a reminder of the corrupt foundations that lie beneath power and splendor. Passages from Pliny and from Heylyn, who also quotes Pliny, probably served Milton's needs here. Milton in turn numbers among the defenders of a Judeo-Christian narrative of the fall who describe the disorder of the ancient pagans of vanished empires that had destroyed themselves, according to seventeenth-century historians. Heylyn attributes the "causes of th[e] desolation" experienced by the "mighty Empires" of the Mediterranean and Middle Eastern regions with "their crying sins[ ]," namely, "the pride of the *Babylonians*, the effeminacy of the *Persians*, the luxury of the *Greeks*, and such an aggregation of vices amongst the *Romans* (or Western *Christians*) before the breaking in of the

barbarous Nations, that they were grown a scandal unto *Christianity*"
("To the Reader" [n.p.]).

The survey of empires in *Paradise Regained* is intended to evoke
the Son's liberationist compulsions. Satan proposes a new revolution
led by a Hebrew deliverer who would apply Parthian military might
against Roman tyranny (3.268ff). If they were freed, the Jews, however, would return to their idolatry, the Son judges; in fact the lesson
about spiritual and moral degradation leading to political downfall is
one that punctuates the history of the Hebrew nation, as well as that
of the New Israel (see PR 3:427, and SA 240). In *Paradise Regained*,
the Jews of Jesus' day are among the nations from the furthest reaches
of the globe (from the Adriatic to the "Blackmoor Sea" [4:72], to
the Ganges, and back again to Europe) who are subject to Rome. The
panorama of "Kingdoms of the world, and all thir glory" (4.89) that
Satan displays at the opening of book 4 is designed to whet Jesus'
appetite for imperial might, but Satan also indicates that the Roman
people require liberation from the tyrant Sejanus, the "wicked
Favorite" (4.95) of the retired emperor Tiberius. But once again, the
Son resists grounds that "military might is ultimately futile for a
people that has," as Balachandra Rajan observed, "surrendered to the
other within itself."[32] The exhibitions of the worldly power then
diminish as the site of contestation is internalized: "What wise and
valiant man would seek to free / These thus degenerate, by themselves enslav'd, / Or could of inward slaves make outward free?"
(4.143–45). This refrain is heard earlier in Milton's 1652 letter to
Philaras about using eloquence to help secure Greek liberation from
Turkish occupation, and invoked in *Paradise Lost* by Michael who
warns Adam about the loss of inward liberty by the nations of the
future (12.97–101).[33] The Son's opening soliloquy in *Paradise
Regained* introduces the theme in the brief epic; tempted by the possibility of "rescu[ing] *Israel* from the *Roman* yoke," Jesus refuses,
holding "it more humane, more heavenly, first / By winning words to
conquer willing hearts, / And make persuasion do the work of fear"
(1.217, 221–23). In what Quint describes as "Milton's most explicit
alignment of his epic poetry with the anti-Virgilian, anti-imperial tradition of Lucan" (326), the Son prophesies that the end of time will
bring about not the establishment but the destruction of all monuments to power. The spiritual Jerusalem will then rise up from the
center of corruption, the ruins of the "Mightiest Empire[s]:" "when
my season comes to sit / On *David's* Throne, it shall be like a
tree / Spreading and overshadowing all the Earth / Or as a stone that
shall to pieces dash / All Monarchies besides throughout the

world, / And of my Kingdom there shall be no end" (4.146–51). The canopy provided by the Throne, which is likened to the sprawling tree, overshadows the satanic Sultan's "high Throne, which under state / Of richest texture spread" (PL 10.445–46).

In the Restoration era when the future of the English monarchy was once again secure, Milton vilified the idolatrous nation that, as he had prophesied, "delivered itself into slavery to its own lusts" and chose "a captain back for Egypt" (CPW 4.684; 7:463). By far the most formidable empire is the empire of the mind, Milton's Satan ultimately recognizes: "Be famous then / by wisdom," he tempts the Son, "as thy Empire must extend, / So let extend thy mind o'er all the world / In Knowledge, all things in it comprehend" (4.221–24). Embracing all of Greek wisdom would "render [Jesus] a King complete" with an empire at his disposal (4.282–84), Satan continues. But the tempter's advances are again frustrated: the words of the prophets alone "in thir majestic unaffected style" (4.359) are the sole support for the nation, and only they "best form a King" (4.362–64), Jesus answers.

By the 1650s Milton descended Mount Atlas, admitting that his blindness now prevented him from perusing maps, "vainly surveying as I do with blind eyes the actual globe of the earth."[34] The global journey is thereupon relocated in the theater of the mind. In his remaining years, the mental traveler struggled with questions of alterity, nationhood, and imperialism in composing an encyclopedic poem that charts the ancient worlds and navigates the Mediterranean and Middle Eastern empires that replaced them. In *Paradise Regained*, however, the Son renounces globe-consuming visions and the temptations of empire, which now originate with Satan, while exposing the self-enslaved condition of a nation that degenerates into what it seeks to renounce. Othello had ironically foreshadowed his tragic demise in the famous question: " 'Are we turned Turks' and to ourselves do that / Which heaven hath forbid the Ottomites?" (2.3.160–61). For Milton too the survey of the theaters of empire leads to the encounter with his own nation's state of barbarism and subjection.

NOTES

1. John H. Elliott, "The Seizure of Overseas Territories by the European Powers," *Theories of Empire, 1450–1800*, ed. David Armitage (Aldershot: Ashgate, 1998), p. 14; originally published in *The European Discovery of the World and its Economic Effects on Pre-Industrial Society, 1500–1800*, ed. Hans Polh (Stuttgart, 1990), pp. 45–6. Twice reprinted in the 1650s and often cited by English writers, *De monarchia Hispanica discursus*, Tommaso Campanella's advice to King Philip II of

Spain, outlines the means for Spain to establish a universal monarchy, which involved "conquer[ing] and subdu[ing] the *Turkish Empire*" (*Tho. [Tommaso] Campanella, A Discourse Touching the Spanish Monarchy... Newly translated into English, according to the Third Edition of this Book in Latine* [trans. Edmund Chilmead] [London, 1654], pp. 11–12). "Empire" refers here to a territorial and legal formation held together by structures of differentiation and containment, and more directly in the case of England, to the domination of a nation over more than one geographical area. See Anthony Pagden, *Lords of All the World: Ideologies of Empire in Spain, Britain and France, c.1500–c.1800* (New Haven: Yale University Press, 1995), p. 14. This definition constitutes the third of three concepts of empire Pagden identifies. See also Lesley B. Cormack, "Britannia Rules the Waves?: Images of Empire in Elizabethan England," in *Literature, Mapping, and the Politics of Space in Early Modern Britain*, ed. Andrew Gordon and Bernhard Klein (Cambridge: Cambridge University Press, 2001), pp. 45–68, esp. pp. 46–7.

2. Bruce McLeod, "The 'Lordly Eye': Milton and the Strategic Geography of Empire," in *Milton and the Imperial Vision*, ed. Balachandra Rajan and Elizabeth Sauer (Pittsburgh: Duquesne University Press, 1999), p. 55.

3. John Milton, *Paradise Lost* in *Complete Poems and Major Prose*, ed. Merritt Y. Hughes (New York: Odyssey Press, 1957), 11. 386–87; *Paradise Regained*, 3.252ff. All citations to Milton's poetry are from the Merritt Hughes edition and cited parenthetically.

4. Paul Stevens recognizes that Milton's major epic "authorizes colonial activity even while it satirizes the abuses of early modern colonialism" (Stevens, "*Paradise Lost* and the Colonial Imperative," *Milton Studies* 34 [1996]: 3). Also see Bruce McLeod, *The Geography of Empire in English Literature 1580–1745* (Cambridge: Cambridge University Press, 1999), p. 134.

5. George Sandys, "To the Prince," *A Relation of a Journey Begun An:Dom: 1610*, 2nd ed. (London, 1615), n.p.

6. Nabil Matar, *Islam in Britain 1558–1658* (Cambridge: Cambridge University Press, 1998), p. 190. Also see Matar's *Turks, Moors, and Englishmen in the Age of Discovery* (New York: Columbia University Press, 1999) and "The Toleration of Muslims in Renaissance England: Practice and Theory," in *Religious Toleration: "The Variety of Rites" from Cyrus to Defoe*, ed. John Christian Laursen (New York: St. Martin's Press, 1999), pp. 127–46 and Daniel Goffman and Christopher Stroop, "Empires as Composite: The Ottoman Polity and the Typology of Dominion," in *Imperialism: Historical and Literary Imagination 1500–1900*, ed. Balachandra Rajan and Elizabeth Sauer (New York: Palgrave Macmillan, 2004), pp. 129–45.

7. McLeod, *The Geography of Empire*, p. 134; McLeod, "The 'Lordly Eye,' " p. 49.

8. John Speed, *The Theatre of the Empire of Great Britaine* (1611). See also Christopher Ivic, "Mapping British Identities: Speed's *Theatre of the Empire of Great Britaine*," in *British Identities and English Renaissance Literature*, ed. David J. Baker and Willy Maley (Cambridge: Cambridge University Press, 2002), pp. 135, 153n3. Evidence of Milton's engagement with Speed is provided by Milton's 31–3 citations of Speed's works in his Commonplace Book (William Riley Parker, *Milton: A Biography*, 2 vols. [Oxford: Clarendon Press, 1968], 2:802).

9. Milton, "The Author's Preface," *A Briefe History of Moscovia* (1682), ed. George B. Parks, *Complete Prose Works of John Milton*, 8 vols., ed. Don Wolfe (New Haven: Yale University Press, 1953–82), 8:474.

10. Two recent and impressive examinations of the catalogues' place names in the epics are Robert Markley's " 'The destin'd Walls / Of *Cambalu*': Milton, China, and the Ambiguities of the East," in *Milton and the Imperial Vision*, ed. Balachandra Rajan and Elizabeth Sauer (Pittsburgh: Duquesne University Press, 1999), pp. 191–213, and John Michael Archer's "Milton and the Fall of Asia," *Old Worlds: Egypt, Southwest Asia, India, and Russia in Early Modern English Writing* (Stanford: Stanford University Press, 2001), pp. 63–99. Both essays, however, focus on the geographical significance of Middle Eastern and Eastern place names.

11. The breakdown of the self-other oppositional relationship is captured in Othello's final long speech: "Set you down this; / And say besides that in Aleppo once, / Where a malignant and turbaned Turk / Beat a Venetian and traduced the state, / I took by th' throat the circumcised dog, / And smote him—thus!" (William Shakespeare, *Othello*, ed. Edward Pechter [New York: Norton, 2004], 5.2.356–61).

12. Richard Helgerson, *Forms of Nationhood: The Elizabethan Writing of England* (Chicago: University of Chicago Press, 1992), esp. pp. 8–18. Helgerson argues that discursive forms of nationhood directed attention away from sovereignty and the power from the monarch to the nation or land (p. 12).

13. Sandys's account of Constantinople, which Milton mentions in his prose and verse—including in the Book 11 catalogue in *Paradise Lost* (11.395)—connects the ancient to the present day empires: Constantine gave the name Constantinople to Byzantium, making it "the seate of his Empire; enduing it with the priviledges [*sic*] of *Rome*." Constantinople remained the key city in the Roman state until 1453, when the Byzantine Empire fell to the Turks. "This Citie by destinie appointed, and by nature seated for Soveraignitie, was first the seate of the *Roman* Emperours, then of the *Greeke*, as now it is of the *Turkish*" (*Relation of a Journey*, 29–30). For Milton's indebtedness to Sandys, see Robert Ralston Cawley, *Milton and the Literature of Travel* (Princeton: Princeton University Press, 1951).

14. Loren E. Pennington, "*Hakluytus Posthumus*: Samuel Purchas and the Promotion of English Overseas Expansion," *The Emporia State Research Studies* 14:3 (1996): 11.

15. See David Armitage, *The Ideological Origins of the British Empire* (Cambridge: Cambridge University Press, 2000), pp. 61–99.

16. Lesley B. Cormack, *Charting an Empire: Geography at the English Universities, 1580–1620* (Chicago: University of Chicago Press, 1997), p. 140.

17. Samuel Purchas, *Purchas His Pilgrimage: or, Relations of the World and the Religions Observed in All Ages and places discovered, from the Creation unto this Present. In foure Partes This First Containeth a Theologicall and Geographicall Historie of Asia, Africa and America* (London, 1613).

18. Peter Heylyn, *Cosmographie: In Four Bookes. Containing the Chorographie and Historie of the Whole World* (London, 1652). Purchas, Raleigh, Heylyn, Ortelius, and others foreground the spatial strategies that Milton wields, thus contributing to a praxis of colonialism.

19. Milton, *Areopagitica, Complete Prose Works of John Milton*, 8 vols., ed. Don Wolfe (New Haven: Yale University Press, 1953–82), 2: 548. Subsequent quotations from the Yale edition of Milton's prose are cited parenthetically as *CPW*.

20. Milton implies that Charles' government was a Turkish tyranny and that Milton hoped for the expulsion of the Turks from Morea—the Peloponnesus. Heylyn notes that Greece was part of the Ottoman Empire that had been ruled since 1648 by Mahomet IV (3.151). On the Turkish monarchy, see also *CPW* 3:453, 574.

21. On the politicization of epic poetry, see David Quint, *Epic and Empire: Politics and Generic Form from Virgil to Milton* (Princeton: Princeton University Press, 1993), p. 8.

22. The national god of the Philistines is among the devils who appear on the scene: Dagon "ad his Temple high / Rear' in *Azotus*, dreaded through the Coast / Of *Palestine*, in *Gath* and *Ascalon*, / And *Accaron* and *Gaza*" frontier bounds (*Paradise Lost* 1. 464–6), five Philistine cities on or near the Mediterranean shore. Sandys' and Purchas's Christianized accounts of Dagon informed Milton's.

23. I am indebted to the notes on this passage provided in *John Milton: Paradise Lost*, ed. John Leonard (London: Penguin, 2000), pp. 424, n431–3, 432, 457. Also see *CPW*, 8:485n44.

24. *Paradise Lost*, 2.1. Also see *CPW*, 8:536.

25. *CPW*, 11:395; Byzantium (Constantinople, Istanbul) was capital of the Ottoman Empire after the falling to the Turks in 1453.

26. Leo Africanus, *The History and Description of Africa*, trans. John Pory (London, 1600, rpt. 1896), p. 16.

27. Sandys, *Relation of a Journey*, 29–30.

28. Heylyn, p. 48. See also P.H. [Peter Heylyn], *Microcosmus, or A Little Description of the Great World: A Treatise Historicall, Geographicall, Politicall, Theologicall* (Oxford, 1621), p. 377. In his 1656 correspondence with Peter Heimbach, Milton complains about the cost of a Bleau-Hondius map, and puns on the name of Atlas as a book of maps: "You write that they ask 130 florins: it must be the Mauritanian mountain *Atlas*, I think and not a book that you tell me is to be bought at so huge a price." In Milton's brief epic, Jesus resists the temptation to rule over the empires of the world, instead predicting their destruction by the "*Atlantic* stone" (*Paradise Regained*, 4.115). The domination of the world's empires, whether discursively or politically, loses its appeal.

29. See Andrew Hadfield, "The English and Other Peoples," in *A Companion to Milton*, ed. Thomas N. Corns (Oxford: Blackwell, 2001), pp. 182–3.

30. Raleigh's account is recorded in Richard Hakluyt, *The Principal Navigations, Voyages, Traffiques and Discoveries of the English Nation* (London, 1598–1600), rpt. Glasgow, 1903, 1st. ed., 3.636.

31. See Stephen Greenblatt, *Marvelous Possessions: The Wonder of the New World* (Chicago: University of Chicago Press, 1991).

32. Rajan, "The Imperial Temptation," in *Milton and the Imperial Vision*, ed. Rajan and Sauer, p. 299.

33. James Harrington offers a gloss for this reading the interior landscape: "the principles of government are twofold; internal, or the goods of the mind; and external, or the gods of fortune;" "if the liberty of a man consists in the empire of his reason, the absence whereof would betray him to the bondage of his passions; then the liberty of a commonwealth consists in the empire of her laws, the absence whereof would betray her to the lust of tyrants" (Harrington, *The Commonwealth of Oceana, Works: The Oceana and Other Works*, ed. John Toland [1720; rpt. London, 1771], pp. 36, 42).

34. Milton, Familiar Letter [Letter 20], "To . . . Peter Heimbach," in *The Works of John Milton*, gen. ed. Frank Allen Patterson (New York: Columbia University Press, 1936), 12:83.

CHAPTER 11

TURNING TO THE TURK:
COLLABORATION AND CONVERSION
IN WILLIAM DAVENANT'S
THE SIEGE OF RHODES

Matthew Birchwood

> *Your name is so eminent in the Justice which you convey through all the different Members of this great Empire, that my* Rhodians *seem to enjoy a better Harbour in the Pacifique* Thames, *than they had on the* Mediterranean; *and I have brought* Solyman *to be arraign'd at your Tribunal, where you are the Censor of his civility and magnificence.*

Appended to the 1663 edition of *The Siege of Rhodes*, Davenant's dedicatory epistle to the Earl of Clarendon makes an overt comparison between the fictive world of the play's Mediterranean setting and the real world of the play's production in London of the early Restoration which amounts to rather more than a playful conceit. As the playwright acknowledges, he has good cause to be grateful for the countenance of so powerful a patron since "Dramatic poetry meets with the same persecution now, from such who esteem themselves the most refin'd and civil, as it ever did from the Barbarous. And yet whilst those virtuous Enemies deny *heroique Plays* to the Gentry, they entertain the People with a Seditious *Farce* of their own counterfeit Gravity." As the epistle makes clear, there is an inverse reciprocity to be drawn between the two worlds: whilst the Turkish sultan manifests a "civility & magnificence" that refutes his archetypal barbarism, those factious elements of contemporary London are charged with affecting a civility that belies their own barbarity. This pre-emptive defense indicates both the persistence of moral opposition to public theater as well as Davenant's characteristic ability to align himself with the prevailing political wind. By the time of the appearance of the play's 1663 edition, Davenant had capitalized upon his position as one of only two playwrights licensed to produce public theater whilst *The Siege of Rhodes* had established him as the first exponent of a strand of "heroic drama" which, taken by Dryden and his imitators, was set to dominate the English stage for the next twenty years. In its various manifestations, Davenant's play spans the gap between two epochs of English theater. The Restoration play now dedicated to Clarendon had its origins in Cromwell's Protectorate and an explosive moment of both political turmoil at home and a correlated fascination with Islamic culture and history in the drama and polemic of the day. The passage of its Mediterranean protagonists to the banks of the "Paciffique Thames" was a stormy one.

In its final form, Davenant's play comprises two parts. The first part of *The Siege of Rhodes* was entered in the Stationer's Register on August 27, 1656 and it seems likely that the play's first performance took place soon afterwards.[1] The venue was Davenant's own Rutland House near Chartehouse although the audiences were charged an entrance fee as in a public theater. The title page implicitly declares its moral and political neutrality, designating itself a "Representation by the Art of Prospective in Scenes, And the Story sung in *Recitative* Musick." In keeping with this diversionary strategy, the conventional divisions of act and scene are replaced with various "entries" each preceded by a section of "Instrumental Musick" and rounded off with a chorus. In his address "To the Reader" which prefaces the first quarto edition of the play, Davenant scrupulously evades the issue of the play's revolutionary status as the first legitimate dramatic production since the 1642 closure and makes no reference to the work as a play at all. Instead, the playwright makes a lengthy apology for its scope, constrained as the producers were by the domestic venue—"the narrowness of the Room" and gives an insight into the logistical difficulties they faced: "so narrow an allowance for the Fleet of *Solyman* the Magnificent, his Army, the Island of *Rhodes*, and the varieties attending the Siege of the City; that I fear you will think, we invite you to such a contracted Trifle as that of the *caesars* carv'd upon a Nut."

Alongside the familiar apology for the inadequacies of the stage to represent the vastness and variety of a history play, is a carefully drawn parallel between Davenant's own "contracted Trifle" and the legitimizing precedent of classical drama. The playwright goes on to justify his use of music, both "Vocal and Instrumental," and emphasizes the innovation of his new style of drama, "being *Recitative*, and therefore unpractised here; though of great reputation amongst other Nations, the very attempt of it is an obligation to our own" and, similarly defends his "frequent alterations of measure" on the grounds that a "variation of Ayres" is more appropriate to the musical accompaniment and better suits the "heroick Argument." Thus, Davenant manages to promote his play as being both seductively novel whilst remaining securely and reassuringly rooted in "Ancient Drammatick" traditions. What is conspicuous by its absence, however, is any acknowledgment of the possible wider significance of the play, for instance, the potential topicality of its subject matter of, indeed, the fact that the limitations of a confined stage may not have been the only constraints the playwright encountered in his attempt to reconcile public theater with the ideological exigencies of Protectorate England. Rather, Davenant's preface assiduously stresses the mundane, the politically inert. The deployment of such a strategy is hardly surprising given the politically hostile conditions in which this groundbreaking play operated and in which, in its moment of production, the play text cannot help but intervene. More surprising, however, is the tendency for subsequent commentators to perpetuate the tacit suggestions of Davenant's somewhat disingenuous preface.

The sheer number of innovations that accompanied Davenant's play justifiably distinguish it as a landmark in the evolution of English drama, but have tended to obscure the possibility of a more historically nuanced appreciation of its portrayal of Mediterranean conflict, perhaps the most dismissive example of which is Chew's verdict that, whilst *The Siege of Rhodes* is "Of much importance in the history of the theatre, it is of little interest in itself."[2] As such, the play has commended critical attention as both the first English opera and, in its first use of moveable scenery as the antecedent to a naturalistic mode of drama.[3] *The Siege of Rhodes* also lays claim to being the first to employ a female actress on the public stage—Mrs Coleman, wife to one of the actors, played the part of Ianthe. Consequently, readings have neglected both the topical allusiveness of the action as well as the multivalent image of the Turk that lies at its heart.[4] For all its innovative deployment of music and scenery and Davenant's supposed eschewal of preexisting theater, the play takes many of its cues from the drama's long-standing fascination with the East. Whilst the impact of French and Italian modes of drama upon Davenant's opera is irrefutable (and acknowledged in the playwright's allusion to other Nations in his address "To the Reader") *The Siege of Rhodes* is also clearly related to a popular strand of English drama. For example, in their portrayal of a specifically feminine Christian virtue, both Bess Bridges of Heywood's *The Fair Maid of the West* (1631) and Despina of Carlell's *Osmond the Great Turk* (1637) suggest themselves as models for Ianthe although Davenant's particular treatment of the binary of Christian maid / Turkish despot represents a distinct development from these prototypes.[5]

Notwithstanding the equanimity of Davenant's preface, it would seem difficult to underestimate the impact of the play's first performance. The curtain was raised on the first legitimate English stage for fourteen years, since the gathering of clouds of civil war had closed the playhouses, and the opening words uttered were a call to arms:

> Arm, Arm, the Bassa's Fleet appears;
> To Rhodes his Course from Chios steers;
> Her shady wings to distant sight,
> Spread like the Curtains of the Night.
> Each Squadron thicker and still darker grows;
> The Fleet like many floating Forrests shows.　(I, 1.1.9–14)[6]

The play narrates the story of the capture of Rhodes by Sultan Suleiman the Magnificent from the Knights of St. John in 1522 for which Davenant's main source seems to have been Richard Knolles' influential work, the *Generall Historie of the Turkes* (1603). Nevertheless, contemporary resonances suffuse the play. Since 1654, the Ottomans had been engaged in the epic siege of another strategic Mediterranean outpost, the Venetian territory of Candia. In June 1656, and shortly before the first appearance of the play, the Turks had suffered an unusual military setback against the Venetian fleet in the Dardanelles, although this does not warrant the commonly made assertion that the Ottoman Empire was already a spent force by mid-century.[7] Accounts of the siege were eagerly consumed in London and reports of the domestic conflict were frequently interspersed with the news from Candia. By the 1650s, English embroilment in the war had become a diplomatically sensitive issue for Cromwell's regime. In 1653, Venice made its first diplomatic overtures to the new Commonwealth of England and Cromwell received the ambassador Paulicci, expressing sympathy for the Venetian cause against the Turk but demurred from offering naval assistance to the Senate on the grounds that English forces were consumed in the current war with the United Provinces and because of the threat any involvement in the conflict would pose to the activities of the Levant Company. Meanwhile, at least one Englishman was strenuously advocating an opportunistic intervention in the war. Writing to the Admiralty Committee from Leghorn in the same year, Charles Longland reported,

> It is rumored that the Turkish fleet has gone out of Rhodes into Candia, and there surprised and taken a strong place from the Venetians, who it is supposed will be forced to quit the island. The Venetians are at Milo. If a good English fleet should appear in the midst of this war between the Turks and Venetians before Constantinople, they might obtain what conditions of trade they pleased from the Turk, even to the exclusion of other nations from the trade, and reserve if for ourselves.[8]

Whilst there is no evidence for state-sponsored piracy on the scale so zealously recommended by Longland, English ships were involved in the war. In a later audience in 1657, the Venetian representative Giavarini complained to Cromwell of an English ship allegedly used in the war against Venice "in the recent action at the Dardanelles." Again it seems that the Protector was cautiously open to entreaty and Giavarini was able to report to the Senate that,

> beyond question, if they do not obtain favorable answers from Constantinople to their demands for the *restitution* of the ship and compensation for the goods, active hostilities will be begun against the Tripolitans, as the merchants there desire, who would be glad to see the destruction not only of Tripoli, but of Algiers, Tunis, and other places on the Barbary Coast, if this would not irritate the Grand Turk and break the peace with the Porte, which they wish to be continued and enlarged.[9]

This final caveat is a far summation of English foreign policy in the Levant; whilst contained action against the Barbary corsairs was feasible, engaging the might of the Ottoman Empire was clearly an entirely different matter. Nevertheless, the robustness of Cromwell's rhetoric does reflect the development of growing English interest and naval confidence in the Mediterranean.

Cromwell's interventionist ambitions in the region were publicized in *A Message sent from His Highness the Lord Protector, to the Great Turk with His Demands and Proposals; and the releasing of the English Captives*

(1654). Having reported Cromwell's decision to "graciously . . . send an Expres to the Governor of Argier," the declaration boasts,

> As touching the influence of the Lord Protector hath gained by his Message to the Turks, 'tis a thing wonderfully to be admired; and indeed, it causeth no little admiration throughout all Christendome; for, true it is, the Argier men of War are become Associates with the English, and will not permit any man of our Nation to be carried captive into thraldome . . . and brings them into Gen Blake who at this very instant, rides triumphant in the Levant Ocean.

In the summer of 1654, Admiral Blake arrived in the vicinity with his formidable squadrons fresh from their decisive victory over the Dutch at the Battle of Portland in the previous year. Dispatched to harry French and Spanish shipping, the English fleet also took the opportunity to quash the troublesome Barbary pirates and, in April 1655, Blake bombarded Tunisian vessels at Porto Farina inflicting significant damage. Gunboat diplomacy of the kind advocated by Blake did, it seems, meet with some temporary success. In the long term, however, attempts to curtail the rogue states of Algeria, Tunisia, and Tripoli both directly and through diplomatic negotiation with the Porte would prove indecisive. What is more telling in the context of Protectorate relations with the Ottomans' regencies is the notion that the traditional enemy might now be counted "Associates with the English," an imaginative repositioning of the Islamic other that feeds directly into Davenant's play. Certainly, news of the Republic's latest incursion in the Mediterranean would have been circulating as Davenant carefully formulated his politic play. In a report "From the city of Tunis," dated April 7, 1655, *Mercurius Politicus* describes the firing of the ships followed by the Dey's defiant response, that "these ships are none of ours, but the Grand Signiors; as also are the Castles where we serve in Garison." The writer's wry comment that "though in this letter they talk of the Grand Seignior, yet it is well known, that he doth not own them, nor will they him, farther, than themselves please here" points toward the delicate balance between defense of the national interest and the continuance of good relations with the Porte so vital to the lucrative Mediterranean trade. Whilst evincing a similar acknowledgment of the Sultan's authority in the region, *The Siege of Rhodes* draws upon and represents the very same sense of complex and entangled allegiances as they were perceived by English observers.

From the outset, the Turkish fleet is represented as both the military and spiritual diametric of the European forces garrisoning the island that is itself imagined as a microcosm of Christendom itself: "Pale shew those Crescents to out bloody Cross? Sink not the Western Kingdoms in our loss" (I, 1.1.49–54). Thus, the fate of the entire "Western Kingdoms" is portrayed as hinging upon the defense of Rhodes. This monumental clash of competing ideologies is described in terms that evoke the prodigious nature of the Turkish hordes, a familiar characteristic of representations of Islamic imperialism that is emblematically proclaimed by their "bright Crescents / . . . that encreasing Empire show; / Which must be still in Nonage and still grow" (I, 1.1.44–6). By contrast, the powers of Christian Europe are palpably on the wane. In the first entry, Alphonso, the heroic soldier-lover of the play, praises the merits of the various Christian contingents who defend the island—"the fiery French," "the grave Italians" and the "cheerfull English" (I, 2.1.27–40) in an evocation of European confederacy that is not borne out by the complacent infighting of the wider western world. Whilst "vainly Rhodes for succour waits," the "triple Diadems, and Scarlet Hats" of Rome are judged guilty of shortsighted parsimony—"Rome keeps her Gold, cheaply her Warriors pays / At first with Blessings, and at last with Praise." Conversely, Catholic Spain is indicted with a profligate imperialism—"By armies, stow'd in Fleets, exhausted Spain / Leave half her Land unplough'd, to plough the Main;/And still would more of the Old World subdue, / As if unsatisfi'd with all the New." Even England is deemed culpable of a vague, but perhaps pertinent dereliction of domestic duties: "the English Lyon ever loves to change/His Walks, and in remoter Forrests range" and thus, "All gaining vainly from each others loss; / Whilst still the Crescent drives away the Cross" (I, 2.1.13–26). The Ottoman forces, however, appear united in their crusading militarism, their expansionism portrayed as a positively religious tenet. In the third entry, Pirrhus, a Turkish pasha echoes the conviction, commonly held among English writers, that the imperial successes of the Ottomans were directly derived from the teachings of Mohammed:

> 'Tis well our valiant Prophet did
> In us not only loss forbid,
> But has conjoyn'd us still to get.
> Empire must move apace.   (I, 3.1.25–30)

The opening exchanges of the play are similarly peppered with allusions to the conventional characteristics of these "Termagant Turks." The rapacious nature of the sultan's "Empire" building is matched by an innate lasciviousness which the Christian forces pledge to defy: "Our Swords against proud Solyman we draw, / His cursed Prophet, and his sensual Law" (I, 1.1.85–6). Solyman's first appearance in the second entry does little to dispel the audience's impression of an archetypal Turk. Infuriated by his army's failure to overrun the valiant Rhodes, Solyman rages at his general Pirrhus, warning that his wrath "must be quench'd by Rhodian blood or thine" (I, 2.2.34). It is, however, the appearance of the captured Ianthe, veiled like "the Morning pictur'd in a Cloud," which jolts Solyman from his wonted nature. Ianthe's captor, the pasha Mustapha, praises the princess for her martial valor in bringing the jewels of her dowry to redeem her besieged husband, and resisting capture in "a bloody Fight." To the play's first audiences, it is plausible that this portrait of the paradigmatic "Christian wife" may well have called to mind the exploits of Henrietta-Maria and her active participation in the civil war.[10] Certainly, Ianthe's exemplary virtue exercises a transformation upon the Sultan that exposes a spiritual fragility in the Rhodian camp. This fracturing of the Christian ideal is synechdochally represented in the corruption of the ostensible epitome of conjugal virtue embodied by Alphonso and Ianthe who appear to be, in the Sultan's words, "such a single pair / As onely equal are / Unto themselves" (I, 4.1.23–5). In fact, this unity soon proves illusive as Alphonso becomes wracked with a jealousy that threatens to undermine the Rhodian cause. By act four, his unwarranted jealousy has spilt over into the public sphere of the play, leading Villerius, the Grand Master of the Knight Hospitallers to read "the sad destruction of our Town" in Alphonso's decline.

However, crucially, the couple's private dialogue in the third act reveals that Alphonso's suspicion is aroused not only by the fact that Ianthe was forced to spend "two whole nights" as Solyman's prisoner, but has been further aggravated by the uncharacteristic nature of the Turk's behavior. In an exchange highly suggestive of the play's sophisticated awareness of preexisting narrative version of the Turk, Ianthe relates her own surprise to Alphonso that, despite "All that of Turks and Tyrants" she had heard, the Sultan "seem'd in civil France, and Monarch there" (I, 3.2.102). Given the indictment of the failure of the various European powers, including France, to come to the succor of Rhodes, expressed earlier in the play, Ianthe's comparison signals an all-important shift in the imaginative positioning of the Islamic counterpart. Here is a further indication of the play's reluctance, or even inability, to enforce a moral distinction between Orient and Occident, a disjunction that feeds upon the fluid and conflicted image of Islam in this decade. Instead, Solyman's apparent appropriation of notionally European patterns of morality and "civil"-ity issues a disorienting challenge to Alphonso, provoking a crisis of identity that the oxymora of his language struggle to contain. Although Ianthe's virtue "seem'd to civilize a barb'rous Foe," Alphonso remains unconvinced and declares "This Christian Turk amazes me" and, in soliloquy, reveals his distrust of such "wondrous Turkish chastity": "Oh Solyman, this mystique act of thine, Does all my quiet undermine" (I, 3.2.141–2). Meanwhile, Alphonso's jealousy continues to be countered by Solyman's "stubborn Honour" in a deliberate and startling substitution of infidel for gallant. On the eve of the Turkish assault on the island, the pashas Pirrhus and Mustapha urge their sultan to punish the Christians for their insolent refusal to accept Solyman's offer of amnesty:

> They in to morrows storm will change their mind,
> Then, though too late instructed, they shall find,
> That those who your protection dare reject
> No humane Power dares venture to protect.
> They are not Foes, but Rebels, who withstand
> The pow'r that does their Fate command. (I, 4.1.7–12)

Here is the recurring stratagem, prevalent throughout the seventeenth century, of conceptualizing the Ottoman Empire as an instrument of "Fate" and the providential scourge of Christendom. Latent within this well-rehearsed thesis, however, is a curious distinction between "Foes" and "Rebels," which has a particular significance in relation to Davenant's own tentative gestures toward the English political situation in this first version of *The Siege of Rhodes*. In their ultimately futile opposition to the inevitability of fate, Ianthe and Alphonso perhaps represent the possibility of virtuous, if misguided rebellion. In the context of 1656, Pirrhus's image appears to mitigate the actions of those who, like the playwright himself, have been swept along with the political tide and forced to accede to the realities of Protectorate government. In this inversion of the standard narrative, it is those who *fail* to turn Turk who are adjudged rebels and traitors to their fate. Whilst the Turkish generals conform to type, Solyman repudiates their blood lust in an evocation of a recognizably Christian conception of ideal government:

> Oh Mustapha, our strength we measure ill,
> We want the half of what we think we have;
> For we enjoy the Beast-like pow'r to save.

> Who laughs at Death, laughs at our highest Pow'r;
> The valiant man is his own Emperour.   (I, 4.1.13–18)

Solyman's self-realization partially derives from contemporary political theory and seems to echo a distinctly Hobbesian analysis of the inherent limitations of a "Beast-like" human nature. The Sultan's final metaphor, however, suggests an evaluation of government based upon a correlation between the individual and society and recapitulates the play's insistent emphasis upon individual responsibility for good self-government. Indeed, if Hotson is correct in his conjecture that the play's first performance took place almost immediately after the play's registration in August 1656, then the Sultan's representation of government legitimized by military might would have been directly applicable to shifting power relations outside the world of the playhouse. By September 1656, Cromwell had called the Second Protectorate Parliament, partly in response to growing civilian pressure to curb the power of the major generals. In this context, the play echoes the possibility of concessive reform to a more consultative form of government of the kind that was mooted in the autumn of 1656.

As a man unable to prove "his own Emperour," therefore, Alphonso conspicuously fails to exercise self-governance; his inability to master his ignoble emotion amounts to a betrayal that is social and political as well as sexual. In the 1656 version, disaster is averted, or at least deferred—Ianthe forgives Alphonso for his "over-cautious love" and a final chorus of soldiers celebrate the Pyrrhic victory of the Rhodians: "Whilst we drink good Wine, and you drink but Coffee" (I, 5.5.32). There remains, however, a tangible sense that the events of the fifth entry have not entirely resolved the unsettling ideological inversions performed in the preceding action. Whilst Solyman vows to starve the "Audacious Town" into submission, Alphonso remains tormented by his jealousy in a final image of contrition: "Draw all the Curtains, and then lead her in; / Let me in darkness mourn away my sin" (I, 5.3.107–8).

Sometimes during the three years following the first performances at Rutland House, Davenant composed the second part of *The Siege of Rhodes* that was itself entered in the Stationer's Register on May 30, 1659. Both parts were ultimately reprinted together in 1663 with "The First Part being lately enlarg'd." However, whether the complete play, in its final augmented two-part form, was ever performed before the Restoration is not clear. The first extant record of a performance is given by Pepys in his diary entry for July 2, 1661 which confirms that the two parts of *The Siege of Rhodes* constituted a principal element of the inaugural program for Davenant's new theater at Lincoln's Inn Fields. It is therefore plausible to imagine that the material had already been tried and tested on audiences at Davenant's embryonic theater at the Cockpit, during the final years of the Commonwealth. Building upon the initial experiment, the second part of *The Siege of Rhodes* dispenses with the diversionary choruses between the "entries," now reestablished as conventional act divisions and develops many of the ideas that begin to emerge in the first.

The scene opens with the Rhodian council bemoaning the continuing inaction of the Western powers to relieve the island and divided in their proposed course of action. Whilst Alphonso presses for action in a last ditch attempt to break the Turkish siege, Villerius counsels caution, reminding the headstrong knights that a reckless attack will leave the town defenseless concluding that "All those attempts of Valour we must shun / Which may the sultan vex; And, since bereft / Of food, there is no help but Treaty left" (II, 1.1.146–8). No sooner is this internal breach repaired, however, than the counsel and the audience are made aware of a wider division on the island, a split that is signaled by the stage direction: "A Shout within, and a Noise of forcing of Doors." Villerius fears that "Our guards will turn confed'rates with the crowd" in an image of anarchic mob rule dangerously abetted by a militant and intractable army. As Alphonso reports, the exercise of war has transformed the people, eroding the deference that sustains the social order. The threat of popular insurrection persuades the Rhodian Council to submit to the people's will and request that Ianthe plead with Solyman on Rhodes behalf since "The people find that they have no defence / But in your Beauty and your Eloquence," once more hazarding the provocation of Alphonso's pernicious jealousy. Again, the growing desperation of the Rhodian people seems to obliquely refer to the experience of civil war. In the second act, the clamor of the "People within" again penetrates the solemn serenity of the counsel chamber, creating a sense that the Rhodian rulers are besieged by their subjects as much as by the Turkish hoards, and provoking a debate about the nature of government. Initially, Villerius evokes an image of ideal, perhaps even democratic government, where "Pow'r is an Arch which ev'ry common hand / Does help to raise to a magnifique height" (II, 2.1.11–12). Six lines later, however, the Grand Master is forced to concede the impracticability of effective government without the consent of the people, since "Those who withstand / The Tide of Flood, which is the Peoples will, / Fall back when they in vain would onward row" (II, 2.1.18–20).

In the second half of the act, the scene turns to Solyman's camp
and resumes the display of Turkish unity that has thus far delineated
Solyman's forces from the Christian contingents of the play. Pirrhus
and Mustapha recite their habitual obsequies to their sultan's "sway,"
but in a key soliloquy, Solyman laments the shifting sands upon which
his authority is founded:

> Of spacious Empire, what can I enjoy?
> Gaining at last but what I first Destroy.
> Tis fatal (Rhodes) to thee,
> And troublesome to me
> That I was born to govern swarms
> Of Vassals boldly bred to arms:
> For whose accurs'd diversion, I must still
> Provide new Towns to Sack, new Foes to Kill.
> Excuse that Pow'r, which by my Slaves is aw'd:
> For I shall find my peace
> Destroy'd at home, unless
> I seek for them destructive Warr abroad.   (II, 2.2.53–64)

Evinced here is the same instinctive militarism of Turks "boldly bred
to arms" which informs much of the first part of the play. In his rendering, however, the conventionally ascribed attribute—an innate
propensity for war—is stood on its head and posited, not as a measure
of the empire's strength, but of its weakness. It is not stretching the
terms of the play's ambivalent mediation of contemporary events too
far to suggest that Davenant's portrait of an isolated and absolute
ruler, forced to conduct a policy of restless imperialism is redolent
of Cromwell's foreign policy in the 1650s and, in particular, the
so-called "Western Design" against Spanish-held territories in the
Caribbean that foundered in the spring of 1655. Here, more than at
any other point in the play, the Sultan's vexed authority recalls
the predicament of the crypto-monarchical figure of Cromwell who as
Lord Protector after 1653, and even more so following the "Humble
Petition and Advice" (1657) began to look increasingly like the
absolute ruler he had striven to overthrow.[11] Indeed, such a blurring
of political identities is well suited to the play's unfolding credo,
manifest in its increasing tendency to represent the Turks and the
Christians along ever-converging lines. In the second part of the play
the distinction between two outwardly inimical systems of government (the absolute rule of the Sultan and the collective oligarchy of
the Rhodian counsel) breaks down and is exposed as an illusion. For
all is specious show of unity, Solyman's "spacious Empire" is, as much

as the Rhodian alliance, subject to the tyranny of the people. The shifting signification of the text constantly resists straightforward allegory, and yet within the play's complex parallelism, the play's distinct preoccupation with the ultimately illusive nature of absolute rule must have seemed particularly germane to contemporary play audiences in the political uncertainty of 1659. On May 24, only six days before the play's registration with the Stationer's Company, Richard Cromwell, the successor Protector ratified by the "Humble Petition and Advice" had resigned, having been forced to dissolve the Third Protectorate Parliament, under Army pressure, and reinstate the "Rump" Parliament of 1653.

When the final version of the play was reprinted in 1663, the first part was advertised as "being lately enlarg'd." In all, Davenant adds six new speaking parts to its original, for Rustan, Haly, the High Marshal and Roxolana as well as sets of attendants for Ianthe and Roxolana. This was in part, no doubt, simply in anticipation of a more commodious stage than that described in the preface of the 1656 play. Similarly, several of Davenant's later additions and emendations to this version are partly made to facilitate their introduction to the audience before they are more fully represented in the succeeding part. Most substantive, however, are the additions that concern the two central women of the play. Before the first chorus, Ianthe is introduced, complete with "Two open Caskets with Jewels" in a new scene that emphasizes her selfless valor and introduces the theme of the transformations wrought by love in war:

> Love a Consumption learns from Chymists Art.
> Saphyrs, and harder Di'monds must be sold
> And turn'd so softer and more current Gold.
> With Gold we cursed Powder may prepare
> Which must consume in smoak and thinner Air.   (I, 1.2.24–8)

The transmutation of Ianthe's jewels into gunpowder underlines that aspect of her story which most closely resembled that of Henrietta-Maria, a comparison Davenant seems more inclined to intimate in his revised version.

More fundamental, however, is the introduction of an entirely new character, that of Roxolana, wife to the Sultan, in three additional scenes before the choruses. At the end of the third entry, she arrives from Licia driven by a dangerous wind, "The Tempest" of her jealous passion. Like Alphonso, she is suspicious of Solyman's motives and is correspondingly compelled to resort to metaphors for inversion and paradox in order to explain the strange influence of this Christian princess upon her husband: "Brave conquest, where the Takers self is taken" (I, 3.3.21).

Roxolana's tirade reiterates the familiar parity between amorous and military conquests that surfaces throughout the play, but also suggests the degree to which identity and "self" are themselves rendered unstable and interchangeable by the crisis of war. With the addition of Roxolana, Davenant expands the theme of the debilitative nature of marital jealousy to symmetrically incorporate the Turkish world of the play. Not only is Solyman compelled to monger war in the name of political expediency, but in a clear reflection of the Rhodian predicament, his foreign policy is hampered by domestic strife, leading the sultan to conclude, "My war with Rhodes will never have success, / Till I at home, Roxana, make my peace" (I, 5.4.19–20). In its original form, the uneasy resolution to the final entry suggested a precarious truce between Alphonso and Ianthe, disaster being narrowly averted by Christian valor on the battlefield. By the 1663 reprint, however, the failure of Solyman's forces to overpower the island defenders is perceived as being as much the consequence of an internalized wrangling in the Turkish encampment, represented by the archetype of a jealous wife, as in any vindication of Christian merit.

In the second part of *The Siege of Rhodes*, Roxolana develops as the main focus for the play's interrogation of the nature of "The cursed Jealousie," an endemic apostasy that comes to infect every sphere of the play action. Having confided in his lieutenants the marital storm that threatens to undo his reputation, Solyman resolves to send Ianthe to her jealous rival's tent, "Such a mysterious Present as will prove / A Riddle both to Honour and to Love" (II, 3.1.146–7). Oscillating between despair and rage, Roxolana derides Mustapha's invocation of duty as "officious fear" and ominously enlists the support of her loyal accomplice, the eunuch Haly. When the audience see Roxolana again, she appears in a dramatic tableau of vengeful jealousy, punctiliously described by Davenant's scene direction: "Being wholly fill'd with Roxolana's Rich Pavilion, Whereing is discern'd at distance, Ianthe sleeping on a Coach . . . Roxolana having a Turkish Embroidered Handkerchief in her left hand, And a naked Ponyard in her right" (II, 4.3.). Deliberately staged, then, this is the sultan's "Riddle" and interpreting this scene, one of the most visually arresting of the entire action, is at the heart of the ways in which the play dramatically rewrites oriental conventions and, in so doing, proclaims its own radical meaning. The setting, the eunuch's presence, the sumptuousness of the décor, the femininity of the handkerchief and the violence of the naked poniard, in fact every detail of this carefully prescribed tableau is designed to evoke the powerful topos of the seraglio. A source of constant fascination to travelers and dramatists alike, the seraglio functions as the locus for an entire range of preconceived notions about the decadence and deviance of the Turkish court. The function of the seraglio as a sexual-political fantasy is central to understanding Roxolana's role in the play.

As much a construction of Western imagination as an immediately identifiable, although ultimately mysterious, representation of Turkish polity, the seraglio is also crucially a site of feminized sovereignty. Moreover, it is the natural stage for disaster and, as Roxolana stands poised to plunge her dagger into the sleeping Ianthe, the play teeters dangerously on the edge of tragedy. Moved to compassion, the eunuch Haly persuades Roxolana to postpone her retribution until she has tried her rival's virtue and the waking Ianthe, resolute in her chasteness, wins the Sultana's mercy. In her account of the play, Bridget Orr characterizes the female opposition of the play as between "a figure of gentle modesty" versus an "ambitious virago"[12] but Roxolana's failure to conform to her Orientalist stereotype is more evidence of the play's reluctance to unconditionally enforce conventional binaries such as this. The fact that tragedy is averted and the twin themes of "honour" and "love" are reaffirmed suggests that generic reform is fundamental to the play's redefinition of a politicized Orient.

When Solyman arrives, Roxolana reproves him for his neglect and, in the ensuing exchange between the Sultan and his wife, Davenant ties up many of the threads of theme and imagery that interlace the play:

> *Roxolana:* You alter ev'ry year the Worlds known face;
> Whilst Cities you remove, and Nations chace . . .
> The various mind will wander very farr,
> Which, more than home, a forein Land preferrs.
> *Solyman:* Strange Coasts are welcome after storms at Sea . . .
> The wise, for quietness, when civil Warr
> Does rage at home, turn private Travailers.
> (II, 4.3.215–28)

Here, more than at any other point in the play, Davenant appears to make reference to his own experience of "civil Warr." The transformations of identity wrought by foreign war are inscribed even upon the "face" of the world. Yet more powerful, however, are the effects of domestic conflict, microcosmically represented by the "Storms" of Roxolana's jealousy, a tempest of such insidious force that the archetype of the invincible Turk becomes transformed into that of the "private Travailer," a figure of exiled virtue reminiscent of many self-characterizations of Royalist luminaries during the 1640s and 1650s, not least those of the Stuart heir and the playwright himself.

As a brief account of Davenant's eventful biography will testify, his life appears inextricably bound up with the life of the nation and its theater in this period. During the 1630s, Davenant became an established playwright for the King's Men and was appointed as successor to Jonson as poet laureate in 1638. In the latter half of the decade, Davenant also achieved distinction as the foremost exponent of a new development in privately staged masques, collaborating with Inigo Jones in the production of splendidly elaborate spectacles for the entertainment of the monarch and his court. As relations between the king and parliament disintegrated, Davenant's allegiance to the monarch engendered the suspicion of parliament and, as early as May 1641, he was arrested for his part in the Army Plot. Having been released on bail, Davenant fled the country and joined Queen Henrietta Maria in her French exile where he acted as emissary to the Queen and organized the passage of arms and supplies to the beleaguered King in England. At the outbreak of open hostilities, Davenant seems to have taken up arms for the King and was knighted at the Siege of Gloucester in 1643. Following the regicide, Davenant remained in exile and began composing his epic poem *Gondibert* but, in May 1650, the poet was appointed Lieutenant Governor of Maryland by the Queen and sent to replace the incumbent governor, a Pariliamentary sympathizer. Davenant and his crew never reached Virginia but were captured whilst still in sight of the French coast by a Parliamentary ship. Davenant was imprisoned initially at Cowes Castle and later in the Tower and was not released until August 1654. The experience of imprisonment seems to have deeply affected Davenant who, judging from his correspondence with Thomas Hobbes and the postscript to his unfinished *Gondibert* (a project "interrupted by so great an experiment as Dying"), fully expected to be executed as an enemy to the new state. The playwright's rehabilitation, at least in the eyes of the authorities, must have been profound: only two years after his release from the Tower, the quondam gun runner and confidante of the Catholic Queen had secured permission to undertake the revolutionary series of plays and representations at Rutland House. By 1660, however, Davenant had come full circle, joining the host of poets eager to add their voice to the adulating throng, exulting in the vanquishing of the tyrant Protector and rejoicing at the return of the rightful heir.[13]

The vicissitudes of the dramatist's life are characteristic of the period and central to an understanding of *The Siege of Rhodes*. Certainly, the play's treatment of notions of betrayal and apparent reversals of allegiance would have seemed particularly resonant to a playgoer of the early Restoration—the question of former loyalties would become a potent preoccupation of the literary thought of the 1660s. Clarendon's own monumental *History of the Rebellion* endeavored to appropriate the events of mid-century in the service of a fundamentally Royalist ethic, the professed purpose of the narrative being to recognize the few who had "opposed and resisted that torrent" in the past in order that they might be distinguished from those who had implicated themselves in the "universal apostasy in the whole nation from their religion and allegiance." Davenant himself was clearly vulnerable to such an impeachment and was accused by Sir Henry Herbert of having "exercised the office of Master of the Revells to Oliuer the Tyrant" by his old adversary Sir Henry Herbert who had himself been reinstated in the post at the Restoration.[14]

Whether mediated on stage, from pulpit or via the polemical press, one of the most abiding preoccupations of English treatments of Islam in the period was the threat of conversion. As the work of Nabil Matar and Daniel Vitkus has shown, rhetorical strategies used to resist the perceived threat of Islamic conversions were readily transferable to other discourses of religious difference, most notably those representing inter-Christian divisions. However, a third and critical meaning emerges in the approach to English constitutional breakdown. To turn Turk in the context of the 1640s did not only encompass literal and figurative defections to the anti-Christian forces of Pope or Prophet, but came to include political and ideological tergiversation within the emerging domestic conflict. From an English perspective, these were clearly related definitions. The image of the renegade had always carried connotations of the enemy within and as religious anxiety concerning the influence of unseen Popish influences mounted, the intensity with which political enemies might be condemned as Turk-like traitors could only increase. In the crisis of allegiance provoked by civil war, this trope was accorded a newly powerful and complex significance, a set of meaning that had been unimaginable before parliament waged war against its sovereign. Of course, just who was the apostate and who the true believer in this scenario was not a matter of consensus. Depending upon one's point of view, the monarch had himself turned, betraying the religious and constitutional ideals of his Protestant people. More commonly expressed after the defeat and execution of the King, however, was the belief that the nation had been overrun with "renegadoes," traitors who had turned Turk and betrayed England to Cromwell's tyranny. Writing in August 1650, for example, John Cleiveland condemned the official Commonwealth journalist Marchmont Nedham as having "reproached our whole nation . . . a three piled apostate, a renegade more notorious than any in Sally or Algier," adding that "there is no such torment to a Christian as to be tyrannized over by a Renegade."[15]

By the time of Davenant's play, England's long-standing fascination with the Orient, or rather with its own construction of Orient had become dislocated, fragmented and rechanneled under the pressures of the Revolution. *The Siege of Rhodes* participates in a preoccupation with Islam that permeated religious, political, diplomatic, and commercial discourses as well as the drama. In theological and political animadversions, the Turk and his religion could be requisitioned in an apparently limitless number of ways; in questions of natural religion, free will, divine revelation, ecclesiastical sovereignty, liberty of conscience, tyranny and toleration, Islam was repeatedly treated. Above all, as a political paradigm, the Islamic model was available to both Royalist and Republican thinkers. The radical indeterminacy this engendered is at the heart of the play's own ideological ambivalence. The ultimate achievement of *The Siege of Rhodes* is clearly much more than the straightforward allegorization of civil war or indeed any consistent system of signification. Rather, Davenant's play takes the topical belief that England might learn from the Turks a crucial step further, performing an extraordinary refraction of identity upon the already acutely politicized Islamic figure. Solyman, the reformed and transformed Turk at the center of the play represents an inversion of orthodox notions of enmity and apostasy directly pertinent to the English situation. In his concluding peroration, the Sultan permits the Rhodians an honorable defeat, granting Ianthe license to make terms form the town, declaiming, "I am content it should recorded be, / That, when I vanquisht Rhodes, you conquered me." In this final confirmation of Solyman's altered identity, a transformation made all the more absolute by his iconic despotism, the Turkish ruler becomes the apogee of a notionally Christian ideal of kingship, the confluence of reason and compassion, honor and love. As the play's reconciliatory finale contends, the answer to the vexed questions of apostasy and allegiance posed in the play lie in a reorientation of long-standing divisions both at home and abroad. Played out against the backdrop of ongoing Mediterranean trade and conflict, English representations of Islamic history and culture would prove instrumental to the ways in which restored drama negotiated the dialectic between past and present, republic and monarchy, long after the return of the king.

NOTES

1. Leslie Hotson speculates that, "it was probably in September, to take advantage of the confluence of gentry to London for the opening of Parliament, and for Michaelmas term at the law courts." *The Commonwealth and Restoration Stage* (New York: Russell & Russell, 1962), p. 131.

2. Samuel Chew, *The Crescent and the Rose: Islam and England During the Renaissance* (New York: Oxford University Press, 1937), p. 496.

3. Conversely, in her study, Laura Brown emphasizes the supposed primitiveness of Davenant's production. Arguing that the stylized nature of the action grows out of the physical conditions of its staging, Brown writes, "The play's form in itself prescribes that distance, elevation, and stasis . . . The enactment of such a standard is inevitably episodic and static, a series of emblematic scenes that display rather than involve." Laura Brown, *English Dramatic Form, 1660–1760: An Essay in Generic History* (New Haven and London: Yale University Press, 1981), p. 6.

4. Susan Wiseman's reading of the play is an important basis for my own although, as I shall argue, the play's representation of the Sultan does not depend upon the diminution of the perceived threat of the Ottoman Empire but a radical reappraisal of its notional relationship with Western Europe and England in particular. Susan Wiseman, *Drama and Politics in the English Civil War* (Cambridge: Cambridge University Press, 1998), p. 153.

5. There seems to have been a particular fascination with the dramatic possibilities of the Orient concentrated in the latter half of the 1650s. Lodovick Carlell's *Osmond the Great Turk*, first performed in 1637, was printed in 1657, one year after the initial performances of *The Siege of Rhodes* and perhaps in response to the revived interest created by Davenant's play. One year earlier, Robert Baron had published his own treatment of Persian history in the shape of *Mirza*, itself a reworking of an earlier play, John Denham's *The Sophy*.

6. This and subsequent quotations are taken from the British Library copy of the two-part edition of the play (1663). The two parts are marked I and II in parentheses.

7. By the time the second part of Davenant's play appeared in the summer of 1659, the Dardanelles had long been reopened and Ottoman armies were once more being mobilized against the Hapsburg territories in Transylvania. Candia itself would finally succumb to the Turks in 1669.

8. *Calendar of State Papers, Domestic, Commonwealth, 1653*, ed., Mary Anne Everett Green (London: H.M.S.O., 1878), pp. 157–8.

9. *Calendar of State Papers. Venetian, 1657*, p. 674.

10. Of the Queen, Wiseman speculates that "the female figures in [Davenant's] plays—such as Ianthe—may perhaps bear traces of his

admiration of her" (*Drama and Politics*, p. 140), whilst Hedbäck asserts that her "activities during the first years of the Civil War parallel strikingly those of Davenant's Ianthe." Ann-Mari Hedbäck, *The Siege of Rhodes: A Critical Edition* (Uppsala: Acta Universitatis Upsaliensis, Studia Anglistica Upsaliensia 14, 1973), p. xxxi.

11. Cromwell famously declined the crown (prompting comparisons with Richard III) and Protectorate government differed from Charles's personal rule in several important ways, not least in how it saw itself. Nevertheless, Cromwell's eventual acceptance of the "Humble Petition" in its revised form (May 25, 1657) did prompt criticism from both Royalists and Republicans alike. For a discussion of the "draft towards kingship" in the 1650s, see David Norbrook, *Writing the English Republic: Poetry, Rhetoric and Politics 1627–1660* (Cambridge: Cambridge University Press, 1999), p. 324.

12. Bridget Orr, *Empire on the English Stage* (Cambridge: Cambridge University Press, 2001), p. 66.

13. The most recent biographer of the playwright is Mary Edmond, *Rare Sir William Davenant* (Manchester: Manchester University Press, 1987).

14. Of course, Davenant never held any such position in an official capacity. Nevertheless, it was reported that songs to the "victor" had accompanied his first piece of licensed theater in the 1650s, *The First Days Entertainment*, whilst the poet had also composed an epithalamium to Cromwell's daughter upon the occasion of her marriage to Lord Falconbridge (entered in the Stationer's Register for December 7, 1657). In this respect, Davenant was in good company—both Waller and Cowley published poetry in praise of Cromwell, whilst Dryden himself had contributed to a collection of verse *Upon the Death of his late Highnesse Oliver Lord Protector of England and Scotland, and Ireland* only to emerge as staunchly Loyalist in the very next year. Alfred Harbage, *Sir William Davenant Poet Venturer 1606–1668* (Philadelphia: University of Pennsylvania Press, 1935), p. 141.

15. John Cleveland, *The Character of Mercurius Politicus* (London, 1650), p. 4. The career of the mercurial Nedham is a good example of the degree to which the tenor of the times transformed public loyalties. For a discussion of *Mercurius Politicus*, see Joseph Frank, *Cromwell's Press Agent: A Critical Biography of Marchamont Nedham, 1620–1678* (Lanham: University Press of America, 1980).

CHAPTER 12

SATIRIZING ENGLISH TANGIER IN SAMUEL PEPYS'S *DIARY* AND *TANGIER PAPERS*

Adam R. Beach

The writings of Samuel Pepys seem an unlikely source for satire of English colonial pretensions in the Restoration period. Little of the English colonial world is given any attention in Pepys's famous *Diary*, and, judging from its nine mundane references to Virginia and New England, the American colonies were simply not an important part of Pepys's mental geography. The only major overseas establishment that consistently held Pepys's attention was the outpost in Tangier (1661–84), which, in most accounts of English colonial history, is considered to be peripheral if it is mentioned at all. In one respect, the focus of seventeenth-century scholars on English overseas activity in the Caribbean, North America, and the East Indies is understandable, given the centrality of those areas to the later British Empire. In contrast, Tangier produced no line of colonial succession, and it was not the staging ground of a later British empire in North Africa, making it easier to underestimate the importance of Tangier to the government of Charles II. It is hard to build a narrative of the "rise of the British empire" on the ruins of English Tangier.

Just outside the Straits of Gibraltar, the fortified North African outpost, along with Bombay and a cash payment, fell into England's possession as part of Charles II's marriage settlement with the Portuguese princess Catherine of Braganza in 1661. As an important official in Charles's government and as a member of the governing Tangier Committee and its eventual Treasurer, Pepys was intimately associated with the project from early on. Pepys was also a participant in the expedition sent out to destroy and abandon Tangier in 1683 and he personally witnessed what little had remained of the approximately 1.6 million pounds of revenue that Charles II had invested in the fortified town and in the expensive and ultimately ineffective mole that was constructed in Tangier harbor. In contrast to other overseas projects run by private companies, chartered entities, or individual proprietors, Charles's cash-strapped government was the sole source of funding and materials for the settlement, including the military establishment that was manned by various Scottish, Irish, and English regiments. The colonists failed miserably in their primary mission of expanding into neighboring territory and establishing Tangier as a trading post and a port for naval operations. Imperialist historians, in fact, bemoan the decision not to turn over Tangier to a private enterprise run by merchants and investors. For example, the editor of Pepys's *Tangier Papers*, Edwin Chappell, exclaims: "there was no antecedent reason why the possession of Tangier should not have led to a great African Empire in the same way that Bombay led to a great Indian Empire. Had Tangier been handed over to a North Africa Company, the history of the World might have been very different."[1] With the increased financial and political pressures of the 1670s and 1680s, Charles could no longer afford the colony, and parliament, fearful of Tangier as a breeding ground for Catholic troops who could support the supposed absolutist aims of the Stuart monarchy, made future funding dependent on the exclusion of James from the throne. Unable to accept such a bargain, Charles decided to abandon Tangier and destroy its fortifications and mole in order to prevent the outpost from falling into enemy hands or becoming another staging ground for Barbary pirates.

In his paradoxical role as both colonial administrator and satirist, Samuel Pepys penned vicious critiques of the Tangier Committee on which he served, darkly humorous accounts of the repetitive military and administrative failures of the English Tangerines, and a vitriolic diatribe on the sexual depravity, monstrous corruption, and frightening absolute power of its military governor, all of which he witnessed first hand during his voyage to the outpost in 1683. This work can be found both in his famous *Diary* and in Chappell's 1935 edition of *The Tangier Papers of Samuel Pepys*, which contains, among other documents, incomplete transcriptions of the shorthand diary and place description he composed during his journey. Taken together, these writings not only represent the unique perspective of a man with direct experience of both the center and periphery of colonial governance, but also furnish further evidence for recent claims that most seventeenth-century English citizens were generally indifferent or outrightly hostile to the old colonial system.

Confirming similar findings by Richard Koebner some thirty years earlier, David Armitage has recently argued that the seventeenth-century colonies were rarely considered to be part of a wider national polity by the small number of English citizens who thought of them at all. Regarding early modern England, Armitage confirms Linda Colley's more general maxim that "empire simply did not loom all that large in the minds of most men and women back in Europe," despite the increasing availability of consumer goods produced in colonial settings.[2] In his recent study of *Paradise Lost* and empire, J. Martin Evans surveys the defensive propaganda put forth by various colonial projectors and concludes that the seventeenth-century colonies were castigated by "a vehemently anticolonial and largely oral subculture that threatened to discredit the whole enterprise."[3] His attention to anticolonial discourse of the period reveals that many Englishmen viewed the colonies as cesspools filled with convicts, Catholics, religious fanatics, political radicals, and other undesirables. No wonder Milton chose to write an epic based on Genesis rather than on the English experiments in America. Peter Linebaugh and Marcus Rediker's delineation of radical and working-class resistance to the overseas projects, both in England and in the colonies themselves, reveals a vehement critique from lower classes that condemned the colonies as vicious labor prisons intended to violently consume the energies of the English poor and African slaves.[4] When reviewing this literature, a picture develops in which some of the only people in England proper who concocted any positive representations of the colonies were those who were trying to make money from them. In the case of Pepys, not even the substantial bribes he received while serving as its treasurer could assuage his feeling that Tangier, and its colonists, were an embarrassment to the nation.

Taking note of such widespread attitudes helps us to place Pepys's writings on Tangier in the context of larger structures of feeling about the colonies that emerged in seventeenth-century England. At the same time, Stuart Sherman's recent reconsideration of the *Diary* has created a space in which we can appreciate Pepys's work as a complex literary composition. Sherman argues that "scholars who consult the diary tend to use it as a resource rather than regard it as a performance, and this has forestalled the possibility of seeing it whole."[5] Even though he does not attend to the satiric performances of the *Diary*, Sherman's work allows for a more attentive reading of the compositional specifics of Pepys's satirical depictions of Restoration government during the disastrous 1660s.Throughout the *Diary*, Pepys demonstrates a keen eye for what is absurd about the English nation, particularly in the years surrounding the disastrous Second Anglo-Dutch War that ended with the shocking 1667 Dutch raid up the Medway River and the destruction of a significant portion of the English Navy. Pepys enjoyed reading satirical poetry about the government which he served and seriously contemplated writing a lampoon on the English failures in the Dutch war, but he wisely contented himself by experimenting with the occasional deadpan satiric entry in the safer privacy of his *Diary*.[6]

While we do not have enough space to examine fully Pepys's representations of Tangier in the *Diary*, satiric or otherwise, it must be noted that he felt that the colony was a complete waste from early on, that it was generally filled with undesirable people of all sorts (4.10.67; 8.160), and that he fully agreed with Sir William Coventry's view that Tangier was an "Excrescence of the earth provided by God for the payment of debts" (5.5.67; 8.201). Along with such scathing references to Tangier, Pepys also gloated about the rich bribes and kickbacks he received during his tenure on the Committee: "But I have good reason to love myself for serving Tanger, for it is one of the best flowers in my garden" (9.26.64; 5.280). Pepys's private writings are refreshing for those used to the obfuscations and rationalizations of most colonial discourse: Tangier appears as both a shameful, unjustifiable venture and a metaphorical blossom in Pepys's garden of corruption. He is not against colonization per se, but he is appalled by its English manifestation in North Africa and finds the colony to be a disgraceful display of the weakness of the Stuart government that he served.

Because he was inside of colonial government, Pepys had first-hand access to information that he could shape into sharp satiric narrative. A pertinent example of his satiric style can be found in the entry for June 2, 1664, in which Pepys recorded one of the most surreal episodes in British colonial history: the massacre of Tangerine soldiers who were led by their Scottish governor Andrew Rutherford, earl of Teviot, into an ambush by local Moorish forces:

> It seems my Lord Tiviotts design was to go out a mile and a half out of the town to cut down a wood in which the enemy did use to lie in ambush. He had sent several spyes; but all brought word that the way

was clear, and so might be for anybody's discovery of an enemy before you are upon them. There they were all snapped, he and all his officers, and about 200 hundred men as they say—there being left now in the garrison but four Captains. This happened the 3rd of May last, being not before the day twelvemonth of his entering into his government there; but at his going out in the morning, he said to some of his officers, "Gentlemen, let us look to ourselfs, for it was this day three years that so many brave Englishmen were knocked on the head by the Moores, when Fines made his sally out." (6.2.64; 5.166–7)

Pepys must have had a chuckle when penning Teviot's infamous last words, as the governor subsequently led his troops into an ambush that was almost identical to the one suffered by the aforementioned Major Fines on May 3, 1662. In this case, Teviot's repetition of Fines's strategic error led to the death, as Pepys later learned, of nearly four hundred men, including the governor himself. Given Pepys's careful composition process, we need to mark the literary style of the piece. In some respects, Andrew Marvell could not have written it better: the passage's deadpan commentary about the failures of the English spies and the dark humor of Teviot's final utterance form part of a fantastic satire on the heroic colonial pretensions of Charles II's Tangerines. Teviot's last declaration seems almost too absurd to be true. Given that Pepys seems to be the only known source of the utterance, we might wonder whether he fictionalized the remarks himself or recorded and shaped an already cutting satirical account of Teviot's final minutes told to him by somebody else.

Yet, my larger claim that Pepys is one of the most important satirists of an early modern English colonial venture rests not only on the perfection of his dark humor, but also on Pepys's rendering of Teviot as the stupid scion of Fines's bumbling. In essence, Pepys creates a descending line of colonial dunces. The morbid comedy of the entry hangs on the suggestion that the English colony is stuck in an uncanny temporal loop whose trajectory tends toward degeneration. The preeminent twentieth-century historian of English Tangier, E.M.G. Routh, speculates that Teviot chose this particular day for his advance because "he no doubt thought that a successful action fought on the fateful May 3 would have double the moral effect of any other time."[7] As the second governor of Tangier, Teviot was clearly hoping to reverse the defeats of the first regime, during which Fines led five hundred men into an ambush and sustained massive casualties. The losses incurred by Fines's blundering contributed to a grotesque body count during the first two years of the English occupation of Tangier and quickly made service there an extremely unpopular option within the army.[8] Rather than inaugurating a new heroic lineage that would reverse the fatal mistakes of the past, the Teviot depicted in Pepys's entry joins an ignoble line of idiotic military leaders whose pretensions are mercilessly exposed by the forces of history and who, by extension, have no right to claim possession of lands in a foreign soil. Similarly, we can recognize a certain satiric spirit in the soldiers of Tangier who enacted a parodic travesty of imperial nomination following the disaster of May 3: the site of the massacre, formerly known as the "Jews' Mount," was thereafter referred to as "Teviot Hill" by the men of the garrison (Routh, p. 68). This gruesome memorialization indicates that Pepys was not the only one to find dark humor in the failed progression and false possession implied by the new place name.

As David Quint has pointed out, circularity is the temporal fate of the vanquished: "To the victors belongs epic, with its linear teleology; to the losers belongs romance, with its random or circular wandering. Put another way, the victors experience history as a coherent, end-directed story told by their own power; the losers experience a contingency that they are powerless to shape to their own ends."[9] We might add that the losers often turn to satire as well, another anNo teleological form, to express their sense of powerlessness. Michael Seidel's provocative study of satire argues that "there is in the satiric act a kind of perverse neutralization of historical progression, a stop without the guarantee of a new start."[10] Seidel's work is especially relevant when examining figures like those of Pepys whose work contests a "rise of empire" narrative and its attendant presentations of time-as-progress and history-as-accumulation. For Seidel, satire is a flexible narrative mode that meditates on temporal movements—regression and circularity—that disrupt or parody the progressive time of the imperial epic and that give birth to an illegitimate, degenerating lineage.

In this light, we can appreciate how Pepys's diurnal form becomes a powerful tool for representing a stagnant sense of time-as-repetition, a temporal feature that is not accounted for in Sherman's investigation of the property, power, and pleasure, that the *Diary* project provided Pepys. When dealing with the affairs of nation and colony, in the historical time that he neither possesses nor controls, Pepys finds himself in a cycle of recurrence in which the repetition of futile tasks and national failures occur in a perpetual series. Any reader of Pepys's *Diary* soon learns that the diurnal form was a perfect vehicle for capturing the inane administrative workings of Restoration government. Consider Pepys's depiction of the desultory meetings of the Tangier Committee that occurred on consecutive days. The first description is from the entry for June 2, 1664, the day he learned of Teviot's blundering: "and so over the park to White-hall to a Committee of Tanger about providing provisions, money and men for Tanger. At it all the afternoon; but it is strange to see how poorly and brokenly things are done of the greatest consequence—and how soon the memory of this great man is gone, or at least out of mind, by the thoughts of who goes next, which is not yet known" (6.2.64; 5:166). The entry for the next day, like the meeting itself, is an exercise in repetition: "At the Committee for Tanger all the afternoon; where a sad consideration to see things of so great weight managed in so confused a manner as it is, so as I would not have the buying of an acre of land bought by—(6.3.64; 5:167)." In this sequence, Pepys presciently captures his experience of the stale, bureaucratic temporality of committee meetings. This lulls all of the participants, the diarist excluded, into a state of amnesia and administrative incompetence: the passive voice ("things are done," "things . . . managed") reinforces the sense that no guiding authority is behind the Tangier project and that events are spiraling out of control of their own accord. The phrase— "it is strange to see"—is emblematic of Pepys's economical representations of the surreal circularity that threatens the disintegration of both the center and the periphery of Stuart government: one useless meeting after another in London is mirrored by one massacre after another in Tangier. This sense that the British community in North Africa was merely an extension of the sick center of English society was only exacerbated upon Pepys's seeing Tangier with his own eyes.

Few of the passages in Pepys's little-studied *Tangier Papers* are as well crafted and darkly humorous as his musings on Teviot, and he tends toward outright condemnation or cutting sarcasm when describing Tangier. However, his participation in the expedition to destroy Tangier in 1683 resulted in a fascinating set of writings in which Pepys continues to play the satirical role outlined by Seidel. What better place could exist in which to document the "perverse neutralization of historical progression" than a failed colony? Consider the following first-person narration in which Pepys recasts an administrative blunder into a meditation on the regressive temporality of English Tangier:

> I speaking with Kirke about want of water . . . [he] adds that at my lord Peterborough's receiving the place from the King of Portugal, there was given him a book (with other customary things) which used among the Portuguese people to be always given from one governor to another, never to be looked into by any other, that did give a secret

account of all the conduit heads and heads of watercourses in and about the town, of which this place was the fullest in the World, every house in the town having a particular well or two, which are now lost and dry, by losing the knowledge whither to go to the conduit head to remedy it. My lord Peterborough having taken away the book with him, and upon being asked for it, has always answered that he has mislaid it and cannot recover it, which is another pretty instance of the fate this place has always, and in everything, met with. (*Tangier Papers*, p. 91)

The regular transfer of important knowledge "from one governor to another" was handled successfully by the Portuguese, but this line of succession grinds to an immediate halt with Peterborough, the first governor of English Tangier, who simply loses its most vital source of knowledge. Having "mislaid" this crucial information, the bungling Peterborough can only pass on what Seidel might call a "satiric inheritance." Pepys's text amounts to a nonfictional satire in which the English in North Africa, just like their counterparts on the Tangier Committee, become parodic figures, unaware of their own incompetence to manage even the most basic administrative tasks. According to Routh, the English were forced to send to Spain for water in 1683, also a year in which the poor quality and quantity of the water supply caused sickness in the garrison (p. 256). The Tangerines allowed wells to be filled in and animals to defecate in their water supply, leading Routh to conclude that "There is no greater blot on the Tangerine administration than its carelessness in this respect" (p. 257). In the face of such mismanagement, Pepys is reduced to sarcasm, and his closing words—"another pretty instance of the fate this place has always, and in everything, met with"—reinforce the sense of the perpetually stagnant time that he discovered in the meetings for the Tangier Committee.

In this respect, déjà vu is the implicit structuring principle of the *Tangier Papers*. In the following paired passages, we can see that Pepys's scathing commentary on the degeneracy of the Tangerines uncannily resembles earlier *Diary* entries that critique the infamous libertine court of Charles II. One travels to Tangier only to witness the sins of Whitehall:

at Court things are in very ill condition, there being so much aemulacion, poverty, and the vices of *swearing, drinking, and whoring*, that I know not what will be the end of it but confusion. (*Diary*, 8.31.61; 2.167)

Nothing but vice in the whole place of all sorts, for *swearing, cursing, drinking and whoring*. (*Tangier Papers*, p. 89)

By and by down to the Chappell again [at Whitehall], where Bishop Morly preached . . . Methought he made but a poor sermon, but long and reprehending the mistaken jollity of the Court for the true joy that shall and ought to be on these days. Perticularized concerning their excess in plays and gameing . . . Upon which, it was worth observing how far they are come from taking the Reprehensions of a Bishop seriously, that *they all laugh in the chapel when he reflected on their ill actions and courses.* (*Diary,* 12.25.62; 3.292–3)

So to church and heard a very fine and season[able] but most unsuccessful sermon from Dr. Ken in reproof particularly of the vices of this town, so as I was in pain for the Governor and the officers about us in the church, *but I perceived they regarded it not.* (*Tangier Papers,* p. 30)

That the talk which these people about our King that I named before have . . . is so base and sordid that it makes the eares of the very gentlemen of back-stairs, I think he called them, *to tingle to hear it spoke in the King's hearing*—and that must be very bad endeed. (*Diary,* 2.22.64; 5.60)

No going by a door almost but you hear people swearing and damning, and the women as much as the men. Insomuch that Capt. Silver, a sober officer of my lord's, belonging to the Ordnance, did say he was *quite ashamed of what he had heard himself in their house,* worse a thousand times than the worst place that ever he was in, in London. (*Tangier Papers,* p. 90; emphasis mine in all preceding citations)

Perhaps Captain Silver had never been to the court of Charles II. Whatever the case, Pepys demonstrates that the putridity of colonial society does not result from a failure to reproduce English civilization in a faraway land, but precisely the opposite. Like Dorimant's shoemaker in *The Man of Mode* or, more pointedly, Pepys himself in the 1660s, the Tangerines have too excitedly taken up the "sins o' the nation"[11] that were openly practiced by the libertine court.

Pepys's analogies between court and colony are not always so implicit. Consider his description of Arthur Herbert, the admiral of the Mediterranean fleet: "W. Hewer tells me of captains submitting themselves to the meanest degree of servility to Herbert when he was at Tangier, waiting at his rising and going to bed, combing his perruque, brushing him, putting on his coat for him, *as the King is served,* he living and keeping a house on shore and his mistresses visited and attended *one after another, as the King's are*"(p. 138; emphasis mine). The national narrative of progress is waylaid into a satiric storyline whereby powerful men dissipate their energies, just like their King, through an unending series of sexual encounters, "one after another," which simultaneously hinders and replaces a succession of military victories or administrative achievements. In this respect, Pepys was working in a venerable Restoration satiric tradition made possible by Charles's politically disturbing sexual behavior and his public championing of both his mistresses and his numerous illegitimate children, which, as James Grantham Turner has noted, allowed Whitehall, with some justification, to be viewed as a mere brothel. Turner has suggestively analyzed the political complications and confusion caused by the "Court's 'wanton talk' and obscene writing, drunken brawling, riot, injury, outrage, insolence, duelling, ruffianly assaults, window-smashing, and wife-snatching—a general state of warfare, both verbal and physical, in which sexuality and disease are the weapons."[12] Turner nicely captures the nihilistic frenzy of the Restoration's libertine ethos and the ways that Pepys was able to both emulate the court in his own sexual adventuring and "dissociate himself from the sins he was copying in miniature" (p. 108). However, in the *Tangier Papers*, none of the ambivalence of the *Diary* is left: Pepys stands aghast at a colonial society that has copied and magnified the worst tendencies of the Stuart court.

The Tangerines flaunt their sexual immoralities before Pepys as if they were as proud of the illegitimate society they had created in Tangier as Charles seemed to be of his own. In Pepys's writings, Tangier resembles a bastard-filled brothel, with the Governor Percy Kirke playing the role of its chief pimp: "I heard Kirke, with my own ears . . . ask the young Controller whether he had had a whore yet since he came into the town, and that he must do it quickly or they would be all gone on board the ships and that he would help him to a little one of his own size, and this openly" (p. 93). Pepys emphasizes his first-hand proximity because he is shocked by Kirke's bravado and his lack of a desire to maintain any reputation in the presence of a dignified visitor from London. Because this disregard of propriety is sanctioned and facilitated by the colony's leadership, a degraded social order has taken shape in Tangier in which sordid sexuality is the public norm. In such an environment, Pepys claims that most of the women in Tangier "are, generally speaking, whores, and think it no extraordinary thing at all, both mothers and daughters being so publicly to one another's knowledge, as to call one another so, commonly" (p. 90). The Tangerines, like the King himself, have created a libertine free-for-all that proclaims itself as such to the shock of ordinary English sinners like Pepys.

At the same time, the culture of the colony not only assaults conventional sexual morality, but also dismisses as dispensable fictions the ideas of legitimacy and paternity that undergird English property law.

Like Charles himself, the Tangerines seem incapable of producing any legitimate progeny, as evidenced by the following anecdote in which Pepys took special interest: "Dr. Balam, their Recorder heretofore, left his servant his estate with the caution that if ever he married a woman of Tangier, or that had ever been there, he should lose it all. I have a copy of his will" (p. 89). Unable to father children himself, Balam at least wishes to keep his estate moving along a steady line of licit successions, a process that would only be endangered by a woman of Tangier. As a fellow man without heirs, one wonders if Pepys must have approved of Balam's own hysterical interdiction against any woman who had "been there," as if merely passing through the outpost would insure the types of illicit births that Seidel argues are the foundation of a satiric lineage.

In describing the rapid decay of the materials used to construct English fortifications, Pepys notes, "Everything runs so to corruption here, that they tell me as an instance that the timber in Pole Fort. . . . do prove more rotten than the like timber in another place would in a great deal longer time in any other place" (p. 91). This maxim about the unnaturally accelerating material deterioration in Tangier clearly applies to aspects of English civilization as well. Early in his journal, Pepys is shocked by the degraded state of the titles that he examines while determining the compensation required to reimburse the displaced Tangerines for their abandoned estates. The satirist finds that the property titles used "such evidence for their security as would not be worth sixpence in Westminster Hall, nor would be here, if any of the right heirs [of] the parties they have their titles from would give them any trouble" (p. 25–6). Evidently, the Tangerines put too much stock in verbal assurances and did not secure proper transmissions of property, much like the Tangier Committee itself, which, as we saw previously, Pepys did not trust to buy a simple acre of land. For Pepys, this disregard for the legal mechanisms of possession renders the colony itself as illegitimate as any child born in its environs.

The decay of the legal written instrument is part and parcel of the absolutist government of Tangier that Pepys represents with as much abhorrence as its libertine culture. Stephen Saunders Webb notes that "Tangier's constitutional place (like that of the American colonies) outside the realm of the common law" allowed Charles to create a local government "subject to absolute, royal, martial authority."[13] Describing the "absolute" powers of the appointed governor in Tangier, Webb notes that he "could commission, discipline, and train the men of his garrison, subdue and slay rebels and traitors, legislate and judge and pardon, license or restrict commerce 'as may best suite with your interests,' restricted only occasionally by royal (that is, ducal) instructions" (p. 23–4). These absolute powers were legally checked to some extent only when the Tangier Committee established a civil government and nonmilitary courts in 1668. Pepys helped to write the constitution for the civil government, part of a general effort to make the town more amenable to trade, to make Tangier law more in step with English custom, and to force the next governor, as Coventry told Pepys, to "go with limitations and rules to fallow, and not to do as he please, as the rest have hitherto done" (*Diary* 4.10.67; 8:160). Upon visiting Tangier, Pepys could see how futile was the effort to control the military governor, whose absolute rule continued relatively unabated, and to what dire ends Kirke would push his prerogative to do as he pleased. Feeble written texts from London had no power to put the genie of Stuart colonial absolutism back into its bottle.

In the *Tangier Papers*, Kirke emerges as something of a seventeenth-century Kurtz, an official who combines an insanely corrupt administration, an insatiable sexual depravity, and a desire for absolute control, the very traits that many English people suspected were part of the Stuart constitution as well. Noting his control over property, his ability to assess illegal fees on all business transactions in the city, and his interference in the civil courts, Pepys represents Kirke as a tyrant who is antithetical to English ideals of liberty and justice and who has become the law unto himself: "And where the Recorder has sometimes told him that such or such a thing was not according to the law of England, he has openly said in Court that it was then according to the law of Tangier" (p. 97). Kirke's supersession of the written English laws and his ability to arbitrarily change the ruling order of things with a mere utterance are indicative of a society where the oral is quickly becoming primary and where the decay of written documentation facilitates absolutist governance. Indeed, Kirke explains to Lord Dartmouth, the leader of the expedition and the highest-ranking officer in Tangier, that "it was not necessary, nor usual here, to have some things done in writing" (p. 94), which increases his absolute authority and precludes the paper trail that would allow outsiders to investigate his administrative practices. Kirke's unchecked power allows him to create a society in which the most base human instincts are given full reign, resulting in an eruption of savagery and human degradation as well as a frightening breakdown of the rule of law. The colonial emulation of the combination of Stuart sexual and absolutist tendencies has resulted in a predatory society in which the only law is that of power and force:

> Capt. Silver told my lord in my hearing what a company of people of
> the King's subjects were in chains, and how long the chains were, when
> my lord came hither and commanded them to be set at liberty. And that
> it was this tyrannical severity of Kirke's that made so many desert the
> place and run to the Moors. And he says there have been 30 or 40 men
> in these chains at a time, and men put into them upon the score of get-
> ting their daughters or wives to come to him to look after their hus-
> bands and fathers where he found them pretty, only to debauch. (p. 92)

A metropolitan elite like Lord Dartmouth can restore some sem-
blance of English standards in this instance, but his granting of
"liberty" to these English captives is no panacea, only a gesture of
improvement before the annihilation of Tangier. Pepys's acquisition
of "one of the very chains . . . that the King's soldiers used to carry
and be made to work in" (p. 92) seems a parody of the tourist
knickknack, a memento of the human degradation everywhere
present in Tangier.

In another case that demonstrates to Pepys the "bestiality of this
place," a man was imprisoned and beaten by Kirke's soldiers while his
property was stolen and his wife repeatedly gang-raped (p. 97–8).
Later on, Pepys writes: "Mr Gargrave tells me of most foul acts done
by Kirke in public, lying with a woman in the market-place, and making another woman be taken from her husband out of her bed and
[14 *words omitted*]" (p. 102–3). The bracketed note is Chappell's, and
he explains in the editor's preface that his publisher demanded the
excision of "ten of the coarsest passages" (p. x). From what Chappell
did include, we can see that Kirke's nihilistic ruling order smashes
through Pepys's notions of private and public and exacts a hideous
price on female bodies in the process. There is a sadistic nastiness in
the reports of Kirke that Pepys collects, including an incident where
Kirke kills a man by having him "tied to a post and then beaten by
himself as long as he could do it, and then by another, and all for bid-
ding a servant of his go to his mistress Mrs. Collier" (p. 96). Besides
demonstrating a perverse pleasure in the torture of others, the colonial governor is also imitating his King who, as Turner observes, could
"launch savage attacks on those who spread prurient gossip or joked
about the royal mistresses" (p. 103). One of the attractions of colonial
service for men like Kirke, as Benedict Anderson has noted of a later
age, is that it allowed them to "play aristocrat off centre court,"[14] and
his brutal regime demonstrates what horrors could be unleashed in

the periphery by those imitating the particularly debased aristocratic culture of the Restoration court.

Pepys finds other troubling correspondences between home and abroad when he realizes that Kirke's "Tangier laws" have forced many of the English out of Tangier altogether, especially those who "desert the place and run to the Moors" (p. 92). Routh reports that English renegades had taken up with the Moorish enemy in such numbers that the Irish troops, whose large Catholic presence in Tangier was another source of concern for parliament, were forced to use Gaelic in the out-lying forts in order to keep their communications a secret from the enemy (p. 170). Pepys must have been reminded of another such dis-solution of the national community during the Dutch incursion into the Medway in 1667 when he was told that English deserters were heard upon enemy vessels crying out: "We did heretofore fight for tickets; now we fight for Dollers!" (*Diary* 6.14.67; 8.267). Finding itself unable to pay its sailors, the Stuart government issued promis-sary notes, or tickets, instead. At least some of the sailors went to the Dutch side in order to receive cash payments, and their presence and expertise in the Medway proved invaluable to Dutch navigation in those tricky waters. In both venues, Englishmen found better accom-modations with the enemy. Given these recurring dynamics, Pepys must have had a feeling of déjà vu all over again.

Mentally drained from continually documenting the same English abuses, Pepys can only imagine a better future for Tangier in the dis-ciplined Islamic men who stand outside its walls. Some of the most intriguing moments in the *Tangier Papers* result from Pepys's interac-tions with the Moors he meets both inside and outside the city. He was drawn early in his stay to a Moorish boy who had fled into Tangier and was asked by Pepys to perform his prayers: "he did it with so much reverence in his manner, speech, the motion of his hands and eyes and [s ?] of his voice and most of all in his prostrations, that I never was more taken with any appearance of devotion in my life in any person of any sort or religion" (p. 21). This sacred display is so striking precisely because of the debauched context in which it occurs. The first real sign of piety that Pepys has encountered in Tangier invades from the outside, prompting Pepys's curiosity about the Islamic people who live beyond the city's gates.

This moment is emblematic of Pepys's representations of the Moors: rather than writing in a derogatory Orientalist vein, as we might expect, he explores their superiority to the bastard English people found in Tangier. Consider, for example, Pepys's description of a meeting between the Alcaid, the local representative of the emperor of Morocco, and a delegation of Englishmen led by Lord Dartmouth: "the Alcaid and his company appearing like very grave and sober men and his discourse and manner of speech very good and with more presence of mind than I thought our master did, though he did also extremely well. Their appearance and habits I liked very well" (p. 27). These are no local savages but exactly the type of men that, in their attention to business and sobriety, seem the rightful possessors of Tangier. In addition, they are able to perform their authority through eloquent speech and a cultivated demeanor, outshining Lord Dartmouth, the highest-ranking Englishman in Tangier. The term "sober" is particularly important to Pepys, especially since, according to Kirke, more English soldiers "had been killed in this place by brandy than by the Moors" (p. 99). In this context, Pepys understands the great disciplinary benefits that might accrue to a people who follow Islam's injunction against alcoholic beverages.

Pepys's attraction to and curiosity about the Moors leads him, on several occasions, to approach the edges of dangerous boundaries. Consider the following two passages: "I walked out into the fields up the hills and there ventured very near the Moors' sentries almost round our bounds, and in the evening too, when they might have come and snapped me and nobody have seen that they took me within our bounds, having only my man with me" (p. 40). "I and de Paz a-horseback. . . . he carried us round the very brinks of our bounds close by the Moors' sentries, to whom we talked and several times out of our bounds, as we were told when we came home, and might have been shot or taken prisoners" (p. 46). As these entries demonstrate, Pepys clearly feels it worthwhile to gain more direct contacts with the Moors, even at the risk of becoming their captive. Yearning to experience a new culture in North Africa and attempting to salvage a most depressing trip, Pepys seems to understand why so many Englishmen decided to go "out of our bounds" and take up with the Moors rather than stay in Kirke's tyrannical Tangier.

To conclude, Srinivas Aravamudan has demonstrated that the postcolonial analysis of early modern texts must deploy a politics of reading that makes for strange bedfellows. Noting that many of the historical figures who are central to the study of colonial discourse in the long eighteenth century cannot be easily identified as pure "colonialist villains or anticolonial heroes," Aravamudan writes, "Rather than use ethical criticism as a form of social therapy, where reading anachronistically leads to rhetorics of condemnation and celebration concerning the political values of texts or the attitudes expressed by their authors, we should identify the institutions and reading practices that determine these shifts of value."[15] Read in this spirit, Pepys can still emerge as a satirist of empire despite the fact that his life's work entailed the militaristic building up of England's navy, that he profited immensely from his service on the Tangier Committee, and that he was not an anti-imperialist in any theoretical sense.

The efficacy of Pepys's satirical representations for postcolonial analysis is further illustrated by the way they puncture the reading practices of twentieth-century historiography, which, in general, has either been silent about Tangier's place in English colonial history or has attempted to resurrect the episode for imperialist narratives about the "rise of the British empire." Pepys's recalcitrant representations are conveniently explained away by both a traditional imperialist historian such as Routh, who dismisses his writings as biased propaganda (p. 276), and a neoimperialist historian such as Webb, who cheerfully claims that the Tangier garrison was typical in the "pleasure" and "temptations" (p. 22) it offered to its soldiers and who hints in an endnote that Pepys's views might be the result of either "shock (or jealously)" (p. 295). In the breathless jingoism of Routh's monograph, we see Pepys's bumbling Teviot cast as "a gallant, if too daring, soldier, and a pioneer of the Empire" (p. 70). In Webb's examination of the role of the famous English general John Churchill and his network of fellow ex-Tangerines in the Glorious Revolution and in the later administration of the English colonies, he claims that the colony "bred Protestant, patriotic, professional military values" (p. 24). Pepys's dark humor, moral outrage, and pessimistic despair are all whitewashed in these narratives that refurbish the Tangier experience and welcome the Tangerines into the heroic genealogies and proud institutions of the British imperial family.

Pepys's vitriolic interpretive practices, his recoiling from the fiscal and human waste produced by foolish imperialists and their overreaching colonial enterprise, and his shock at the vicious animality of the absolutely ruled Tangerine society should be continually juxtaposed with such efforts to interpret Tangier as a noble breeding ground for the empire. For Pepys, the story of Tangier is part of a larger narrative about the fall of English civilization into the furthest depths, as he indicates in a personal letter composed in Tangier that it "is a place of the world I would last send a young man to, but to hell."[16] The movement of the English to North Africa and the bestowal of absolute authority on the colonial governor unleash the forces of ineptitude and barbarity already brewing in the imperial center of Stuart England. One leaves Pepys's *Diary* and *Tangier Papers* with an idea of the dangerous pretensions and sadistic depravity of the few who directed early English colonialism, its insatiable appetite for human flesh, and the despair and exploitation of the men and women caught in its tenacious grip.

In the end, Pepys is an effective satirist of Tangier precisely because he himself is not innocent of its vices of corruption and lust. Seidel instructs us to see the satirist as already contaminated by the evils he rails against and to attend to the strategies by which he "works to distance himself from the debasing, deforming, encroaching, and contaminating nature of his subjects by placing surrogate figures into his fictions" (p. 14). Pepys's subtle re-creation of himself as an Old Testament prophet is a particularly good example: "being a little ill and troubled at so much loose company at table, my lord not being there, I dined in my chamber and Dr. Ken for the same reason came and dined with me there. And a great deal of good discourse we had upon the viciousness of this place and its being time for God Almighty to destroy it" (p. 49). English Tangier becomes like the Old Testament cities of Sodom and Gomorrah, a nauseating place that needs to be annihilated from the face of the earth in order to appease an angry God. From our historical vantage point, we could see this as the self-serving rhetoric of a man who contributed to and profited from the human misery in the English colony in North Africa. Yet, Pepys's moral outrage, however tainted, produces a haunting image for postcolonial analysis, and his prophet-surrogate should be entered into our evolving genealogy of those who have given witness to the dark comedy and the even darker tragedy spawned by the British empire.

NOTES

1. Edwin Chappell, introduction to *The Tangier Papers of Samuel Pepys*, ed. Edwin Chappell (London: Navy Records Society, 1935), p. xx. All subsequent citations will be found in the text.
2. Linda Colley is quoted in Armitage, *The Ideological Origins of the British Empire* (Cambridge: Cambridge University Press, 2000), p. 16. Colley's full argument is found in "The Imperial Embrace," *Yale Review* 81:4 (1993): 92–8, an insightful review of Edward Said's *Culture and Imperialism*. For more on the general indifference to the English colonies, see Koebner, *Empire* (Cambridge: Cambridge University Press, 1961), pp. 93–6.
3. J. Martin Evans, *Milton's Imperial Epic: Paradise Lost and the Discourse of Colonization* (Ithaca: Cornell University Press, 1996), p. 14.
4. Peter Linebaugh and Marcus Rediker, *The Many-Headed Hydra: Sailors, Slaves, Commoners, and the Hidden History of the Revolutionary Atlantic* (Boston: Beacon Press, 2000).

5. Stuart Sherman, *Telling Time: Clocks, Diaries, and English Diurnal Form, 1660–1785* (Chicago: University of Chicago Press, 1996), p. 30.

6. See *The Diary of Samuel Pepys*, 11 vols., ed. Robert Latham and William Matthews (Berkeley: University of California Press, 1971–1983), 1.20.67; 8.21 and 7.15.66; 7.207, for an example of Pepys's pleasure in the "Advice to a Painter" satires and for his thoughts about writing a lampoon on the Stuart conduct of the war. All subsequent citations will be found in the text in the above format, which indicates the date of the passage first, followed by volume number and page number.

7. E.M.G. Routh, *Tangier: England's Lost Atlantic Outpost, 1661–1684* (London: John Murray, 1912), p. 66. All subsequent citations will appear in the text.

8. See John Childs, *The Army of Charles II* (London: Routledge & Kegan Paul, 1976), pp. 121–4, for the high mortality rates in the garrison and for Tangier's terrible reputation among English soldiers and officers.

9. David Quint, *Epic and Empire: Politics and Generic Form from Virgil to Milton* (Princeton: Princeton University Press, 1993), p. 9.

10. Michael Seidel, *Satiric Inheritance: Rabelais to Sterne* (Princeton: Princeton University Press, 1979), p. 21. All subsequent citations will appear in the text.

11. George Etherege, *The Man of Mode, or, Sir Fopling Flutter* in *The Dramatic Works of Sir George Etherege*, ed. H.F.B. Brett-Smith (Oxford: Basil Blackwell, 1927), 2; I.i.271–2.

12. James Grantham Turner, "Pepys and the Private Parts of Monarchy," in *Culture and Society in the Stuart Restoration*, ed. Gerald MacLean (Cambridge: Cambridge University Press, 1995), p. 105. All subsequent citations will appear in the text.

13. Stephen Saunders Webb, *Lord Churchill's Coup: The Anglo-American Empire and the Glorious Revolution Reconsidered* (Syracuse: Syracuse University Press, 1998), pp. 21–2. All subsequent citations will appear in the text.

14. Benedict Anderson, *Imagined Communities: Reflections on the Origin and Spread of Nationalism*, rev. ed. (London: Verso, 1991), p. 150.

15. Srinivas Aravamudan, *Tropicopolitans: Colonialism and Agency, 1688–1804* (Durham: Duke University Press, 1999), pp. 14–15.

16. This letter to Mr. Houblon, dated October 19, 1683, can be found in *The Tangier Journal of Samuel Pepys*, intro. A.P. Asaph (London: The Doppler Press, 1980), p. 65. The edition gives no information on the source of the transcription and is generally poor, but it is helpful as it contains several letters that Pepys wrote from Tangier.

CHAPTER 13

FROM INVASION TO INQUISITION: MAPPING MALTA IN EARLY MODERN ENGLAND

Bernadette Andrea

[W]hat is unrepresentable about space is not only the pressure of diverse social maps multiplying space toward infinity but the additional pressure of what is hidden, encrypted, repressed, or unspoken in global and local histories. And this repression is exacerbated by the quiddity and seeming impenetrability of created local space.

In thus theorizing "The Strange Effects of Ordinary Space," Patricia Yaeger points toward a fundamental aporia in literary and cultural studies of early modern Malta: the always-already effaced indigenes of the island.[1] As in Shakespeare's *The Tempest*, numerous colonial and countercolonial contests striate this profoundly overdetermined locale, positioned roughly between the coast of Sicily and the coast of modern Libya (the site of early modern Tunis and ancient Carthage). In *The Tempest*, a similarly situated Mediterranean island stages the struggle between Prospero, the newest invader, and Caliban, the previous invader now subject to the current colonial hegemony. The indigenes of the island, however, emerge in the play as "what is hidden, encrypted, repressed, or unspoken" through Caliban's famous paean: "Be not afeard. The isle is full of noises, / Sounds, and sweet airs, that give delight and hurt not."[2] Similarly, Maltese history from antiquity through the early modern period involves successive invasions by the

Phoenicians (ninth century BC), the Carthaginians (eighth and seventh century BC), the Romans (fourth century BC to sixth century AD, with an influential landing by St. Paul in the first century and a possible occupation by the North African Vandals in the fifth century), the Byzantine Greeks (the sixth century AD), the Muslim Arabs (from AD 870, establishing the Maltese language as a cognate of Arabic), the Normans (from AD 1061), and the Aragonese (from AD 1283). The Knights of St. John—first the Knights Hospitaller of Jerusalem, subsequently the Knights of Rhodes, and finally the Knights of Malta—occupied the island in 1530 after their ignominious expulsion from Rhodes by the Ottoman Sultan Suleiman the Magnificent in 1522.[3] By the seventeenth century, the island was firmly under the rule of the Knights, who repelled ensuing attacks by the Ottomans on their Maltese stronghold—most famously, during the siege of 1565 marking "the furthermost expansion of the Ottoman Empire into the Mediterranean and Europe." As confirmed by Voltaire's famous assessment, "[n]othing is better known than the siege of Malta," the island remained among the most overdetermined geographical of spaces for the Western European imaginary well into the eighteenth century.[4] The framework of this essay accordingly complicates Emily Bartels's widely cited conclusion that the overlords, governors, and "the citizens [of the island] are of such diverse or undetermined nationalities that it is impossible to know who, if anyone, has prior claim to the island." While I recognize Bartels is focusing on the imaginative world of Marlowe's Malta, the premise that the island constitutes a leveling "multinational melting pot" potentially occludes the deeper native claims encrypted in early modern European accounts (p. 91).[5]

In the only study, thus far, to engage the discursive construction of Malta in the early modern period, Helen Vella Bonavita argues that "histories of the siege [of 1565] retained religious and political meaning for a considerable length of time" beyond the siege's immediate political and military efficacy.[6] As Vella Bonavita documents using sources from the middle to the end of the sixteenth century in Italian, Latin, and English, Western European attention to Malta throughout the sixteenth century conflates the exploits of the Knights with the geographical space of Malta at the expense of both the global history of the island's successive colonizations and its local histories as conceptualized by the Maltese. Yet, the social geography of the island under the Knights was never monolithic. Malta from the sixteenth through the eighteenth century presented a morass of competing sites of power, including (but not limited to) the Knights, the Office of the

Inquisition under the Holy See, the independent Bishop of Malta, the disaffected Maltese aristocracy (deriving from the thirteenth-century invasion of the Aragonese, who were nevertheless excluded from the "international" aristocratic order that ruled the island since the sixteenth century), the Maltese peasantry (many of whom manned the brisk corsair trade that brought the island the bulk of its revenue and its less savory reputation during the seventeenth century). In this essay, I address the hitherto effaced complexity of Malta in English printed texts from the mid-sixteenth century through the early eighteenth century to extend Vella Bonavita's thesis that the sixteenth century archive evinces "the manner in which the siege of Malta became a contested area, a locus where competing narratives of the same event struggled to attain the status of orthodoxy" (p. 1027). While Vella Bonavita confines her study to sixteenth-century responses, ending with Thomas Mainwaringe's unpublished *Caelius Secundi Curio his historie of the warr of Malta* (composed during the late 1570s), my examination ranges from contemporary reports of the "Great Siege" of 1565, when the Maltese people under the Knights of Malta resisted the combined might of the Ottoman army and navy to the belated 1633 publication of Christopher Marlowe's popular *The Jew of Malta*, first performed on the London stage in 1592 and to the multiple editions of the widely read account by two Quaker women, Katharine Evans and Sarah Chevers, of their *Cruel Sufferings ... in the Inquisition in the Isle of Malta*, first published in 1662 and reissued in 1663 and 1715. Dwelling on the multiple editions of Evans and Chevers's testimonial-cum-history, I conclude that its successive revisions most fully illuminate the displacement of the Maltese in early modern Anglocentric cultural, political, and religious discourses.

PRONOUNCEMENTS AND PRAYERS, 1565

Customarily, studies of Malta mark its modern history as beginning in 1565 with the Knights of St. John leading the defense of the island against its potential colonization by the Ottomans. In his magisterial study of *The Mediterranean and the Mediterranean World in the Age of Philip II*, which encompasses the second half of the sixteenth century, Fernand Braudel follows the celebrationist tendency of his entirely Christian sources in labeling the 1565 siege of Malta as "a trial of strength" and concluding that its consequences "made it one of the great events of the century."[7] Reinforcing this assessment of the siege as a singularly epochal moment, he remarks that "[t]he loss of Malta would undoubtedly have been a disaster for Christendom" (vol. 2, p. 1017). By contrast, Vella Bonavita maintains the results of the "successful" defense of Malta in 1565 were far from conclusive, since the previously disastrous history of the Knights in Rhodes suggested the Ottomans would attempt a second siege (as the King of Spain was prudent enough to recognize) and, given their history, they would achieve their goal the second time around (p. 1024). This uncertainty about the intentions and direction of Ottoman expansionism flavors several newsletters from the siege translated into English. To follow Vella Bonavita's calculations, "[b]etween 1565 and 1570 more than seventy narratives were published in German, Latin, French, and Italian." However, as she continues: "accounts of the siege of Malta sent to England tended to remain in their original languages" (p. 1026). While Vella Bonavita cites the lengthy titles of the English language newsletters, she does not provide any analysis of their content. Such print publications reached a wide audience, including the mass of illiterates who could appreciate an oral presentation, yet also retained the contradictory discursive construction of Malta through textual apparatus such as title pages. A close contextualized reading of these newsletters therefore provides a necessary antidote to the traditional "myth of Malta" purveyed most influentially by Braudel.

A closer reading of *Certayn and tru good nues, fro[m] the syege of the Isle Malta* and *A copie of the last advertisement that came from Malta, of the miraculous deliverie of the Isle, from the longe siege of the Turke, both by sea and lande*—two extant newsletters printed in English in 1565—reveals initial reports from the siege did not construct a fait accompli, to contrast with the retrospective myth of Malta suggested by their titles.[8] As its complete title page indicates, the earliest of the two newsletters, *Certain and tru good nues*, was "translat owt of Frenche yn to Englysh" and "prented yn Gaunt, the 27 of August." In other words, the tract presents an assessment of the ongoing siege when the odds were with the Ottomans. Moreover, though presented as a letter from the Grand Master, it establishes a supplicatory tone rather than the triumphalism suggested by its title. The "Relation made by Orlando Magro pilot to the chyff galley of the great master coma[n]der of the Rhodes, now Malta the wyche aryued at Messina the .xxvij. day of Iune 1565" appended to the Grand Master's letter similarly offers a pragmatic inventory rather than assurances of a certain victory. As such, this report concludes ambivalently with the image of "the hardiness of one valiant knyght hauing a two handed swerd yn hys hand, saying that he wold dye for the Cristian fayth, gave to all the rest suche curage, that they obtayned at last the victori" in what was nevertheless a preliminary sortie. Immediately followed by "Item that the great master was veari sorrowful for the death of Capitayn mirande," the provisional victory of this knight is further qualified. The pragmatics of a siege not (yet) represented as a fait accompli rather than the pieties of Christian providentialism determines the initial reports shaping the imaginary geography of Malta for an English vernacular audience.[9]

Hence, while *A copie of the last advertisement that came from Malta* presents the running title, "The deliuery of Malta from the Turke," the tract actually features an abjectly wounded soldier in need of patronage after sacrificing his livelihood in the devastating battle at St. Elmo castle. Following the salutation to "My right honorable Lorde and gossip," this soldier details, "it hath pleased the goodness of God to suffer me to lyve with twoo harquebushe [shot] in my body," one in his left thigh and the other in his right arm, "whiche is to a man of warre matter of importance." The tract continues with a cursory description of the battle and a list of the attending knights. The codicil to this report, or more accurately a plea for patronage, consists of a postscript to a letter dated September 28, less than a month after the conclusion of the siege on September 8. Notably, while this codicil acknowledges "it is great meruayle that euer our men could kepe" the walls of the remaining fortresses of Borgo (Birgu) and St. Michael's, it does so with a less than reassuring tone. Since the last sentence of the tract records "howe that Don garcia de Toledo, did imbarke 4000. souldiours of the bandes of Sicilia, Naples, and Corsica, and Departed from Malta with 58. Galies after the Turkish army: God send hym good success," it is clear the tottering walls of the two fortresses do not stand for a confirmed victory. Rather, they signify the possibility of a terrifying defeat and suggest the function of this report issued in the immediate aftermath of the siege was to seek patronage not simply for one crippled soldier but for a vastly crippled "bastion of Christendom."[10]

The several prayers issued by the Anglican liturgy "for the delivery of those Christians that are now invaded by the Turk" from the same year have been frequently cited as instances of newly Protestant England's rapprochement with the largely Catholic powers of Western Europe during a moment of potential crisis for Christendom as a whole. As Samuel Chew declares in his monumental study of Islam and England during the Renaissance, "[e]ven Protestant England responded" to the Pope's plea for prayers.[11] Chew promotes the view that "a common sense of imminent peril transcend[ed] the prejudices of sectarian divisions" during the 1565 siege (p. 123). Nonetheless, just as contemporaneous newsletters construct a contradictory social cartography for Malta, which as easily might have become a bastion of Ottoman expansionism as of Christian resistance, the prayers of the British islanders for the island of Malta display an uncanny dynamic of identification and disavowal.[12] The preface to *A Form to be used in common prayer every Wednesday and Friday, within the city and Diocese of Sarum: to excite all godly people to pray unto God for the delivery of those Christians that are now invaded by the Turk*, which became the prototype for subsequent prayers inspired by the 1565 siege, delivers the double message: "it is our parts, which for distance of place cannot succour them with temporal relief, to assist them with spiritual aid."[13] When the preface warns, "[i]f they should prevail against the Isle of *Malta*, it is uncertain what further peril might follow to the rest of Christendom," it thus displays less than good faith in justifying the primary logistical problem threatening besieged Malta: the lack of material support from Western Christian sovereigns, including the Most Catholic King, Philip II, and the Defender of the Protestant Faith, Elizabeth I. Playing both sides of this potentially deadly game, the preface evokes fear in its domestic audience (a useful mechanism, as we see in our historical moment, for enacting social controls at home) even as it dissimulates Elizabethan England's "ecumenical" economic, diplomatic, and even military alliances with the Ottomans and Moroccans against Catholics such as the Maltese and the Spanish.[14]

The accompanying prayers similarly evoke hyperbole to heighten English fear of invasion, even as the state-sponsored drafters of these prayers acknowledge in their prefaces the unlikelihood of this event. *A Form to be used in common prayer every Wednesday and Friday, within the city and Diocese of Sarum* opens with the threat, "[b]etter it is for us to fall into thy [God's] hands, than into the hands of men, and especially into the hands of Turks and Infidels thy professed enemies, who now invade thine inheritance." It closes with the pledge, "The Turk goeth about to set up, to extol, and to magnify that wicked monster and damned soul Mahumet above thy dearly beloved Son Jesus Christ, whom we in our heart believe, and with mouth confess, to be our only Savior and Redeemer" (p. 522). Christendom's enemies, presumed to be God's as well, are thus counterpoised against Muslims in general. Significantly, this prayer does not register divisions within Christendom, even as it derives from a state church deemed "heretical" by the Catholic Church of Rome. By contrast, the more widely disseminated *A Short Form of Thanksgiving to God for the delivery of the Isle of Malta from the invasion and long siege thereof by the great army of the Turks both by sea and land, and for sundry other victories lately obtained by the christians against the said Turks* undermines the binary oppositions of the former prayer by gloating, "[God] hast of late most sharply corrected and scourged our christian brethren thy servants with terrible wars and dreadful invasions of most deadly and cruel enemies, Turks and Infidels" (p. 526). Infidels, presumably Catholics and other Non-Anglican Christians, are here aligned with the Turks.[15]

Importantly, these are the prayer services that the generation that came of age at the end of the sixteenth century was mandated to attend during their developmental years by the Acts of Uniformity promulgated by the Elizabethan state church. Yet, a complicating discourse around Malta was simultaneously broadcast by newsletters trumpeting victory though their lengthy titles, but revealing uncertainty through their fractured content. As we turn to several popular histories and plays in English from the end of the sixteenth century through the early decades of the seventeenth century, these contradictions increasingly inform the imaginary geography of Malta as a Mediterranean(ist) locale. Malta, that is, remains a bastion of Christendom under the formerly celebrated Knights, who nevertheless double in seventeenth-century Anglocentric discourse as the monstrous corsairs of a specifically Catholic Malta.

HISTORIES AND TRAGEDIES, 1592–1633

After the initial outpouring of interest in Malta during the five years following the "Great Siege," the pace of print productions in English focusing on the island dwindled to insignificance. After all, Malta had become a bastion, not of Christendom in general, but of Catholicism against the forces of "the Turks" and "the Lutherans." The English, as far as the Spanish crown and its Maltese protectorate were concerned, seemed barely indistinguishable from either category. As Andrew P. Vella documents in his fascinating study of *An Elizabethan-Ottoman Conspiracy*, the Protestant English, under the direction of Sir Francis Walsingham and with the consent of Queen Elizabeth, had considered a joint venture with the Ottomans to colonize Catholic Malta. Vella concludes, "[h]ad it been successful the English power would have gained a vital foothold in the center of the Mediterranean 220 years before British rule in Malta was in fact established."[16] English shipping in the Mediterranean flagged during the early decades of Elizabeth's reign due to Ottoman depredations in the eastern half of the region and a combination of Barbary, Maltese, and Spanish depredations in the western half. However, by the late 1570s the English were eagerly courting Ottoman trade, receiving the lucrative capitulations that allowed them to operate independently of the

French in 1581. Deemed by the Catholic powers of continental Europe to be "Protestant Turks," though seeing themselves as defenders of a purified Christianity, the English thus retained Malta in its cultural imaginary as the bastion of Christendom enshrined as the myth of Malta after 1565 even as they overlaid this mythos with connotations of corruption, cruelty, and lawlessness associated with the ultra-Catholic Knights, the Inquisition, and the corsairs of Malta.[17]

The late sixteenth-century revival of this island in the English imaginary is epitomized by the popular production of Christopher Marlowe's *The Jew of Malta*.[18] Written in the late 1580s, a period when England constantly feared and eventually "fought off" an invasion from imperialist Spain, Marlowe's play turns to the 1565 siege to present a tale of corruption, mercantile capitalism, and Machiavellian compromise. As Thomas Healy remarks in his *Christopher Marlowe*, a lucid study of the playwright, the logic of primitive accumulation in this play "allows the transgression of spatial organizations" (p. 47). The space of the emerging global marketplace, which can "inclose / Infinite riches in a little room," nevertheless functions to efface not only the particularity of place, along with the local labor alienated through the logic of commodification, but also the specificity of history.[19] As numerous critics have noted, Marlowe "errs" in representing the 1565 siege as successful for the Ottomans when, in fact, the reverse was true. Moreover, the device of the tribute demanded by the Turkish forces is pure fantasy, since the only tribute the Knights ever paid was the celebrated Maltese falcon to their feudal overlord, the King of Aragon. Finally, the presence of a Jewish community is anachronistic for the sixteenth century, as this community was expelled from Malta in 1492 as part of the wave of persecution associated with the consolidation of the Aragonese and Castillian crowns into the expansionist Spanish empire.[20] As Healy brilliantly argues, Marlowe's play parallels the celebrated compendium by the imperialist propagandist Richard Hakluyt, *The Principall Navigations, Voiages and Discoveries of the English Nation* (1599–1600), since both purveyed colonialist scenarios "without foundation in actuality" at the time of their enunciation (p. 47). This parallel therefore answers Roma Gill's question in her recent edition of Marlowe's play, "WHY—why *Malta?*"[21] Perhaps the question to ask, however, is not why Marlowe represented Malta in his play, but why he misrepresented its history and, even more so, why he could misrepresent this history to his late sixteenth-century English audience. Was it the gap of three decades from the "Great Siege" in the 1560s to the first staging of Marlowe's play in the 1590s—decades involving the consolidation of the Elizabethan state and its church in opposition to the expansionist empire of Catholic Spain (and therefore led to English alliances with the Muslim counterforces of the Ottoman Empire and Morocco)—that enabled Marlowe to reshape the myth of Malta to enable the "double vision" Bartels locates throughout Marlowe's oeuvre? Broadly speaking, "while the demonization of Oriental rulers provided a highly charged impetus for England's own attempts to dominate the East, their valorization provided a model for admiration and imitation, shaming or schooling the English into supremacy, or providing an excuse for defeat."[22] More specifically—and in a significant departure from his sources—Marlowe depicts the ostensibly "occidental" Malta via this "double vision" as simultaneously admirable and abominable.

In charting the double vision regarding Malta in early modern England, Marlowe's play further functions as a benchmark due to its delayed publication, first being performed in 1592 but not appearing in print until 1633. The publication of this popular play thirty-five years after its debut persists as a complication for its numerous editors, who have vigorously debated Marlowe's authorship (especially of the latter acts). Thomas Heywood, who was responsible for the staging of the play in the early 1630s leading to its publication and who framed the play with his own dedication, prologue, and epilogue, has been deemed a likely candidate for writing, revising, or at least modifying all or part of Marlowe's play.[23] Elsewhere Heywood displayed an active interest in the interface between England and the Islamic powers of the Mediterranean, which he featured in his paired plays, *The Fair Maid of the West* (1604; pub. 1631).[24] Hence, whatever his involvement in shaping Marlowe's printed play, Heywood's pivotal role in its revival (and preservation) signals the continuing interest in Malta's strategic position within colonialist discourses on the Mediterranean—what Jon P. Mitchell in his analysis of the Maltese as *Ambivalent Europeans* calls "Mediterraneanism." Related to Orientalism, Mediterraneanism presents difference as inferiority on a north-south axis, involving "exoticizing," "homogenizing," and "restricted comparativism."[25] In this context, the printed version of *The Jew of Malta* emblematizes early modern England's ambivalent positioning within the ostensibly antagonistic waters of the Mediterranean as ruled by Catholics (with whom the English nevertheless identified in moments of crisis such as the "Great Siege") and Muslims (whom the English scorned ideologically, but sought as a diplomatic counter-weight against the Catholic forces of the Mediterranean). I consequently adduce the dates of the first performance and first publication of Marlowe's play to frame a series of foundational histories published in the early seventeenth century focusing on the Ottoman Empire, with significant attention drawn to Malta. As I shall argue, these histories—Ralph Carr's *The Mahumetan or Turkish History* (1600), Richard Knolles's *The Generall Historie of the Turkes* (1603), and George Sandys's *A Relation of a Iourney begun An: Dom: 1610* (1615)—formalize the shift between the Malta of the Great Siege and the Malta of the Marlovian moment.

Ralph Carr's *The Mahumetan or Turkish Historie, containing three Bookes*, the third of which focusing on "the warres and seege of Malta, which Solyman the Great made to the great Maister and brothers of that order," initiates a significant shift in the English vernacular understanding of the island by translating "from the French & Italian tongues" at least two treatises on Malta. As Vella Bonavita documents, this "third book" is largely derived from *Caelii Secundi Curionis de Bello Melitensi a turcis gesto historia nova* (pp. 1028–9). As such, it recapitulates the discursive construction of early modern Malta via the revisionist Protestant historiography initiated by Curio, who muted the emphasis in his Italian source text on the divine endorsement of the *Catholic* defenders of Malta and replaced it with the more neutral "human interest" aspect of the siege. As the patently Christian humanist Carr indicates in his dedicatory letter to the volume, he views his published translation of the history of Ottoman expansionism, halted by the successful defense of Malta in 1565, as a public service (sigs. Aij^v–Aiij). Aware of the advancing power of the Ottoman Empire, which he describes as having "made themselues now conquerours ouer the whole East; & in fine are become euen the terror of the West" with unprecedented speed and scope (sig. Aiij^v), Carr proposes the thesis of the rise and fall of empires to predict the limits of the Ottoman reach. In pursuing a mode of humanist historiography based on empiricism rather than moralism, Carr brackets the customary reasons for the Ottomans' victories, such as the punishment of Christians for their moral failings (sig. Aiiiij). He thereby shifts his focus on Malta from the successful defense of 1565 to the contemporary need for Christian political unity, a motif he borrows from Curio.

In the dedicatory letter to the second book of this volume, Carr reiterates his contemporary focus by referencing "the present Hungarian wars and the often assemblies of the Germaine Princes to prouide some remedy for their feared harms" (sig. I^v). Clearly, Carr does not view this volume as antiquarian, but as the foundation for current strategizing about an effective response to the imperialist push of the Ottomans into Europe. Thus, the position of the third book as the culmination of a linear history, beginning with the establishment of Islam in the eighth century to the continuous attacks on the Maltese archipelago from 1560, provides not simply a catalogue of resistance but sounds more like a final warning that Ottoman expansionism would not halt with the "successful" defense of Malta in 1565. The Turks may have been routed, but "they set sayle and departed towards *Grecia*, leauuing the Iland of *Malta*, shamefully wasted and enpouerished" (p. 101).[26] This history does not conclude, moreover, with a celebration of the (Catholic) Christian victors, but with a description of subsequent Ottoman conquests in Eastern Europe. In positioning Malta as "placed beetwixt *Africk* and *Sicilia*, and doubted whether it should belonge to *Africk* or *Europe*, if it had not ben that the ancient inhabitants of *Melita* time out of minde, hauing vsed the common language of those of *Africk*, haue alwaies reputed the Iland to bee a member of *Africk*" (p. 57ᵛ), Carr presents the island as a profoundly liminal space to support his revisionist Protestant historiography. He further contests St. Paul's shipwreck in Malta (p. 58), a claim that previously enshrined this ultra-Catholic island within the lineage of "pure" Christianity. Since the Reformation churches considered themselves the quintessence of Christianity, and consequently considered Catholicism a corruption, denying Malta its place in the Pauline genealogy foregrounds the tensions underlying Protestant representations of this overdetermined locale.

Like Carr's, Knolles's account of the 1565 siege of Malta in *The General Historie of the Turkes* relies largely on Curio's foundational account. Issued in seven editions over the seventeenth century, Knolles's "mainstream" dissemination of Curio's revisionist history suppresses the island's Catholicism by questioning the status of the Maltese as "genuine" Europeans.[27] Mention of Malta significantly frames the long chapter on "The Life of Solyman, the Fourth and most Magnificent Emperor of the Turks," which begins with the expulsion of the Knights of St. John from Rhodes in 1522 (thus anticipating their ultimate tenure as the Knights of Malta) and ends with a description of the siege of 1565. By embedding his description of Malta within the context of Ottoman political history, Knolles modifies Carr's strictly ideological focus on the rise of Islam in contest with Christianity. He further presents the 1565 siege of Malta within a continuum of engagements characterizing the "*eternal* war" of Mediterranean piracy during the sixteenth century.[28] Unlike Carr, he details earlier raids on the Maltese archipelago, especially the devastating capture of almost the entire population of Gozo in 1551 and the definitive capture of Tripoli from the Knights the same year. The capture of the Christian fleet at

Zerbi in 1560, which resulted in many high-ranking Knights being sent to Istanbul in chains, further adds to the image of the Ottomans as implacable.[29] Yet, the Knights of Malta are simultaneously represented, albeit through the words of Suleiman while rousing his troops, as "crossed pyrats" (p. 793). As Peter Earle stresses in *Corsairs of Barbary and Malta*, the Maltese slave market vied with those of Algiers, Tunis, and Tripoli as entrepôts for the spoils of the mutual piracy of Christians and Muslims in the Mediterranean.[30] Thus, while the Knights of Malta remain champions of Christendom in Knolles's history, they also appear as seagoing predators who differ little from Muslims.

As in Carr's account, such tensions in Knolles's history ultimately manifest in the representation of Malta as a liminal place positioned "betwixt Africa and Sicilia." Knolles extends Carr's description by commenting, it "might be doubted whether it [Malta] were to be accounted in Africk or Europ, but that the antient cosmographers and the Moors language, which the Maltese haue alwaies vsed, claime it for Africke" (p. 795). This reference to the native Maltese expands in Knolles to include an ethnographic description informed by emerging English models of racialized difference: "The Inhabitants are so burnt with the Sun, that they differ little in colour from the Ethyopians: they are of a wholsom constitution of body, spare of dyet, industrous, rather painful than warlike, dying more for age than of sicknes" (p. 795). Echoing Carr, who echoes Curio, Knolles concludes his description by casting doubt on the Christian genealogy of the island, traditionally traced to St. Paul's shipwreck of AD 59 (p. 795). (Catholic) Malta is thus removed in the popular imagination from its central place in Christian history, even as its status as the "Bulwark of Christendom" continues to inform accounts of the 1565 siege (p. 793). Once again, Knolles has Suleiman the Magnificent describe Malta as a bulwark in his "oration to his captains for the invading" of the same (p. 793). As in the Marlovian myth, such a rendering reinforces the view of Malta as a bastion of Christendom, even as it erodes this view by casting it through the heightened rhetoric of an enemy commander-in-chief rousing his troops. Finally, as in Carr's history, Knolles necessarily follows the apparent defense of Malta with an account of the successive victories of the Ottomans in "the Island of Chios" and "the kingdome of Hungary" (p. 819). Together, Carr's and Knolles's histories suggest Malta, marked by its cultural, geographical, and racialized position between Europe and Africa, can secure neither the Mediterranean nor Eastern Europe from the dark forces of Islam *and* Catholicism.

George Sandys's *Relation* combines the humanist emphasis of Carr's history with the popularity of Knolles's to present an imaginary geography of Malta recast by the distinctly spatialized structure of an itinerary. Malta appears in Sandys's text, not through the chronological rendition of the past, characteristic of Carr's and Knolles's histories, but through the present tense of a journey that begins in Venice, winds through the eastern Mediterranean, extends into Asia Minor as far as Constantinople, dwells in the Holy Land of the Christians, Muslims, and Jews, and finally returns to Venice (and, nondiegetically, to England) with a significant stop in Malta. While Sandys sequences his personal travels chronologically, with the surface events of the narrative covering just over a year, the time of the text is profoundly archeological: the eras of classical Greece and Rome, of Christianity, of Islam, and of contemporary European politics layer significantly as Sandys extracts deeply rooted etymologies for the places he traipsed through. Malta, as in Knolles, is first encountered in Rhodes, with the displacement of the expelled Knights from the eastern to the western Mediterranean rendered proleptically through the description of their defeat: "Such as would, according to composition were suffered to depart: who from hence remoued vnto *Malta*" (p. 72). Malta continues to be mentioned in association with the Knights throughout Sandys's journey, particularly as he explicates their origin in Jerusalem as a crusading order (p. 168) and their initial displacement to Acre (p. 205) with the fall of the Christian kingdom of Jerusalem in the time of "our *Richard* the first, and *Philip* the French King" (p. 205). When Sandys lands in Malta on his homeward journey his reader might expect the conventional effacement of the natives of the island in favor of the Knights as in the previous histories by Carr and Knolles. The associative flow of an itinerary, rather the chronological pressure of a history, nevertheless enables Sandys to present a vividly personal Maltese landing.

Sandys begins with an extended description of the native people before returning to the conventional recounting of the Knights' history as it intersects with Malta's. Specifically, his first encounter with Malta is shaped by the lore linking danger to the waters surrounding the island, so that he (and his shipmates) mistake an English ship for a hostile man-of-war and an anonymous "litle ship" is "supposed a Pirat" (p. 226). When they land at Malta, trying to escape a storm, they are not allowed to leave because the Knights-cum-pirates of Malta are conducting a raid on the North African corsairs' havens. Yet, when the English ship insists on braving the storm, and the ire of the Knights, Sandys refuses to go along. As he entertainingly writes, "no intreatie could get me aboard; choosing rather to vndergo all hazards and hardnesse whatsoeuer, then so long a voyage by sea, to my nature so irksome." This resolution, at once comic and heroic, leaves him stranded "on a naked promontorie right against the Citie, remote from the concourse of people, without prouision, and not knowing how to dispose of my selfe." Shifting to the pastoral romance mode, the narrative continues with a party of "two old women," "a Gallant," and "his two *Amarosaes*, attired like Nymphs, with lutes in their hands" preparing a picnic (p. 227).[31] Once Sandys is discovered by this group, he is invited to eat with them; he subsequently receives succor from "a *Maltese*, whose father was an English man." As he records, "[s]o I came into the Citie, and was kindly entertained in the house of the aforesaid *Maltese*; where for three weeks space, with much contentment I remained" (pp. 227–28).

Only after this scene of hospitality and human interaction across cultural barriers, albeit one rendered through the conventions of pastoral romance, does Sandys provide the requisite description of Malta and its Knights. His discussion of St. Paul, though couched in his characteristic skepticism through the disclaimer "where they say Saint *Paul* lay when hee suffered ship-wrack," is rendered plausible through the "great devotion" of the Maltese (p. 180). Nevertheless, class distinctions, informed by racialized hierarchies, eventually undermine the broadmindedness of Sandys's description, as when he records, "[t]he *Maltese* are little lesse tawny then the *Moors*, especially those of the countrey, who go half clad, and are indeed a miserable people: but the Citizens are altogether Frenchified; the Great Master, & major part of the Knights, being French-men" (p. 183). Hence, while Sandys is certainly an "anti-pilgrim," Daniel Vitkus's resonant term for those Protestant Englishmen (and, as we shall see, women) who traveled to the Mediterranean as Christians but who expressed skepticism (and even condemnation) of the primarily Catholic occupation of this space, he suspends his judgment when describing Malta in a manner as yet unvoiced in English discourse on the island.[32] Still, he ultimately represents the Maltese as essentially different, whether religiously or racially, from the Protestant English. Even his relatively sympathetic representation of Malta therefore joins with the foundational histories by Carr and Knolles to presage the radical shift in early modern England's myth of Malta as a space of prodigies during the so-called Puritan Revolution of the mid-seventeenth century.

PROPHECIES AND PERSECUTION, 1637–1715

If the imaginary geography of Malta in the first decades of the seventeenth century moved from the retrospective fantasy of Marlowe's popular play to the strained presentism of the trio of foundational histories cited above, the mapping of Malta that emerges in English printed texts during the civil war period of the 1640s, through the uneasy tenure of the republican "rule of saints" during the 1650s, into the restoration of limited monarchy during the 1660s, presents its most radical rupture. Beginning with *Newes from Babylon: Of a New-Found Prince, that as soone as he was borne, spake, and wrought Miracles by word of mouth. Sent from thence to the Grand Master of Malta, by his Lieger Ambassador resident there, and from Malta disperst into most parts of Christendome* (1637) to the multiple editions of *A Short Relation of Some of the Cruel Sufferings (For the Truths Sake) of Katharine Evans & Sarah Chevers, in the Inquisition in the Isle of Malta* (1662, 1663, 1715), the Anglocentric discourse charting the island takes a turn toward the supernatural rather than the cynical, the apocalyptic rather than the empirical.[33] I shall argue in the remainder of this essay that print productions about purported prophets of Malta during the mid-seventeenth century provide a hitherto unexamined basis for Evans and Chevers's construction of themselves as prophet figures. At the same time, as prophets "of Malta" in the sense Bartels specifies when situating Marlowe's title character in a grid of "colonialist competitions," Evans and Chevers promulgate the discourse of Mediterraneanism to support the expanding British global imperial project even as they challenge patriarchal norms at home and abroad. A symptomatic reading of their *Short Relation* accordingly reveals "to be of Malta" cannot simply be deconstructed to mean "in effect, not to be, originally, of Malta" (though in Marlowe's play, such an erasure arguably may be complete) (p. 102).[34] Specifically, as Evans and Chevers become prophets "of Malta," they inadvertently reveal the presence of an indigenous "other" who continues to resist Anglo-Protestant proselytizing in the Maltese homeland.

To reiterate, Malta for the radical sectarians of mid-seventeenth-century England had become a place of marvels and perils rather than the bastion of Christendom celebrated by mythographers of the "Great Siege" and sullied (but not abandoned) in Marlowe's popular play and the frequently reprinted seventeenth-century histories touching upon the island. The aforementioned *Newes from Babylon*, for instance, displaces prodigiousness, and even monstrosity, onto Malta through diplomatic channels and geographic description. As Christopher Hill outlines in *The Century of Revolution*, the year 1637 (the year of this tract's publication) was marked by a cluster of events presaging England's devastating civil wars: "In 1637 a papal agent was received at Whitehall. The Puritans blamed Laud for this policy, and for England's failure to give support to the Protestant cause in the Thirty Years' War. Simultaneously critics of the state were savagely punished. In 1637 the lawyer William Prynne, the Reverend Henry Burton,

and Dr John Bastwick were mutilated, heavily fined, and imprisoned
for life." The year 1637 was also the year of the infamous Ship Money
crisis and the disastrous introduction of the Anglican Prayer Book into
Scotland.[35] These cumulative events sparked the conflagration of civil
war in the British Isles over the subsequent decade. *Newes from
Babylon*, as a print production in the English vernacular, encodes the
anxiety of a nation on the brink of a religiously inflected war by dis-
placing the horror of the Antichrist not simply onto the East, as in
Orientalism, but more disturbingly onto the borders of the West, as in
Mediterraneanism. The tract begins by evoking "[t]he unparalleld
pride and ambition of *Lucifer*" in inducing "the Birth of a Newfound
Antichrist born in *Babylon*, in *Caldea* or *Assyria*" (sigs. A3, A3^v).
Citing scriptural prophecy to corroborate the supposed birthplace of
the Antichrist in the Middle East, the tract next seeks to address "the
mayn question," which "is, how the supposed news of this Bable of
Babel, should be spread and rumourd through the Christian World"
(sig. A4). At this point, Malta becomes a repository not merely of the
news of this monstrous birth, as in the introductory "Letter to the
Great Master of *Malta*, wherin is advertised to the Princes of
Christendom, of the Birth of Antichrist" (sig. A4^v), but transmutes by
association into a place of strangeness itself. In assuming a lapse in the
historical memory of the island as a bastion of Christendom, the
author of this tract describes a now estranged Malta: "Yet because
mention is made of *Malta*, and of the Grand or Great Master there,
and that many of the Readers are ignorant what *Malta* is, or what
place or dignity the Great Master bears, it is not amisse that somthing
touching these points be described" (sig. C2). The reader learns that
"Malta is an Island in the Mediterranean Sea, farre within the
straights, almost betwixt that part of the World called *Africa*, and the
Island or Kingdome of *Sicilia*, the naturall borne people there are
black, (but they are Christians)" (sigs. C2–C2^v). A hasty survey of St.
Paul's association with the island, the defense of Malta against the
Ottomans in 1565, and the vow of the Knights of Malta "in defence
and service of their faith against all *Mahometans*, *Pagans*, or *Infidels*
whatsoever" confirm the island as a liminal space in the seventeenth-
century English imaginary (sig. C3). Here a Protestant "infidel"
could be persecuted as easily as a Muslim; here an antichrist might be
decried as readily as a defender of Christendom celebrated.

   In 1641, with the impending war between England's king and its
parliament, a related tract was published under the title, *New News
and Strange News from Babylon, or, The coppy of a letter which was sent
from the master of Malta, to a gentleman and kinsman of his resident*

here in England: wherein is related the birth of a very strange Prophet,
with his manner of living, actions, and great wonders performed by him:
Also his departure from thence, threatning with terrour and feare the
Countries Desolation. The title of this tract, which begins descriptively
but ends by prophesying doom, thus enacts the transition from the
empiricism of the early seventeenth-century historiographers to the
apocalypticism of radical sectarian discourse from the civil war period.
A five-page pamphlet imbued with primal fear of "very many strange
things," it describes the birth of a prodigy who horribly recapitulates
the life of Christ: a monstrous rather than a miraculous birth, an itin-
erant ministry with "a douzen or fourteen ugile, and illshapen
fellows" as disciples, and a career of perverted prophesying (pp. 1–2).
Appropriating the language of *Revelation* (the book of the Apocalypse),
it warns: "at his death there should be warrs, and rumours of warrs, in
so much that all the westerne countreys shall be laid desolate, but this
Countrey shall flourish like a bay tree even in the middest of the winter of misfortunes" (p. 2). Clearly, the Malta being constructed for the
radical sectarian reader appears thoroughly abominable, with none of
the residual admiration constituting the "double vision" of Malta in
turn-of-the-seventeenth-century public discourse. It is easy to see,
moreover, how the fear of the English people in their divided island is
being mapped onto this monstrous projection. Other tracts from the
period similarly evoke the primal fear political instability instantiated
in the prophetic writing of the period. *News from the Great Turke. A*
Blasphemous Manifestation of the Grand Seignior of Constantinople,
against the Christians; of his entrance into Christendome, and the
Particulars of his Great Armie (1645) translates the still current continental view of Malta as a bastion of Christendom, even as it concludes with terrifying pessimism. Despite the preparations of the
Catholic powers, "[i]n the meane time, the Great *Turke* goeth on his
way, bringing all under his Power where he comes, whilest they feed
themselves with these offers" (p. 5).[36] In sum, Malta falls in these
prophetic tracts from its vaunted position as the ultimate defense of
Christendom against Ottoman expansionism in the Mediterranean
(and, by extension, in all of Western Europe and perhaps even the
Americas).[37]

The fall of Malta as defender of Christendom to a site of corruption
in mid-seventeenth-century English discourse on the island is reflected
in the merchant Samuel Boothhouse's *A Brief Remonstrance of*
Several National Injuries and Indignities perpetrated on the Persons
and Estates of publick Ministers and Subjects of this Common-wealth, by
the Dey of Tunis in Barbary: By reason of the Captivity of an English

Ship by the Friers Hospitalers, commonly called Cavaliers of Malta (1653), which emphasizes the decay of the glorious Knights of the sixteenth century into the crass pirates of the seventeenth century. Boothhouse condemns "the unexampled insolence of the *Friars Hospitallers* (now assuming the title of *Cavaliers of Malta*) who by their institution ought not to offend any *Christian banner*" (sig. A2–A2ᵛ). The Knights have become little better than Turks, and seem strikingly similar to the royalists the current English republic had replaced.[38] Finally, on the eve of the first edition of Evan and Chevers's *A Short Relation*, a pamphlet appeared with the title *Europes Wonder: or, The Turks Overthrow . . . With a great Victory lately obtained against the Turks, by His Majesty the King of Great Brittain's Royal Navy, under the command of the Right Honourably the Lord G. Montagu: The entring of the Famous Port of Guienne, the taking of the Strong Fort of Agria; & the coming of the Knights of Malta and Venecians to the assistance of the English Fleet; with a brief Narrative of their Bloody Fight, and the chief particulars thereof* (1661). Printed in The Hague, this tract collects "several *Prophecies* of *Paul Grebner*," "a laborious *Devine*" who published at least two other apocalyptic tracts during the previous volatile decade (p. 1). Malta's transformation into an island of prophecy, whether deriving from the island or directed toward it, is thus consolidated as part of accelerating British imperialist efforts in the Mediterranean. Like Hakluyt, though in a prophetic rather than an empirical mode, Grebner functions as a propagandist for a new mapping of the Mediterranean with the English fleet in the lead.

Consequently, by the time Katharine Evans and Sarah Chevers began their unintentional journey toward Malta, having originally been inspired by "the Inner Light" to travel to Alexandria along with other Quaker missionaries infiltrating the Mediterranean during the seventeenth century, the imaginary mapping of the island from a radical sectarian perspective had shifted to a region primed for prophecy.[39] As we have seen, prior to Evans and Chevers's thoroughly documented sojourn, such prophesying for an English audience was associated with Maltese monstrosity, as in the infamous "Antichrist" from the tracts of the 1630s and 1640s, and Maltese corruption, as in the tracts of the 1650s and 1660s focusing on the Knights in their decline. The full title for the first edition of Evans and Chevers's *Short Relation* accordingly constructs an itinerary for their inadvertent landing in Malta that precisely encapsulates the Mediterraneanist logic of simultaneous aggrandizement and deprecation. In the first of three long paragraphs constituting this title, Malta is presented through the

"Black Legend of the Inquisition" as a place of intense pain, cruelty, and death, with the word "suffering" reiterated three times within the first sentence.[40] The "Inhabitants" of the island are additionally characterized as inhospitable apostates. Yet, Malta as an imaginary geography for Christian missionaries, and particularly missionaries of radical Protestant strains such as the Quakers, offered a positive significance as, to reference the second paragraph of the title, the island where "*Paul* suffered shipwreck there among the barbarous people," as recorded in Acts 27 and 28. Though some scholars have quibbled over the association of St. Paul with Malta, the view of the island as one of the earliest and most sustained sites of Christianity (from AD 59, approximately five centuries before Christian missionaries began their conversion of the Anglo-Saxons in AD 597) was firmly entrenched in the early modern geographies of the region. This precedent would certainly appeal to Quaker missionaries such as Evans and Chevers, who like other radical Protestants sought to restore the "primitive church" of Paul's era to replace the accretions and distortions of the Roman Church. Evans and Chevers accordingly become manifestations of Paul, with the Maltese people caught in the Mediterraneanist stasis of "barbarous people" from over 1600 years ago. Concomitantly, the two English women emphasize their calling to "save" the Maltese people: they declare upon disembarking from the ship, "there came many to see us, and we call'd them to repentance, and many of them were tender; but the whole City is given to Idolatry" (p. 3). Evans and Chevers continue to cast aspersions on the Maltese as part of their proselytizing project. Being cast into the prison of the Inquisition thus fits perfectly, if not congenially, into their layered mapping of the island as an archetypal site of present cruelty and past purity.

Given the layered geography of the tract's title page, how does Malta figure in the narratives, prophecies, and poetry produced by Evans and Chevers for this compendium? To start, the vantage point assumed in the primary narrative of *A Short Relation* is very much that of the "walker" rather than the "voyeur" Michel de Certeau specifies in "Spatial Practices."[41] This narrative moves from Plymouth in the south of England, to Leghorn on the northwest coast of the Italian peninsula, toward Alexandria with a significant deviation into the Grand Harbor at Malta, to the house of the English counsel on the island, into the streets of the harbor city where the two women distributed Quaker pamphlets, and eventually to the council chambers of the Inquisition. However, this trajectory is not open to radical alterity in the way Certeau theorizes; rather, the movement of the two women toward the central space of their *Short Relation*—"an inner room in the Inquisition" (p. 6)—seems tendentious from a providentialist perspective. For instance, despite the English Counsel's clear warning "there was an Inquisition" in Malta (p. 3), the two women persist in their illegal proselytizing. Correspondingly, up to this point in their narrative the Maltese people remain objects of deprecation even as the mission of Paul remains a topic of aggrandizement. As C.V. Wedgwood speculates, because Evans and Chevers were "[u]nused to Mediterranean crowds," the sight of "the walls of the City . . . full of people" with "some [who] stood on the top of the walls" to observe the arrival of the "Dutch ship" in which the two women traveled presents the first of many moments of cultural dissonance (pp. 2, 3).[42] Rather than expressing incomprehension, or a desire to comprehend Maltese culture on its own terms, the English women assume the waiting crowd stared "as if something had troubled them" (p. 2).[43] In the remainder of their narrative, the Maltese people intrude only as impersonal pronouns: "them" (p. 3), "they" (p. 31), "some" (p. 37), and so on. The gendered spatial motif of the Maltese nunnery, to which Evans and Chevers are frequently invited, furthers this representation of corrupt confinement in the name of religion. Their enclosure in an unbearably "hot room" (pp. 8, 13), which also becomes a highly gendered space as the language of domesticity imbues the English women's missionary activity, directly counters the place of honor in the nunnery promised them if they convert to Catholicism (p. 75). The Inquisitor's recourse to "[a]ll the men and women of Malta" (p. 14), who continuously pray for Evans and Chevers's conversion, thus casts the native population as fundamentally wicked. When the Inquisitor appears as the head of the penal panopticon—in their words, "the Inquisitor came up into a Tower, and lookt down upon us as if he would have eaten us" (p. 29)—we reach the climax of this proto-feminist, proto-imperialist relation. By the conclusion of the 1662 narrative, "Written in the Inquisition-Prison in the Isle of *Malta*" (p. 44), Evans and Chevers are predicting their arrival in Rome to complete the path of Paul (p. 41).

Having become a cause célèbre in the wake of their published relation, Evans and Chevers's release was obtained through the agency of the Quaker leader George Fox (not by Daniel Baker, editor of the first edition, who after three weeks in Malta traveled to Gibraltar, was imprisoned upon his return to England in early 1662 and eventually enslaved in Morocco from 1679–1682).[44] Wisely, Fox sought the support of Lord d'Aubigny, a prominent Catholic in the court of Charles II, who was able to secure the women's release after three years "in the Inquisition-Prison in the Isle of Malta" (their famous tag line).[45] Since the women were released before they died, as implied by the 1662 title page, the 1663 edition offers a thoroughly revised title page to celebrate "[h]ow God at last by his Almighty Power effected their Deliverance." Malta in this edition is thus conflated with the Inquisition as a place of "Great Tryals," "Cruel Sufferings," and "Confinement." The reference to St. Paul is noticeably absent from this title, which not only confirms the deprecation of Malta as a malign locale in the English imaginary but also effaces the agency of the two Quaker women, who had identified themselves with primarily masculine prophets.[46] The penultimate "[B]rief Account of their further Tryals, and how God at last by his Almighty Power effected their Deliverance, and brought them again into the Land of their Nativity" (pp. 228–77), written alternately by Evans and Chevers, provides an outward itinerary from Malta, to Tangiers (where the two women again sought to proselytize the "natives"), and finally to England.[47] The structural revisions to the tract nevertheless contain the subversive prophetic voice achieved by the two women on Malta, with *A Short Relation from George Robinson, of the Sufferings that befel him in his Journey to Jerusalem* having the last word in this account.

The containment of Evans and Chevers's radical agency as women missionaries, thoroughly imbricated with their complicity in the beginnings of the Anglocentric imperialist project in the Mediterranean, continues in the third edition of their account, retitled *A Brief History of The Voyage of Katharine Evans and Sarah Cheevers, to the Island of Malta*.[48] The 1715 title page restores the emphasis on "the Island of Malta, Where the Apostle Paul Suffer'd Shipwreck," though the focus on the Inquisition in this Enlightenment history is subordinated to a linear chronology of the women's experiences. Arguing "[t]he former RELATION, out of which the following HISTORY is collected, was with much Difficulty written, by the Hands of these poor Sufferers, Katharine Evans and Sarah Cheevers, in the Cruel Inquisition of Malta, wherein they were deprived of Ink and Paper for the greatest Part of their Confinement there" (pp. iii–iv), the editor demotes the women from the position of authorship (however inspired) by completely reworking their writings. Basing his comments on the restored patriarchalism of the second period of Quakerism and the intensifying skepticism of the Enlightenment toward prophetic discourse, this editor treats Evans and Chevers's narratives as mere "source" material for a "history" that completely effaces the women's authorial agency.[49] As the editor of the third edition condescends in his "Preface to the Reader," "The Historical Part hereof being thus interwoven in their Letters and Epistles, and brokenly related through the whole, render'd it very obscure and hard in the former Impression to come to a true Understanding thereof: tho' considering the great Disadvantages they had in their close Confinement, it was probably done as well as they could" (pp. iv–v). Even the women's first-person voice is rendered in the third person! Hence, while they are quoted selectively in this "history," their own representation of their heroic resistance, providential power, and discursive agency is effectively muted. Moreover, only their narrative accounts are mined for quotes, while their doctrinal pronouncements, manifested through their visions, dreams, and verse, are completely erased.

Ironically, just as Evans and Chevers confronted the Maltese people with the imperialist combination of absolute incomprehension and complete confidence in the superiority of their foreign cultural system, English male editors progressively mute the women's material and discursive agency by deeming their original relation incomprehensible and subordinating it to the (masculinist) historical method. This analysis of the silencing of the Maltese people by Evans and Chevers in their relation, and the silencing of Evans and Chevers by these editors, thus comprehends a complicated grid of gender, cultural, religious, and imperialist investments. Mapping Malta in studies of early modern England, therefore, must not accede to the "Black Legend" of the Maltese Inquisition or to the celebrationist mythos drawn from cursory accounts of the "Great Siege." Yet, neither must sophisticated theoretical approaches to English literature on Malta from the sixteenth through the eighteenth century simply deconstruct this binary opposition to conclude to be "of Malta" means to be always already from elsewhere. The Maltese indigene, however complexly constituted, must remain on the horizon of our analyses of this early modern imaginary geography. "Them," "they," and "some," the effaced Maltese in Evans and Chevers's account, accordingly emerge as subjects of their own history rather than as perennial objects of imperialist conflict.[50]

NOTES

1. Patricia Yaeger, "Introduction: Narrating Space," *The Geography of Identity* (Ann Arbor: University of Michigan Press, 1996), pp. 1–38; epigraph p. 25; citation p. 1.
2. For Caliban's assertion of his current subjection and his former sovereignty, see *The Tempest*, 1.2.344–7 and 3.2.40–1. For his paean, see 3.2.130–8.

3. Brian Blouet in *A Short History of Malta* (New York: Frederick A. Praeger, 1967), 26–67. Subsequent colonists included the French and the English in 1798. The Maltese achieved national independence in 1964.

4. Ernle Bradford, *The Great Siege* (New York: Harcourt, Brace and World, 1961), p. vii. My use of the psychoanalytic model of the "imaginary," rather than the traditional term "imagination," references imperialist subject formation as theorized by Robert J.C. Young in *Colonial Desire: Hybridity in Theory, Culture and Race* (London: Routledge, 1995), pp. 159–82.

5. Emily C. Bartels, "Capitalizing on the Jew: The Third Term in *The Jew of Malta*," *Spectacles of Strangeness: Imperialism, Alienation, and Marlowe* (Philadelphia: University of Pennsylvania Press, 1993), pp. 82–108. On the subject position of the "native," see "Ethnicity and Indigeneity," in *The Post-Colonial Studies Reader*, ed. Bill Ashcroft, Gareth Griffiths, and Helen Tiffin (London: Routledge, 1995), pp. 213–45, esp. Terry Goldie, "The Representation of the Indigene," pp. 232–6.

6. Helen Vella Bonavita, "Key to Christendom: The 1565 Siege of Malta, Its Histories, and Their Uses in Reformation Polemic," *Sixteenth Century Journal* 33 (2002): 1021–43; citation p. 1021.

7. Fernand Braudel, *The Mediterranean and the Mediterranean World in the Age of Philip II*, 2 vols., trans. Siân Reynolds (New York: Harper and Row, 1972), vol. 2, p. 1014.

8. Unless otherwise indicated, all primary sources may be found in *Early English Books Online*.

9. For Christian providentialism as a response to Ottoman imperialism, see Jonathan Burton, "English Anxiety and the Muslim Power of Conversion: Five Perspectives on 'Turning Turk' in Early Modern Texts," *Journal of Early Modern Cultural Studies* 2 (2002): 35–67.

10. Braudel, vol. 2, p. 1014, reiterates this commonplace. A.J. Arberry, in his Introduction to *A Maltese Anthology* (Oxford: Clarendon Press, 1960), refers to Malta as "a bastion of Western civilization" (p. xxxvii).

11. Samuel C. Chew, *The Crescent and the Rose: Islam and England During the Renaissance* (New York: Oxford University Press, 1937), p. 123. Cf. Elizabeth I's warning, "If the Turks should prevail against the Isle of Malta, it is uncertain what further peril might follow to the rest of Christendom" (Bradford, *The Great Seige*, p. vii).

12. On the parallel between England and Malta, see Vella Bonavita, "Keys to Christendom," pp. 1040–3.

13. The English prayers for the 1565 siege of Malta may be found in *Liturgies and Occasional Forms of Prayer set forth in the Reign of Queen Elizabeth*, ed. W.K. Clay (Cambridge: Parker Society, 1847), pp. 519–37, citation p. 519.

14. Braudel, vol. 1, pp. 625–6, discusses "Anglo-Turkish negotiations, 1578–1583." For Anglo-Moroccan diplomatic and cultural negotiations,

see Jack D'Amico, *The Moor in English Renaissance Drama* (Tampa: University of South Florida Press, 1991).

15. For a similar privileging, see *A Form to be used in common prayer . . . through the whole Realm: To excite and stir all godly people to pray unto God for the preservation of those Christians and their Countries, that are now invaded by the Turk in Hungary, or elsewhere* (*Liturgies*), pp. 527–37.

16. Andrew P. Vella, *An Elizabethan-Ottoman Conspiracy* (Malta: Royal University of Malta, 1972), p. 5.

17. The Maltese held the comparable view of Elizabeth as "an ultra-Protestant queen" and of English seaman as disruptive forces in the Mediterranean (Vella, *An Elizabethan-Ottoman*, p. 8).

18. As Thomas Healy notes in *Christopher Marlowe* (Plymouth: Northcote House Publishers, 1994), "the *Jew of Malta* was the most frequently performed play between 1592 and 1597" (p. 10). It continued to be revived throughout the first three decades of the seventeenth century, culminating in the publication of the play in a quarto volume in 1633.

19. *The Jew of Malta* 1.1.36–7, in Christopher Marlowe, *Complete Plays and Poems*, ed. E.D. Pendry (London: J.M. Dent, 1976).

20. Stefan Goodwin, *Malta, Mediterranean Bridge* (Westport, CT: Bergin and Garvey, 2002), p. 34.

21. Roma Gill, Introduction in *The Complete Works of Christopher Marlowe. Volume IV: The Jew of Malta* (Oxford: Clarendon Press, 1995), p. ix.

22. Bartels, "The Double Vision of the East: Imperialist Self-Construction in Marlowe's *Tamburlaine, Part One*," *Renaissance Drama* new series, 23 (1992): 3–24, citation 5. Bartels extends this paradigm to the rest of Marlowe's oeuvre in *Spectacles of Strangeness*.

23. See N.W. Bawcutt's Introduction to *The Jew of Malta* (Manchester University Press, 1978), pp. 16–37, for the debate over the play's authorship that he resolves in Marlowe's favor. Bawcutt nevertheless presumes "the hypocrisy and double standards of Maltese society" without clarifying that the world of Marlowe's play does not correspond to historical Malta (p. 35).

24. John Fletcher and Philip Massinger's *The Knight of Malta* (1618) is the only extant English play of the seventeenth century, other than Marlowe's published version, to reference Malta in its title.

25. On "Mediterraneanism," see Peregrine Horden and Nicolas Purcell, *The Corrupting Sea: A Study of Mediterranean History* (Oxford: Blackwell, 2000), pp. 486–8, 522–3; citation 486–7; Jon P. Mitchell, *Ambivalent Europeans: Ritual, Memory, and the Public Sphere in Malta* (London: Routledge, 2002), pp. xi–xii; and Michael Herzfeld, *Anthropology through the Looking-Glass: Critical Ethnography in the Margins of Europe* (Cambridge University Press, 1987), pp. 13–16, 64–70.

26. As Blouet notes, as late as the 1640s, the Maltese lived in fear of a Turkish attack to parallel the attempt of 1565 (p. 121).

27. For the relationship between Curio's and Richard Knolles's histories, see Vella Bonavita, "Key to Christendom," pp. 1029–30.

28. In *Corsairs of Malta and Barbary* (London: Sidgwick and Jackson, 1970), Peter Earle contrasts the "*eternal* war" (p. 3), his term for the chronic guerrilla warfare in the Mediterranean through the late eighteenth century or "the war of the corsairs," with Braudel's *grand guerre* or the more formalized conflict between Islam and Christendom in the Mediterranean that ended in the 1580s (p. 72).

29. Knolles describes the raid on Gozo on p. 752 and the capture of Tripoli on p. 753 of the 1638 edition; he details the capture of the Christian fleet at Zerbi on pp. 783–87.

30. Peter Earle documents Malta as "[t]he Capital of Christian Piracy" well into the eighteenth century (pp. 97–122). Bradford corroborates that the Knights during the sixteenth century "lived by what can only be called 'organized piracy' " (*The Great Seige*, p. 11).

31. The women of Malta, observes George Sandys, go veiled in public, "converse not with men, and are guarded according to the manner of *Italy*." The numerous prostitutes of the island, who Sandys claims are "for the most part *Grecians*," constitute the flip side of this immurement (p. 183). Maltese women, though they remain anonymous figures in most histories of the island, are nevertheless celebrated for their participation in the defense of Malta during the 1565 siege (Bradford, *The Great Seige*, p. 176, Blouet, *A Short History*, p. 84). Blouet also records an uprising of Maltese women in 1644 when the Knights planned to abandon the ancient capital, Mdina, in anticipation of another threatened Turkish attack (p. 117).

32. Daniel J. Vitkus, "Trafficking with the Turk: English Travelers in the Ottoman Empire During the Early Seventeenth Century," in *Travel Knowledge: European "Discoveries" in the Early Modern Period*, ed. Ivo Kamps and Jyotsna G. Singh (New York: Palgrave, 2001), pp. 35–52; citation p. 41.

33. On similarly fraught locales for the radical sectarians, see *The Apocalypse in English Renaissance Thought and Literature*, ed. C.A. Patrides and Joseph Wittreich (Ithaca: Cornell University Press, 1984).

34. Bartels initiates her explication of the previously overlooked nomen "of Malta" in "Malta, the Jew, and the Fictions of Difference: Colonialist Discourse in Marlowe's *The Jew of Malta*" (1990), *Critical Essays on Christopher Marlowe* (New York: G.K. Hall, 1997), pp. 97–109; citation p. 99.

35. Christopher Hill, *The Century of Revolution, 1603–1714* (New York: Norton, 1980), p. 9. For a "revisionist" perspective, see Conrad Russell, "England in 1637," *Reformation to Revolution: Politics and Religion in Early Modern England*, ed. Margo Todd (London: Routledge, 1995), pp. 116–41.

36. The title page of this tract indicates that it was *"Published by Authoritie*; that all Christians may take notice of the great Pride and horrid Blasphemy of the *Turkes.*"

37. *News from the Great Turke* (1645), for instance, lists among the Ottoman Sultan's numerous honorifics, "of *America*" (sig. A2). While Knolles in the sixth edition of *The Generall Historie of the Turkes* (1687) establishes the Americas as outside the reach of Ottoman expansionism ("only *America* being free from him" [p. 981]), popular culture believed the Ottoman Empire to be global. For Ottoman interest in the Americas during the early modern period, see Bernadette Andrea, "Columbus in Istanbul: Ottoman Mappings of the 'New World,' " *Genre: Forms of Discourse and Culture* 30 (1997): 135–65.

38. A movement was afoot in seventeenth-century England to restore the English Knights of Malta, as detailed in D.F. Allen, "Attempts to Revive the Order of Malta in Stuart England," *The Historical Journal* 33 (1990): 939–52.

39. For background on Evans and Chevers, see Bernadette Andrea, "The Missionary Position: Seventeenth-Century Quaker Women and Global Gender Politics," *In-Between: Essays and Studies in Literary Criticism* (2003): 71–87.

40. Ann Jacobson Schutte proposed the model of the "Black Legend of the Inquisition" at the NEH (National Endowment for the Humanities) Summer Institute, "A Literature of Their Own?: Women Writing—Venice, London, Paris—1500–1700" (directed by Albert Rabil at the University of North Carolina, Chapel Hill, in July 2001). For Schutte's further explorations of this model, see his *Aspiring Saints: Pretense of Holiness, Inquisition, and Gender in the Republic of Venice, 1618–1750* (Baltimore: Johns Hopkins University Press, 2001). Also note the discussion of the Maltese Inquisition, originally an offshoot of the Spanish Inquisition in Sicily and subsequently comprehended under the Roman Inquisition in 1574, in Charles Henry Lea, *The Inquisition in the Spanish Dependencies* (London: Macmillan, 1908; 1922), pp. 44–7, and in Andrew P. Vella, *The Tribunal of the Inquisition in Malta* (Royal University of Malta, 1964). Lea mentions Evans and Chevers's encounter with the Maltese Inquisition on p. 47; Vella provides a more thorough analysis of their case using the trial records of the Inquisition, pp. 30–7, balancing Evans and Chevers's inevitably one-sided account.

41. Michel de Certeau, "Spatial Practices," *The Practice of Everyday Life*, trans. Steven F. Rendall (Berkeley: University of California Press, 1984), pp. 91–130.

42. C.V. Wedgwood, "The Conversion of Malta," *Velvet Studies* (London: Jonathan Cape, 1946), p. 130.

43. For the imperialist implications of this response, see Tzvetan Todorov, *The Conquest of America: The Question of the Other*, trans. Richard Howard (New York: Harper and Row, 1984), p. 30.

44. Kenneth L. Carroll mentions Baker in "Quaker Captives in Morocco, 1685–1701," *The Journal of the Friends' Historical Society* 55 (1983): 67–79.

45. D'Aubigny just as famously responded to their gratitude for his intervention, "Good women, for what service or kindness I have done you, all that I shall desire of you is that when you pray to God, you will remember me in your prayers" (quoted in Wedgwood, "The Conversion," p. 137).

46. As Phyllis Mack notes in *Visionary Women: Ecstatic Prophecy in Seventeenth-Century* (Berkeley: University of California Press, 1992), the prophetic voice of first generation Quaker women such as Evans and Chevers recalls that of "the aggressive, male Old Testament hero" rather than the subdued "mother in Israel" of the second generation (pp. 127–64).

47. The most tolerant pronouncement in the entire narrative was voiced by the brother of the Grand Master of Malta, who was on the outbound ship of Evans and Chevers: "he spake to the Captain often that we might not want any thing that was in the Ship, and he told us: if we were at *Malta* again we should not be persecuted so; for as soon as he saw our faces he said, *he would not differ with us*; he and some other of them said to the Captain, *If we went to Heaven one way, and they another, yet we should all meet together at the last.*" To this broad tolerance, Evans and Chevers retorted, "But we held out Christ Jesus the Light of the World, to be the *alone way* to the Father" (p. 255). At Tangiers, Evans and Chevers strove to convert "the *Moors* their Enemies" (p. 259), but were prevented from doing so by the Governor of the besieged fort. For a description of this strained colonial outpost, see E.M.G. Routh, "The English at Tangier," *The English Historical Review* 26 (1911): 469–81.

48. *The Eighteenth Century* microfilm collection, reel 1275:11.

49. See William C. Braithwaite, *The Second Period of Quakerism* (Cambridge University Press, 1961), companion volume to *The Beginnings of Quakerism*, 2nd ed. (Cambridge University Press, 1961). For the intensifying patriarchalism of this period, see Mack, *Visionary Women*, pp. 265–304.

50. For two studies that represent the early modern Maltese as subjects of their own history, see G. Grech, "The Ransoming of the Maltese," and Dun Karm, "The Great Victory," *A Maltese Anthology*, comp. A.J. Arberry, pp. 49–51 and 52–7.

AFTERWORD

Daniel Goffman

This collection of essays concerns the role of the Mediterranean in the development of an early modern English identity. It attempts to chart, through English literature, how the rest of the world helped the English define who they were and what place they held in that world. More specifically, most of the articles in this volume are about how the English mentally mapped a particular place—the Mediterranean—at a particular time—the late sixteenth and seventeenth centuries. Their authors set out to show that the Mediterranean propelled a developing English sense of self, a sense that lay at the core of English identity and British imperialism. The essays, in their examination of a series of specific works and approaches, make a strong case for this assessment.

Even though the collection concerns itself with Mediterranean influences upon the English, it does not attempt to highlight one particular influence over another. In the regional relations between the English and Mediterranean cultural and political forces, however, the Ottoman Empire rises above its neighbors to haunt the consciousness of the English. Indeed, the Ottoman presence flickers in and out of the reader's awareness, but always inhabiting the periphery of our vision. This presence is particularly fascinating for a historian of the Ottoman Empire, such as me, because, even though the Ottomans are always hovering about, they remain so amorphous that the appearance of the empire and its people is unclear even if we could focus our gaze upon them. One author seems to reference the imperial monarch, the sultan or padishah, as the empire personified; a second focuses upon the Ottoman capital, Istanbul, as representative of the polity as a whole; a third touches upon a fearsome Ottoman phantom drifting across the Mediterranean seas plundering Christian, and especially English, ships and capturing English subjects; a fourth examines the imperial heartlands in Anatolia or the Balkans; and a fifth turns to Tangiers or some other distant and semiautonomous hinterland of northwest Africa. Not only does the Ottoman Empire rarely solidify as an object of study in this collection, but many of the essays also reflect their subjects' uncertainties about just who these Ottomans were or what this Ottoman world was to the early modern Englishman. This persistent incorporeality of the Mediterranean and Ottoman worlds hinders analysis of the English *mentalité*. Most of the essays admirably discuss the specifics of a particular play, travel narrative, or English writer. None, however, grapples with the specifics of their subjects' Mediterranean objects. Recent contemplations on postcolonial theory, especially in its application to the Americas and India, urge us to examine the object as well as the subject of proto-imperialism, colonialism, and imperialism. This object, whether it is the Mediterranean, the Moor, the Turk, the Muslim, or the Ottoman, remains absent, or at least silent, in most of these pieces.

In a sense, it is fitting that the Ottomans remain marginal. After all, this book is not about the Mediterranean or the Ottomans. It is a study of how the Mediterranean world influenced the English. Its authors are not trying to ascertain Ottoman or Mediterranean realities through Ottoman chronicles, narratives, archives, or poems. Rather, they seek to understand how the English portrayed that world, and how that depiction may have conditioned the development of English theater, literature, and, more generally, a sense of self as that people began acquiring an overseas empire (which, ironically, did not for centuries incorporate either the Ottomans or other parts of the Mediterranean basin).

These essays succeed in conveying English ambivalence toward various aspects of the Mediterranean, the Ottoman Empire, and/or Islam, and in analyzing how that ambivalence translated into an evolving English sense of self. For example, in "Mapping Malta," Bernadette Andrea incisively traces images of the Ottoman siege of that island in 1565 in English writings in the late sixteenth and seventeenth centuries. The author presents Malta as an "overdetermined geographic area," its definition disputed by individuals, religions, and states. In her hands, it becomes both a bastion of Christendom, as well as a representation of the fraudulent and corrupt Catholic rendition of the Christian faith, where Catholic intolerance reigned in the guise of the Inquisition and corsairs, who preyed upon the English and other Protestants. Andrea concludes that Malta's physical position in the middle of the Mediterranean combined with its ideological uncertainties (the English could identify comfortably with neither its Catholic inhabitants nor its Muslim invaders) generated both a fascination for and ambivalence toward the island. English writers consequently evince an evolving and sometimes contradictory assessment of that space, and use it to consolidate their own identities.

Goran Stanivukovic, meanwhile, writes of an English imagined colonization of an unconquerable East, apparent especially in the prose romances of the Renaissance period. He argues that such texts constitute a "discourse of contact," proposing not the ambivalence of a place, such as Malta, but the ambivalence of English thought as the island's travelers and writers constructed a vision that "othered" the East. Stanivukovic compellingly demonstrates that prose romances become "cultural texts" that recount an East in which the culturally forbidden becomes normal, in which the sexually forbidden can be explored even as it is deplored.

Unlike most of the other English writers explored in this volume, the subject of Adam Beach's essay, Samuel Pepys, had experienced life in the Mediterranean—in Tangiers. Perhaps because of this familiarity, Beach is able to draw upon Pepys' writings to introduce a fascinating explanation for why so many Englishmen living in that English outpost found it seductive. Pepys satirized the administration of the English governor, Kirke, in Tangiers, and presented English actions (and English failures) in that place as a reflection of English society. As the English situation in Tangiers eroded, Beach argues, Pepys became aware that oral pronouncements more and more replaced written law, and absolutist rule replaced legal and consultative government. In such circumstances, many Englishmen grew to prefer the "Moor" to Kirke's tyrannical rule, a turn of events that Pepys bitingly satirizes.

While Beach's argument suggests that the experiences of Englishmen in the Mediterranean seas helped to temper and even to problematize the ideological opposition to the Moor (and by implication other peoples and societies in that historic basin), Emily Bartels generalizes this observation in her discussion of George Peele's play *The Battle of Alcazar*, inspired by an event that predated by almost a century the Tangierine events lampooned by Pepys. Bartels argues that the battle coincided with a moment of uncertainty in English identity, and provided an opportunity for the English to reexamine their place in the world. As a result, Englishmen overseas learned to "make choices," and Englishmen in general learned to "go global" in their sense of themselves. In other words, their experiences helped them overcome parochialism and to envision for themselves a role outside of their Atlantic archipelago.

Both Andrea and Stanivukovic see an evolving image of the Mediterranean, the "Turk," and the East in English writings. Neither author, however, juxtaposes such images against Mediterranean or

Ottoman realities (as well as we can reconstruct them). Nor do Beach and Bartels concretely explore the Mediterranean in their discussions of particular places in that sea. In other words, even as these essays skillfully flesh out our understandings of English minds, its imaginings of the East, and what those images tell us about the English, they also suggest lacunae in our knowledge of how early modern English texts might distort and obscure their Mediterranean and Ottoman objects of study.

Jonathan Burton not only explicitly recognizes the Mediterranean world with which early modern Englishmen established contact, but also suggests ways for us to investigate it. He argues that we still tend to view the Mediterranean (read Ottoman Empire?) as a "passive reflection of contemporary knowledge," by which he is suggesting that scholars should move beyond an engagement with that world only through Western (and principally English) sources, and instead should acknowledge its own "multiple voices." He proposes that one root difficulty in such an enterprise is an imbalance between English and Ottoman sources, and believes that attempts to deal with this problem have been lacking. In other words, despite our best efforts we have not yet found ways to articulate an authentic Ottoman voice.

In order to resolve this quandary, Burton suggests that we read English and Ottoman sources against each other and allow such documents to condition our models, rather than vice versa. He also provides an example of how to do so in his recounting of the conquest of Constantinople in 1453, where he juxtaposes John Foxe's "The History of the Turks" against Evliya Çelebi's *Seyahatname*. Burton's conclusions are helpful in understanding how differently an Englishman and an Ottoman envisioned that event. He also usefully reminds us through a critique of Nabil Matar's *In the Lands of the Christians* that no one version of history can wholly take the place of another, or can reveal a universal truth.[1] These are essential reminders, though, rather than a new theoretical approach. Burton's proposal to emplot the Mediterranean world, it seems to me, boils down to what every historian tries to do. It is basic historical methodology (dressed, perhaps, in literary clothing).

One fascinating and essential aspect of reading cross-cultural sources against each other concerns the translation of language and text and, through it, the transformation of ideas. Edmund Campos addresses this issue in his examination of England's resistance to the fact that the Spanish language constituted the lingua franca of the age of early exploration. He also links an explosion in translation from Spanish to English to a development in English imperialism, and argues insightfully that translation renders worlds "knowable, translatable, transferable, and ultimately bestowable." Translation, of course, also changes meaning. The ultimate power of translation, I would argue, is not merely that it bestows knowledge (and power?), but that it transforms the very significance of that knowledge. It is in this sense that Campos makes a profound, if indirect, contribution to our understanding of the English perception of the Ottoman world. For, if the English needed to learn Spanish in order to survive in an imperial setting in the Iberian dominated Atlantic world, the English also had to learn Turkish in order to survive in the Ottoman-dominated Mediterranean world. When they were unable or unwilling to do so, they relinquished to dragomans (interpreters) and others control over the dialogue between themselves and the Ottoman world. Examining how and why the English transformed Turkish words and Islamic concepts such as *tercüman*, pasha, and qadi should help us to decipher the English appropriation of knowledge. Identifying those areas where the English failed to recognize the nuances of language or situation, of Ottoman customs and usages, should help us understand English bewilderment at the world in which they found themselves.

In other words, Campos is on to something essential here about the slippery nature of cross-cultural communications. If the English struggled to translate and grasp Spanish words and ideas, how much more difficult it must have been for them to comprehend Ottoman ones. In fact, the English confusions about Ottoman society and political structures were frequent, and, often through the very writings that the essays in this volume examine, these misapprehensions were popularized and transformed into stereotypes and, eventually, imperialistic constructs. According to Richard Wilson, Christopher Marlowe, for one, was very much aware of the complications of the Mediterranean world, and used this realization to good effect in his play, *The Jew of Malta*. Marlowe's Jew serves the English as an interpreter of an opaque Mediterranean world; his Malta becomes a type of middle ground between the East and the West. This character and this place, both of which act as foils for a Spanish Catholic threat, serve to problematize English/Ottoman relations. Malta in particular, Wilson argues, subverted "the dichotomies of Renaissance ideology," and broke down the binaries between English religion and culture and those of the "others."

Marlowe may have envisioned Malta and the Jew at the core of transforming English conceptions of religion and trade, and of the place of England in the world. Nevertheless, surely there were "middle grounds" other than Malta in the English Mediterranean, and groups other than Jews whom the English exploited to penetrate that world. Tangiers, Venice, Izmir, and Istanbul are other sites at which the English had to negotiate in myriad ways, and Venetians, Armenians, Greeks, and Muslims (while themselves problematic constructs) are other communities with whom the English had to negotiate. Furthermore, we have concepts and vocabularies through which to explore these relationships. After all, the English did not so much emulate the Jewish and other communities themselves, as they did the type of trading diasporas that they had constructed, and they borrowed from the Ottomans concepts such as "dragoman" (*tercüman* in Ottoman Turkish).[2]

Whereas most of these essayists limit their analyses of English transforming experiences to Mediterranean locations, Alan Stewart argues that productions in English theater suggest that London itself was becoming a "Mediterranean mix" in this period. As in Wilson's discussion, Stewart's evidence for this shift in urban image concerned Jews rather than Venetians, Turks, or Muslims. Second generation Jewish immigrants blurred the definitions of London's citizenry, and helped the city to perceive itself as "religiously diverse and commercially vibrant." This essay carries the richness and confusion of the Mediterranean world to London in the person of the Jew, and replicates a characteristically early modern mixing of the idea of the Jew with the conception of "Mediterranean," "Turk," or "Ottoman" in its depiction of that early modern city. This conflation of identity also suggests the provocative notion that, whereas early modern Englishmen in the Mediterranean may have been able to distinguish between these groups, in London and the rest of England, the "Jew" became a trope for all things Mediterranean, all things Eastern, and even all things Islamic.

Whereas Stuart might consider the Jew of early modern London as the eclectic Mediterranean personified, Elizabeth Sauer argues that at least some influential Englishmen distinguished this people from others of the Mediterranean world. John Milton, for one, perceived Jews as fundamentally distinct from both Catholics and "Turks" because they, unlike either of the other groups, could be saved through conversion. Furthermore, Milton envisioned an emerging English nationhood as a response not to Jews but to Catholics and Turks, who he associated (through the Mediterranean) with the demonic.

Another possibility, suggested by Daniel Vitkus, is that the English in this period may have transformed the East itself into a trope for contamination and disease (again, carried partially in the person of the Jew). Vitkus proposes that such a representation did occur, largely as a result of England's struggle to develop its own identity in the midst of strong, even hegemonic entities such as the Spanish and Ottoman Empires. Vitkus argues that, in the early modern period, the English were not contemplating future colonization. Rather, they were struggling hard not to lose their own identities, and to avoid "turning Turk" in the senses of religious conversion, cultural transformation, and even physical, figurative alteration. As Vitkus puts it, "pockets of expatriate Englishmen were forced to adapt to other cultures where there were no Protestant churches at all, and where, in the case of the Levant, cultural heterogeneity and mixture surrounded and perplexed them." Elizabethan theater manifests these struggles and becomes a medium through which to examine how the English negotiated change and tracked cultural behavior.

It is heartening that Vitkus and other authors in this volume are aware how marginal the Ottomans remain in most current scholarship. It is even more encouraging that they are struggling to find ways to integrate the Ottoman Empire into their writings. In fact, several of these critics state categorically that the Ottoman world looms much larger in early modern London theater than has been hitherto acknowledged. Others go so far as to assert that the idea of the "Turk" imposed itself in important ways not only upon popular entertainment, but also upon domestic politics. For example, Matthew Birchwood argues that royalist veterans of the English Civil War applied the idea of "turning Turk" to Cromwell's tyranny during the 1650s. He further domesticates the idea of the Ottomans by arguing that plays, such as William Davenant's *The Siege of Rhodes*, about Süleyman's attack on Rhodes in 1522, are really about the Veneto-Ottoman struggle over the island of Crete in the mid-1650s, and that they also constitute a statement on Cromwell's simultaneous "Western Design." This particular play, according to Birchwood, resists conventional East-West binaries, especially in its depiction of Süleyman's wife Hurrem (in the play and in the West known as Roxolana), whom, in a revised edition of the play, the playwright curiously inserts into actions that occurred a decade before she was historically significant. This and other unabashed historical inaccuracies confirm that most such writers were utterly absorbed in their own English rather than other, worlds, and used them only as channels to describe their own state, society, and compatriots.

Birchwood's presentation of Hurrem is representative of how several of these essays attempt to complicate overly simplistic scholarly understandings of English perceptions of the Ottomans. Indeed, one of this volume's principal lessons concerns the highly ambiguous nature of

English attitudes toward the Ottomans (and the Mediterranean world in general). Several of the articles persistently attack, or at least attempt to complicate, the long-standing notion of the binaries of East versus West, Christian versus Muslim, or good versus evil.

Not all scholars, even in this volume, would agree with the assessment of English perceptions of the Ottomans. Leeds Barroll, for example, provocatively argues that Marlowe wrote his play, *The Jew of Malta*, as if the Ottomans had taken the island in 1565 (in fact, they were thrown back after a fierce and bloody siege), not because of wishful thinking, but because he wanted to trivialize that empire (in this regard, his interpretation of *The Jew of Malta* differs markedly from Richard Wilson's discussion of this same play). Barroll believes that playwrights such as Marlowe intentionally misrepresented history in part—first to demonize various others, including the Jew and the Black, and second to present what the public wanted to believe about the Ottomans. In other words, fear of the Ottomans compelled English popular imagination to trivialize, poke fun at, and revile the threatening entity. In order to substantiate his arguments about English misrepresentation of the Ottomans, Barroll presents a sustained rendition of Ottoman history.[3] His Ottoman sketch, however, limits itself to high politics, an arena in which the foreign visitor rarely intervened. In order to gauge the Ottoman role in English texts, we need to get a handle not only on the actions of sultans, but also on the less exalted culture and society in which Englishmen abroad were living.

Such a reconstruction of the English milieu in Ottoman domains is critical not only to make sure that the modern reader understands how the English stereotyped and distorted the Ottoman world, but also because such an attempt to expose Mediterranean realities will help us deconstruct and comprehend the foundations of the habitually wild misrepresentations of Mediterranean societies that English writers produced. Understanding why Marlowe, Shakespeare, Milton, and others chose the particular fictions that they did in their depictions of the Ottoman Empire and Mediterranean basin should, in turn, provide considerable insight into the construction of an early modern English identity and nation.

Just as useful will be a thorough comparison between early modern English perceptions of the Mediterranean and other parts of the world. Constance Relihan's essay begins this process, and her work suggests how fertile such cross-cultural investigations can be. She examines Barnaby Riche's writings on Ireland, and concludes that Ireland itself was effectively absent from his work. For Riche, the Irish were merely a channel through which to attack Catholicism. He wanted to prove that the Pope, and not the Jews or the "Great Turk," was anti-Christ. In other words, Riche approached the Irish in much the same way as other early modern English writers approached the Mediterranean, as objects through which to discuss other concerns. Relihan's essay is the exception. In general, this volume attests how firmly the gaze of Renaissance literary critics is now fixed upon the Ottoman world, and how such commentators have embraced the idea that the Ottomans loomed large in the imagination of Renaissance English writers. Critics have found this presence in myriad English plays, poems, essays, and travel accounts. In some cases, such as *Selimus, Emperor of the Turks*, a play about the Ottoman sultan Selim I, the protagonist himself is Ottoman; in others, such as *A Christian Turn'd Turk* and *The Renegado*, the protagonist must confront the Ottomans (or an Ottoman surrogate) directly; and in a third and more familiar case, such as *Othello*, the Ottomans remain shadowy, usually threatening, and often serve as a *deus ex machina* in the plot's twists and turns.[4] The Ottoman world was often present in these works, but it was rarely clearly delineated, remaining instead generally undifferentiated and hazy, and serving mainly as a backdrop.

Furthermore, in those few cases when a playwright did focus directly upon the Ottomans, as in *Selimus*, the author's concrete observations about the Ottomans are often blatantly, and possibly deliberately, inaccurate. In this play, Robert Greene presents a monarch as protagonist, and his vision was of a cruel, autocratic, and profane ruler. Greene's chief purpose in this historical tragedy in which Selim poisons his father and murders his siblings even as he repudiates his faith, was doubtlessly to entertain and even to titillate an English audience. Nevertheless, the play also served to distance the English from this Mediterranean foe and help forge an English identity by emphatically stating what an Englishman was not.

Selimus certainly exhibits no more interest in the realities of its subject's life than did other early modern English plays. Unexplored (and unacknowledged) is the Ottoman political use of fratricide. Nor does the work examine the struggles of Bayezid I (Selim's father) to win the throne over a more competent and better-loved brother, Cem, who himself spent decades in exile in Rhodes, Egypt, France, and Italy, trying always to overthrow Bayezid. The play's mangling of Islam—typical in a time and place that did not have access even to the Qur'an, that most basic text of Islam—the religion that legitimized Ottoman rule, further demonstrates the writer's ignorance of his subject matter. We should not be surprised that this and other early modern English writings on the Ottoman world were disconnected from their remote and poorly understood heroes and scoundrels, who typically constituted little more than a trope for English mores and concerns.

The essays in this volume do, however, show that those Englishmen who did embark into the Mediterranean had to contend with a vast, established, and resilient world in which the Ottomans played a central role, and that these adventurers successfully impressed upon their compatriots a need to take that empire most seriously. Their encounters in those lands taught the English (and other foreigners) about Ottoman administration and peoples, and how to establish themselves in strange realms. The Genoese, the Venetians, the French, the Dutch, and the English—all fashioned booming foreign districts in Ottoman cities such as Istanbul, Aleppo, and, later, Izmir (Smyrna). This fact of settlement is not so startling. More unexpected for those of us who study later British expansion and imperialism is that they were not able to do so on their own terms, but instead had to accommodate their conduct, sometimes in extraordinary ways, to the demands of their hosts.[5] The essays in this volume make clear how feeble the influence of the English in fact was, and how Englishmen negotiating the eastern Mediterranean world had to adapt themselves to the powerful and sophisticated polity that the Ottomans had constructed.

One example of such accommodation is in the realm of worship. In most of early modern Western European society, there was little room for emotional or physical expressions of alien faiths. In Ottoman port cities, however, the Anglican English, the Catholic French, and other Christians quickly took as absolute their rights not only to roam and worship freely, but also to repair and even build chapels and churches. They did so in environments that also boasted soaring minarets and public and well-appointed synagogues. Several of the essays in this volume emphasize not only the ambivalence that the English developed toward the Ottoman, Muslim, and Jewish worlds, but also the English hatred and fear of Catholics. How, then, does one assess the impact on these people of an environment in which the English were forced to live and trade with these very groups that they so reviled and failed to understand?

A second example of adaptation concerned the employment of foreigners in Ottoman realms. Whereas much of early modern Western Europe discouraged the employment of foreigners in political and commercial administration, the early modern Ottoman world was crowded with non-Ottoman administrators. Alvise Gritti, for one, was the son of a Venetian doge who became an Ottoman official who in the 1520s led an Ottoman army against the Hungarians and was a close friend of the Ottoman grand vizier Ibrahim pasha.[6]

Remapping the Mediterranean World in Early Modern English Writings has much to say about English ambivalence, as it persuasively works to break down a series of reductive constructs concerning English relations with and perceptions of the outside world as the English set about mapping it. Before the English even considered a presence in the Mediterranean seas, however, Venetians were forced to become a very model of ambivalence in their own mappings of the Ottoman world. Venice was a profoundly Mediterranean city, but certainly not an Ottoman one. Indeed, for much of the early modern period this Catholic city-state constituted the Ottomans' principal Mediterranean rival, as that Islamic empire expanded into the Aegean and other parts of those seas largely at Venetian expense. Gritti and countless other Venetians responded to this expansion through adaptation. When the English assaulted the Mediterranean basin in the late sixteenth century, they encountered the vestiges of a Venetian seaborne empire. This empire had not simply faded away, however. The Venetians instead had managed to fashion a formidable trading network in those very areas where its corporeal empire had previously existed.

Wherever the English went, they met Venetian merchants with deep roots in Mediterranean commerce, and learned from them and others how to negotiate the Ottoman world. Englishmen also had to adapt and, despite our current fascination with captivity narratives,[7] enslavement was not the only, or even the principal, way that English men (and occasionally women) learned about and merged themselves into Ottoman society. For example, though Henry Hyde, was the English consul of the Morea (the Peloponnesian peninsula) in the 1630s, he simultaneously carved out considerable influence in Ottoman administration. Even as he served as representative for his compatriots, Hyde also purchased a *voyvodalık* in the region surrounding Patras, a position that granted him virtually the authority of an Ottoman pasha. He also bought a *bacdarlık* that transformed him into an Ottoman collector of customs.[8] Hyde thus was able to establish what amounted to a small fiefdom, even building a large house and chapel on a Morean promontory overlooking the island of Zante. He served as one of the most important English representatives in the Ottoman world, responsible for exporting wildly popular currants to England, even as he commanded a body of janissary guards who helped him collect taxes on these very same currants for the Ottoman government and impose Ottoman customs duties on his English compatriots. When English Levant Company officials became cognizant of his actions, they responded by ordering his replacment as consul. Hyde staved off this dismissal for several years through recourse to the Ottoman court system, where the municipal judge of Patras heard as witnesses an array of Ottoman officials, Frenchmen, Jews, Turkish Muslims, Greek Orthodox Christians, and others, as well as to Ottoman pashas and the imperial government in Istanbul.

At every turn, Hyde outmaneuvered his ostensible replacement, Gyles Ball, whom the Company sent to oust him. For example, when, despite letters from company, king, and ambassador, Hyde refused either to resign his office or to surrender the capitulations that defined and legitimized his authority, Ball struggled to get his government to exert its authority. He exclaimed in a communication to the English ambassador that Hyde used his authority as *voyvoda* and *bacdar* to disrupt Ball's commerce, forcing him "to visit the Caddee, once or twice a day & my Druggerman half a score times a day," and that Hyde followed Ball around with five janissaries and a regiment of bandits in order to harass him, abuse his servants, and underbid him in all his dealings. Among many other ventures, Hyde also one night sent a boatload of janissaries aboard Ball's vessel, the *Defence*, in a search for contraband. Ball further maintained that, though he could not restrain Hyde alone, "the Caddee can but will not without commands, the common people would but dare not, without the Caddee's warrant, & to attempt ought of force by the hands of soldiers. . . . I rather am content to bear the weight of this heavy burden awhile."[9]

Perhaps unwittingly, Ball had thrown himself against a hopeless challenge. His rival enjoyed not only support from English merchants, but also rank as an Ottoman official, patronage from powerful native merchants and administrators, and a profound grasp of the composition of the Ottoman legal and political worlds. Hyde had rooted himself firmly in that social and economic order, an accommodation that cannot be explained by English society alone, or by the tracts and plays about the Ottomans that the English produced. Rather, it was the civilization of the eastern Mediterranean that forged cultural chameleons such as Henry Hyde and hundreds of other Englishmen.

That world is only beginning to become less undifferentiated and hazy to literary scholars. Not only has it remained indistinct, but there has also been a persistent and regrettable tendency to conflate the Ottoman with the Mediterranean world, and, even more problematically, to fail to differentiate between places, classes, and cultures surrounding the vast and diverse Mediterranean sea. More troubling, perhaps, has been the enduring readiness with which scholars have accepted and thereby perpetuated their subjects' stereotyping of the Ottomans.

Recently, I heard an erudite and well-attended lecture on early seventeenth-century-"Turk plays." The presenter (echoing many of the authors in this volume) convincingly argued the centrality of such plays to a developing sense of English identity, and evoked the relatively few English plays on the Americas in support of the argument that the Mediterranean loomed far larger than did the greater Atlantic in early modern popular English consciousness. Woven into the presenter's analysis of the genre were colorful references to scimitars and turbans, sultans and sultanas, and also the description of a scene (meant as a contrasting case) from a play about the Americas in which Native Americans speak "gibberish." The audience, several hundred strong, remained silent and attentive during the passages dealing with Eastern exotica, but laughed knowingly during the narration on the babble of Native Americans. This contrast strikes me as telling, for I perceive in it modern academicians who, on one hand, have critically engaged with and succeeded in deconstructing the representation of an American people whose civilization and history European imperialists had virtually erased from the historical record. On the other hand, this same audience, in its inability or unwillingness to see the English labeling of the Ottomans for what it was—a combination of ignorance and an attempt at appropriation—seems to have digested and still embraced that very view of the Ottoman world that early modern English writers had deceptively manufactured.

The essays in *Remapping the Mediterranean World in Early Modern English Writings* make clear that an important element in the English imperial endeavors of the sixteenth and seventeenth centuries was the transformation of Mediterranean and Ottoman culture through translation of words, concepts, and especially fundamental ideas. The prolific literary output of these years represents one consequence of this transformation. What we see before us, then, is a nascent and proto-imperial English vision of the Ottoman world, one that is surprisingly still reflected in contemporary scholarship. Our primary job, as literary critics and historians, is to become aware of these transformations, understand how and why the English undertook them, and recognize the differences between the worlds that existed and English representations of those worlds.

NOTES

1. However one-sided Matar's approach maybe, his aggressive revisionism and that of and a handful of others have effectively forced an essential reassessment of our sources and our approaches.

2. The idea of dragoman is especially worth exploring. Such a figure was often not so much a translator of language as an interpreter (and consequently a transformer) of Ottoman customs and practices.

3. Barroll's presentation of the Ottomans could be more precise. His claim, for instance, that the Ottomans regarded Europe as barbarous (based, it seems, almost exclusively upon the disputed analyses of Bernard Lewis) is simultaneously too broad and too reductive. Barroll is also inaccurate in his discussion of imperial Ottoman customs of murder. It was never expected that a sultan should kill his sons, as this author suggests. Rather, the codified practice was for a sultan to kill his brothers (fratricide rather than filicide).

4. See, as examples of the growing literature on these plays, Gerald McLean, "On Turning Turk, or Trying To: National Identity in Robert Daborne's *A Christian turn'd Turke,*" *Explorations in Renaissance Culture* 29.2 (Winter 2003): 225–52 and Daniel Vitkus, *Turning Turk: English Theater and the Multicultural Mediterranean, 1570–1630* (New York and Houndmills, Basingstoke, Hampshire, England: Palgrave Macmillan, 2003).

5. Gerald MacLean has coined the phrase "imperial envy" to characterize early modern English attitudes toward the Ottomans. He also suggests the term "Ottomanism" to distinguish English (and western European) relations with the East from the very different relationship suggested by the term Orientalism. See MacLean, "Performing East: English Captives in the Ottoman Maghreb," *Actes du Ier Congrès International sur Le Grande Bretagne et le Maghreb: Etat de Recherche et contacts culturels* (*Zaghouane,* Tunisia: Fondation Temimi, 2001), p. 1.

6. Gülru Necipoğlu, "Süleyman the Magnificent and the Representation of Power in the Context of Ottoman-Hapburg-Papal Rivalry," *Art Bulletin* 71.3 (1989): 401–27. Eric R. Dursteler has recently taken up the general ambivalence of Venice toward the Ottomans as well as the complexity of their relationship. See his "The Bailo in Constantinople: Crisis and Career in Venice's Early Modern Diplomatic Corps," *Mediterranean Historical Review* 16.2 (2001): 1–30; and "Commerce and Coexistence: Veneto-Ottoman Trade in the Early Modern Era," *Turcica* 34 (2002): 105–33.

7. On which, see Linda Colley, *Captives: Britain, Empire, and the World, 1650–1800* (New York: Pantheon, 2002; and Daniel Vitkus, ed., *Piracy, Slavery, and Redemption: Barbary Captivity Narratives from Early Modern England* (New York: Columbia University Press, 2001).

8. British Library, Egerton MS 2541, fos. 300–2 and 316.

9. British Library, Egerton MS 2541, fos. 318–19. Over the next decade, Hyde, a fervent royalist, continued to use his understanding of the Ottoman world to stir trouble for the English, on which see Daniel Goffman, *Britons in the Ottoman Empire, 1642–1660* (Seattle, Washington: University of Washington Press, 1998), passim.

INDEX

Elizabeth I, Queen of England, 7,
    17n16, 79, 81, 84–6, 99–100,
    109, 118, 127, 146, 151–2,
    163, 168–9, 250–1
England, 1, 5, 7–9, 19n32, 32,
    46–8, 51–3, 65, 89–1, 97–8,
    101, 103, 107, 112, 146, 159,
    167, 170, 191, 227, 229, 253,
    259–60, 263, 282
erotic ethnography, 61
Evans, J. Martin, 229
Evans, Katharine, 247, 259, 262–4,
    266, 271n47
Ezard, John, 17n16

Ferrara, 185
Fez, 97
Flanders, 163–4
Fleischer, Cornell, 39n21
Fletcher, John
    The Wild-Goose Chase, 45
Fletcher, John and Philip Massigner
    The Knight of Malta, 268n24
Fletcher, Phineas
    "Upon the picture of Achmat the
        Turkish tyrant", 4
Florence, 131
Florio, John, 76
Foxe, John, 27–8
    "The History of the Turks", 27
France, 5, 8, 52, 100, 163, 214, 281
Frank, Joseph, 226
Frobisher, Martin, 80, 86
Fuchs, Barbara, 51, 57n36, 73n22
Fuller, Mary, 106
Fuller, Thomas
    History of the Worthies of England,
        101, 106
Furnivall, F.J., 158

Galata, 172
Garber, Marjorie, 134
Genoa, 132, 185
Gibraltar, the Straits of, 21
Gil Harris, Jonathan, 46
Gill, Roma, 252

Glucester, Siege of, 222
Glover, Thomas, 68
Goffman, Daniel, 2, 16n3, 18n25,
    28, 287n9
Goldberg, Jonathan, 76
Goodall, Baptist
    "The Tryall of Travell", 42
Gosson, Stephen, 170
Gozo, 255
Grech, G., 271n50
Greece, 4, 17n14, 63, 186, 195–6,
    257
Greeks, 278
Greenblatt, Stephen, 77, 92n6, 150,
    199
Greene, Robert, 281
Gresham, Thomas, 84–6, 91
Greville, Fulke, 124
Gritti, Alvise, 282
Guiana, 198
Guilmartin, J., 121
Gunpowder Plot, the, 150

Hadfield, Andrew, 11, 16n13,
    19n38
hajj, 25
Hakluyt, Richard, 88, 99, 146, 150,
    193–4, 252, 262
    The Principal Navigations, 5, 78
Hall, Joseph, Bishop, 42, 50
Hamburg, 163
Harbage, Alfred, 226
Harborne, William, 148, 168
Harrington, James, 205n33
Harrison, John, 98
Healy, Thomas, 252
Henslowe, Philip, 127
Herodotus (Helikarnasseus), 198
Heylyn, Peter, 194–5, 199
Hoby, Edward, 89
Hoby, Thomas, 75–6
Holland (the Netherlands), 8, 88
Holy Land, 257
Harrington, James, 205n33
Harrison, William, 161
Haughton, William, 171

Mendoza, Bernardino de, 87
Mesopotamia (Iraq), 191
Mignolo, Walter D., 28, 38n14
Milton, John, 13, 191, 194–6,
204n20, 205n28, 280
  Eikonoklastes, 195
  Paradise Lost, 15, 192, 197,
  199, 229
  Paradise Regained, 15, 192,
  197, 200–1
Minsheau, John, 89–91, 94n40–1,
95n43
Mitchell, Jon P., 253
Montaigne, Michel de, 98
Moors, 107, 112, 125–6, 240, 274
Morocco, 69, 102, 108, 112, 121,
123, 125, 128, 241
Moryson, Fynes, 30, 39n18, 65
Mount Atlas, 198, 201
Mully Mollocco, 10
Munday, Anthony, 100
Murad III, Sultan, 168
Muscovy Company, 162
Muslims, 14, 27, 48, 60, 131–2,
143, 149, 157, 159, 167–8,
170, 192, 194, 224, 250, 253,
255, 260, 274, 277–8, 282,
284
  and intolerance and bigotry, 34
  and proselytism, 35

Napoleon, Bonaparte, 143
Nashe, Thomas, 41–4
  The Unfortunate Traveller, 41–2,
  45, 148
Neale, Thomas, 4–3
Nebrija, Antonio, 78
New England, 227
New World, the, 30, 77–8, 87, 123
  and cannibalism, 29
Nicolay, de Nicholas, 66, 68
Norbrook, David, 226n11

O'Neill, Shane, 100
Orient, the, 221, 224, 225n5
Orientalism, 221, 253, 260

Ortelius, Abraham, 63, 193
Ottoman Empire, the, 4–6, 7–9, 11,
14–15, 24, 27–31, 52, 60, 65,
71, 117–8, 120, 122, 124–5,
127–8, 140, 146, 150–1, 157,
161, 168, 170, 191–2, 196,
198, 210, 213, 215, 246, 248,
250, 252–4, 261, 273–4, 276,
278–9, 281–3, 285
Ovid (Ovidius Publius Naso), 64
  The Metamorphoses, 68

Pacific Ocean, 137
Palestine, 143, 195–6
Palmer, Sir Thomas, 50
Pamuk, Orhan, 59, 72n2, 131
Parry, William, 45
Pathomachia, 70
Patrides, C. A., 149, 269n33
Pavia, 185
Peele, George, 101, 103–5, 107–8
  The Battle of Alcazar, 10, 98–9,
  107, 109, 112, 125, 127–8,
  275
Pepys, Samuel, 13, 218, 227–8,
231, 236–7, 239, 242, 275
  Diaries, 15, 227, 229, 232–3,
  235, 238, 240
  Tangier Papers, 15, 233–6
Percivale, Richard, 87–9
Persia, 69, 169, 198–9
Persian language, 23
Philaras, Leonard, 196
Philip II, King of Spain, 17n16, 78,
81, 89–90, 100, 121–3, 132–3,
135, 137, 142, 144–5, 250
Phillips, Adam, 62, 72n11
Pliny (Gaius Plinius Secundus), 199
Polemon, John, 98
Portugal, 17n15, 100, 122, 132,
144
  and privateering, 80–1
Purchas, Samuel, 193

Quint, David, 232
Qur'an, the, (Koran), 25–6, 34, 134